The Thoughtful Reader

The Thoughtful Reader Fifth Edition

Mary C. Fjeldstad

LaGuardia Community College
City University of New York

WADSWORTH
CENGAGE Learning

Australia • Brazil • Japan • Korea • Mexico • Singapore • Spain • United Kingdom • United States

The Thoughtful Reader, Fifth Edition
Mary C. Fjeldstad

Director, Developmental English
& College Success: Annie Todd

Development Editor: Cathy Richard Dodson

Assistant Editor: Kate Remsberg

Marketing Manager: Kirsten Stoller

Content Project Manager: Jessica Rasile

Art Director: Linda Helcher

Senior Print Buyer: Betsy Donaghey

Text Permissions Manager: Margaret
Chamberlain-Gaston

Senior Image Manager: Deanna Ettinger

Production Service/Compositor:
International Typesetting
and Composition

Cover Designer: Brian Salisbury

Cover Image: © Digital Vision/Media
Bakery

For product information and technology assistance, contact us at
Cengage Learning Academic Resource Center, 1-800-423-0563

For permission to use material from this text or product, submit all requests online at **www.cengage.com/permissions**
Further permissions questions can be e-mailed to
permissionrequest@cengage.com

Library of Congress Control Number: 2008921087

ISBN-13: 978-1-4130-3347-2
ISBN-10: 1-4130-3347-4

Wadsworth Cengage Learning
25 Thomson Place
Boston, MA 02210
USA

Cengage Learning products are represented in Canada by Nelson Education, Ltd.

For your course and learning solutions, visit **academic.cengage.com**

Purchase any of our products at your local college store or at our preferred online store **www.ichapters.com**

Printed in the United States of America
1 2 3 4 5 6 7 12 11 10 09 08

Contents

UNIT ONE
READING AND THINKING ABOUT EDUCATION

Think about the kind of world you want to live and work in. What do you need to know to build that world? Demand your teachers teach you that.
—Prince Kropotkin

for doing it, and educators worry that increased cheating reflects a world that is growing more corrupt.

UNIT TWO
READING AND THINKING ABOUT CULTURE

Culture is that which binds men together.
—Ruth Benedict

UNIT THREE
READING AND THINKING ABOUT LANGUAGE

All words are pegs to hang ideas on.
—Henry Ward Beecher

UNIT FOUR
READING AND THINKING ABOUT WORK
AND THE WORLD OF BUSINESS

The more I want to get something done, the less I call it work.
—Delacorte

UNIT FIVE
CRITICAL READING AND THINKING ABOUT
CONTROVERSIAL ISSUES

He who knows only his own side of the cause knows little.
—John Stuart Mill

UNIT SIX
READING AND THINKING ABOUT TEXTBOOKS

Knowledge itself is power.
—Francis Bacon

LEARNING STRATEGIES

Alternate Contents

A Note to the Instructor

Can you imagine a life without reading? Without the consolation of a good book to crawl into after a disheartening day? Without that thrill of picking up the morning newspaper and, for just a moment, feeling the whole world in your hands? To us avid readers, a life without reading is nearly unimaginable.

What Are You Reading?

If you're like me, you've got at least one book going, probably two. The morning newspaper. A weekly newsmagazine. I'm studying Spanish, so I'm also in the middle of a novel by a young Argentinean writer. Oh, and a short story by García Márquez. A new *Atlantic Monthly* is due but I haven't finished last week's *New Yorker* yet. But I do want to check out that great BBC news website before I do anything else. . . . What does your list look like? If it's even longer than this, I envy and pity you—there aren't enough hours in the day to read all we want to read and need to read.

But now let's ask our students the same question: what are you reading? Some will say, nothing. Some, too few, will say the newspaper. Others are reading a book for their English classes. Textbooks will probably fill out the list. What's the point? Reading is like any other skill—you have to practice it to improve it. Over the years we avid readers have become effortless, fluent readers. We don't think about the process of reading, only the product—"The President said *what*?" "A new drug is being developed for arthritis. . . . Hope it will be out in time for me." "Hopeful news from Haiti? At last. . . ." "Only three more weeks 'til spring training!" "Tuition is going up again?"

For our students, the experience is vastly different. For them the **process** is all-important and sometimes so exhausting it overwhelms the **product**. They struggle through a page, a chapter, encountering unfamiliar words, unfamiliar names, titles, events, and allusions. By the time they finish, they are too overwhelmed to make use of the ideas in the text.

When we avid readers read, we unconsciously call into play all we've read before. If we read a sociology text, we already have a vast store of knowledge about the nature of society and societies, human behavior, the debate over nature versus nurture, and a million other things we read in the past. When we read about business, we call on our knowledge of different forms of economic systems, the structure of capitalism, the impact of technology, the debate over free trade, and a million other things. Now think about reading without the benefit of all this background knowledge. Every article you read, every chapter you studied, every story, would be a heroic task: every unfamiliar word would have to be puzzled out, its definition laboriously considered, its context analyzed; every fact would have to be painstakingly decoded, examined, and somehow integrated with others being learned at the same time. This daunting task is what faces our students in much of their college work and, of course, in their outside reading.

How can we help our students to be more fluent readers? The first and most obvious answer is to ask them to read. The more they read, the better they will read. Just try to improve your tennis game, your golf stroke, your skills in the kitchen without practice. Why should reading be any different? So let's have our students read a lot. But unlike what many of them have experienced, let's not make reading a chore, a boring assignment, a frustrating exercise with no benefit other than a grade. Let's try to make reading for them what it is for us—an exhilarating part of our lives.

This book is full of interesting relevant stories, essays, and articles. The reading selections and the exercises that accompany them are geared to adults and adult interests. They treat issues important to all of us—education, our life as human beings living in societies, language, work, and topics of current controversy. Students will enjoy reading, thinking, talking, and writing about the stories. The book is organized according to themes. Because students don't have stores of background knowledge, they rarely experience the joy of reading fluently. Because most of what they read is unfamiliar, they constantly struggle as novices rather than fluent readers. But by reading deeply in one theme, students can build a fund of knowledge that will allow them to read at a higher, more sophisticated level.

The Fifth Edition

The fifth edition has been enhanced by the addition of many new readings: thoughts on how the educational system has failed our poorest children by Jonathan Kozol; a lively piece considering the meaning of "intelligence" by Isaac Asimov; a discussion of cheating in American schools; the search for a unique identity by Muslim American teens; Sandra Cisneros' musing on the meaning of being an "only daughter" in a family of seven children. Unit Four, on work and the world of business, includes several new and appealing readings: an essay by Barbara Ehrenreich, the author of *Nickel and Dimed: On Not Getting By in America* explains her effort to experience and record the struggles of people trying to get by on minimum wage; an article about a young mother trying to survive on what she earns at Burger King ("Nothing special. Nothing much," she says of herself); a lively discussion of the joys and sorrows of multitasking (what else are you doing right now? Listening to the radio? Looking at your e-mail? Making a phone call?). Unit Five, on controversial issues, adds a heartbreaking essay by a young woman who must decide if and when to have the test for Huntington's disease, knowing she has a 50–50 chance of being a victim. Finally, Unit Six includes three completely new textbook excerpts.

The philosophy behind the text has not changed—thematic organization, high-interest readings, challenging exercises, emphasis on the connection between reading and writing. And although the "Learning Strategies" section is at the end of the book, these strategies should be at the forefront of our thinking. Previewing text, annotating text, summary writing, and the understanding of figurative language are crucial to our students' development as college readers. The format of the text is flexible—the teacher can turn to the strategies whenever it is appropriate and comfortable—but the skills are indispensable.

Why These Themes?

The five themes—education, culture, language, work, and controversial issues—were selected for five reasons. First, they are topics our students already know about; second, they are interesting—students like to read about them; third, connections can easily be drawn between the information in one section and that in another, as well as to what students read in newspapers and magazines; fourth, each theme lends itself to exposition in a variety of sources and styles—in each unit you will find selections from newspapers, magazines, essays, narratives, and textbooks; fifth, the content is presented in a way similar to that of college texts—for example, a history, psychology or business course. Thus the skills students learn here easily transfer to their other courses.

Many of the reading selections in this book are challenging. Students are insulted and demeaned when they are given materials they see as childish. They are challenged and engaged when presented with work they see as college level.

Writing and Reading

An important assumption of this book is that reading and writing are inextricably linked. Writing helps students become co-creators of the texts they read. In creating their own written versions and interpretations of, and reactions to, the content, they become masters of what they read. Writing about what they read allows them to monitor their own progress, to check whether they really understand what they read. It forces them to infer structure and make connections between the varying levels of information in the selection itself and their own background knowledge. In simple terms, writing can help readers make sense of what they read.

The book is also meant to be a "course model." Much as in a textbook for history, literature, sociology, or business, the reading selections contain information that students are expected to master; they read and study the selections with several goals similar to those of a college content course: learning vocabulary and information specific to a field, producing reaction and argumentation papers, and, finally, passing exams. The major difference is that, in the reading course, students are given more support from the textbook and from the teacher. The strategies and knowledge that students gain can transfer immediately to their primary concern—the concepts and processes of their content courses.

Organization

The readings in this book are not arranged in an artificial sequence of increasing complexity—this does not happen in real life. Rather, they are arranged in a logical order one might expect in a college textbook. The ideas in each selection build upon those that came before. To provide the greatest support to students as they read these real and challenging materials, each unit contains the following features:

Thinking about the Theme. Each unit begins by inviting students to think about the subject they are about to read. There are pertinent quotations, a brief introduction to the theme, and some questions to engage students' interest. They are challenged to remember what they already know about the topic, to imagine some new aspect of the topic, and to think about how the topic affects them personally. In short, they are helped to "turn on the engines" of their minds and get ready to read.

Introduction to the Reading Selection. Each selection is briefly introduced—first to encourage students to activate the knowledge they already have about the specific subject at hand; second, in some cases, to provide them with crucial information they may lack; and finally, to stimulate their interest in what they are about to read.

Vocabulary. Because they are drawn from real sources, many of the selections contain fairly complex language. Students will be able to figure out many of the words from their context, but they will need the dictionary for many others. Several words from each reading are targeted, and students are asked to use a special vocabulary strategy to figure out its meaning: read the word in context, try to guess its meaning, evaluate the guess, and, finally, confirm the guess by checking the dictionary or other source. This strategy most closely resembles the way fluent readers naturally learn new words. Students are also encouraged to target other words they may find hard to understand and use the same strategy.

Guide Questions. The questions have several goals. First, they guide students to a basic understanding of the major ideas presented in the text. Thus some questions are aimed at the lowest levels of cognitive activity—knowledge and comprehension. Second, students are asked to apply the new ideas presented to their own experiences or to other situations they may read or hear about. Students then may be asked to synthesize the new information with ideas they had before or, where appropriate, evaluate the new ideas. The main ideas are generally addressed in the same sequence in which they appear, thus students discern text organization in a natural way.

Application. The themes addressed in this book are of high interest to most college students and lend themselves to application to students' own lives and experiences. Transferring information to novel situations is an excellent way to promote and demonstrate mastery of the content. Application questions are personal, interesting, and even enjoyable ways of stretching the mind.

Marking Text. Marking text is one of the most valuable learning strategies students can use to master the ideas in their textbooks. Marking text means to underline important ideas and make notes in the margins to label those ideas and to write personal comments and questions. Marking text is explained in the special "Learning Strategies" section at the end of the book.

Learning Strategies. Students learn to identify, underline, and annotate. This ensures that they understand what they have read; it helps them to remember what they've learned; and it is a big help when exam time comes along—students have their very own personalized study guide, making test prep a breeze.

Writing. Students should be encouraged to see the connections among all the communication skills, but there is a special emphasis here on writing. The guide questions are meant to be answered in writing and discussed and argued about in class. Some of the readings naturally lend themselves to creative writing assignments, others to summary writing.

Collaborative Learning
At the end of Units One through Four are two reading selections with no attached exercises. Students are asked to work in small groups to master the information on their own. Following the model of the earlier chapters, students create their own exercises—vocabulary, guide questions, writing. This kind of collaborative activity reinforces active learning.

Special Projects
At the end of Units Two through Five are projects that will allow students to use the knowledge they've gained by reading the unit and to investigate topics independently.

Short Takes
Sprinkled throughout the book are short readings—little stories, examples, or explanations—related to ideas presented in the unit. They are included for their high interest, because they add to the topic, or just because they'll elicit a smile.

Unit 5
This unit, *Critical Reading and Thinking about Controversial Issues,* presents several topics of current controversy—interesting and stimulating issues for students to learn about and discuss. At the end of the unit, students are asked to work in groups to research and write an essay arguing for or against a position on a particular issue. This kind of concluding exercise calls on students to use higher-level thinking skills, including synthesis, evaluation, and application, and encourages them to operate as fluent readers and thinkers.

Unit 6
This unit, *Reading and Thinking about Textbooks,* is different from the first five. Here, students tackle real college textbook chapters. Instructions guide them through previewing, reading, and marking the chapters. Then actual review, discussion, and exam questions are presented. Students can see what they will face in a college content course.

Please note that the answers to the exam questions in Unit Six can be found in the instructor's manual that accompanies this textbook.

Flexibility

An important feature of this book is its flexibility. Instructors may choose any theme they wish. It is not necessary to complete the first unit in order to understand the following units. If a particular reading selection does not appeal to the instructor, it can be skipped without any significant problem. (Note, however, that after the first reading in each unit, the directions for vocabulary and guide questions are abbreviated.) Learning strategies such as previewing, using direction words, marking text, summarizing, and others are taught in a separate section at the end of the book and may be presented at any point the teacher considers appropriate. Too often, textbooks are set up so rigidly that instructors have very little say in their own curricula and are forced to teach topics that bore them or that they don't feel confident teaching. This book offers a wide range of subjects that can be organized to suit the individual teacher and class. In addition, it offers both collaborative and independent activities that can be assigned to accommodate the learning styles of individual students.

Acknowledgments

Teaching is hard work. Writing textbooks is hard work. Sometimes there are not enough hours, not enough energy; sometimes the obstacles seem overwhelming. When disheartening feelings steal in, I think of my students. They come to class after working all day (or all night), after caring for their children, after cleaning the house and cooking the dinner. They struggle with the language, with exhausting class schedules, with the constant pressure of tests, and with financial worries I can only imagine. But come to class they do, and work they do, and succeed they do. If this book is of some small help to them, all the effort is more than worthwhile. They are my heroes.

A Note to the Student

Are you a good basketball player? Or a good singer? Can you cook well? Perhaps you are a computer whiz? Great! Now, answer this: How did you get so good at what you do? That's right—you practiced. No one ever got to be a good tennis player, golfer, swimmer, singer, or photographer without endless hours of practice.

Now here's another question: are you a good reader? Could you be better? How do you think you could become a better reader? Right again—by practicing. Reading is a skill like any other—you improve by practice. So, if you want to improve as a reader, you must read. But just like your tennis game or your computer skills, the practice can be fun. And the better you get, the more fun it is. If you get into the habit of reading, if you expand your vocabulary so that you are not running to the dictionary constantly, if you build enough background knowledge so that your reading is fast and fluent, then you will find that reading is not work, not a boring school requirement, but rather one of life's great pleasures.

In this book, you can read about many subjects that you are already familiar with—education; people and their customs; language, work, and careers; and some of the controversial issues of our time. You will find these topics interesting and entertaining to read. You will also learn things that will help you in the other courses you take in college and things that will be useful in your life.

How to Use This Book

Themes

This book is organized around five themes: (1) education, (2) culture, (3) language, (4) work and the world of business, and (5) controversial issues.

Thinking About

Each of the five thematic units of this book begins with a section called *Thinking About.* In this introductory section, ideas are presented to get you thinking about what you will be reading and studying. Often, you will find questions to stimulate you to remember what you already know about the subject the unit will cover. These questions will help you "turn on the engine" of your mind and get ready to learn.

Introduction

A short introduction precedes each reading selection. You should read it and answer any questions it contains. This will help you get ready to read.

The Reading

The reading selection itself then follows. You should read it straight through one time without stopping. Then go back and read it a second time, underlining important ideas, making notes, and marking any words you don't know.

Vocabulary

Each reading selection is followed by a list of important words selected from the text and instructions to help you figure out their meanings. These words were chosen because they are crucial to your understanding of the selection.

Guide Questions

Each reading selection is also followed by guide questions. Their purpose is to "guide" your understanding of the text. Some of the questions are simple fact questions, meant to ensure that you understand the basic information the author is trying to get across. Other questions are more sophisticated and ask you to *analyze* information, to *synthesize* information, to *evaluate* information.

Application

Following the guide questions for each reading are one or more questions that ask you to take some of the things you have learned and apply them to some different situation or to your own life. The ability to apply information to new situations is a high-level thinking skill. It proves that you truly comprehend what you have read.

Writing

Because reading and writing are closely linked, each chapter includes one or more writing assignments. Writing is the skill most college students need to develop.

Writing about what you have read is an interesting and valuable way to make the new information truly yours. As with all the features just described, your instructor will select which exercises you are to do and will give you all the support you need to complete them successfully.

How to Begin?

Don't begin by jumping right in. When you are reading a college textbook, you need to *prepare* to read and learn. The best way to prepare is to *preview* the book before you read any of the selections you are assigned. To learn how, turn to page 407 and read "Learning Strategy I—Previewing." Then do the exercise "Previewing a Textbook" on page 409.

Do this now and then come back here.

Now that you've previewed your textbook, you'll be able to read it more easily and comfortably. Similarly, previewing each *reading* will help you to read it well. Let's try it out. Preview the first reading selection, "What True Education Should Do," by answering the questions to "Previewing a Chapter" on page 410.

When you have finished, come back here.

Now you're ready to read! So, let's read and study the first selection in Unit One, *Reading and Thinking about Education:* "What True Education Should Do," by Sydney Harris. Read the introduction before the reading selection. (Always read these introductions and, if there are questions, answer them.) Here we see the author compares students to *sausages* and *oysters.* Sounds strange. How can a person be like a sausage? Think about what you already know about sausages. Well, they can be tasty—but I doubt that's what Harris means. Just what is a sausage anyway? It is a casing filled with chopped meat and other filler. How could this be like a student? With this question in mind, keep reading.

When you finish, you may still be confused about Harris's point—keep going. Move on to the vocabulary exercises. By going over any unfamiliar words, you'll go deeper into the text and clear up confusion as you go along.

Be sure to follow the directions carefully.

Now, let's do the first word as a practice. The word *animate* is in paragraph 1.

> *When most people think of the word* education, *they think of a pupil as a sort of animate sausage casing. Into this empty casing, the teachers are supposed to stuff "education."*

The author is comparing a pupil to a "sort of animate sausage casing" into which teachers stuff education. What kind of sausage casing could "animate" be? Empty? A good guess—the sentence would then read ". . . they think of a pupil as a sort of [empty] sausage casing." Could be right. But then note the following sentence: "Into this empty casing, the teachers are supposed to stuff 'education.'" Why would the author repeat this notion of "empty"? No, *animate* probably means something else. If you are stuck, your next move should be to the dictionary, where you will find something like "alive" or "living" as meanings of *animate.*

Does this make sense? Read the sentence again: ". . . they think of a pupil as a sort of [living] sausage casing." Sounds good, makes sense—it's probably right. Write it in the margin of the text. Then be sure to confirm your definition or synonym by looking up the word in a dictionary or thesaurus. When you get to class, check your meanings with your instructor. Then enter your correct meanings in the chart.

If you find other words you don't know, follow the same procedure with them. A box at the end of the vocabulary chart says "Others?" Enter any other unfamiliar words you've found, and check their meanings in the same way you would the key words. For example, you may want to check the meaning of the word *cultivate* in paragraph 10.

Remember to write the meanings of all the new words in the margin of the text. When you finish the vocabulary section, your text should look something like the example on page xxxi.

In the following reading selection, the author says students are usually treated as if they were sausages to be "stuffed" with information. He urges, instead, that students be treated as oysters—that is, something that education should "open" to reveal the riches within.

WHAT TRUE EDUCATION SHOULD DO

Sydney J. Harris

empty
living

When most people think of the word *education,* they think of a pupil as a sort of animate sausage casing. Into this empty casing, the teachers are supposed to stuff "education." 1

drawing out

But genuine education, as Socrates knew more than two thousand years ago, is not inserting the stuffings of information into a person, but rather eliciting knowledge from him; it is the drawing out of what is in the mind. 2

*I think
elicit is
explained
here*

"The most important part of education," once wrote William Ernest Hocking, the distinguished Harvard philosopher, "is this instruction of a man in what he has inside of him." 3

And as Edith Hamilton has reminded us, Socrates never said, "I know, learn from me." He said, rather, "Look into your own selves and find the spark of truth that God has put into every heart, and that only you can kindle to a flame." 4

In the dialogue called the "Meno," Socrates takes an ignorant slave boy, without a day of schooling, and proves to the amazed observers that the boy really "knows" geometry—because the principles and axioms of geometry are already in his mind, waiting to be called out. 5

useless

So many of the discussions and controversies about the content of education are futile and inconclusive because they are concerned with what should "go into" the student rather than with what should be taken out, and how this can best be done. 6

*briefly
+
clearly*

The college student who once said to me, after a lecture, "I spend so much time studying that I don't have a chance to learn anything" was succinctly expressing his dissatisfaction with the sausage-casing view of education. 7

He was being so stuffed with miscellaneous facts, with such an indigestible mass of material, that he had no time (and was given no encouragement) to draw on his own resources, to use his own mind for analyzing and synthesizing and evaluating this material. 8

*not yet
developed*

Education, to have any meaning beyond the purpose of creating well-informed dunces, must elicit from the pupil what is latent in every human being—the rules of reason, the inner knowledge of what is proper for men to be and do, the ability to sift evidence and come to conclusions that can generally be agreed to by all open minds and warm hearts. 9

*make them
grow*

Pupils are more like oysters than sausages. The job of teaching is not to stuff them and then seal them up, but to help them open and reveal the riches within. There are pearls in each of us, if only we knew how to cultivate them with ardor and persistence. 10

Key Word	Paragraph	Meaning
1. animate	1	*living/alive*
2. eliciting	2	*drawing out/bringing out*
3. futile	6	*useless*
4. succinctly	7	*briefly and clearly*
5. latent	9	*not yet developed/potential*
Others?		
cultivate	*10*	*make something grow*

When you have completed the vocabulary section, go on to the next section, *Guide Questions.* Read the directions carefully.

Notice that some of the questions are quite simple and straightforward, while others are much more demanding. Some may ask you to consider your own experience or knowledge of the world in answering, not just to consider ideas from the text.

Read the first guide question:

1. Write what you think is Harris's definition of a "true education."

No one sentence in the selection directly states Harris's definition of a true education, but it is certainly clear that he expects true learning to come from within the student rather than to be imposed by the teacher. The comments he makes in paragraph 9 begin to answer the question:

> Education, to have any meaning beyond the purpose of creating well-informed dunces, must elicit from the pupil what is latent in every human being—the rules of reason, the inner knowledge of what is proper for men to be and do, the ability to sift evidence and come to conclusions that can generally be agreed to by all open minds and warm hearts.

But to properly answer, you should create your own conclusion of *what you think Harris would say if he were asked this question.* In other words, draw an inference based on all the information in the selection.

Complete the guide questions. Note that the third question asks you to take the ideas from the chapter and apply them to your own life.

Go on to the next section, called "Application." This section will vary with each selection. Here, you will be asked to think about the education you have received so far and discuss with your classmates what you would still like to learn.

Last is a section called "Writing." Here, you have two questions to consider. Your instructor will tell you whether to do one or both. In one, you are asked to write a short essay based on the ideas you generated in the Application section. In the second, you are asked to *react* to Harris's view of education. To *react* means to respond with your point of view and the reasons you feel the way you do.

Many of the questions in this book begin with special *direction words.* These are words you see frequently on college assignments and exams. Some examples are *cite, define, paraphrase, summarize,* and so on. It is important to respond accurately to these words. Turn to page 423 to study and practice using direction words.

Special Projects

At the end of Units Two through Five in the text you will find a special project. The goal of each project is to allow you to use the knowledge and skills you have gained from reading extensively about one particular topic.

Unit Six

Unit Six of the text, *Reading and Thinking about Textbooks,* is different from the first five parts. Here, you will work with actual excerpts from college textbooks. With these chapters, you can practice your reading and studying skills with "the real thing." You can even test yourself by answering the actual exam questions that teachers ask on tests.

The Thoughtful Reader

UNIT ONE

READING AND THINKING ABOUT EDUCATION

Think about the kind of world you want to live and work in. What do you need to know to build that world? Demand your teachers teach you that.

—Prince Kropotkin

In oneself lies the whole world, and if you know how to look and learn, then the door is there and the key is in your hand. Nobody on earth can give you either that key or the door to open, except yourself.

—J. Krishnamurti

Thinking about Education

As you begin this new chapter in your college career, take a moment to reflect. Why are you in college? You may answer that you are "getting an education." But what does the word *education* really mean? Do you envision learning lots of new facts, memorizing them, and repeating them back to the instructor on exams? Is the possession of a piece of paper (a degree or certificate) your only goal? Is education simply a stepping-stone to a well-paying job? Or is it the key to becoming a happier, more fulfilled person? Perhaps education means something different to you. Take a few moments to think about your definition of education before you read this section of the book.

In the following reading selection, the author says students are usually treated as if they were sausages to be "stuffed" with information. He urges, instead, that students be treated as oysters—that is, something that education should "open" to reveal the riches within.

WHAT TRUE EDUCATION SHOULD DO

Sydney J. Harris

1   When most people think of the word *education,* they think of a pupil as a sort of animate sausage casing. Into this empty casing, the teachers are supposed to stuff "education."

2   But genuine education, as Socrates knew more than two thousand years ago, is not inserting the stuffings of information into a person, but rather eliciting knowledge from him; it is the drawing out of what is in the mind.

3   "The most important part of education," once wrote William Ernest Hocking, the distinguished Harvard philosopher, "is this instruction of a man in what he has inside of him."

4   And as Edith Hamilton has reminded us, Socrates* never said, "I know, learn from me." He said, rather, "Look into your own selves and find the spark of truth that God has put into every heart, and that only you can kindle to a flame."

5   In the dialogue called the "Meno," Socrates takes an ignorant slave boy, without a day of schooling, and proves to the amazed observers that the boy really "knows" geometry—because the principles and axioms of geometry are already in his mind, waiting to be called out.

6   So many of the discussions and controversies about the content of education are futile and inconclusive because they are concerned with what should "go into" the student rather than with what should be taken out, and how this can best be done.

7   The college student who once said to me, after a lecture, "I spend so much time studying that I don't have a chance to learn anything" was succinctly expressing his dissatisfaction with the sausage-casing view of education.

8   He was being so stuffed with miscellaneous facts, with such an indigestible mass of material, that he had no time (and was given no encouragement) to draw on his own resources, to use his own mind for analyzing and synthesizing and evaluating this material.

---

*Socrates (469–399 BC) was a Greek philosopher who profoundly affected Western thought. Socrates believed that *discussion* and *self-examination* were the best ways to develop the mind and the spirit. He spent most of his life engaging in dialogue and argument with anyone who would listen and would engage in his question-and-answer form of teaching. He believed he could best serve his country as a teacher, encouraging the people of Athens to engage in self-examination and in tending to their souls.

Socrates believed that discussion was more important than writing, and so we have no written record of his thinking. Most of what we know about him we learn through the writings of his famous student, the philosopher Plato.

Education, to have any meaning beyond the purpose of creating well-   9
informed dunces, must elicit from the pupil what is latent in every human being—
the rules of reason, the inner knowledge of what is proper for men to be and do,
the ability to sift evidence and come to conclusions that can generally be agreed
to by all open minds and warm hearts.

Pupils are more like oysters than sausages. The job of teaching is not to stuff   10
them and then seal them up, but to help them open and reveal the riches within.
There are pearls in each of us, if only we knew how to cultivate them with ardor
and persistence.

Vocabulary

Directions: Find each of the key words in the reading selection. Study each word in its
context and try to determine its meaning. Write what you think it means in the margin
of the text, near the word. Then read over the sentence, mentally substituting your guess
for the key word. Does the sentence still make sense? Does it retain its original meaning?
If it does, you've probably figured out the meaning of the key word correctly. In any case,
confirm your guess by checking a dictionary or thesaurus.

If you take your meaning from a dictionary or thesaurus, be sure the definition
includes words you already know and feel comfortable using. If it doesn't, you will be
worse off than when you started—you will have begun with one word you didn't know
and ended with *two* words you don't know!

Record the new words you've learned in the following chart.

Key Word	Paragraph	Meaning
1. animate	1	
2. eliciting	2	
3. futile	6	
4. succinctly	7	
5. latent	9	
Others?		

Guide Questions

Directions: These questions will guide your analysis of the text. Your thoughtful answers
will ensure that you understood the main ideas the author wanted to convey. Some questions ask you simply to find the stated facts in the reading selection; others ask you to

do more difficult tasks, such as paraphrasing information (putting the author's ideas into your own words), synthesizing several ideas into one complex thought, evaluating (making judgments about) an idea, or taking information from the reading and applying it to a new situation or to your own life.

Write answers to the questions in your notebook or on a separate sheet of paper if your instructor wishes to collect it. Your answers will form the basis of class discussion.

1. Write what you think is Harris's definition of a "true education."
2. Explain what Harris means by his comparison of students to sausages and oysters.
3. Have teachers treated you like a sausage or like an oyster? Would a different comparison better describe your personal experience? Explain.

Application

Directions: Read the following observations by Alan Watts on what he feels would have been an ideal education for him; then answer the questions that follow.

It is perhaps idle to wonder what, from my present point of view, would have been an ideal education. If I could provide such a curriculum for my own children they, in their turn, might find it all a bore. But the fantasy of what I would have liked to learn as a child may be revealing, since I feel unequipped by education for problems that lie outside the cloistered, literary domain in which I am competent and at home. Looking back then, I would have arranged for myself to be taught survival techniques for both natural and urban wildernesses. I would want to have been instructed in self-hypnosis; in *aikido* (the esoteric and purely self-defensive style of judo); in elementary medicine; in sexual hygiene; in vegetable gardening; in astronomy, navigation, and sailing; in cookery and clothesmaking; in metalwork and carpentry; in drawing and painting; in printing and typography; in botany and biology; in optics and acoustics; in semantics and psychology; in mysticism and yoga; in electronics and mathematical fantasy; in drama and dancing; in singing and in playing an instrument by ear; in wandering; in advanced daydreaming; in prestidigitation; in techniques of escape from bondage; in disguise; in conversation with birds and beasts; in ventriloquism; in French and German conversation; in planetary history; in morphology; and in classical Chinese. Actually, the main thing left out of my education was a proper love for my own body, because one feared to cherish anything so obviously mortal and prone to sickness.

1. What do you think Watts does for a living? What evidence in the paragraph supports your guess?
2. When Watts says there is one area in which he feels competent and at home, what does he mean by "at home"?

3. In a small group, discuss the ideas addressed in this essay. Choose a director for your group whose job is to ask group members to discuss their own personal lists of (1) the areas where they feel "competent and at home"; and (2) things they wish they had been taught. At the end of the discussion, each person should have two lists that can be developed into the essay described in writing assignment 1 below.

Writing

1. Write a short essay similar to the one by Alan Watts. In the first paragraph, describe, as Watts does, the areas in which you feel "competent." In the second paragraph, name and describe the things you wish you had been taught.

2. React to the argument presented in Sydney J. Harris's "What True Education Should Do." Do you agree or disagree with the author? Write one paragraph stating your reaction, giving reasons to support your opinion.

3. Here are comments on education by three famous writers. Read and think about each one of them. Then write your own definition or description of education.

> Education is not the filling of a pail, but the lighting of a fire.
>
> —*William Butler Yeats*

> Education is a companion which no misfortune can depress, no crime can destroy, no enemy can alienate, no despotism can enslave. At home, a friend, abroad, an introduction, in solitude, a solace and in society, an ornament. It chastens vice, it guides virtue, it gives at once grace and government to genius. Without it, what is man? A splendid slave, a reasoning savage.
>
> —*Joseph Addison*

> Education is the movement from darkness to light.
>
> —*Alan Bloom*

SHORT TAKE

Hope Helps

Just beginning college? Just sent your son or daughter off to school? Here is a scary statistic: there is approximately a 50% chance that you (or your beloved child) will drop out, most likely in the first year.

Is there anything that can help to improve your odds?

Research has shown that high hopes can make a difference. The students who scored "most hopeful" on tests tended to stay in school and to do better academically than those who described themselves as more pessimistic. In fact, students' perceptions of their likelihood of success were better predictors of success than standardized tests. Students with low expectations generally achieved averages of C while those with higher hopes averaged Bs.

More students who began with high hopes graduated at a higher rate than others.

So, look on the bright side—it couldn't hurt and may well help.

Mortimer Adler was well known for many things: he was the chairman of the Board of Editors of Encyclopaedia Britannica; *he was a prolific writer, perhaps most famous for his series of "Great Ideas" books in which he discussed six ideas—truth, beauty, equality, justice, goodness, and liberty—in ways that every reader could understand and enjoy. He originated the "Great Books" program in which people from all backgrounds met to read and discuss the classics. Dr. Adler was a philosopher who believed that "philosophy is everybody's business" and that a better understanding of great ideas is essential if we are to cope with the political, moral, and social issues that we all confront.*

Dr. Adler, who died in 2001 at the age of 98, wrote extensively about the joys of reading and the "how-to's" of reading. In this essay, which appeared in the Saturday Review of Literature *in 1940, he offers timeless advice on how to "own" a book.*

HOW TO MARK A BOOK

Mortimer Adler

You know you have to read "between the lines" to get the most out of anything. I want to persuade you to do something equally important in the course of your reading. I want to persuade you to "write between the lines." Unless you do, you are not likely to do the most efficient kind of reading. 1

I contend, quite bluntly, that marking up a book is not an act of mutilation but of love. 2

You shouldn't mark up a book which isn't yours. Librarians (or your friends) who lend you books expect you to keep them clean, and you should. If you decide that I am right about the usefulness of marking books, you will have to buy them. Most of the world's great books are available today, in reprint editions. 3

There are two ways in which one can own a book. The first is the property right you establish by paying for it, just as you pay for clothes and furniture. But this act of purchase is only the prelude to possession. Full ownership comes only when you have made it a part of yourself, and the best way to make yourself a part of it is by writing in it. An illustration may make the point clear. You buy a beefsteak and transfer it from the butcher's icebox to your own. But you do not own the beefsteak in the most important sense until you consume it and get it into your bloodstream. I am arguing that books, too, must be absorbed in your bloodstream to do you any good. 4

Confusion about what it means to *own* a book leads people to a false reverence for paper, binding, and type—a respect for the physical thing—the craft of the printer rather than the genius of the author. They forget that it is possible for a man to acquire the idea, to possess the beauty, which a great book contains, without staking his claim by pasting his bookplate inside the cover. Having a fine library doesn't prove that its owner has a mind enriched by books; it proves nothing more than that he, his father, or his wife, was rich enough to buy them. 5

There are three kinds of book owners. The first has all the standard sets and best-sellers—unread, untouched. (This deluded individual owns woodpulp and ink, not books.) The second has a great many books—a few of them read 6 through, most of them dipped into, but all of them as clean and shiny as the day they were bought. (This person would probably like to make books his own, but is restrained by a false respect for their physical appearance.) The third has a few books or many—every one of them dog-eared and dilapidated, shaken and loosened by continual use, marked and scribbled in from front to back. (This man owns books.)

7   Is it false respect, you may ask, to preserve intact and unblemished a beautifully printed book, an elegantly bound edition? Of course not. I'd no more scribble all over a first edition of *Paradise Lost* than I'd give my baby a set of crayons and an original Rembrandt! I wouldn't mark up a painting or a statue. Its soul, so to speak, is inseparable from its body. And the beauty of a rare edition or of a richly manufactured volume is like that of a painting or a statue.

8   But the soul of a book *can* be separated from its body. A book is more like the score of a piece of music than it is like a painting. No great musician confuses a symphony with the printed sheets of music. Arturo Toscanini reveres Brahms, but Toscanini's score of the C-minor Symphony is so thoroughly marked up that no one but the maestro himself can read it. The reason why a great conductor makes notations on his musical scores—marks them up again and again each time he returns to study them—is the reason why you should mark your books. If your respect for magnificent binding or typography gets in the way, buy yourself a cheap edition and pay your respects to the author.

9   Why is marking up a book indispensable to reading? First, it keeps you awake. (And I don't mean merely conscious; I mean wide awake.) In the second place, reading, if it is active, is thinking, and thinking tends to express itself in words, spoken or written. The marked book is usually the thought-through book. Finally, writing helps you remember the thoughts you had, or the thoughts the author expressed. Let me develop these three points.

10   If reading is to accomplish anything more than passing time, it must be active. You can't let your eyes glide across the lines of a book and come up with an understanding of what you have read. Now an ordinary piece of light fiction, like say, *Gone with the Wind,* doesn't require the most active kind of reading. The books you read for pleasure can be read in a state of relaxation, and nothing is lost. But a great book, rich in ideas and beauty, a book that raises and tries to answer great fundamental questions, demands the most active reading of which you are capable. You don't absorb the ideas of John Dewey the way you absorb the crooning of Mr. Vallee. You have to reach for them. That you cannot do while you're asleep.

11   If, when you've finished reading a book, the pages are filled with your notes, you know that you read actively. The most famous active reader of great books I know is President Hutchins, of the University of Chicago. He also has the hardest schedule of business activities of any man I know. He invariably reads with a pencil, and sometimes, when he picks up a book and pencil in the evening, he finds himself, instead of making intelligent notes, drawing what he calls "caviar factories" on the margins. When that happens, he puts the book down. He knows he's too tired to read, and he's just wasting time.

But, you may ask, why is writing necessary? Well, the physical act of writing, with your own hand, brings words and sentences more sharply before your mind and preserves them better in your memory. To set down your reaction to important words and sentences you have read, and the questions they have raised in your mind, is to preserve those reactions and sharpen those questions.   12

Even if you wrote on a scratch pad, and threw the paper away when you had finished writing, your grasp of the book would be surer. But you don't have to throw the paper away. The margins (top and bottom, as well as side), the end-papers, the very space between the lines, are all available. They aren't sacred. And, best of all, your marks and notes become an integral part of the book and stay there forever. You can pick up the book the following week or year, and there are all your points of agreement, disagreement, doubt, and inquiry. It's like resuming an interrupted conversation with the advantage of being able to pick up where you left off.   13

And that is exactly what reading a book should be: a conversation between you and the author. Presumably, he knows more about the subject than you do; naturally, you'll have the proper humility as you approach him. But don't let anybody tell you that a reader is supposed to be solely on the receiving end. Understanding is a two-way operation; learning doesn't consist in being an empty receptacle. The learner has to question himself and question the teacher. He even has to argue with the teacher, once he understands what the teacher is saying. And marking a book is literally an expression of your differences, or agreements of opinion, with the author.   14

There are all kinds of devices for marking a book intelligently and fruitfully. Here's the way I do it: 15

1. *Underlining:* of major points, of important or forceful statements.
2. *Vertical lines at the margin:* to emphasize a statement already underlined.
3. *Star, asterisk, or other doo-dad at the margin:* to be used sparingly, to emphasize the ten or twenty most important statements in the book. (You may want to fold the bottom corner of each page on which you use such marks. It won't hurt the sturdy paper on which most modern books are printed, and you will be able to take the book off the shelf at any time and, by opening it at the folded-corner page, refresh your recollection of the book.)
4. *Numbers in the margin:* to indicate the sequence of points the author makes in developing a single argument.
5. *Numbers of other pages in the margin:* to indicate where else in the book the author made points relevant to the point marked; to tie up the ideas in a book, which, though they may be separated by many pages, belong together.
6. *Circling of key words or phrases.*
7. *Writing in the margin, or at the top or bottom of the page, for the sake of:* recording questions (and perhaps answers) that a passage raised in your mind; reducing a complicated discussion to a simple statement; recording the sequence of major points right through the books. I use the end-papers at

the back of the book to make a personal index of the author's points in the order of their appearance.

16   The front end-papers are, to me, the most important. Some people reserve them for a fancy bookplate. I reserve them for fancy thinking. After I have finished reading the book and making my personal index on the back end-papers, I turn to the front and try to outline the book, not page by page, or point by point (I've already done that at the back), but as an integrated structure, with a basic unity and an order of parts. This outline is, to me, the measure of my understanding of the work.

17   If you're a die-hard anti-book-marker, you may object that the margins, the space between the lines, and the end-papers don't give you room enough. All right. How about using a scratch pad slightly smaller than the page-size of the book—so that the edges of the sheets won't protrude? Make your index, outlines, and even your notes on the pad, and then insert these sheets permanently inside the front and back covers of the book.

18   Or, you may say that this business of marking books is going to slow up your reading. It probably will. That's one of the reasons for doing it. Most of us have been taken in by the notion that speed of reading is a measure of our intelligence. There is no such thing as the right speed for intelligent reading. Some things should be read quickly and effortlessly, and some should be read slowly and even laboriously. The sign of intelligence in reading is the ability to read different things according to their worth. In the case of good books, the point is not to see how many of them you can get through, but rather how many can get through you—how many you can make your own. A few friends are better than a thousand acquaintances. If this be your aim, as it should be, you will not be impatient if it takes more time and effort to read a great book than it does a newspaper.

19   You may have one final objection to marking books. You can't lend them to your friends because nobody else can read them without being distracted by your notes. Furthermore, you won't want to lend them because a marked copy is a kind of intellectual diary, and lending it is almost like giving your mind away.

20   If your friend wishes to read your *Plutarch's Lives,* Shakespeare, or *The Federalist Papers,* tell him gently but firmly to buy a copy. You will lend him your car or your coat—but your books are as much a part of you as your head or your heart.

Vocabulary

Directions: Locate each of the key words in the reading selection. Try to figure out each word's meaning by using the context. Confirm your guess by checking the dictionary or thesaurus. Write the meanings of the words in the margin of the text. Then record the meanings in the following chart.

Key Word	Paragraph	Meaning
1. mutilation	2	
2. intact	7	
3. indispensable	9	
4. invariably	11	
5. die-hard	17	
Others?		

Guide Questions

Directions: These questions will guide your understanding of what you have read. Write your answers in your notebook, or on a separate sheet of paper if your instructor wishes to collect it. Your answers to these questions will be the basis of class discussion.

1. Cite two ways to "own" a book, according to Adler.
2. List the three types of book owners.
3. Explain Adler's statement: "the soul of a book *can* be separated from its body."
4. Why is marking indispensable?
5. React to Adler's statement: "Reading a book should be a conversation between you and the author."
6. Which of the seven devices for marking a book do you think would be valuable to you?
7. Explain why Adler says that even though marking books will slow up your reading, that's OK.
8. Explain how you would mark these books differently:
   a. a romance novel
   b. a psychology textbook
   c. a "how-to" manual for using a digital camera
   d. a philosophy textbook
9. Assume you are still a die-hard anti-book-marker. Can you think of any other ways to get the benefits of marking text? (Hint: Think *post-it notes.*)

Application

Use the tips in Adler's essay to mark his essay.

Making Connections

Consider the first reading selection in this unit, "What True Education Should Do" by Sydney J. Harris (pages 2–3). Which do you think Mortimer Adler would support—the "sausage" or "oyster" view of education?

SHORT TAKE

The First Book

Rita Dove

Open it.

Go ahead, it won't bite.
Well, maybe a little.

More a nip, like. A tingle.
It's pleasurable, really.

You see, it keeps on opening.
You may fall in.

Sure, it's hard to get started;
Remember learning to use

Knife and fork? Dig in:
You'll never reach bottom.

It's not like it's the end of the world—
Just the world as you think

You know it.

Richard Wright's story of his life caused a sensation when it was first published in 1937.
Until then it had been unthinkable that a black man would dare to tell the truth about the
poverty, hunger, fear, and hatred that dominated the lives of black Americans in the racially
segregated South. In his book, Wright describes his own reaction to the brutality that sur-
rounded him. He tells how he learned to hate, lie, steal, drink, and perhaps worst of all,
to pity himself.

Eventually, through reading, Wright learned to understand himself and his situation.
Through his writing, he helped the world understand the cruel society bred by racism.

BLACK BOY

Richard Wright

I entered the library as I had always done when on errands for whites, but I felt   1
that I would somehow slip up and betray myself. I doffed my hat, stood a respect-
ful distance from the desk, looked as unbookish as possible, and waited for the
white patrons to be taken care of. When the desk was clear of people, I still
waited. The white librarian looked at me.

"What do you want, boy?"   2

As though I did not possess the power of speech, I stepped forward and simply   3
handed her the forged note, not parting my lips.

"What books by Mencken does he want?" she asked.   4

"I don't know, ma'am," I said, avoiding her eyes.   5

"Who gave you this card?"   6

"Mr. Falk," I said.   7

"Where is he?"   8

"He's at work, at the M———— Optical Company," I said. "I've been in here   9
for him before."

"I remember," the woman said. "But he never wrote notes like this."   10

Oh, God, she's suspicious. Perhaps she would not let me have the books? If   11
she had turned her back at that moment, I would have ducked out the door and
never gone back. Then I thought of a bold idea.

"You can call him up, ma'am," I said, my heart pounding.   12

"You're not using these books, are you?" she asked pointedly.   13

"Oh, no, ma'am. I can't read."   14

"I don't know what he wants by Mencken," she said under her breath.   15

I knew now that I had won; she was thinking of other things and the race   16
question had gone out of her mind. She went to the shelves. Once or twice she
looked over her shoulder at me, as though she was still doubtful. Finally she came
forward with two books in her hand.

"I'm sending him two books," she said. "But tell Mr. Falk to come in next   17
time, or send me the names of the books he wants. I don't know what he wants
to read."

I said nothing. She stamped the card and handed me the books. Not daring   18
to glance at them, I went out of the library, fearing that the woman would call

me back for further questioning. A block away from the library I opened one of the books and read a title: *A Book of Prefaces*. I was nearing my nineteenth birthday and I did not know how to pronounce the word "preface." I thumbed the pages and saw strange words and strange names. I shook my head, disappointed. I looked at the other book; it was called *Prejudices*. I knew what that word meant; I had heard it all my life. And right off I was on guard against Mencken's books. Why would a man want to call a book *Prejudices*? The word was so stained with all my memories of racial hate that I could not conceive of anybody using it for a title. Perhaps I had made a mistake about Mencken? A man who had prejudices must be wrong.

19   When I showed the books to Mr. Falk, he looked at me and frowned.

20   "That librarian might telephone you," I warned him.

21   "That's all right," he said. "But when you're through reading those books, I want you to tell me what you get out of them."

22   That night in my rented room, while letting the hot water run over my can of pork and beans in the sink, I opened *A Book of Prefaces* and began to read. I was jarred and shocked by the style, the clear, clean, sweeping sentences. Why did he write like that? And how did one write like that? I pictured the man as a raging demon, slashing with his pen, consumed with hate, denouncing everything American, extolling everything European or German, laughing at the weaknesses of people, mocking God, authority. What was this? I stood up, trying to realize what reality lay behind the meaning of the words . . . Yes, this man was fighting, fighting with words. He was using words as a weapon, using them as one would use a club. Could words be weapons? Well, yes, for here they were. Then, maybe, perhaps, I could use them as a weapon? No. It frightened me. I read on and what amazed me was not what he said, but how on earth anybody had the courage to say it.

23   Occasionally I glanced up to reassure myself that I was alone in the room. Who were these men about whom Mencken was talking so passionately? Who was Anatole France? Joseph Conrad? Sinclair Lewis, Sherwood Anderson, Dostoyevsky, George Moore, Gustave Flaubert, Maupassant, Tolstoy, Frank Harris, Mark Twain, Thomas Hardy, Arnold Bennett, Stephen Crane, Zola, Norris, Gorky, Bergson, Ibsen, Balzac, Bernard Shaw, Dumas, Poe, Thomas Mann, O. Henry, Dreiser, H. G. Wells, Gogol, T. S. Eliot, Gide, Baudelaire, Edgar Lee Masters, Stendhal, Turgenev, Huneker, Nietzsche, and scores of others? Were these men real? Did they exist or had they existed? And how did one pronounce their names?

24   I ran across many words whose meanings I did not know, and I either looked them up in a dictionary or, before I had a chance to do that, encountered the word in a context that made its meaning clear. But what strange world was this? I concluded the book with the conviction that I had somehow overlooked something terribly important in life. I had once tried to write, had once reveled in feeling, had let my crude imagination roam, but the impulse to dream had been slowly beaten out of me by experience. Now it surged up again and I hungered for books, new ways of looking and seeing. It was not a matter of believing or disbelieving

what I read, but of feeling something new, of being affected by something that made the look of the world different.

As dawn broke I ate my pork and beans, feeling dopey, sleepy. I went to work, but the mood of the book would not die; it lingered, coloring everything I saw, heard, did. I now felt that I knew what the white men were feeling. Merely because I had read a book that had spoken of how they lived and thought, I identified myself with that book. I felt vaguely guilty. Would I, filled with bookish notions, act in a manner that would make the whites dislike me?   25

I forged more notes and my trips to the library became frequent. Reading grew into a passion. My first serious novel was Sinclair Lewis's *Main Street.* It made me see my boss, Mr. Gerald, and identify him as an American type. I would smile when I saw him lugging his golf bags into the office. I had always felt a vast distance separating me from the boss, and now I felt closer to him, that I could feel the very limits of his narrow life. And this had happened because I had read a novel about a mythical man called George F. Babbitt.   26

The plots and stories in the novels did not interest me so much as the point of view revealed. I gave myself over to each novel without reserve, without trying to criticize it; it was enough for me to see and feel something different. And for me, everything was something different. Reading was like a drug, a dope. The novels created moods in which I lived for days. But I could not conquer my sense of guilt, my feeling that the white men around me knew that I was changing, that I had begun to regard them differently.   27

Whenever I brought a book to the job, I wrapped it in newspaper—a habit that was to persist for years in other cities and under other circumstances. But some of the white men pried into my packages when I was absent and they questioned me.   28

"Boy, what are you reading those books for?"   29

"Oh, I don't know, sir."   30

"That's deep stuff you're reading, boy."   31

"I'm just killing time, sir."   32

"You'll addle your brains if you don't watch out."   33

I read Dreiser's *Jennie Gerhardt* and *Sister Carrie* and they revived in me a vivid sense of my mother's suffering; I was overwhelmed. I grew silent, wondering about the life around me. It would have been impossible for me to have told anyone what I derived from these novels, for it was nothing less than a sense of life itself. All my life had shaped me for the realism, the naturalism of the modern novel, and I could not read enough of them.   34

Steeped in new moods and ideas, I bought a ream of paper and tried to write; but nothing would come, or what did come was flat beyond telling. I discovered that more than desire and feeling were necessary to write and I dropped the idea. Yet I still wondered how it was possible to know people sufficiently to write about them? Could I ever learn about life and people? To me, with my vast ignorance, my Jim Crow station in life, it seemed a task impossible of achievement. I now knew what being a Negro meant. I could endure the hunger. I had learned to live with hate. But to feel that there were feelings denied me, that the very   35 breath of life itself was beyond my reach, that more than anything else, hurt, wounded me. I had a new hunger.

36   In buoying me up, reading also cast me down, made me see what was possible, what I had missed. My tension returned, new, terrible, bitter, surging, almost too great to be contained. I no longer *felt* that the world about me was hostile, killing; I *knew* it. A million times I asked myself what I could do to save myself, and there were no answers. I seemed forever condemned, ringed by walls.

37   I did not discuss my reading with Mr. Falk, who had lent me his library card; it would have meant talking about myself and that would have been too painful. I smiled each day, fighting desperately to maintain my old behavior, to keep my disposition seemingly sunny. But some of the white men discerned that I had begun to brood.

38   "Wake up there, boy!" Mr. Olin said one day.

39   "Sir!" I answered for the lack of a better word.

40   "You act like you've stolen something," he said.

41   I laughed in the way I knew he expected me to laugh, but I resolved to be more conscious of myself, to watch my every act, to guard and hide the new knowledge that was dawning within me.

42   If I went north, would it be possible for me to build a new life then? But how could a man build a life upon vague, unformed yearnings? I wanted to write and I did not even know the English language. I bought English grammars and found them dull. I felt that I was getting a better sense of the language from novels than from grammars. I read hard, discarding a writer as soon as I felt that I had grasped his point of view. At night the printed page stood before my eyes in sleep.

43   Mrs. Moss, my landlady, asked me one Sunday morning:

44   "Son, what is this you keep on reading?"

45   "Oh, nothing. Just novels."

46   "What you get out of 'em?"

47   "I'm just killing time," I said.

48   "I hope you know your own mind," she said in a tone which implied that she doubted if I had a mind.

49   I knew of no Negroes who read the books I liked and I wondered if any Negroes ever thought of them. I knew that there were Negro doctors, lawyers, newspapermen, but I never saw any of them. When I read a Negro newspaper I never caught the faintest echo of my preoccupation in its pages. I felt trapped and occasionally, for a few days, I would stop reading. But a vague hunger would come over me for books, books that opened up new avenues of feeling and seeing, and again I would forge another note to the white librarian. Again I would read and wonder as only the naïve and unlettered can read and wonder, feeling that I carried a secret, criminal burden about with me each day.

Vocabulary

Directions: Locate each of the key words in the reading selection. Try to figure out each word's meaning by using the context. Confirm your guess by checking the dictionary or thesaurus. Write the meanings of the words in the margin of the text. Then record the meanings in the following chart.

Key Word	Paragraph	Meaning
1. forged	3	
2. extolling	22	
3. reveled	24	
4. steeped	35	
5. buoying	36	
6. brood	37	
7. yearnings	42	
Others?		

Guide Questions

Directions: These questions will guide your understanding of what you have read. Write your answers in your notebook or on a separate sheet of paper if your instructor wishes to collect it. Your answers to these questions will be the basis of class discussion.

1. Jim Crow laws are not defined, but merely alluded to, in this story.
   a. Go through the story and find examples of unequal treatment of black Americans in the South during the first few decades of the twentieth century.
   b. Go to your encyclopedia or use the Internet to find a complete description of Jim Crow laws.
2. Blacks were forbidden to use public libraries, yet young Wright managed to get the books he so desperately wanted. How did he do this?
3. What can we infer about Mr. Falk and his attitude toward Wright's desire to read?
4. Wright managed to take out some books by H. L. Mencken. What effect did Mencken's words have on him?
5. In paragraph 23, Wright says, "Occasionally I glanced up to reassure myself that I was alone in the room." Why does he say this?

6. On several occasions, Wright refers to his "guilt" (see paragraph 27, for example). What does he feel guilty about?

7. In paragraph 35, Wright says, "I now knew what being a Negro meant." What do you think it meant to him?

Application

Wright makes extraordinary use of figurative language, for example in paragraph 22: "slashing with his pen," and "Could words be weapons?" How many other powerful examples of figurative language can you find in the story? Go through the story and note all the examples you find. Then compare your examples with those of your classmates. What effect does the use of this kind of language have on the reader? (Figurative language is introduced and explained on pages 427–429, Learning Strategy VI.)

Writing

Directions: Choose one of these assignments.

1. Wright feels that he was "saved" by reading and writing. What might have happened to him if he had not discovered books? Write two or three paragraphs.

2. Imagine if the Richard Wright in this story were 19 years old today. How would his life be different? Write two or three paragraphs.

SHORT TAKE

Examples of "Jim Crow" Laws

From the 1880s into the 1960s, a majority of American states enforced segregation through "Jim Crow" laws (so called after a black character in minstrel shows). From Delaware to California, and from North Dakota to Texas, many states (and cities, too) could impose legal punishments on people for associating with members of another race. The most common types of laws forbade intermarriage and ordered business owners and public institutions to keep their black and white clientele separated.

Here is a sampling of laws from various states.

Buses All passenger stations in this state operated by any motor transportation company shall have separate waiting rooms or space and separate ticket windows for the white and colored races. **Alabama**

Restaurants It shall be unlawful to conduct a restaurant or other place for the serving of food in the city, at which white and colored people are served in the same room, unless such white and colored persons are effectually separated by a solid partition extending from the floor upward to a distance of seven feet or higher, and unless a separate entrance from the street is provided for each compartment. **Alabama**

Toilet Facilities, Male Every employer of white or negro males shall provide for such white or negro males reasonably accessible and separate toilet facilities. **Alabama**

Intermarriage The marriage of a person of Caucasian blood with a negro, Mongolian, Malay, or Hindu shall be null and void. **Arizona**

Intermarriage All marriages between a white person and a negro, or between a white person and a person of negro descent to the fourth generation inclusive, are hereby forever prohibited. **Florida**

Education The schools for white children and the schools for negro children shall be conducted separately. **Florida**

Burial The officer in charge shall not bury, or allow to be buried, any colored persons upon ground set apart or used for the burial of white persons. **Georgia**

Amateur Baseball It shall be unlawful for any amateur white baseball team to play baseball on any vacant lot or baseball diamond within two blocks of a playground devoted to the Negro race, and it shall be unlawful for any amateur colored baseball team to play baseball in any vacant lot or baseball diamond within two blocks of any playground devoted to the white race. **Georgia**

Circus Tickets All circuses, shows, and tent exhibitions, to which the attendance of more than one race is invited or expected to attend shall provide for the convenience of its patrons not less than two ticket offices with individual ticket sellers, and not less than two entrances to the said performance, with individual ticket takers and receivers, and in the case of outside or tent performances, the said ticket offices shall not be less than twenty-five (25) feet apart. **Louisiana**

Promotion of Equality Any person . . . who shall be guilty of printing, publishing or circulating printed, typewritten, or written matter urging or presenting for public acceptance, or general information, arguments or suggestions in favor of social equality or of intermarriage between whites and negroes, shall be guilty of a misdemeanor and subject to fine not exceeding five hundred (500.00) dollars or imprisonment not exceeding six (6) months or both. **Mississippi**

Libraries The state librarian is directed to fit up and maintain a separate place for the use of the colored people who may come to the library for the purpose of reading books or periodicals. **North Carolina**

Lunch Counters No persons, firms, or corporations, who or which furnish meals to passengers at station restaurants or station eating houses, in times limited by common carriers of said passengers, shall furnish said meals to white and colored passengers in the same room, or at the same table, or at the same counter. **South Carolina**

Grace Paley (1922–2007) was one of America's most beloved writers. In much of her work, she explored the lives of women—mostly Jewish, mostly New Yorkers—in all their dailiness, ordinary women muddling through everyday lives. Her stories are marked by close attention to language, with its tonal rise and fall, hairpin rhetorical reversals and delicious understatement. Like "Traveling," many of her stories are written in the first person and beg to be read aloud. A self-described "somewhat combative pacifist and cooperative anarchist," Ms. Paley was an advocate of liberal causes. During the Vietnam War she was jailed several times for protests; in later years she lobbied for women's rights, against nuclear proliferation, and, most recently, against the war in Iraq. Ms. Paley taught for many years at Sarah Lawrence College and the City College of New York.

Paley lived what she called the "push-pull life" of a wife, mother, professor, peace activist, and, of course, writer. Many called her a "great American writer," but as Jamaica Kincaid says, that is too specific; "she was just simply great."

As you read this profoundly moving story, try to appreciate its simple, graceful language.

TRAVELING

Grace Paley

1   My mother and sister were traveling south. The year was 1927. They had begun their journey in New York. They were going to visit my brother, who was studying in the South Medical College of Virginia. Their bus was an express and had stopped only in Philadelphia, Wilmington, and now Washington. Here, the darker people who had gotten on in Philadelphia or New York rose from their seats, put their bags and boxes together, and moved to the back of the bus. People who boarded in Washington knew where to seat themselves. My mother had heard that something like this would happen. My sister had heard of it, too. They had not lived in it. This reorganization of passengers by color happened in silence. My mother and sister remained in their seats, which were about three-quarters of the way back.

2   When everyone was settled, the bus driver began to collect tickets. My sister saw him coming. She pinched my mother: Ma! Look! Of course, my mother saw him, too. What frightened my sister was the quietness. The white people in front, the black people in back—silent.

3   The driver sighed, said, You can't sit here, ma'am. It's for them waving over his shoulder at the Negroes, among whom they were now sitting. Move, please.

4   My mother said, No.

5   He said, You don't understand, ma'am. It's against the law. You have to move to the front.

6   My mother said, No.

7   When I first tried to write this scene, I imagined my mother saying, That's all right, mister, we're comfortable. I can't change my seat every minute. I read this invention to my sister. She said it was nothing like that. My mother did not try to be friendly or pretend innocence. While my sister trembled in the silence, my mother said, for the third time, quietly, No.

Somehow finally, they were in Richmond. There was my brother in school   8
among so many American boys. After hugs and my mother's anxious looks at her
young son, my sister said, Vic, you know what Mama did?

My brother remembers thinking, What? Oh! She wouldn't move? He had a   9
classmate, a Jewish boy like himself, but from Virginia, who had had a public
confrontation with a Negro man. He had punched that man hard, knocked him
down. My brother couldn't believe it. He was stunned. He couldn't imagine a
Jewish boy wanting to knock anyone down. He had never wanted to. But he
thought, looking back, that he had been set down to work and study in a nearly
foreign place and had to get used to it. Then he told me about the Second World
War, when the disgrace of black soldiers being forced to sit behind white German
POWs shook him. Shamed him.

About fifteen years later, in 1943, in early summer, I rode the bus for about three   10
days from New York to Miami Beach, where my husband in sweaty fatigues,
along with hundreds of other boys, was trudging up and down the streets and
beaches to prepare themselves for war.

By late afternoon of the second long day, we were well into the South, beyond   11
Richmond, maybe South Carolina or Georgia. My excitement about travel in the
wide world was damaged a little by a sudden fear that I might not recognize Jess
or he, me. We hadn't seen each other for two months. I took a photograph out of
my pocket; yes, I would know him.

I had been sleeping waking reading writing dozing waking. So many hours,   12
the movement of the passengers was something like a tide that sometimes ebbed
and now seemed to be noisily rising. I opened my eyes to the sound of new people
brushing past my aisle seat. And looked up to see a colored woman holding a large
sleeping baby, who with the heaviness of sleep, his arms so tight around her neck,
seemed to be pulling her head down. I looked around and noticed that I was in the
last white row. The press of travelers had made it impossible for her to move farther
back. She seemed so tired and I had been sitting and sitting for a day and a half at
least. Not thinking, or maybe refusing to think, I offered her my seat.

She looked to the right and left as well as she could. Softly said Oh no. I became   13
fully awake. A white man was standing right beside her, but on the other side of
the invisible absolute racial border. Of course, she couldn't accept my seat. Her
sleeping child hung mercilessly from her neck. She shifted a little to balance the
burden. She whispered to herself, Oh, I just don't know. So I said. Well, at least
give me the baby. First, she turned, barely looking at the man beside her. He
made no move. So, to my surprise, but obviously out of sheer exhaustion, she dis-
engaged the child from her body and placed him on my lap. He was deep in
child-sleep. He stirred, but not enough to bother himself or me. I liked holding
him, aligning him along my twenty-year-old young woman's shape. I thought
ahead to that holding, that breathing together that would happen in my life if
this war would ever end.

I was so comfortable under his nice weight. I closed my eyes for a couple of   14
minutes, but suddenly opened them to look up into the face of a white man talking.

In a loud voice he addressed me. Lady, I wouldn't of touched that thing with a meat hook.

15   I thought, Oh, this world will end in ice. I could do nothing but look straight into his eyes. I did not look away from him. Then I held that boy a little tighter, kissed his curly head, pressed him even closer so that he began to squirm. So sleepy, he reshaped himself inside my arms. His mother tried to narrow herself away from the dangerous border, too frightened at first to move at all. After a couple of minutes, she leaned forward a little, placed her hand on the baby's head, and held it there until the next stop. I couldn't look up into her mother face.

16   I write this remembrance more than fifty years later. I look back at that mother and child. How young she is. Her hand on his head is quite small, though she tries by spreading her fingers wide to hide him from the white man. But the child I'm holding, his little face as he turns toward me, is the brown face of my own grandson, my daughter's boy, the open mouth of the sleeper, the full lips, the thick little body of a child who runs wildly from one end of the yard to the other, leaps from dangerous heights with certain experienced caution, muscling his body, his mind, for coming realities.

Vocabulary

Directions: Locate each of the key words in the reading selection. Try to figure out each word's meaning by using the context. Confirm your guess by checking the dictionary or thesaurus. Write the meanings of the words in the margin of the text. Then record the meanings in the following chart.

Key Word	Paragraph	Meaning
1. fatigues	10	
2. trudging	10	
3. ebbed	12	
Others?		

Guide Questions

Directions: These questions will guide your understanding of what you have read. Write your answers in your notebook or on a separate sheet of paper if your instructor wishes to collect it. Your answers to these questions will be the basis of class discussion.

1. Paley recounts several anecdotes in "Traveling." What happened in each story? Who were the characters in each?
   a. The mother's story
   b. The brother's story
   c. The young wife's story
   d. The grandmother's story

2. Reread paragraph 12. Did you notice that in the first sentence Paley doesn't use commas where normally you would? Read the sentence out loud, first with commas where they would be, and then again without the commas. What is the difference? Why do you think Paley left out the commas?

3. Interpret the last sentence of "Traveling," especially the phrase "muscling his body, his mind, for coming realities."

Application

In paragraph 15, Paley writes, "I thought Oh, this world will end in ice." This is an allusion (a reference) to the famous poem by Robert Frost called *Fire and Ice*:

> Some say the world will end in fire,
> Some say in ice.
> From what I've tasted of desire
> I hold with those who favor fire.
> But if it had to perish twice,
> I think I know enough of hate
> To know that for destruction ice
> Is also great
> And would suffice.

What do you think Frost is saying in his poem? Do you think Paley shares Frost's meaning when she says, " . . . this world will end in ice"?

Making Connections

Make a connection between "Traveling" and "Black Boy." Both of the selections are narratives. Review the characteristics of a narrative on page 411. Then compare and contrast the two stories by analyzing the characters, setting, events, tone, and relevance of each story.

Barbara Jordan was born in Texas in 1936 and died there in 1996. She began her life in the largest black ghetto in the biggest state of the union. She graduated magna cum laude from Texas Southern University and went on to Boston University Law School. She was the first woman and the only black member of the Texas State Senate; she was the first woman and the only black member of the U.S. Congress from Texas; she was the first woman and the only black member of Congress from the entire South. To quote Molly Ivins's essay on Jordan, which appeared in The New York Times, *"The degree of prejudice she had to overcome by intelligence and sheer force of personality is impossible to over-estimate. She wasn't just black and female: she was homely, she was heavy, and she was dark black. When she first came to the Texas Senate, it was considered a great joke to bring racist friends to the gallery when B. J. was due to speak. They would no sooner gasp, 'Who is that nigger?' than she would open her mouth and out would roll language Lincoln would have appreciated. Her personal dignity was so substantial even admirers hesitated to approach her. No one will ever know how lonely she was at the beginning." Jordan won national acclaim for her intelligence and oratory during the House Judiciary Committee's proceedings to impeach President Richard Nixon in 1974 and later for her keynote speech to the Democratic National Convention in 1976. She retired from Congress after three terms and became an immensely popular and respected teacher at the University of Texas. In 1992, Jordan returned to the podium of the Democratic National Convention and electrified the nation with her speech. She spoke of her fierce passion for her country and for its ideals. She proclaimed, "My faith in the Constitution is whole, it is complete, it is total." To quote Ivins again, "She sounded like God." Suffering from multiple sclerosis and other ailments, Barbara Jordan died on January 17, 1996. President Clinton called her death the "loss of a national treasure." Today, she is the first and only black woman buried in the Texas State Cemetery.*

In this excerpt from her autobiography, Jordan describes learning to "think and read and understand and reason."

BECOMING EDUCATED

Barbara Jordan

1   So I was at Boston University in this new and strange and different world, and it occurred to me that if I was going to succeed at this strange new adventure, I would have to read longer and more thoroughly than my colleagues at law school had to read. I felt that, in order to compensate for what I had missed in earlier years, I would have to work harder, and study longer, than anybody else. I still had this feeling that I did not want my colleagues to know what a tough time I was having understanding the concepts, the words, the ideas, the process. I didn't want them to know that. So I did my reading not in the law library, but in a library at the graduate dorm, upstairs where it was very quiet, because apparently nobody else there studied. So I would go there at night after dinner. I would load my books under my arm and go to the library, and I would read until the wee hours of the morning and then go to bed. I didn't get much sleep during those years.

I was lucky if I got three or four hours a night, because I had to stay up. I had to. The professors would assign cases for the next day, and these cases had to be read and understood or I would be behind, further behind than I was.

I was always delighted when I would get called upon to recite in class. But   2 the professors did not call on the "ladies" very much. There were certain favored people who always got called on, and then on some rare occasions a professor would come in and would announce: "We're going to have Ladies Day today." And he would call on the ladies. We were just tolerated. We weren't considered really top drawer when it came to the study of the law.

At some time in the spring, Bill Gibson, who was dating my new room-   3 mate, Norma Walker, organized a black study group, as we blacks had to form our own. This was because we were not invited into any of the other study groups. There were six or seven in our group—Bill, and Issie, and I think Maynard Jackson—and we would just gather and talk it out and hear ourselves do that. One thing I learned was that you had to talk out the issues, the facts, the cases, the decisions, the process. You couldn't just read the cases and study alone in your library as I had been doing; and you couldn't get it all in the classroom. But once you had talked it out in the study group, it flowed more easily and made a lot more sense.

And from time to time I would go up to the fourth floor at 2 Rawley Street   4 to check on how Louise was doing. She was always reading *Redbook*. Every time I was in there and wanted to discuss one of the cases with her, she was reading a short story in *Redbook*. I don't know how she could do that. She was not prepared in class when the professors would call on her to discuss cases, but that did not bother her. Whereas it was a matter of life and death with me. I had to make law school. I just didn't have any alternatives. I could not afford to flunk out. That would have been an unmitigated disaster. So I read all the time I was not in class.

Finally I felt I was really learning things, really going to school. I felt that   5 I was getting educated, whatever that was. I became familiar with the process of thinking. I learned to think things out and reach conclusions and defend what I had said.

In the past I had got along by spouting off. Whether you talked about   6 debates or oratory, you dealt with speechifying. Even in debate it was pretty much canned because you had, in your little three-by-five box, a response for whatever issue might be raised by the opposition. The format was structured so that there was no opportunity for independent thinking. (I really had not had my ideas challenged ever.) But I could no longer orate and let that pass for reasoning. Because there was not any demand for an orator in Boston University Law School. You had to think and read and understand and reason. I had learned at twenty-one that you couldn't just say a thing is so because it might not be so, and somebody brighter, smarter, and more thoughtful would come out and tell you it wasn't so. Then, if you still thought it was, you had to prove it. Well, that was a new thing for me. I cannot, I really cannot describe what that did to my insides and to my head. I thought: I'm being educated finally.

Vocabulary

Directions: Locate each of the key words in the reading selection. Then read and study each word in its context and try to determine its meaning. Use a dictionary or thesaurus to check your guess. Write the meanings of the words in the margin of the text.

Record the new words you've learned in the following chart.

Key Word	Paragraph	Meaning
1. compensate	1	
2. top drawer	2	
3. unmitigated	4	
4. spouting off	6	
5. oratory	6	
Others?		

Guide Questions

Directions: These questions will guide your understanding of what you have read. They also will help you to analyze and evaluate the author's ideas and apply them to the real world and your own life.

Write answers to the questions in your notebook or on a separate sheet of paper if your instructor wishes to collect them. Your answers will form the basis of class discussion.

1. What can you infer from this story about the status of women and minorities in law schools at the time Barbara Jordan attended Boston University?
2. What did Jordan learn about the value of studying with a group of fellow students while she was at Boston University?
3. At the end of the piece, Jordan says, "I'm being educated finally." What had happened to make her feel this way?

Application

Directions: Learn a little more about this interesting American, Barbara Jordan. Visit these websites: http://www.elf.net/bjordan, http://www.pbs.org/newshour/bb/remember/jordan_1-17.html, or any of the hundreds of sites devoted to Barbara Jordan. Share what you discover with your classmates.

Writing

Directions: Complete these two assignments.

1. Do you ever feel discouraged about school? Many students juggle work and family responsibilities as well as college. Many students find their course work just plain hard! Try this mental exercise: Write a letter to Barbara Jordan. Describe the problems you are having. Try to be specific: Is scheduling a problem? Do you have difficulty finding enough time to study? Are your classes extremely difficult? Is the material too advanced? Is there a problem with an instructor? Or with other students? Are your grades lower than you would like? Try to define and describe any trouble you are having. Write at least a page—you may need to write more.
2. Put the letter you wrote in assignment 1 in a drawer for a few days. Then take it out and read it carefully. Imagine you are Barbara Jordan and write an answer to your letter. What do you think she might say in response to you?

Making Connections

Read the selection "Darkness at Noon" by Harold Krents on page 260. Write a letter to yourself from Mr. Krents in which he responds to the letter you wrote in writing assignment 1.

This story appeared in The New York Times *in May 2000.*

AN UNRELENTING DRIVE, AND A HARVARD DEGREE

Jacques Steinberg

1   CAMBRIDGE, Mass., May 15—The honors thesis that Brooke Ellison presented earlier this spring at Harvard University, "The Element of Hope in Resilient Adolescents," was a scientific analysis steeped in data.

2   But her own story would have made a good case study.

3   Struck by a car on her first day in the seventh grade and given little chance of survival, Ms. Ellison awoke, after 36 hours in a coma, as a quadriplegic, one whose first words included the questions, "When can I get back to school?" and "Will I be left back?"

4   Though she would regain no sensation below her neck, Ms. Ellison never missed a grade, and early next month she will cap her improbable educational odyssey by graduating from Harvard with an A⁻ average and a bachelor's degree in psychology and biology.

5   A smiling 21-year-old woman with a strong, sometimes scratchy voice, Ms. Ellison said there is nothing extraordinary about her accomplishments, whether it is piloting her wheelchair (as well as the cursor on her computer screen) by touching her tongue to a keypad in a retainer on the roof of her mouth, or being selected by her peers to address them on senior class day on June 7.

6   And do not even try to tell her that she is, as near as university officials can tell, the first quadriplegic to graduate from Harvard.

7   "This is just the way my life is," Ms. Ellison said over the clicking of a ventilator that forces air through her trachea and into her lungs 13 times a minute. "I've always felt that whatever circumstances I confront, it's just a question of continuing to live and not letting what I can't do define what I can."

8   Those looking for a hero in this story, Ms. Ellison suggested, should focus on her mother, Jean Marie, 48, who has sat at her daughter's side in every class since the eighth grade.

9   After Ms. Ellison was admitted to Harvard, the family decided, reluctantly, that Mrs. Ellison would temporarily leave her husband and teenage son in Stony Brook, N.Y., and move into a dormitory suite with her daughter. The two have hardly been out of earshot, for even a moment, since.

10   "If I'm with friends or want to be alone," Ms. Ellison said, "she knows when to give me my space."

11   Mrs. Ellison, whose first—and last—day as a special education teacher was the day of her daughter's accident, has been much more than a 24-hour nurse. Though Ms. Ellison dictated her term papers into a voice-activated computer and did whatever research she could on the Internet, her mother turned the pages of books like "Heart of Darkness" ("I don't have a particular signal," Ms. Ellison said, "I just say, 'Mom, turn the page now.'"), and served as her daughter's

surrogate right hand, raising hers high when Ms. Ellison had something to say in class.

As a tribute, the mother received a mock degree in "virtual studies" from the seniors in her daughter's house.   12

"I'm the brawn," Mrs. Ellison said. "She's the brains."   13

The mother added that her daughter "can't understand what all the hoopla is about, which is refreshing."   14

Though she has never known the freedom of tossing a Frisbee across the Yard, Ms. Ellison insisted that hers had been a fairly typical Harvard existence. She has, for example, occasionally sipped a beer at Brew Moon in Harvard Square, though she has hardly made a habit of it.   15

"I'd be drinking and operating my wheelchair at the same time," she said. "That would classify me as a d.w.i."   16

Ms. Ellison lived on campus all four years (the last three in the boxy, 30-year-old Currier House), studied with renowned professors such as Alan Dershowitz and Stephen Jay Gould, founded a student advocacy group on behalf of the disabled and attended her house's senior formal.   17

But she is the first to say that her mother—as well as her father, younger brother and older sister—were only the starting lineup on a team deep in talent that made her graduation possible.   18

Her dormitory room was custom-fitted by Harvard technicians with a hospital bed, small hydraulic lift, panic button and electronic door opener. When she signed up for a class on the history of opera, it had to be moved because the building was inaccessible with a wheelchair.   19

And though she and her date stayed at the senior formal well past midnight, they had to be chaperoned by her mother (Ms. Ellison's brother, Reed, was his mother's escort) and were ferried from the party not in a white limousine but a white van with an open cargo bay.   20

Kevin Davis, a retired Cambridge police detective who would often drive Ms. Ellison to class, said: "Brooke's captured my heart. It's inspiring to know a person of her character."   21

Like one of her idols, the actor Christopher Reeve, Ms. Ellison conceded that she does have moments of sadness, particularly when her sleep is interrupted by dreams of the dance classes that were her childhood passion. (A poster in her dorm room, brought from home, showed five pint-size ballerinas at a dance bar, the middle girl desperately trying to stretch to reach as high as the other four.)   22

She said she has never wanted to meet the man whose car hit her as she walked home from school, an accident that fractured her skull, her spine and almost every major bone in her body. But she said she holds no grudge.   23

"If I were to harbor anger for 10 years," she said, "it'd be too exhausting."   24

Even though she was a formidable student in high school who scored 1510 out of a possible 1600 on her College Board exams (she filled in the bubbles by dictating to a teacher), Ms. Ellison never expected to get into Harvard, which was the only college to which she applied other than the State University of New York at Stony Brook. "I thought if I got accepted, I would put the letter in a frame," she said.   25

26   But once she was admitted, she said, Harvard, which costs more than $30,000 a year, made herculean efforts to ensure that she would attend. The university provided her with scholarships not only to supplement her father's salary as an administrator in a Social Security office but also to pay for her costly medical needs.

27   Ms. Ellison is keeping the text of her class day address a secret, but does allow that it will touch on the many friendships she forged in Cambridge. Among the first to approach her, on the way to an early morning language class, was Neil Holzapfer, 22, then a freshman from Kingston, N.H., who majored in government and Russian studies.

28   "I was struck by the courage that it would take for her to be in this kind of atmosphere, which is stressful and intense under the best conditions," Mr. Holzapfer recalled.

29   Four years later, Mr. Holzapfer said that his friend had become his role model, her love of the bubble gum rocker Bryan Adams notwithstanding. "Brooke is living a life that is out there," he said, "instead of closing up and looking inward."

30   After spending the summer getting to know her family again, Ms. Ellison intends to write her autobiography (she already has an agent at William Morris) and hopes to travel as a motivational speaker.

31   "Anywhere people feel they need encouragement," she said, "that's where I hope to be."

Vocabulary

Directions: Locate each of the key words in the reading selection. Try to figure out each word's meaning by using the context. Confirm your guess by checking the dictionary or thesaurus. Write the meanings of the words in the margin of the text. Then record the meanings in the following chart.

Key Word	Paragraph	Meaning
1. resilient	1	
2. odyssey	4	
3. brawn	13	
4. advocacy	17	
5. formidable	25	
6. herculean	26	
Others?		

Guide Questions

Directions: These questions will guide your understanding of what you have read. Write your answers in your notebook or on a separate sheet of paper if your instructor wishes to collect it. Your answers to these questions will be the basis of class discussion.

1. "An Unrelenting Drive" is the story of an extraordinary young woman and her family. Summarize the major facts of their story.
2. Each of the major characters in this story shows remarkable determination and effort. Think about each and describe their contributions to the "happy ending" of a Harvard degree.
   a. Brooke Ellison
   b. Ms. Ellison's mother, Jean
   c. Ms. Ellison's father, brother, and sister
   d. Harvard University
3. Imagine you are the person at *The New York Times* who writes the headlines. Write your own headline for this story.

Application/Writing

1. The following two letters appeared in *The New York Times* in response to "An Unrelenting Drive, and a Harvard Degree." Each focuses on a different aspect of the story. Write one sentence for each letter, summarizing its main point.

Disabled in America, Beyond Harvard

To the Editor:
Re "An Unrelenting Drive, and a Harvard Degree" (front page, May 17):
   It seems that you missed the real significance of this story. The fact that Brooke Ellison is a quadriplegic who is graduating from Harvard, and that her story is worthy of coverage, tells us a lot about the general lack of equal opportunity for disabled people in this country.
   The fact that her mother had to quit work to become her daughter's full-time attendant through high school and college demonstrates the appalling lack of support given to disabled people.
   What if her mother had been unable or unwilling to do so? What would have become of Ms. Ellison then?

Douglas Baynton
Iowa City, May 18, 2000
The writer is an assistant professor of history at the University of Iowa.

A Student's Promise

To the Editor:
Re "An Unrelenting Drive, and a Harvard Degree" (front page, May 17):
   The beautiful thing about inclusion of people with disabilities is that it is a classic "win-win" situation. Brooke Ellison gets to fulfill her fullest potential; Harvard gets to cultivate a broader intellectual and social climate than would otherwise be the case, benefiting everyone.

Ms. Ellison's classmates obviously recognize the degree to which their lives are enriched by exposure to her unique ideas, abilities and perspective; I presume that is why they voted for her to present a senior class day speech.

Harvard is to be commended for recognizing why inclusion of Ms. Ellison was a win-win. (Now it should make sure that all of its buildings are accessible to wheelchairs.)

Other institutions should take note of the fact that everyone benefits from an inclusive policy toward people with disabilities.

Barbara Quackenbos
Maplewood, N.J., May 17, 2000

2. Write your own letter, either to the *Times* or to Brooke Ellison, reacting to the story.
3. Brooke Ellison graduated from Harvard in 2000. Since then she has been very busy. Go to the Internet to find out what Ellison has been doing for the past several years.

Making Connections

Compare and contrast the stories of Richard Wright ("Black Boy") and Brooke Ellison ("An Unrelenting Drive, and a Harvard Degree"). How are they similar? How are they different?

Jonathan Kozol, a graduate of Harvard University, is a writer, educator, and activist. He is best known for his books on social justice, especially the inequalities of public education. He writes that despite the struggles of the Civil Rights era and the efforts of the courts, our nation's public schools are still separate and still unequal. Author of many books, including Savage Inequalities *and* Amazing Grace, *for the past several decades Kozol has devoted his life to exposing the shame of a system that ignores its poorest. He writes about the children of the poor, saying these are "good children sent to us by God and not yet soiled by the knowledge that their nation does not love them."*

This selection from Kozol's book, Illiterate America, *describes the consequences of a failed education system.*

ILLITERATE AMERICA

Jonathan Kozol

"You have to be careful not to get into situations where it would leak out. . . . If somebody gives you something to read, you make believe you read it."

He is meticulous and well-defended.   1

He gets up in the morning, showers, shaves, and dresses in a dark gray business suit, then goes downstairs and buys a *New York Times* from the small newsstand on the corner of his street. Folding it neatly, he goes into the subway and arrives at work at 9 a.m.   2

He places the folded *New York Times* next to the briefcase on his desk and sets to work on graphic illustrations for the advertising copy that is handed to him by the editor who is his boss.   3

"Run over this with me. Just make sure I get the gist of what you really want."   4

The editor, unsuspecting, takes this as a reasonable request. In the process of expanding on his copy, he recites the language of the text: a language that is instantly imprinted on the illustrator's mind.   5

At lunch he grabs the folded copy of *The New York Times,* carries it with him to a coffee shop, places it beside his plate, eats a sandwich, drinks a beer, and soon heads back to work.   6

At 5 p.m., he takes his briefcase and his *New York Times,* waits for the elevator, walks two blocks to catch an uptown bus, stops at a corner store to buy some groceries, then goes upstairs. He carefully unfolds his *New York Times*. He places it with mechanical precision on a pile of several other recent copies of *The New York Times*. There they will remain until, when two or three more copies have been added, he will take all but the one most recent and consign them to the trash that goes into a plastic bag that will be left for pickup by the truck that comes around during the night and, with a groaning roar, collects and crushes and compresses all the garbage of the occupants of this and other residential buildings of New York.   7

Then he returns upstairs. He opens the refrigerator, snaps the top from a cold can of Miller's beer, and turns on the TV.   8

9   Next day, trimly dressed and cleanly shaven, he will buy another *New York Times,* fold it neatly, and proceed to work. He is a rather solitary man. People in his office view him with respect as someone who is self-contained and does not choose to join in casual conversation. If somebody should mention something that is in the news, he will give a dry, sardonic answer based upon the information he has garnered from TV.

10   He is protected against the outside world. Someday he will probably be trapped. It has happened before; so he can guess that it will happen again. Defended for now against humiliation, he is not defended against fear. He tells me that he has recurrent dreams.

11   "Somebody says: WHAT DOES THIS MEAN? I stare at the page. A thousand copies of *The New York Times* run past me on a giant screen. Even before I am awake, I start to scream."

12   If it is of any comfort to this man, he should know that he is not alone. Twenty-five million American adults cannot read the poison warnings on a can of pesticide, a letter from their child's teacher, or the front page of a daily paper. An additional 35 million read only at a level which is less than equal to the full survival needs of our society.

13   Together, these 60 million people represent more than one third of the entire adult population.

14   The largest numbers of illiterate adults are white, native-born Americans. In proportion to population, however, the figures are higher for blacks and Hispanics than for whites. Sixteen percent of white adults, 44 percent of blacks, and 56 percent of Hispanic citizens are functional or marginal illiterates. Figures for the younger generation of black adults are increasing. Forty-seven percent of all black seventeen-year-olds are functionally illiterate. That figure is expected to climb to 50 percent by 1990.

15   Fifteen percent of recent graduates of urban high schools read at less than sixth grade level. One million teenage children between twelve and seventeen cannot read above the third grade level. Eighty-five percent of juveniles who come before the courts are functionally illiterate. Half the heads of households classified below the poverty line by federal standards cannot read an eighth grade book. Over one third of mothers who receive support from welfare are functionally illiterate. Of 8 million unemployed adults, 4 to 6 million lack the skills to be retrained for hi-tech jobs.

16   The United States ranks forty-ninth among 158 member nations of the U.N. in its literacy levels.

17   In Prince George's County, Maryland, 30,000 adults cannot read above a fourth grade level. The largest literacy program in this county reaches one hundred people yearly.

18   In Boston, Massachusetts, 40 percent of the adult population is illiterate. The largest organization that provides funds to the literacy programs of the city reaches 700 to 1,000 people.

19   In San Antonio, Texas, 152,000 adults have been documented as illiterate. In a single municipal district of San Antonio, over half the adult population is

illiterate in English. Sixty percent of the same population sample is illiterate in Spanish. Three percent of adults in this district are at present being served.

In the state of Utah, which ranks number one in the United States in the percent of total budget allocated to the education sector, 200,000 adults lack the basic skills for employment. Less than 5 percent of Utah's population is black or Hispanic.   20

Together, all federal, state, municipal, and private literacy programs in the nation reach a maximum of 4 percent of the illiterate population. The federal government spends $100 million yearly to address the needs of 60 million people. The President has asked that this sum be reduced to $50 million. Even at the present level, direct federal allocations represent about $1.65 per year for each illiterate.   21

In 1982 the Executive Director of the National Advisory Council on Adult Education estimated that the government would need to spend about $5 billion to eradicate or seriously reduce the problem. The commission he served was subsequently dismissed by presidential order.   22

Fourteen years ago, in his inaugural address as governor of Georgia, a future President of the United States proclaimed his dedication to the crisis of Illiterate America. "Our people are our most precious possession . . . Every adult illiterate . . . is an indictment of us all . . . If Switzerland and Israel and other people can end illiteracy, then so can we. The responsibility is our own and our government's. I will not shirk this responsibility."   23

Today the number of identified nonreaders is three times greater than the number Jimmy Carter had in mind when he described this challenge and defined it as an obligation that he would not shirk.   24

On April 26, 1983, pointing to the literacy crisis and to a collapse in standards at the secondary and the college levels, the National Commission on Excellence in Education warned: "Our Nation is at risk."   25

Vocabulary

Directions: Find each of the key words in the essay. Try to figure out each word's meaning by using the context. Confirm your guess by checking the dictionary. Write the meanings of the words in the margin of the text, near the word. Then record the meanings in the following chart.

Key Word	Paragraph	Meaning
1. meticulous	1	
2. gist	4	
3. consign	7	
4. sardonic	9	

Key Word	Paragraph	Meaning
5. recurrent	10	
6. indictment	23	
7. shirk	23 and 24	
Others?		

Guide Questions

Directions: These questions will guide your understanding of what you have read. Write your answers in your notebook or on a separate sheet of paper if your instructor will collect it. Your answers will be the basis of class discussion.

1. Who is the subject of the story Kozol tells in the first eleven paragraphs? What do we know about him?
2. Why do you think the author gives so much detail about the man's handling of *The New York Times*?
3. What do you think the author means when he says the man is "well defended"? (paragraph 1)
4. Summarize the statistics Kozol gives about illiteracy among Americans.
5. Does the story about the unnamed illiterate man leave you with any questions? What would you ask him if you could speak with him?
6. Use the Internet to find the current statistics on illiteracy among United Nations members. Is the United States still in forty-ninth place on the list? List some of the countries that place higher in the list.

Writing

1. What is your reaction to the story? Write a paragraph or two.
2. According to the United Nations, the definition of a literate person is *"someone who can with understanding both read and write a short simple statement on his everyday life. A person is illiterate who cannot with understanding both read and write a short simple statement on his everyday life."*

   What do you think a person needs to be able to read and understand in order to function well in today's society?

Application

The book in which this reading appeared was written more than 20 years ago. Do some research to see how (or if) things have changed. Choose two of the statistics cited in the reading, and find the same information for today.

Making Connections

If you read the story "Black Boy," write a brief essay (at least one paragraph) on the following topic: Imagine you are Richard Wright. What would you say to the unnamed illiterate man in this reading?

Isaac Asimov (1920–1992) was an exceptionally prolific writer. Best known for his science fiction, he wrote or edited more than 500 books. (According to some sources, he also wrote an estimated 90,000 letters and postcards, and he has works in nine of the ten major categories of the Dewey Decimal System.) He had an ability to explain complex science in a simple and often humorous way.

This essay is from Asimov's autobiography. Before you read it, write an answer to this question: **What is intelligence?**

WHAT IS INTELLIGENCE, ANYWAY?

Isaac Asimov

1   What is intelligence, anyway? When I was in the Army, I received a kind of aptitude test that all soldiers took and, against a normal of 100, scored 160. No one at the base had ever seen a figure like that, and for two hours they made a big fuss over me. (It didn't mean anything. The next day I was still a buck private with KP—kitchen police—as my highest duty.)

2   All my life I've been registering scores like that, so that I have the complacent feeling that I'm highly intelligent, and I expect other people to think so, too. Actually, though, don't such scores simply mean that I am very good at answering the type of academic questions that are considered worthy of answers by the people who make up the intelligence tests—people with intellectual bents similar to mine?

3   For instance, I had an auto repairman once, who, on these intelligence tests, could not possibly have scored more than 80, by my estimate. I always took it for granted that I was far more intelligent than he was. Yet, when anything went wrong with my car I hastened to him with it, watched him anxiously as he explored its vitals, and listened to his pronouncements as though they were divine oracles—and he always fixed my car.

4   Well, then, suppose my auto repairman devised questions for an intelligence test. Or suppose a carpenter did, or a farmer, or indeed, almost anyone but an academician. By every one of those tests, I'd prove myself a moron. And I'd *be* a moron, too. In a world where I could not use my academic training and my verbal talents but had to do something intricate or hard, working with my hands, I would do poorly. My intelligence, then, is not absolute but is a function of the society I live in and of the fact that a small subsection of that society has managed to foist itself on the rest as an arbiter of such matters.

5   Consider my auto repairman, again. He had a habit of telling me jokes whenever he saw me. One time he raised his head from under the automobile hood to say: "Doc, a deaf-and-mute guy went into a hardware store to ask for some nails. He put two fingers together on the counter and made hammering motions with the other hand. The clerk brought him a hammer. He shook his head and pointed to the two fingers he was hammering, the clerk brought him nails. He picked out the sizes he wanted, and left. Well, doc, the next guy who came in was a blind man. He wanted scissors. How do you suppose he asked for them?"

Indulgently, I lifted my right hand and made scissoring motions with my first   6
two fingers. Whereupon my auto repairman laughed raucously and said, "Why you
dumb jerk, he used his *voice* and asked for them." Then he said, smugly, "I've been
trying that on all my customers today." "Did you catch many?" I asked. "Quite a
few," he said, "but I knew for sure I'd catch *you*." "Why is that?" I asked. "Because
you're so goddamned educated, doc, I *knew* you couldn't be very smart."

And I have an uneasy feeling he had something there.   7

Vocabulary

Directions: Find each of the key words in the essay. Try to figure out each word's meaning by using the context. Confirm your guess by checking the dictionary. Write the meanings of the words in the margin of the text, near the word. Then record the meanings in
the following chart.

Key Word	Paragraph	Meaning
1. buck private	1	
2. complacent	2	
3. hastened	3	
4. oracles	3	
5. foist	4	
6. raucously	6	
Others?		

Guide Questions

Directions: Answer these questions to make sure that you understand what you've read.
Write your answers in your notebook or on a separate sheet of paper if your instructor
will collect it. Your answers will be the basis of class discussion.

1. Asimov tells us that he scores very high on IQ tests. For example, he
   scored 160 on an intelligence test the army gave him. How does he interpret his high score?
2. Asimov assumed his auto repairman was not very intelligent because he
   would not score high on a similar test. What made Asimov reconsider his
   opinion of the repairman's intelligence?

3. Under what circumstances does Asimov say he'd be considered "a moron"?
4. Explain the lesson Asimov learns from the auto repairman's joke.
5. Would you revise your definition of intelligence after reading this story?

Marking Text

Directions: Review how to mark text on page 413. Then mark the important ideas in "What Is Intelligence, Anyway?"

Writing

1. Use your marked text to write a summary of "What Is Intelligence, Anyway?" Remember, summary writing is explained on page 417.
2. What is your opinion of IQ tests? Do you think they accurately measure a person's intelligence? Do they measure all kinds of intelligence? Have you ever taken an IQ test? How did you feel about the results? Write one or two paragraphs.

Application

1. Have you ever had an experience similar to the one Asimov describes in the story? Write a few paragraphs describing what happened and what you learned.
2. Isaac Asimov was a beloved figure in American culture. He came to the United States when he was 3 years old when his family emigrated from Russia. He taught himself to read when he was five. Asimov earned a doctorate in biochemistry but pursued many other interests. He led a full and prolific life. Go to the Internet and learn more about this fascinating man. Collect several facts about him. Then work with classmates to create a full biography. You will need to be succinct—there is a great deal to say about Asimov.

After decades of war and years of oppression by the Taliban in Afghanistan, attention is beginning to be paid to the education of women. Literacy classes are opening all over the country, and the long-denied students are responding with enthusiasm.

This story appeared in The New York Times *in September 2002.*

LONG IN DARK, AFGHAN WOMEN SAY TO READ IS FINALLY TO SEE

Carlotta Gall

MAZAR-I-SHARIF, Afghanistan, Sept. 19—The female voices ring out clear and confident across the courtyard as a class recites the Afghan alphabet, "Alef, Be, Te. . . ." But the surprise is that inside the simple mud-brick house, the pupils sitting on the floor before their teacher are adult women, some nursing babies or pushing aside noisy toddlers. 1

In their greedy embrace of the government's back-to-school campaign after the prohibitive years under the Taliban, Afghanistan's women are as eager to get an education for themselves as for their children. Hundreds of women's literacy classes are forming in the back streets of this town in northern Afghanistan— faster than the government can register them—as women meet in neighborhood houses to learn to read and write. 2

"I wanted to know something and help my children," said Mahgul, 45, a widow and mother of six. "I have no knowledge, and so I am not a useful person. If I can get some knowledge, I can help my children more." 3

Zainab, 50, sitting next to her, said it was watching her own children read and write that made her want to learn, too. Her husband, sick with tuberculosis and also illiterate, urged her to come to the free lessons starting in the neighborhood. "He said, 'You are getting older, and you should know something and help your children so they do not grow up blind like you,'" she said. 4

"Blind" is the word many of these illiterate women use to describe themselves, and it speaks to the confusion and difficulties that they encounter as uneducated members of a society already harshly discriminatory against women. 5

"Without knowledge, I am blind; I do not know white from black," said Torpikay, 30. "In town, I do not know where is the hospital, or the baths or the washroom, and I will take my dishes into the wrong place, because we just follow other women and don't know where we are going." That last comment raised laughter from the entire class. 6

The women most often complain of not being able to decipher street signs, even for the bathroom, and not being able to understand medical prescriptions, says Mariya, one of the teachers who have started literacy classes for adult women in an impoverished neighborhood known as Ali Chupan, on the east side of Mazar-i-Sharif. 7

Silent, shadowy figures in public, Afghan women, dressed in the all-compassing burka, often are too timid to approach strangers to ask for directions. 8

9   One woman said she could not tell the difference between government money and the money widely used in the north, which looks almost the same but is worth half the value. "She was sometimes cheated because of that," Mariya said.

10   And the women, especially those without men in the family, say they are ill equipped to manage the daily difficulties of running the household and feeding their families.

11   In each of four classes visited in Ali Chupan, there were widows and young women fending for themselves, and they all said they wanted to become literate so they could find employment.

12   Three sisters, who live alone with their widowed mother, said they made a living weaving carpets, but could barely earn enough to survive. "I really want to learn and get work, maybe in an office," said Nasi, 20. Tears welled up as she described her life, how she had never been to school and how the family fled to the mountains when the Taliban came. But after only a few days of classes, she and her sister, Shaqila, 18, were rapidly writing down the alphabet.

13   Another reason the women often gave for attending classes is that they wanted to read letters from members of the family who because of the years of conflict, often live miles apart, or abroad as refugees.

14   Basira, 17, said her in-laws, who live with her, had urged her to come to classes because her father-in-law, the only one in the family who can read and write, was having trouble with his eyes.

15   "He suggested I learn to read so I could read the letters when they come," she said. "My mother-in-law becomes happy when I read something to them. She says, 'When we have a problem, you are the youngest of this house, and you will be able to solve the problem.'"

16   Some of the older women stare uncomprehendingly at the makeshift blackboards that teachers have arranged in their houses, one on the bare plastered wall, one on an old broken door.

17   But some women are fascinated and clearly hungry to learn. When they received new notebooks, they huddled in groups and helped each other write the letters.

18   "The best thing is being able to write my name," says Siddiqa, 18, who studied the Koran in her village but never went to school.

19   Some estimates have put women's illiteracy in Afghanistan as high as 85 percent, and the new government has begun a broad program not only to get all children back to school, but also to address the adult literacy problem by paying schoolteachers in the cities to instruct adults in their homes after school lets out.

20   Mazar-i-Sharif already has 172 registered adult literacy classes, and more are opening all the time as teachers hope to earn some extra pay, and women pile in to receive the free lessons. "We are happy about this, a lot of people want to come to the classes," said Palwasha Rafat of U.N.-Habitat, a United Nations aid organization that works with the Afghan government on education.

21   Governments that preceded the Taliban had organized women's literacy classes, but the surge of interest now after years of women's exclusion has surpassed anything before, she said. "People realized that the reason for all these years

of war was the lack of education in the country," she said. "Both the men and the women realize this now and want to change that."

Vocabulary

Directions: Locate each of the key words in the reading selection. Try to figure out each word's meaning by using the context. Confirm your guess by checking the dictionary or thesaurus. Write the meanings of the words in the margin of the text. Then record the meanings in the following chart.

Key Word	Paragraph	Meaning
1. decipher	7	
2. fending	11	
3. makeshift	16	
Others?		

Guide Questions

Directions: These questions will guide your understanding of what you have read. Write your answers in your notebook or on a separate sheet of paper if your instructor wishes to collect it. Your answers will be the basis of class discussion.

1. In a sentence or two, summarize the main points of this article.
2. Explain what Torpikay means when she describes herself as "blind."
3. Relate the women's description of being blind to the title of the article.
4. What kinds of problems do the women encounter because of their illiteracy?
5. What are some of the goals the women have?
6. What is your reaction to the story? Write a few sentences.

Application

What is the illiteracy rate of women in Afghanistan? Use the Internet to find the illiteracy rate of both women and men and the illiteracy rate in the United States. If you are from another country, check the statistics from your home country.

Making Connections

Imagine that Richard Wright ("Black Boy," page 13) visited one of the women's literacy classes in Afghanistan. Write what you think he would say to the Afghan women in the class.

In recent years, the number of older people returning to school has grown enormously. Many return to improve their employment potential. Others return simply for the pleasure of learning. In this essay, we learn of a 30-year-old woman who feels handicapped by her lack of education—and of her determination to help herself overcome it.

OVERCOMING AN INVISIBLE HANDICAP

Thomas J. Cottle

1   On her thirtieth birthday, Lucille Elmore informed her husband that she was going through a crisis. "I was thirty years old, active, in good health—and I was illiterate," she recalls. "I didn't know books, I didn't know history, I didn't know science. I had the barest understanding of the arts. Like a physical condition, my knowledge limped, my intelligence limped."

2   She was not only the mother of two young children but also was working full time as an administrative assistant in a business-consulting firm. Nevertheless, at age thirty, with her husband's agreement, Lucille Elmore enrolled in college. "I thought getting in would be difficult," she says. "It was easy. I thought I couldn't discipline myself, but that came. Half the people in the library the first day thought I was the librarian, but that didn't deter me."

3   For Lucille, the awareness of her invisible limp came only gradually. As a young woman, she had finished high school, but she had chosen not to go on with her education. Her parents, who had never completed high school themselves, urged her to go to college but she refused. At the time, she was perhaps a bit timid and lacked a certain confidence in her own intellectual or academic abilities. Besides, a steady job was far more important at that point to Lucille than schooling; she felt she could read on her own to make up for any lack of education.

4   At twenty, working full time, she married Ted Elmore, a salesman for a foodstore chain, a man on his way to becoming more than modestly successful. There was no need for her to work, but she did so until her first child was born; she was then twenty-two. A second child was born two years later, and three years after that, she went back to work. With her youngest in a day-care program, she felt no reservations about working, but her lack of education began to nag at her as she approached the age of thirty. She thus gave up her job, entered a continuing-education program at a nearby university, and began what she likens to a love affair.

5   "I'm carrying on an open affair with books, but like a genuinely good lover, I'm being guided. Reading lists, suggested reading, recommended readings—I want them all. I must know what happened in the twelfth, thirteenth, and eighteenth centuries. I want to know how the world's major religions evolved. Papal history, I know nothing of papal history and succession, or the politics involved. I read the Bible, but I never studied it. It's like music: I listened, but it wasn't an informed listening. Now all of this is changing.

6   "I must tell you, I despise students when they talk about 'the real world,' as if college were a dream world. They simply don't understand what the accumulation of

knowledge and information means. Maybe you have to be thirty at least, and going through a personal crisis, to fully appreciate what historical connections are.

"A line of Shakespeare challenges me more than half the jobs I'll be equipped for when I'm finished. I'm having an affair with him, too, only it's called Elizabethan Literature 606. I think many people prefer the real world of everyday work because it's less frightening than the larger-than-life world of college. 7

"There's a much more important difference between the rest of the students and me. We don't agree at all on what it means to be a success. They think in terms of money, material things. I suppose that's normal. They don't understand that, with a nice home, and decent job prospects, and two beautiful children, I know I am a failure. I'm a failure because I am ignorant. I'm a failure until I have knowledge, until I can work with it, be excited by and play with ideas. 8

"I don't go to school for the rewards down the line. I want to reach the point at which I don't measure knowledge by anything but itself. An idea has value or it doesn't. This is how I now determine success and failure. 9

"'How can I use it?' That's what students ask. 'What good will this do me?' They don't think about what the question says about them, even without an answer attached to it. Questions like that only build up competition. But competition is the bottom line for so many students, I guess, getting ahead, getting a bit of a step up on the other guy. I know, it's my husband's life. 10

"I'll tell what I think I like most about my work: the library. I can think of no place so exclusive and still so open and public. Millions of books there for the taking. A chair to sit in, a row of books, and you don't need a penny. For me, the library is a religious center, a shrine. 11

"Students talk about the real world out there. What about the free world in here? Here, no one arrests you for what you're thinking. In the library, you can't talk, so you have to think. I never knew what it meant to think about something, to really think it through. I certainly never understood what you had to know to even begin to think. I always thought it was normal to limp." 12

Vocabulary

Directions: Locate each of the key words in the reading selection. Then read and study each word in its context and try to determine its meaning. Use a dictionary or thesaurus to check your guess. Write the meanings of the words in the margin of the text.

Record the new words you've learned in the following chart.

Key Word	Paragraph	Meaning
1. deter	2	
2. shrine	11	
Others?		

Guide Questions

Directions: These questions will guide your understanding of what you have read. They will also help you to analyze and evaluate the author's ideas and apply them to the real world and your own life.

Write answers to the questions in your notebook or on a separate sheet of paper if your instructor wishes to collect them. Your answers will form the basis of class discussion.

1. Define the word *illiterate* as it is generally used; then define *illiterate* as it is used by Elmore in this essay.
2. Why did half of the people in the library on the first day think Elmore was the librarian?
3. In this essay, Elmore uses powerful comparisons in describing her return to school: a "handicap," or "limp," and a "love affair." Explain each of these comparisons.
4. In paragraph 8, Elmore describes herself as a failure. Why does she say this? Do you agree that she was a failure?
5. Contrast Elmore's view of what it means to be a success with the view of her fellow students.
6. a. Why does Elmore say she despises students when they talk about "the real world"?
   b. List some of the other differences of opinion between Elmore and her younger classmates.
7. a. Why does Elmore describe the library as "a religious center"?
   b. Compare and contrast your opinion of the library with Elmore's.

Making Connections

Compare Lucille Elmore's view of education with that of Sydney Harris's ("What True Education Should Do"). Would they agree on the purpose of education? Give evidence to support your answer. Write at least one paragraph.

Writing

If you are a "returning student" (say, returning to school after an absence of five or more years), discuss your view of education with a younger student (someone who came to college directly from high school). If you are a young student, discuss education with an older classmate. Then write one or two paragraphs comparing and contrasting your views.

COLLABORATIVE LEARNING

Working in Groups to Guide Your Own Reading

All of the reading selections so far in this unit have been accompanied by questions and exercises meant to help you understand and use what you've read. However, in much of your college reading (not to mention in your real life), you will be expected to master the material on your own.

Research has shown that one of the most effective ways to learn is in *groups*. In college, working with classmates can help you to master the material of a college course. The give-and-take that comes naturally when working with other people helps us to avoid falling into bad habits like *passive reading*. (We have all had the awful experience of reading a whole chapter, then realizing that we don't remember one single thing we've read.) Working with other students will help you to avoid such problems. For this assignment, form groups of approximately four students. In your group, read and think about the two following reading selections: "The Teacher Who Changed My Life," by Nicholas Gage, and "A Cheating Crisis in America's Schools," from ABC News Internet Ventures. Then, create your own vocabulary chart, guide questions, and application and writing assignments.

Follow these steps to complete the assignment:

1. Preview the selection before you read—look at and think about the title, any headings or subheadings, the first paragraph, the last paragraph, and the first sentence of each paragraph.
2. Read through the selection one time quickly.
3. Read the selection a second time, more carefully. This time mark the text. Review how to do this by turning to page 413, "Learning Strategy III—Marking Text."
4. Brainstorm with your group. Ask yourselves: What important issues is the author discussing? What new information did you learn? Can the issues discussed in the selection be connected to those you have already studied? Can any of the information here be applied to situations in your own life?
5. Now, create a set of exercises similar to those you have completed in previous chapters of this book:
   a. **Vocabulary.** Make a list of key words from the text. Set them up in chart format as on page 3.
   b. **Guide Questions.** Write questions that will guide understanding of the major ideas in the reading.
   c. **Application.** Prepare an application exercise that takes one or more of the important ideas in the reading and relates it to real life.
   d. **Writing.** Create a writing assignment to conclude the chapter.

Before you begin, it would be a good idea to review the questions and exercises in the previous reading selections in this book.

When you are finished, submit your work to your instructor. Your instructor may review and combine the work of all the groups and return the exercise to the class. You will then have the opportunity to *answer* the questions you and your classmates have developed.

Now, use your skills as an active, independent reader to tackle the following reading selections. Good luck!

"If it weren't for her . . ." says Nicholas Gage as he speaks of Miss Hurd, the English teacher and school newspaper-club advisor who changed the whole course of his life. She was "the catalyst that sent me into journalism and indirectly caused all the good things that came after." This powerful and emotional story comes from Gage's book, A Place for Us. *In it, he describes his life after coming to the United States at the age of nine. Earlier, during the Greek civil war, Gage's mother had been captured and killed for sending her children to safety and freedom in America. It was Miss Hurd who "directed [his] grief and pain into writing," inspired him to become an investigative reporter, foreign correspondent, and writer of the much-acclaimed book about his mother's life,* Eleni. *Can you recall a teacher who had a special effect on your life?*

THE TEACHER WHO CHANGED MY LIFE

Nicholas Gage

1   The person who set the course of my life in the new land I entered as a young war refugee—who, in fact, nearly dragged me onto the path that would bring all the blessings I've received in America—was a salty-tongued, no-nonsense school-teacher named Marjorie Hurd. When I entered her classroom in 1953, I had been to six schools in five years, starting in the Greek village where I was born in 1939.

2   When I stepped off a ship in New York Harbor on a gray March day in 1949, I was an undersized nine-year-old in short pants who had lost his mother and was coming to live with the father he didn't know. My mother, Eleni Gatzoyiannis, had been imprisoned, tortured, and shot by Communist guerrillas for sending me and three of my four sisters to freedom. She died so that her children could go to their father in the United States.

3   The portly, bald, well-dressed man who met me and my sisters seemed a foreign, authoritarian figure. I secretly resented him for not getting the whole family out of Greece early enough to save my mother. Ultimately, I would grow to love him and appreciate how he dealt with becoming a single parent at the age of fifty-six, but at first our relationship was prickly, full of hostility.

4   As Father drove us to our new home—a tenement in Worcester, Massachusetts—and pointed out the huge brick building that would be our first school in America, I clutched my Greek notebooks from the refugee camp, hoping that my few years of schooling would impress my teachers in this cold, crowded country. They didn't. When my father led me and my eleven-year-old sister to Greendale Elementary School, the grim-faced Yankee principal put the two of us in a class for the mentally retarded. There was no facility in those days for non-English-speaking children.

5   By the time I met Marjorie Hurd four years later, I had learned English, been placed in a normal, graded class and had even been chosen for the college preparatory track in the Worcester public school system. I was thirteen years old when our father moved us yet again, and I entered Chandler Junior High shortly after the beginning of seventh grade. I found myself surrounded by richer, smarter, and better-dressed classmates who looked askance at my strange clothes

and heavy accent. Shortly after I arrived, we were told to select a hobby to pursue during "club hour" on Fridays. The idea of hobbies and clubs made no sense to my immigrant ears, but I decided to follow the prettiest girl in my class—the blue-eyed daughter of the local Lutheran minister. She led me through the door marked "Newspaper Club" and into the presence of Miss Hurd, the newspaper advisor and English teacher who would become my mentor and my muse.

A formidable, solidly built woman with salt-and-pepper hair, a steely eye, and a flat Boston accent, Miss Hurd had no patience with layabouts. "What are all you goof-offs doing here?" she bellowed at the would-be journalists. "This is the Newspaper Club! We're going to put out a *newspaper*. So if there's anybody in this room who doesn't like work, I suggest you go across to the Glee Club now, because you're going to work your tails off here!"

I was soon under Miss Hurd's spell. She did indeed teach us to put out a newspaper, skills I honed during my next twenty-five years as a journalist. Soon I asked the principal to transfer me to her English class as well. There, she drilled us on grammar until I finally began to understand the logic and structure of the English language. She assigned stories for us to read and discuss; not tales of heroes, like the Greek myths I knew, but stories of underdogs—poor people, even immigrants, who seemed ordinary until a crisis drove them to do something extraordinary. She also introduced us to the literary wealth of Greece—giving me a new perspective on my war-ravaged, impoverished homeland. I began to be proud of my origins.

One day, after discussing how writers should write about what they know, she assigned us to compose an essay from our own experience. Fixing me with a stern look, she added, "Nick, I want you to write about what happened to your family in Greece." I had been trying to put those painful memories behind me and left the assignment until the last moment. Then, on a warm spring afternoon, I sat in my room with a yellow pad and pencil and stared out the window at the buds on the trees. I wrote that the coming of spring always reminded me of the last time I said good-bye to my mother on a green and gold day in 1948.

I kept writing, one line after another, telling how the Communist guerrillas occupied our village, took our home and food, how my mother started planning our escape when she learned that the children were to be sent to re-education camps behind the Iron Curtain and how, at the last moment, she couldn't escape with us because the guerrillas sent her with a group of women to thresh wheat in a distant village. She promised she would try to get away on her own, she told me to be brave, and hung a silver cross around my neck, and then she kissed me. I watched the line of women being led down into the ravine and up the other side, until they disappeared around the bend—my mother a tiny brown figure at the end who stopped for an instant to raise her hand in one last farewell.

I wrote about our nighttime escape down the mountain, across the minefields, and into the lines of the Nationalist soldiers, who sent us to a refugee camp. It was there that we learned of our mother's execution. I felt very lucky to have come to America, I concluded, but every year, the coming of spring made me feel sad because it reminded me of the last time I saw my mother.

11   I handed in the essay, hoping never to see it again, but Miss Hurd had it published in the school paper. This mortified me at first, until I saw that my classmates reacted with sympathy and tact to my family's story. Without telling me, Miss Hurd also submitted the essay to a contest sponsored by the Freedoms Foundation at Valley Forge, Pennsylvania, and it won a medal. The Worcester paper wrote about the award and quoted my essay at length. My father, by then a "five-and-dime-store chef," as the paper described him, was ecstatic with pride, and the Worcester Greek community celebrated the honor to one of its own.

12   For the first time I began to understand the power of the written word. A secret ambition took root in me. One day, I vowed, I would go back to Greece, find out the details of my mother's death and write about her life, so her grandchildren would know of her courage. Perhaps I would even track down the men who killed her and write of their crimes. Fulfilling that ambition would take me thirty years.

13   Meanwhile, I followed the literary path that Miss Hurd had so forcefully set me on. After junior high, I became the editor of my school paper at Classical High School and got a part-time job at the Worcester *Telegram and Gazette.* Although my father could only give me $50 and encouragement toward a college education, I managed to finance four years at Boston University with scholarships and part-time jobs in journalism. During my last year of college, an article I wrote about a friend who had died in the Philippines—the first person to lose his life working for the Peace Corps—led to my winning the Hearst Award for College Journalism. And the plaque was given to me in the White House by President John F. Kennedy.

14   For a refugee who had never seen a motorized vehicle or indoor plumbing until he was nine, this was an unimaginable honor. When the Worcester paper ran a picture of me standing next to President Kennedy, my father rushed out to buy a new suit in order to be properly dressed to receive the congratulations of the Worcester Greeks. He clipped out the photograph, had it laminated in plastic and carried it in his breast pocket for the rest of his life to show everyone he met. I found the much-worn photo in his pocket on the day he died twenty years later.

15   In our isolated Greek village, my mother had bribed a cousin to teach her to read, for girls were not supposed to attend school beyond a certain age. She had always dreamed of her children receiving an education. She couldn't be there when I graduated from Boston University, but the person who came with my father and shared our joy was my former teacher, Marjorie Hurd. We celebrated not only my bachelor's degree but also the scholarships that paid my way to Columbia's Graduate School of Journalism. There, I met the woman who would eventually become my wife. At our wedding and at the baptisms of our three children, Marjorie Hurd was always there, dancing alongside the Greeks.

16   By then, she was Mrs. Rabidou, for she had married a widower when she was in her early forties. That didn't distract her from her vocation of introducing young minds to English literature, however. She taught for a total of forty-one years and continually would make a "project" of some balky student in whom she

spied a spark of potential. Often these were students from the most troubled homes, yet she would alternately bully and charm each one with her own special brand of tough love until the spark caught fire. She retired in 1981 at the age of sixty-two but still avidly follows the lives and careers of former students while overseeing her adult stepchildren and driving her husband on camping trips to New Hampshire.

Miss Hurd was one of the first to call me on December 10, 1987, when President Reagan, in his television address after the summit meeting with Gorbachev, told the nation that Eleni Gatzoyiannis's dying cry, "My children!" had helped inspire him to seek an arms agreement "for all the children of the world."   17

"I can't imagine a better monument for your mother," Miss Hurd said with an uncharacteristic catch in her voice.   18

Although a bad hip makes it impossible for her to join in the Greek dancing, Marjorie Hurd Rabidou is still an honored and enthusiastic guest at all family celebrations, including my fiftieth birthday picnic last summer, where the shish kebab was cooked on spits, clarinets and *bouzoukis* wailed, and costumed dancers led the guests in a serpentine line around our Colonial farmhouse, only twenty minutes from my first home in Worcester.   19

My sisters and I felt an aching void because my father was not there to lead the line, balancing a glass of wine on his head while he danced, the way he did at every celebration during his ninety-two years. But Miss Hurd was there, surveying the scene with quiet satisfaction. Although my parents are gone, her presence was a consolation, because I owe her so much.   20

This is truly the land of opportunity, and I would have enjoyed its bounty even if I hadn't walked into Miss Hurd's classroom in 1953. But she was the one who directed my grief and pain into writing, and if it weren't for her I wouldn't have become an investigative reporter and foreign correspondent, recorded the story of my mother's life and death in *Eleni,* and now my father's story in *A Place for Us,* which is also a testament to the country that took us in. She was the catalyst that sent me into journalism and indirectly caused all the good things that came after. But Miss Hurd would probably deny this emphatically.   21

A few years ago, I answered the telephone and heard my former teacher's voice telling me, in that won't-take-no-for-an-answer tone of hers, that she had decided I was to write and deliver the eulogy at her funeral. I agreed (she didn't leave me any choice), but that's one assignment I never want to do. I hope, Miss Hurd, that you'll accept this remembrance instead.   22

Vocabulary

Directions: Mark any important words in the reading selection that you don't know. Then list them in the following chart along with their paragraph numbers. Try to figure out each word's meaning by reading over the context carefully for clues to help you guess the meaning of the unfamiliar word. Check your dictionary or thesaurus to confirm your guess. After you discuss the words with your group members, write the meanings in the margin of the text, near the word. Then enter them in the chart as well.

Key Word	Paragraph	Meaning

Guide Questions

Directions: Develop a list of questions that elicit the important ideas in the reading selection. Start at the beginning and work your way sequentially through the text until you have addressed all of the author's major ideas.

Application

Directions: When you have a list of guide questions, read through the selection again. This time, write one or more questions that require application of the information in the text to a situation in the real world.

Writing

Directions: Your last task is to prepare a writing assignment. For example, you might ask for a paragraph in which the writer comments on the ideas in the reading selection. You might also ask for a summary of the selection.

Cheating has always been a problem in schools, but many say that technology is making it easier and more tempting. Students who cheat offer many reasons for doing it, and educators worry that increased cheating reflects a world that is growing more corrupt.

A CHEATING CRISIS IN AMERICA'S SCHOOLS

ABC News Internet Ventures

Angelo Angelis, a professor at Hunter College in New York City, was recently grading some student papers on the story of Paul Revere when he noticed something strange. 1

A certain passage kept appearing in his students' work, he said. 2

It went like this, Angelis told Primetime's Charles Gibson: "Paul Revere would never have said, 'The British are coming, the British are coming,' he was in fact himself British, he would have said something like, 'the Red Coats are coming.'" 3

Angelis typed the words into Google, and found the passage on one Web site by a fifth-grade class. Half a dozen of his college students had copied their work from a bunch of elementary school kids, he thought. 4

The Web site was very well done, Angelis said. For fifth graders, he would give them an "A." But his college students deserved an "F." 5

Lifting papers off the Internet is one of the newer trends in plagiarism and technology is giving students even more ways to cheat nowadays. 6

Authoritative numbers are hard to come by, but according to a 2002 confidential survey of 12,000 high school students, 74 percent admitted cheating on an examination at least once in the past year. 7

In a six-month investigation, Primetime traveled to colleges and high schools across the country to see how students are cheating, and why. The bottom line is not just that many students have more temptation but they seem to have a whole new mindset. 8

Get Real

Joe is a student at a top college in the Northeast who admits to cheating regularly. Like all of the college students who spoke to Primetime, he wanted his identity obscured. 9

In Joe's view, he's just doing what the rest of the world does. 10

"The real world is terrible," he told Gibson. "People will take other people's materials and pass it on as theirs. I'm numb to it already. I'll cheat to get by." 11

Primetime heard the same refrain from many other students who cheat: that cheating in school is a dress rehearsal for life. They mentioned President Clinton's Monica Lewinsky scandal and financial scandals like the Enron case, as well as the inconsistencies of the court system. 12

"Whether or not you did it or not, if you can get the jury to say that you're not guilty, you're free," said Will, a student at one of the top public high schools in the nation. 13

14   Mary, a student at a large university in the South, said, "A lot of people think it's like you're not really there to learn anything. You're just learning to learn the system."

15   Michael Josephson, founder of the Josephson Institute for Ethics, the Los Angeles-based organization that conducted the 2002 survey, said students take their lead from adults.

16   "They're basically decent kids whose values are being totally corrupted by a world which is sanctioning stuff that even they know is wrong. But they can't understand why everybody allows it."

An Issue of Expediency

17   Even if the world were more ethical, students still have reasons for cheating. Some said they cheat because they're graded on a curve so that their score is directly affected by how other students do.

18   "There's other people getting better grades than me and they're cheating. Why am I not going to cheat? It's kind of almost stupid if you don't," said Joe.

19   The pressure for good grades is high. "Grades can determine your future, and if you fail this then you're not going on to college, you're going to work at McDonald's and live out of a car," said high school student Spike.

20   A business student at a top state university said, "Everything is about the grade that you got in the class. Nobody looks at how you got it." He graduates in a few weeks and will go on to a job with a top investment firm.

21   Others see it as a sort of moral relativity. Some students feel it is perfectly OK to cheat in some situations and in some courses.

22   "You'll have an engineer say, 'You know, what do I need to know about English literature? I shouldn't have to take this course,'" said Don McCabe, a professor who heads the center for academic integrity at Rutgers University in New Jersey.

23   For Mary's classmate Pam, it was a different sort of prioritizing. "You don't want to be a dork and study for eight hours a day. You want to go out and have fun."

24   And some professors make it easy, students said. They overlook even the most obvious instances.

25   In fact, McCabe says, a survey of more than 4,000 U.S. and Canadian schools revealed half of all faculty members admitted ignoring cheating at least once.

Tech War

26   Still, one of the main elements of cheating is doing it in secret. There are the tried and true methods:

27   Many sororities and fraternities maintain a file of term papers for reuse— take one, turn it in.

28   The old rubber band trick—stretch one out and write everything you need on it, and when it shrinks back to shape, no one will be the wiser.

29   But students today also have more technologically sophisticated options open to them:

A favorite device is the graphing calculator, which most professors allow stu-   30
dents to bring into an exam and and into which students can download all kinds
of material.

Another is an iPAQ—a handheld computer similar to a Palm Pilot which   31
can also download information.

Cell phones—to take pictures of notes, or among the more wily, to text-   32
message friends for answers.

Even a two-way pager can be used to cheat. For one student whose campus   33
has wireless Internet access, he used it as a mini-computer to access the entire
Internet during his test.

And then there are Internet-based clearing houses for term papers, such as   34
Papers4Less, Cheathouse.com and Schoolsucks.com.

Fortunately, educators have technological options too. Schools have been   35
subscribing to a service called Turnitin.com, which can help teachers compare
students' papers to all the available literature in its database.

"It's typically 30 percent of all the papers submitted have significant levels   36
of plagiarism," said John Barrie, founder of Turnitin.com.

Where Is the Tipping Point?

"We are in a crisis," said Josephson. But he added, "I don't think it has to stay   37
that way."

He said he was waiting for the tipping point, like Enron with business   38
ethics, where there would be a sea change in attitudes towards cheating.

An ABC News poll found hopeful signs but worrying ones as well.   39

In a random sample of high school students aged 15 to 17, 36 percent admitted   40
to having cheated themselves, fewer than in Josephson's survey.

But seven in 10 kids also say they have friends who cheat, and only one-third   41
of students has ever had a serious talk with their parents about cheating.

"We need to promote integrity. We need to get students to understand why   42
integrity is important, as opposed to policing dishonesty and then punishing
that dishonesty. Because they can beat the system," McCabe said.

Josephson emphasized that college teaches students many things: how to   43
learn, behave, overcome challenges, and succeed.

"And if they approach it honestly, they'll learn far more in college than they   44
think they can," he said. "But more than that, they'll come out of it better,
stronger people."

Vocabulary

Directions: Mark any important words in the reading selection that you don't know. Then
list them in the following chart along with their paragraph numbers. Try to figure out
each word's meaning by reading over the context carefully for clues to help you guess
the meaning of the unfamiliar word. Check your dictionary to confirm your guess. After
you discuss the word with your group members, write the meanings in the margin of the
text, near the word. Then enter them in the chart as well.

Key Word	Paragraph	Meaning

Guide Questions

Directions: Create a list of questions that elicit the important ideas in the reading selection. Start at the beginning and work your way sequentially through the text until you have dealt with all of the author's major ideas.

Application

Directions: When you have a list of guide questions, read through the reading selection again. This time, write one or more questions that require application of the information in the text to a new situation or perhaps to your own life.

Writing

Directions: Your last task is to create a writing assignment. For example, you might ask your classmates to write a paragraph commenting on the ideas in the reading selection—but be sure to write directions that are specific to the ideas in the reading selection. Make sure your classmates know what to do.

UNIT TWO

READING AND THINKING ABOUT CULTURE

As the traveler who has once been from home is wiser than he who has never left his own doorstep, so a knowledge of one other culture should sharpen our ability to scrutinize more steadily, to appreciate more lovingly, our own.

—Margaret Mead

Reading makes immigrants of us all. It takes us away from home, but most important, it finds homes for us everywhere.

—Hazel Rochman

Culture regulates our lives at every turn. From the moment we are born until we die there is, whether we are conscious of it or not, constant pressure upon us to follow certain types of behavior that other men have created for us.

—Clyde Kluckhohn

Thinking about Culture

Before you begin this part of the textbook, think about the following brief descriptions. Then answer the question at the end.

A small group of people called *hijras* live in India. *Hijras* are men who live as women. They wear female clothing and jewelry and their body language is feminine. They earn their living by asking for alms and receiving pay for blessing newborn babies. They believe in a goddess named Bahuchara Mata and identify with her totally. They undergo emasculation as a way of expressing their devotion to the goddess.

The Mundugumor people of New Guinea live a life of extreme individualism and hostility. They live in subdivided households and there is little community life. Babies are kept in hard uncomfortable baskets. When they cry, the mothers do not pick them up and hold them. Instead, they make scratching noises on the side of the basket. If the child continues to cry, the mother will feed it, standing up, in an awkward manner. As soon as the child has eaten, it is immediately returned to the basket.

The Wodaabe of West Africa hold a celebration every year before which the unmarried men spend days styling their hair, donning elegant robes, and applying elaborate and enormous amounts of make-up. As a result they are transformed into very feminine-looking young men. Nevertheless, the young women of the village are enchanted by the sight of these men, who most Americans would take for women. A beauty contest is then held to choose the most "beautiful" man. Then, if they agree, the winner and the most eligible young woman of the village may wed.

These are snapshots of people living in various cultures. Do these people seem very different from you and your family? Can you imagine that they would find *your* customs to be strange indeed? How can we account for the great differences among human beings all over the world? After all, we are all basically the same animal, with a few differences in skin color, height, hair texture, eye shape, and so on. The major differences seem to be in the *culture* each group has developed. Think about this question:

What is culture?

Now, write your own definition or explanation of culture.

Anthropologist Clifford Geertz says in his book, The Interpretation of Cultures, *"There is no such thing as a human nature independent of culture. Men without culture . . . would be unworkable monstrosities with very few useful instincts, fewer recognizable sentiments, and no intellect: mental basket cases."*

In this section, you will be introduced to the basic elements of culture and will take a look at different groups of people to see how they are different from us—and how they are the same.

CULTURE

Clyde Kluckhohn

Why do the Chinese dislike milk and milk products? Why would the Japanese die willingly in a Banzai charge [in World War II] that seemed senseless to Americans? Why do some nations trace descent through the father, others through the mother, still others through both parents? Not because different peoples have different instincts, not because they were destined by God or Fate to different habits, not because the weather is different in China and Japan and the United States. Sometimes shrewd common sense has an answer that is close to that of the anthropologist: "because they were brought up that way." By *culture,* anthropology means the total life way of a people, the social legacy the individual acquires from his group. Or *culture* can be regarded as that part of the environment that is the creation of man.

This technical term has a wider meaning than the *culture* of history and literature. A humble cooking pot is as much a cultural product as is a Beethoven sonata. In ordinary speech a man of culture is a man who can speak languages other than his own, who is familiar with history, literature, philosophy, or the fine arts. In some cliques that definition is still narrower. The cultured person is one who can talk about James Joyce, Scarlatti, and Picasso. To the anthropologist, however, to be human is to be cultured. There is culture in general, and then there are the specific cultures, such as Russian, American, British, Hottentot, Inca. The general abstract notion serves to remind us that we cannot explain acts solely in terms of the biological properties of the people concerned, their individual past experience, and the immediate situation. The past experience of other men in the form of culture enters into almost every event. Each specific culture constitutes a kind of blueprint for all of life's activities.

One of the interesting things about human beings is that they try to understand themselves and their own behavior. While this has been particularly true of Europeans in recent times, there is no group which has not developed a scheme or schemes to explain man's actions. To the insistent human query "why?" the most exciting illumination anthropology has to offer is that of the concept of culture. Its explanatory importance is comparable to categories such as evolution in biology, gravity in physics, disease in medicine. A good deal of human behavior can be understood and, indeed, predicted, if we know a people's design for living. Many acts are neither accidental nor due to personal peculiarities nor caused by supernatural forces nor simply mysterious. Even those of us who pride ourselves on our individualism follow most of the time a pattern not of our own making. We brush our teeth on arising. We put on pants—not a loincloth or a grass skirt. We eat three meals a day—not four or five or two. We sleep in a bed—not in a hammock or on a sheep pelt. I do not have to know the individual and his life history to be able to predict these and countless other regularities, including many in the thinking process, of all Americans who are not incarcerated in jails or hospitals for the insane.

4   To the American woman a system of plural wives seems "instinctively" abhorrent. She cannot understand how any woman can fail to be jealous and uncomfortable if she must share her husband with other women. She feels it "unnatural" to accept such a situation. On the other hand, a Koryak woman of Siberia, for example, would find it hard to understand how a woman could be so selfish and so undesirous of feminine companionship in the home as to wish to restrict her husband to one mate.

5   Some years ago I met in New York City a young man who did not speak a word of English and was obviously bewildered by American ways. By "blood" he was American, for his parents had gone from Indiana to China as missionaries. Orphaned in infancy, he was reared in a remote village. All who met him found him more Chinese than American. The facts of his blue eyes and light hair were less impressive than a Chinese style of gait, Chinese arm and hand movements, Chinese facial expression, and Chinese modes of thought. The biological heritage was American, but the cultural training had been Chinese. He returned to China.

6   Another example of another kind: I once knew a trader's wife in Arizona who took a somewhat devilish interest in producing a cultural reaction. Guests who came her way were often served delicious sandwiches filled with a meat that seemed to be neither chicken nor tuna fish yet was reminiscent of both. To queries she gave no reply until each had eaten his fill. She then explained that what they had eaten was not chicken, not tuna fish, but the rich, white flesh of freshly killed rattlesnakes. The response was instantaneous—vomiting, often violent vomiting. A biological process is caught in a cultural web.

7   A highly intelligent teacher with long and successful experience in the public schools of Chicago was finishing her first year in a [North American] Indian school. When asked how her Navaho pupils compared in intelligence with Chicago youngsters, she replied, "Well, I just don't know. Sometimes the Indians seem just as bright. At other times they just act like dumb animals. The other night we had a dance in the high school. I saw a boy who is one of the best students in my English class standing off by himself. So I took him over to a pretty girl and told them to dance. But they just stood there with their heads down. They wouldn't even say anything." I inquired if she knew whether or not they were members of the same clan. "What difference would that make?"

8   "How would you feel about getting into bed with your brother?" The teacher walked off in a huff, but, actually, the two cases were quite comparable in principle. To the Indian, the type of bodily contact involved in our social dancing has a directly sexual connotation. The incest taboos between members

of the same clan are as severe as between true brothers and sisters. The shame of the Indians at the suggestion that a clan brother and sister should dance and the indignation of the white teacher at the idea that she should share a bed with an adult brother represent equally nonrational responses, culturally standardized unreason.

All this does not mean that there is no such thing as raw human nature. The   9 very fact that certain of the same institutions are found in all known societies indicates that, at bottom, all human beings are very much alike. The files of the Cross-Cultural Survey at Yale University are organized according to categories, such as "marriage ceremonies," "life crisis rites," "incest taboos." At least seventy-five of these categories are represented in every single one of the hundreds of cultures analyzed. This is hardly surprising. The members of all human groups have about the same biological equipment. All men undergo the same poignant life experiences, such as birth, helplessness, illness, old age, and death. The biological potentialities of the species are the blocks with which cultures are built. Some patterns of every culture crystallize around focuses provided by the inevitables of biology: the difference between the sexes, the presence of persons of different ages, the varying physical strength and skill of individuals. The facts of nature also limit culture forms. No culture provides patterns for jumping over trees or for eating iron ore.

Vocabulary

Directions: Find each of the key words in the reading selection. Study the word in its context and try to determine its meaning. Write your guess in the margin of the text, near the word. Then read over the sentence, mentally substituting your guess for the key word. Does the sentence still make sense? Does it retain its original meaning? If it does, you've probably figured out the meaning of the key word correctly. In any case, confirm your guess by checking a dictionary or thesaurus.

If you take your meaning from a dictionary or thesaurus, be sure the definition includes words you already know and feel comfortable using. If it doesn't, you will be worse off than when you started—you will have begun with one word you didn't know and ended with *two* words you don't know!

Record the new words you've learned in the following chart.

Key Word	Paragraph	Meaning
1. legacy	1	
2. cliques	2	
3. insistent	3	
4. abhorrent	4	
5. gait	5	

Key Word	Paragraph	Meaning
6. instantaneous	6	
7. poignant	9	
Others?		

Guide Questions

Directions: These questions will guide your analysis of the text. Your thoughtful answers will ensure that you have understood the main ideas the author wanted to convey. Some of the questions require you simply to find the stated facts in the reading selection; others will ask you to do more difficult tasks, such as paraphrasing information (putting the author's ideas into your own words), synthesizing several ideas into one complex thought, evaluating (making judgments about) an idea, or taking information from the reading and applying it to a new situation or to your own life.

Write answers to the questions in your notebook or on a separate sheet of paper if your instructor wishes to collect it. Your answers will form the basis of class discussion.

1. Kluckhohn states that the term *culture* can have two different meanings, depending on the context. What does *culture* mean in ordinary speech? What does *culture* mean to an anthropologist?
2. a. Many people feel that the way we eat, drink, marry, walk, and talk are somehow "instinctual" or "natural." Give some examples from the text that contradict this.
   b. Explain what Kluckhohn means by his description of people's reaction to eating rattlesnake: "A biological process is caught in a cultural web."
3. Kluckhohn cites many institutions that have been found in every single one of the hundreds of cultures that have been studied. How does he explain these many similarities among the peoples of the world?
4. Explain what Kluckhohn means by his final point, "the facts of nature also limit culture forms."

Application

Directions: Consider each of the following little stories, which describe the traditional behavior of a group of people in a certain situation. Compare and contrast these with how you and the members of your culture would act in the same situation.

Work in small groups to complete this assignment. First, choose a *group leader,* who will be responsible for directing the conversation and ensuring that every member participates. Next, choose a *reader,* who will read each of the stories out loud before the group discusses it. Next, choose a *secretary,* who will record the group's answers to the questions following each story. Finally, choose a *timekeeper,* whose job is to "keep the ball rolling" and make sure the group works efficiently. When you finish, your instructor may want you to hand in your answers.

1. *Finding a Wife.* A Chiricahua man, young and unmarried, goes to visit an old woman, the grandmother of an unmarried girl:

> I went to her place that night. I had heard the old lady had some *tiswin* (a fermented liquor made of corn). When I got there she told me to have a drink. As we talked she told me that I was single and needed a wife. She mentioned this girl (her grandchild) and said it was worth two horses to get her. I had never seen the girl before. When I got home I started to think about it seriously. I talked it over with my relatives. An uncle of mine gave me a mule, and a cousin gave me a horse.
>
> The next day I went to the home of a certain woman, a middle-aged woman. She was eating when I arrived. I called her outside and hired her to speak for me to this girl's grandmother. This woman lived just on the other side of a stream from the girl and her grandmother. The next day my go-between demanded two good horses. My go-between thanked the grandmother and came to tell me what had been said. I gave her the horse and the mule to lead to the old woman, and the next day I went to the girl.

Morris E. Opler, *An Apache Life-Way,* p. 157

Describe how a member of your culture finds a wife. List the similarities and differences between the way you would do it and the way the Chiricahua did it. (The Chiricahua are North American Indians.)

2. *A Husband Discovers His Wife Has Been Unfaithful.* A Chiricahua man is expected to take drastic action:

> A wronged husband who does not show some rancor is considered unmanly. . . . The woman, since she is close at hand, is likely to be the first to feel the husband's wrath. A beating is the least punishment she suffers. If there is no one to intercede for her, her very life may be forfeit, or she may be subjected to mutilation. . . . The husband is just as insistent that the man who has disrupted his home be punished. After the husband has punished or killed his wife, he will go after the man and kill him.

An Apache Life-Way, p. 410

List the similarities and differences between how a member of your culture would handle this situation and how the Chiricahua behaved.

3. *A Wedding in Tahiti.*

> Tahitian weddings generally last two days, the law allowing two days off from work, with pay. The civil ceremony takes place at the mayor's office. If there is a religious ceremony, it takes place later at the church. The reception is usually at the home of a family member. The decorations include a temporary covered terrace (in case of rain), posts wrapped in coconut leaves with flowers inserted into them; flowers and greenery everywhere. The bride and groom are welcomed to the reception with flower garlands and leis. Tahitians do not serve a wedding cake or throw a wedding bouquet or the garter. The festivities include eating, storytelling, singing, spoontapping, and dancing. At the reception the couple is given their new name, the "marriage name" by which they will henceforth be called. Usually the name is selected by the family and is the name of an ancestor or a name from the Bible. The names of the couple's first and second children are also selected.

Describe the similarities and differences between a wedding in Tahiti and a wedding in your culture.

4. *A Funeral among the Teton-Dakota Indians.*

> At the death of an individual, his relatives and friends gathered at his tepee to mourn. The women spent four days in intermittent wailing. Parents often gashed themselves or severed a finger to express their grief. A bereaved father might wander from camp, singing a death song, to shoot down the first person whom he met and then kill himself. A give-away of the family's property to the mourners was part of the funeral ceremony, and another give-away ended the year of mourning.
>
> > Gordon MacGregor, *Warriors without Weapons: Society and Personality Development of the Pine Ridge Sioux,* p. 94

Describe a funeral ritual in your society. How is it similar to and different from a funeral among the Teton-Dakota Indians? (The Teton-Dakotas are North American Indians.)

5. *Birth Ceremonies of the Hmong.*

> Hmong women try not to cry or show pain during labor. Moments after birth, the baby is given a silver necklace to warn away bad spirits. In some Hmong communities, women make caps with flower designs to fool the spirits into thinking the baby is a flower.
>
> The placenta is buried beneath the central pole of the house. If the firstborn is a boy, the umbilical cord is dried and boiled with a piece of oak. It is then used as medicine.
>
> For the first month of life, the new mother eats only freshly killed chicken, boiled, with broth and rice three times a day.

When the baby is three days old, a naming ceremony takes place. The family calls back the child's soul, which may have been frightened away during birth. White strings are tied around the baby's wrist to protect him or her from the spirits. The strings prevent the soul from being stolen, and they remain in place until they fall off or disintegrate. Traditionally, the Hmong do not compliment a baby, believing evil spirits will then take the baby away.

Describe the rituals surrounding the birth of a child in your culture. Compare and contrast them with the traditions of the Hmong. (The Hmong live in Southeast Asia, principally in Laos and Cambodia.)

Writing

Directions: Return to the definition of culture that you were asked to write on page 58, "Thinking about Culture." Evaluate your definition in light of what you learned from this selection. Compare your definition to Kluckhohn's explanation of *culture*. Is your definition sufficient? Is it accurate? How would you rewrite it? Write a few sentences in response to these questions.

In Japan, when two businessmen meet, they automatically bow to one another; in the United States, two men in the same situation would shake hands. In Iran, men and women eat separately, while in most Western countries, men and women have their meals together. Fish is used as a food by most American Indian tribes; but some, including the Navajos and Apaches of New Mexico, consider it nauseating and unfit for human consumption. The aboriginal tribes of Australia and the Indians of Tierra del Fuego wear almost no clothing at all; the Baganda people of East Africa must be fully clothed from neck to ankles. Among the Navajos of the American Southwest, a man was not supposed to speak to or even look at his wife's mother. In northwestern India, married older brothers were not expected to show jealousy when younger brothers slept with their brides. Countless other cultural differences exist among human societies. When asked, for example, why they eat with knives and forks rather than with chopsticks, most Americans would reply, "Because that's the way we do it," or perhaps "Because it's the 'right' way to eat," or even "I don't know." Such answers are not very informative. Most people don't think about these common patterns of social behavior—they simply obey the rules. As anthropologist Clyde Kluckhohn says, "Culture regulates our lives at every turn. From the moment we are born until we die there is, whether we are conscious of it or not, constant pressure on us to follow certain types of behavior that other men have created for us."

In this selection we learn about the rules—imposed by culture—called norms.

NORMS*

Mary Fjeldstad

1   Why do we behave in controlled and predictable ways? Because we are members of a society of human beings, our actions are controlled by *norms*—shared guidelines that prescribe the appropriate behavior in a particular situation. Norms define how we are expected to behave in specific circumstances in a specific society. Many norms are unwritten rules that regulate even the smallest details of social life. Usually, we are not even aware that we are obeying norms; they are simply a part of us. Such norms include knowing when to speak, how to address other people (Sir, Mr. Jones, or Bobby), when to sit or stand and when to leave. We learn these norms through the process of *socialization*—the education of individuals in society's customs and beliefs through the family, the school, professional organizations, and so on.

2   We generally only think about a norm when someone departs from it. For example, if, in a restaurant, someone were to suddenly begin eating with his hands, we would all be surprised, or distressed, or even amused by this departure from the American norm of using silverware to eat. Our criticism of the person, or ridicule, or even request for him to leave would be our way of applying sanctions to him. When we visit people from other cultures, we quickly become aware that they do things according to their own set of rules, which may be very different from ours. If we were to visit a village in Burkina Faso in Africa,

---

*This selection is based in part on information in Ian Robertson's *Sociology*.

for example, we would probably find ourselves the victim of sanctions if we did not use our hands to eat, as is the custom there.

What is the purpose of norms? Norms help society to function smoothly. They give guidelines to follow in our own behavior and help us anticipate how others will behave. Imagine how difficult life would be if we had no norms! Each time you encountered a novel situation, you'd have to figure out anew how you were going to act. Take a job interview, for example: should you wear a T-shirt or a jacket? Should you stand or sit? Or why not kneel down or lie on the floor? How can you expect the interviewer to act? Will he or she speak first? Or wait for you to begin? Will the interviewer direct the conversation? Shake your hand or bow? Or perhaps kiss your cheek? All of these questions are answered by our knowledge of the rules of our society. Life would indeed be stressful if we could not rely on norms. 3

The function of norms — regulating social behavior — is so crucial to day-to-day life that there is always pressure on people to conform. 4

There are two major types of norms. The first, *folkways,* are the ordinary rules of everyday life. We expect conformity to folkways, but accept a great deal of nonconformity. For example, in the United States, we expect people to bathe frequently, speak quietly in a library, wait for their turn in line. If people do not follow such rules, they are sanctioned, or "punished," by being criticized, or laughed at, but they are not considered criminal or depraved. Society is generally not outraged when someone violates a folkway. 5

On the other hand, *mores,* much more powerful norms, are treated more seriously. Rules against theft, murder, and rape are examples of mores. People believe that their mores are crucial to the decent and orderly functioning of society and are deeply outraged by violations of them. Penalties for those who disobey mores are serious and can range from monetary fines to physical attack to imprisonment or commitment to a mental institution. 6

One special type of more is the *taboo* — a powerful prohibition against acts that society considers loathsome. In most cultures, for example, the eating of human flesh is a taboo, one that is rarely broken. 7

Most mores are formally encoded and thus are also laws. A *law* is simply a rule of conduct that a society has officially recorded and that is enforced by the power of the state. Laws are written to codify existing norms, to specify the requirements and the exact penalties for violations of them. Penalties can vary widely both within a culture and from one culture to another. For example, in Iran, adultery may be punished by death, while in the United States violations of this law are usually ignored by the authorities. Within the United States the penalties for violations of laws vary from state to state. For example, drug abuse in certain states, such as Texas, is punished more severely than in many other states. The penalty for speeding while driving in New York is a heavy fine, as much as $500, while in the state of Montana the fine until recently was only $5, no matter how fast the driver was going. The penalty for drunk driving can be as severe as a $1,000 fine plus a year in jail (in South Dakota) or as light as a $100 fine and ten days in jail (in Oklahoma). 8

9   Sometimes legislators introduce new laws in an attempt to alter existing norms. For example, in 1919 a constitutional amendment outlawing the manufacture and sale of alcoholic beverages was passed. Such laws are often ineffective if they run counter to a society's norms. In this case, the prohibition law was routinely violated until it was repealed fourteen years later. Other examples of ineffective laws are those prohibiting stores from being open on Sunday and those forbidding the personal use of certain drugs.

10   Norms are not fixed, however. Social protest and political movements may bring about changes in social norms—for example, abortion-law reform, treatment of homosexuals by society, and changes in the roles of women. Unlike Prohibition, certain laws that oppose social norms have survived. A notable example is the civil-rights laws passed in the 1960s and 1970s, which were aimed at changing the traditional behaviors of white-dominated society, especially in the South. Laws that required equal access to public facilities for people of all races ran counter to traditional norms and provoked great resistance. Eventually, however, the norms began to change to conform to the civil rights laws and great differences in folkways and mores have occurred in the past few decades. Traditional modes of behavior in the South, such as requiring blacks to sit at the rear of public buses, use separate public toilet facilities, or eat at lunch counters reserved for "colored," have changed through the strict enforcement of new laws as well as the efforts of civil rights groups.

Vocabulary

Directions: Find each of the key words in the reading selection. Study the word in its context and try to determine its meaning. Write your guess in the margin of the text, near the word. Then read over the sentence, mentally substituting your guess for the key word. Does the sentence still make sense? Does it retain its original meaning? If it does, you've probably figured out the meaning of the key word correctly. In any case, confirm your guess by checking a dictionary or thesaurus.

If you take your meaning from a dictionary or thesaurus, be sure the definition includes words you already know and feel comfortable using. If it doesn't, you will be worse off than when you started—you will have begun with one word you didn't know and ended with *two* words you don't know!

Record the new words you've learned in the following chart.

Key Word	Paragraph	Meaning
1. sanctions	2	
2. conform	4	
3. depraved	5	
4. crucial	6	

Key Word	Paragraph	Meaning
5. loathsome	7	
6. run counter to	9	
Others?		

Guide Questions

Directions: These questions will guide your analysis of the text. Your thoughtful answers will ensure that you have understood the main ideas the author wanted to convey. Some of the questions require you simply to find the stated facts in the reading selection; others will ask you to do more difficult tasks, such as paraphrasing information (putting the author's ideas into your own words), synthesizing several ideas into one complex thought, evaluating (making judgments about) an idea, or taking information from the reading and applying it to a new situation or to your own life.

Write answers to the questions in your notebook or on a separate sheet of paper if your instructor wishes to collect them. Your answers will form the basis of class discussion.

1. Define the term *norms*.
2. It is a norm in American society for men to shake hands upon meeting one another. Give an example of a different norm in some other society that regulates the same situation.
3. How do we learn the norms of our society?
4. Explain the purpose of norms.
5. Give some examples of what your day-to-day life would be like if we did not have norms.
6. List the two major types of norms discussed in the text.
7. a. Give an example of a folkway mentioned in the text.
   b. Give an example of a folkway not mentioned in the text.
8. Describe the type of pressure that is put on people to conform to folkways.
9. How do mores differ from folkways?
10. Give some examples of mores in American society.
11. Describe the type of pressure that society puts on people to conform to mores.
12. What are taboos?
13. Define the term *laws*.
14. Explain why the Prohibition amendment was not effective.
15. What can cause the norms of a society to change?

Application

1. Norms vary from society to society (as you probably already know if you are from another country or if you know people from other countries). One example of this variation in norms is that, in the United States, marriage is thought of as a private arrangement between a man and a woman who are motivated by romantic love. Do you know of other cultures where marriage is *not* a product of romantic love? Where the bride and groom have no control over whom or when they marry? If you do, write a paragraph describing this different kind of marriage. Be sure to name the society you are describing. You may need to do some research on marriage customs in the culture you choose.

2. Choose a social situation (other than marriage), and in two paragraphs describe how it is articulated in two different societies: the United States and some other society. In the first paragraph, describe the situation and the norm that regulates it in the United States; in the second paragraph, describe how the situation is regulated in some other society. For example, you might write one paragraph describing how Americans eat dinner using plates, knives, forks, and spoons, and a second paragraph describing how the Chinese use different utensils for their meals.

3. Write at least one paragraph in response to the following statement: Norms are constantly changing, especially in a dynamic society such as the United States. List as many norms as you can that have changed in your lifetime, or since your parents' youth. Then explain *how* each norm has changed. For example, you might consider how norms regarding premarital sex, smoking, or dress have changed in the past several years.

Marking Text

Turn to page 413, "Learning Strategy III—Marking Text." Read and study the information on how to mark your text. Then mark the selection "Norms" using what you've learned. To get you started, here is a model of how you might mark the first section of the essay. Finish marking the selection on your own.

NORMS

Mary Fjeldstad

1   Why do we behave in controlled and predictable ways? <u>Because we are members of a society of human beings, our actions are controlled by *norms*</u>—shared guidelines that prescribe the appropriate behavior in a particular situation. Norms define how we are expected to behave in specific circumstances in a specific society. Many norms are <u>unwritten rules</u> that regulate even the smallest details of social life. <u>Usually, we are not even aware that we are obeying norms</u>; they are simply a part of us. Such norms include knowing when to speak, how to address other people (Sir, Mr. Jones, or Bobby), when to sit or stand and when to leave. <u>We learn these norms through the process of *socialization*</u>—the education of individuals in

Norms definition

Socialization defined

society's customs and beliefs through the family, the school, professional organizations, and so on.

We generally only think about a norm when someone departs from it. For example, if, in a restaurant, someone were to suddenly begin eating with his hands, we would all be surprised, or distressed, or even amused by this departure from the American norm of using silverware to eat. Our criticism of the person, or ridicule, or even request for him to leave would be our way of applying sanctions to him. When we visit people from other cultures, we quickly become aware that they do things according to their own set of rules, which may be very different from ours. If we were to visit a village in Burkina Faso in Africa, for example, we would probably find ourselves the victim of sanctions if we did not use our hands to eat, as is the custom there.

Sanctions?

2

What is the purpose of norms? Norms help society to function smoothly. They give guidelines to follow in our own behavior and help us anticipate how others will behave. Imagine how difficult life would be if we had no norms! Each time you encountered a novel situation, you'd have to figure out anew how you were going to act. Take a job interview, for example: should you wear a T-shirt or a jacket? Should you stand or sit? Or why not kneel down or lie on the floor? How can you expect the interviewer to act? Will he or she speak first? Or wait for you to begin? Will the interviewer direct the conversation? Shake your hand or bow? Or perhaps kiss your cheek? All of these questions are answered by our knowledge of the rules of our society. Life would indeed be stressful if we could not rely on norms.

3 *Why do we have norms?*

(I never thought of this before!)

The function of norms — regulating social behavior — is so crucial to day-to-day life that there is always pressure on people to conform.

4

There are two major types of norms. The first, *folkways,* are the ordinary rules of everyday life. We expect conformity to folkways, but accept a great deal of nonconformity. For example, in the United States, we expect people to bathe frequently, speak quietly in a library, wait for their turn in line. If people do not follow such rules, they are sanctioned, or "punished," by being criticized, or laughed at, but they are not considered criminal or depraved. Society is generally not outraged when someone violates a folkway.

5 *2 Types:*
1-folkways

Exs of folkways

?

On the other hand, *mores,* much more powerful norms, are treated more seriously. Rules against theft, murder, and rape are examples of mores. People believe that their mores are crucial to the decent and orderly functioning of society and are deeply outraged by violations of them. Penalties for those who disobey mores are serious and can range from monetary fines to physical attack to imprisonment or commitment to a mental institution.

6

2-mores

Exs of mores

Now, finish, marking the chapter yourself.

Which is more important to you—winning that tennis game or making sure your friend has a good time playing? Both reflect values important to most Americans—winning and friendship. Sometimes we must decide between two equally desirable things, and it can be tough!

Most Americans would say they value honesty very highly. But what if it comes into conflict with some other value, like friendship? For example, if you saw your friend cheating on an exam, and he begged you not to tell, would you? You are caught in a conflict of two important values. What would you do?

Many Americans expect to work hard, overtime if necessary, to make decisions fast, and implement them quickly. If Americans try to work "as usual" in another culture where a long, relaxed lunch is the norm, and speedy implementation of decisions is unknown, they may become upset and frustrated because their values conflict with those of their new culture. Which values are at work here?

In this excerpt from a textbook chapter we learn about values, the principles that underlie a society's ideas and behavior.

VALUES

Ian Robertson

1   The norms of a society are ultimately an expression of its values—socially shared ideas about what is good, right, and desirable. The difference between values and norms is that values are abstract, general concepts, whereas norms are specific guidelines for people in particular kinds of situations.

Importance of Values

2   The values of a society are important because they influence the content of its norms. If a society values education highly, its norms will make provision for mass schooling. If it values a large population, its norms will encourage big families. In principle at least, all norms can be traced to a basic social value. For example, the norms that require a student to be more polite and formal to a professor than to other students express the value our society places on respect for authority and learning. The mid-20th century norms that insisted on short hair for men reflected the high value placed on men's "masculinity" in American culture—a value that was threatened by long hair because it was regarded as "effeminate."

3   Although all norms express social values, many norms persist long after the conditions that gave rise to them have been forgotten. The folkway that requires us to shake hands, especially when greeting a stranger, seems to have originated long ago in the desire to show that no weapon was concealed in the right hand. The folkway of throwing rice or confetti over a bride and groom may seem rather meaningless, but it actually stems from an ancient practice of showering newly-weds with nuts, fruits, and seeds as symbols of fertility.

American Values

Unlike norms, whose existence can easily be observed in everyday behavior, values are often more difficult to identify. The values of a society have to be inferred from its norms, so that any analysis of social values relies heavily on the interpretations of the observer. The United States presents a particular problem, for it has a heterogeneous culture drawn from many different racial, ethnic, religious, and regional traditions, and so lacks the unquestioned consensus on values that smaller, traditional communities tend to display. Sociologists have therefore concentrated on detecting "core" values that appear to be shared by the majority of Americans. The most influential of these attempts is that of Robin Williams, who found fifteen basic value orientations in the United States:

1. *Achievement and success.* The society is highly competitive, and great value is placed on the achievement of power, wealth, and prestige.
2. *Activity and work.* Regular, disciplined work is highly valued for its own sake; those who do not work are considered lazy and even immoral.
3. *Moral orientation.* Americans tend to be moralists, seeing the world in terms of right and wrong and constantly evaluating the moral behavior of others.
4. *Humanitarianism.* Americans regard themselves as a kindly, charitable people, always ready to come to the aid of the less fortunate or the underdog.
5. *Efficiency and practicality.* Americans believe that problems have solutions, and they are an intensely practical people; the ability to "get things done" is widely admired.
6. *Progress.* Americans look to the future rather than the past, sharing a conviction that things can and should get better; their outlook is fundamentally optimistic.
7. *Material comfort.* Americans value the "good life," which they define in terms of a high standard of living and the possession of material goods.
8. *Equality.* Americans claim to believe in human equality, particularly in equality of opportunity; they generally relate to one another in an informal, egalitarian way.
9. *Freedom.* The freedom of the individual is regarded as one of the most important values in American life; Americans believe devoutly that they are and should remain "free."
10. *External conformity.* Despite their expressed belief in "rugged individualism," Americans tend to be conformist and are suspicious of those who are not.
11. *Science and rationality.* Americans believe deeply in a scientific rational approach to the world and in the use of applied science to gain mastery over the environment.
12. *Nationalism–patriotism.* Americans are proud of their country and its achievements; the "American way of life" is highly valued and assumed to be the best in the world.

13. *Democracy.* Americans regard their form of government as highly democratic, and believe that every citizen should have the right of political participation.
14. *Individual personality.* To be a responsible, self-respecting individual is very important, and Americans are reluctant to give the group priority over the individual.
15. *Group-superiority themes.* A strong countervalue to that of individual personality is the one that places a higher value on some racial, ethnic, class, or religious groups than on others.

6   It is obvious that some of these values are not entirely consistent with one another. Many of them, too, are accepted by some Americans but rejected by others. Also, Williams's list does not exhaust all the possibilities, and other writers have identified rather different values. James Henslin, for example, includes several items on Williams's list but adds others, such as education, religiosity, male supremacy, romantic love, monogamy, and heterosexuality. Moreover, values change over time, and some of those listed by Williams may be eroding. Questions have been raised, for example, about the meaning of "progress," and about new problems posed by science and technology, such as pollution of the environment. There is perhaps less insistence now on the value of conformity, and certainly less emphasis on group superiority, than there was a few decades ago.

Vocabulary

Directions: Locate each of the key words in the reading selection. Then read and study each word in its context and try to determine its meaning. Use a dictionary or thesaurus to check your guess. Write the meanings of the words in the margin of the text.

Record the new words you've learned.

Key Word	Paragraph	Meaning
1. inferred	4	
2. heterogeneous	4	
3. consensus	4	
4. eroding	6	
Others?		

Guide Questions

Directions: These questions will guide your understanding of what you have read. They also will help you to analyze and evaluate the author's ideas and apply them to the real world and your own life.

Write answers to the questions in your notebook or on a separate sheet of paper if your instructor wishes to collect them. Your answers will form the basis of class discussion.

1. Contrast the definitions of *values* and *norms* according to the information given in the first paragraph.
2. Give two examples of values that you personally hold.
3. a. Cite a few of the examples of values from the selection and the norms that result from them.
   b. Based on your understanding of question 3a, how would you describe the *relationship* between values and norms?
4. Discuss the point made in paragraph 4 of the selection: "The United States presents a particular problem, for it has a heterogeneous culture. . . ." What does the author mean by "a heterogeneous culture"? How can we account for the fact that the United States is so heterogeneous?
5. In the introduction and in paragraph 6, you read that we often must choose between two values in the same situation—for example, between honesty and friendship when your friend asks you to help her cheat on an exam. Can you think of some other situations in which two values are in conflict?
6. It is important to remember that values are different in different societies. The Tangu, a group of people who live in New Guinea, play a game called *taketak,* which is similar to bowling. The goal of the game is not for one team to score more points than the other, but rather for both sides to score the *same* number of points. The Tangu place a high value on *equivalence* and think that winning generates ill will. In fact, when the Europeans introduced soccer to New Guinea, the Tangu changed the rules so that the object of the game was for the two teams to score the same number of goals. Sometimes their soccer games went on for days! Americans, of course, value competition and winning and insist on winners and losers. Living among the Tangu would certainly be very different from living in the United States. What might be some of the *advantages* of living in a society where equivalence is valued and winning is disapproved of? What might the *disadvantages* be?
7. A major distinction between values and norms is that values are abstract concepts and norms are concrete rules for behavior. Using the chart that follows, give several examples of abstract values and some of the concrete norms that are derived from them. Some information is already filled in to get you started. You can use the values in Williams's list and/or your own personal list of values.

The Value	The Norm
Honesty	*I pay my taxes.*
	I will not cheat on Tuesday's exam.
Efficiency	*I make a list of "things to do" every day.*
Thrift	
Punctuality	

Application

1. Did you know that in Mexico clocks do not "run," they "walk"? And that Mexicans do not say they "missed" the bus, but rather the bus "left" them? In three or four sentences, explain what you think these two examples tell us about the differing values of the United States and Mexico.

2. Work in small groups to complete this exercise. Here are brief descriptions of people in specific situations. Read the descriptions out loud, then discuss with your group members which American value is reflected in each little story.

   a. A mother says angrily to her young child, "You march right back to that bathroom—and this time use soap!"

   b. A boss looks at the clock as an employee arrives at work. The clock says 9:25 a.m. The boss says, "Well, good *afternoon!*"

   c. A girl wins an essay-writing contest sponsored by a nearby university. When told of her prize, she smiles and says, "Oh, it was nothing—anyone could have done it."

   d. A father takes his young daughter outside to practice baseball every night, rain or shine. When the girl is beaten by another child in a ball game, they increase the length of their practice sessions. When the girl is chosen "Most Valuable Player" of her league, the father and daughter are happy and proud.

e. A male executive hears there may be layoffs in his company, so he decides to look for another job. Before going on his first interview, he visits a hair-styling salon to have his gray hair dyed back to its original brown color.

Add the values you identify in this question to the chart of values and norms you created for guide question 7.

Marking Text
Mark the chapter, "Values." (Marking text is explained on page 413.)

Making Connections
Connect the ideas in "Values" with those in the previous selection, "Norms." How did the information in "Norms" help you to understand "Values"? What did you learn in "Values" that clarified or enhanced your understanding of "Norms?"

The diversity of behavior among the peoples of the world is tremendous. For example, in some societies, bending your finger toward your body means "come here," while in other cultures, it means "go away." In India, cows wander freely through the streets, something Americans find offensive; in the United States, dogs run freely in homes, something visitors from India would find disgusting. Most Americans teach their children not to fight. "Solve your problems with words, not fists," they counsel. Among the Yanomamo of South America, a father deliberately teases and goads his son until the child, in desperation, strikes him in the face. The father cries out in approval. Why have humans all over the world, who are so similar physically, developed such different ways of living? Cultural anthropologists try to discover why people behave as they do. In this chapter we learn that our culture is only one alternative among the many designs for living. No one group of people has developed the "right" way of living. "Other fields, other grasshoppers," say the Javanese.

UNITY IN DIVERSITY

Donald Light and Suzanne Keller

1   What is more basic, more "natural" than love between a man and woman? Eskimo men offer their wives to guests and friends as a gesture of hospitality; both husband and wife feel extremely offended if the guest declines. The Banaro of New Guinea believe it would be disastrous for a woman to conceive her first child by her husband and not by one of her father's close friends, as is their custom.

2   The real father is a close friend of the bride's father. . . . Nevertheless the first-born child inherits the name and possessions of the husband. An American would deem such a custom immoral, but Banaro tribesmen would be equally shocked to discover that the first-born child of an American couple is the offspring of the husband.

3   The Yanomamo of northern Brazil, whom anthropologist Napoleon A. Chagnon named "the fierce people," encourage what we would consider extreme disrespect. Small boys are applauded for striking their mothers and fathers in the face. Yanomamo parents would laugh at our efforts to curb aggression in children, much as they laughed at Chagnon's naiveté when he first came to live with them. To be officially considered a man, a Yanomamo boy must compile a record of successful battles, and if he is to be taken seriously, by the time he reaches puberty his body must be covered with scars. Older men, hardened to injury, duel with each other constantly in an effort to prove which man has the greater capacity to bear pain. Even women do not escape tribal savagery since men will frequently prove just how fierce they are by beating, mutilating, or wounding their wives. A wife cannot even escape to her family because, to the family, the husband's behavior is simply part of a long tradition.

4   The variations among cultures are startling, yet all peoples have customs and beliefs about marriage, the bearing and raising of children, sex, and hospitality—to name just a few of the universals anthropologists have discovered in their

cross-cultural explorations. But the details of cultures do indeed vary: in this country, not so many years ago, when a girl was serious about a boy and he about her, she wore his fraternity pin over her heart; in the Fiji Islands, girls put hibiscus flowers behind their ears when they are in love. The specific gestures are different but the impulse to symbolize feelings, to dress courtship in ceremonies, is the same. How do we explain this unity in diversity?

Cultural Universals

Cultural universals are all of the behavior patterns and institutions that have   5
been found in all known cultures. Anthropologist George Peter Murdock identified over sixty cultural universals, including a system of social status, marriage, body adornments, dancing, myths and legends, cooking, incest taboos, inheritance rules, puberty customs, and religious rituals.

The universals of culture may derive from the fact that all societies must per-   6
form the same essential functions if they are to survive—including organization, motivation, communication, protection, the socialization of new members, and the replacement of those who die. In meeting these prerequisites for group life, people inevitably design similar—though not identical—patterns for living. As Clyde Kluckhohn wrote, "All cultures constitute somewhat distinct answers to essentially the same questions posed by human biology and by the generalities of the human situation."

The way in which a people articulate cultural universals depends in large   7
part on their physical and social environment—that is, on the climate in which they live, the materials they have at hand, and the peoples with whom they establish contact. For example, the wheel has long been considered one of humankind's greatest inventions, and anthropologists were baffled for a long time by the fact that the great civilizations of South America never discovered it. Then researchers uncovered a number of toys with wheels. Apparently the Aztecs and their neighbors did know about the wheel; they simply didn't find them useful in their mountainous environment.

Adaptation, Ethnocentrism, and Cultural Relativity

Taken out of context, almost any custom will seem bizarre, perhaps cruel, or just   8
plain ridiculous. To understand why the Yanomamo encourage aggressive behavior in their sons, for example, you have to see things through their eyes. The Yanomamo live in a state of chronic warfare; they spend much of their time planning for and defending against raids with neighboring tribes. If Yanomamo parents did not encourage aggression in a boy, he would be ill-equipped for life in their society. Socializing boys to be aggressive is **adaptive** for the Yanomamo because it enhances their capacity for survival. "In general, culture is . . . adaptive because it often provides people with a means of adjusting to the physiological needs of their own bodies, to their physical–geographical environment and to their social environments as well."

9   In many tropical societies, there are strong taboos against a mother having sexual intercourse with a man until her child is at least two years old. As a Hausa woman explains,

> A mother should not go to her husband while she has a child she is suck-
> ling. . . . [I]f she only sleeps with her husband and does not become preg-
> nant, it will not hurt her child, it will not spoil her milk. But if another
> child enters in, her milk will make the first one ill.

10   Undoubtedly, people would smirk at a woman who nursed a two-year-old child in our society and abstained from having sex with her husband. Why do Hausa women behave in a way that seems so overprotective and overindulgent to us? In trop-ical climates protein is scarce. If a mother were to nurse more than one child at a time, or if she were to wean a child before it reached the age of two, the youngster would be prone to kwashiorkor, an often fatal disease resulting from protein deficiency. Thus, long post partum sex taboos are adaptive. In a tropical environment a post partum sex taboo and a long period of breast-feeding solve a serious problem.

11   **Ethnocentrism** is the tendency to see one's own way of life, including behaviors, beliefs, values, and norms as the only right way of living. Robin Fox points out that "any human group is ever ready to consign another recognizably different human group to the other side of the boundary. It is not enough to pos-sess culture to be fully human, you have to possess our culture." Although the error of this way of thinking about culture may seem self-evident today, it is a lesson that anthropologists and the missionaries who often preceded them to remote areas learned the hard way, by observing the effects their best intentions had on peoples whose way of life was quite different from their own. In an arti-cle on the pitfalls of trying to "uplift" peoples whose ways seem backward and inefficient, Don Adams quotes an old Oriental story:

> Once upon a time there was a great flood, and involved in this flood
> were two creatures, a monkey and a fish. The monkey, being agile and
> experienced, was lucky enough to scramble up a tree and escape the
> raging waters. As he looked down from his safe perch, he saw the
> poor fish struggling against the swift current. With the very best inten-
> tions, he reached down and lifted the fish from the water. The result was
> inevitable.

12   No custom is good or bad, right or wrong in itself; each one must be examined in light of the culture as a whole and evaluated in terms of how it works in the context of the entire culture. Anthropologists and sociologists call this **cultural relativity.**

13   The Tangu, who live in a remote part of New Guinea, play a game called *taketak,* which, in many ways, resembles bowling. The game is played with a top that has been fashioned from a dried fruit and with two groups of coconut stakes that are driven into the ground (more or less like bowling pins). The players divide into two teams. Members of the first team take turns throwing the top into the

batch of stakes; every stake the top hits is removed. Then the second team steps to the line and tosses the top into their batch of stakes. The object of the game, surprisingly, is not to knock over as many stakes as possible. Rather, the game continues until both teams have removed the same number of stakes. Winning is completely irrelevant.

In a sense, games are practice for "real life"; they reflect the values of the culture in which they are played. **Values** are the criteria people use in assessing their daily lives, arranging their priorities, measuring their pleasures and pains, choosing between alternative courses of action. The Tangu value equivalence: the idea of one individual or group winning and another losing bothers them, for they believe winning generates ill will. In fact, when Europeans brought soccer to the Tangu, they altered the rules so that the object of the game was for two teams to score the same number of goals. Sometimes their soccer games went on for days! American games, in contrast, are highly competitive; there are always winners and losers. Many rule books include provisions for overtime and "sudden death" to prevent ties, which leave Americans dissatisfied. World Series, Superbowls, championships in basketball and hockey, Olympic gold medals are front-page news in this country. In the words of the late football coach Vince Lombardi, "Winning isn't everything, it's the only thing."   14

Norms

Norms, the rules that guide behavior in everyday situations, are derived from values, but norms and values can conflict, as we have seen. You may recall a news item that appeared in American newspapers in December 1972, describing the discovery of survivors of a plane crash twelve thousand feet high in the Andes. The crash had occurred on October 13; sixteen of the passengers (a rugby team and their supporters) managed to survive for sixty-nine days in near-zero temperatures. The story made headlines because, to stay alive, the survivors had eaten parts of their dead companions. Officials, speaking for the group, stressed how valiantly the survivors had tried to save the lives of the injured people and how they had held religious services regularly. The survivors' explanations are quite interesting, for they reveal how important it is to people to justify their actions, to resolve conflicts in norms and values (here, the positive value of survival versus the taboo against cannibalism). Some of the survivors compared their action to a heart transplant, using parts of a dead person's body to save another person's life. Others equated their act with the sacrament of communion. In the words of one religious survivor, "If we would have died, it would have been suicide, which is condemned by the Roman Catholic faith."   15

Vocabulary

Directions: Locate each of the key words in the reading selection. Then read and study each word in its context and try to determine its meaning. Use a dictionary or thesaurus to check your guess. Write the meanings of the words in the margin of the text.

Record the new words you've learned in the following chart.

Key Word	Paragraph	Meaning
1. derive	6	
2. baffled	7	
3. chronic	8	
4. smirk	10	
5. wean	10	
6. pitfalls	11	
Others?		

Guide Questions

Directions: These questions will guide your understanding of what you have read. They also will help you to analyze and evaluate the authors' ideas and apply them to the real world and your own life.

Write answers to the questions in your notebook or on a separate sheet of paper if your instructor wishes to collect them. Your answers will form the basis of class discussion.

1. Why did the Yanomamo laugh at Chagnon when he first went to live with them? Why did they think he was "naive"?
2. Define *cultural universal*.
3. Cite several examples of cultural universals.
4. The authors state that the *details* of cultural universals may vary from society to society. Give examples of cultural universals that are acted out differently in different cultures.
5. Explain why cultural universals exist.
6. According to the authors of the selection, what determines the way people articulate cultural universals?
7. Define or describe the concept of *adaptation*.
8. Explain why the Hausa postpartum sex taboo is *adaptive*.
9. Define *ethnocentrism*.
10. What moral or lesson can we learn from the Oriental story quoted in the selection?
11. Define *cultural relativity*.
12. Explain the conflict of values and norms cited in the story of the Andes plane-crash survivors.

Application

Directions: Read the following excerpt from the essay "Body Ritual among the Nacirema" by anthropologist Horace Miner:

> The Nacirema have an almost pathological horror of and fascination with the mouth, the condition of which is believed to have a supernatural influence on all social relationships. Were it not for the ritual of the mouth, they believe that their teeth would fall out, their gums bleed, their jaws shrink, their friends desert them, and their lovers reject them. They also believe that a strong relationship exists between oral and moral characteristics. For example, there is a ritual ablution of the mouth for children which is supposed to improve their moral fiber.   1
>
> The daily body ritual performed by everyone includes a mouth-rite. Despite the fact that these people are so punctilious about care of the mouth, this rite involves a practice which strikes the uninitiated stranger as revolting. It was reported to me that the ritual consists of inserting a small bundle of hog hairs into the mouth, along with certain magical powders, and then moving the bundle in a highly formalized series of gestures.   2
>
> In addition to the private mouth-rite, the people seek out a holy mouth-man twice a year. These practitioners have an impressive set of paraphernalia, consisting of a variety of augers, awls, probes, and prods. The use of these objects in the exorcism of the evils of the mouth involves almost unbelievable ritual torture of the client. The holy mouth-man opens the client's mouth and, using the above-mentioned tools, enlarges any holes which decay may have created in the teeth. Magical materials are put into these holes. If there are not naturally occurring holes in the teeth, large sections of one or more teeth are gouged out so that the supernatural substance can be applied. In the client's view, the purpose of these ministrations is to arrest decay and to draw friends. The extremely sacred and traditional character of the rite is evidenced by the fact that the natives return to the holy mouth-man year after year, despite the fact that their teeth continue to decay.   3

If you feel that living among the people who practice such bizarre customs would be strange and horrifying, then reexamine the excerpt *after* you read the name of the tribe—Nacirema—backwards!

Note the formal, highly technical language used to describe ordinary, everyday things. To understand the passage, "translate" the following phrases into everyday language.

1. In paragraph 2:
   mouth-rite—
   small bundle of hog hairs—
   magical powders—
   moving the bundle in a highly formalized series of gestures—

2. In paragraph 3:
   holy mouth-man—
   exorcism of the evils of the mouth—
   magical materials are put into these holes—
   large sections . . . are gouged out—
3. In paragraph 1:
   What is Miner referring to at the end of paragraph 1 when he says "there is a ritual ablution of the mouth for children which is supposed to improve their moral fiber"?

Why does Miner describe our dental habits in such a "foreign" way? What point is he making here?

Writing

1. a. Consider this custom of the Thompson Indians (a North American Indian tribe): Their puberty ritual includes a long period of fasting, sweating, and beating of the teenaged boys to prepare them to take on the responsibilities of manhood. Write a few sentences describing the reactions of ethnocentric individuals upon learning of this ritual. How would they feel about it? What would they say? What might they do about it?
   b. Now write a similar short paragraph from the perspective of a person who believes in the concept of cultural relativity.
2. The authors tell us in paragraph 6 that cultural universals developed from the requirements for survival in group life. Why do they specify *group* life? Why would these concepts not apply to *individual* life—say, to a hermit living alone on a deserted island?
3. To fully understand the important concepts presented in "Unity in Diversity," you must make the ideas your own. In your own words, write definitions of the key concepts: cultural universals, adaptation, ethnocentrism, cultural relativity, norms, and values.

Marking Text
Mark the chapter "Unity in Diversity." (Marking text is explained on page 413.)

Making Connections
Return to the selection "Culture" (page 59) and reread paragraph 9. Compare the information in paragraph 9 to the information in paragraphs 5, 6, and 7 in "Unity in Diversity." What are the similarities? Are there any differences?

Imagine going from a life of slavery, a life so primitive that you had never seen a light bulb, flushed a toilet, or eaten an apple to a life in 21st-century America. Can you imagine having to learn to use a refrigerator, lock a door, take out a lease, or use a cell phone—to name just a tiny part of a very long list? In this story, we learn about the Bantu people of Somalia who are hoping to leave a life of poverty and discrimination for a new life in the United States. They know they have a lot to learn.

AFRICA'S LOST TRIBE HOPES TO DISCOVER AMERICA

Rachel L. Swarns

KAKUMA, Kenya—The engines rumbled and the red sand swirled as the cargo plane roared onto the dirt airstrip. One by one, the dazed and impoverished refugees climbed from the belly of the plane into this desolate wind-swept camp.   1

They are members of Africa's lost tribe, the Somali Bantu, who were stolen from the shores of Mozambique, Malawi and Tanzania and carried on Arab slave ships to Somalia two centuries ago. They were enslaved and persecuted until Somalia's civil war scattered them to refugee camps in the 1990s.   2

Yet on this recent day, the Bantu people were rejoicing as they stepped from the plane into the blinding sun. They were the last members of the tribe to be transferred from a violent camp near the Somali border to this dusty place just south of Sudan. They knew their first trip in a flying machine was a harbinger of miracles to come.   3

Over the next two years, nearly all of the Somali Bantu refugees in Kenya— about 12,000 people—are to be flown to the United States. This is one of the largest refugee groups to receive blanket permission for resettlement since the mid-1990s, State Department officials say.   4

The refugees will be interviewed by American immigration officials in this camp, which is less violent than the camp near Somalia. The interview process has been slowed by security concerns in the aftermath of Sept. 11. Despite the repeated delays, the preparations for the extraordinary journey are already under way.   5

Every morning, dozens of peasant farmers take their seats in classrooms in a simple one-story building with a metal roof. They study English, hold their first notebooks and pens, and struggle to learn about the place called America. It is an enormous task.   6

The Bantu, who were often denied access to education and jobs in Somalia, are mostly illiterate and almost completely untouched by modern life. They measure time by watching the sun rise and fall over their green fields and mud huts.   7

As refugees, they have worked the soil, cooked, cleaned and labored in back-breaking construction jobs, filling about 90 percent of the unskilled jobs in the camp in Dadaab, Kenya, where most Bantu people lived until they were transferred here last year. But most have never turned on a light switch, flushed a toilet or held a lease.   8

So the students here study in a classroom equipped with all the trappings of modern American life, including a gleaming refrigerator, a sink, a toilet and a   9 bathtub. They are learning about paper towels and toilet cleanser and peanut butter and ice trays, along with English and American culture.

10 Refugee officials here fear that the Bantu's battle to adjust to a high-tech world will only be complicated by American ambivalence about immigrants since the terrorist attacks in the United States.

11 The Bantu are practicing Muslims. Women cover their hair with brightly colored scarves. Families pray five times a day. In Somalia, they were in a pre-dominantly Muslim country often described as a breeding ground for terrorists.

12 The American government requires refugees from such hot spots to undergo a new series of security clearances before they can be resettled in the United States. The new system has delayed the arrival of thousands of refugees, leaving them to languish in camps where children often die of malnutrition.

13 But most people here are willing to do what it takes to live in a country that outlaws discrimination. While they wait, they learn about leases and the separa-tion between church and state, and they practice their limited English.

14 About 700 Bantu have gone through this cultural orientation. By the end of September, State Department officials say, 1,500 are expected to be resettled in about 50 American cities and towns, including Boston; Charlotte, N.C.; San Diego; and Erie, Pa.

15 In America, the refugees tell each other, the Bantu will be considered human beings, not slaves, for the first time.

16 "It's scary," said Haw Abass Aden, a peasant farmer still trembling as she stepped off her first flight through the clouds. She clung tightly to a kerosene lamp with one hand and her little girl with the other. But she regained her com-posure as she considered her future.

17 "We are coming here to be resettled in the United States," said Ms. Aden, 20, speaking through a translator. "There, we will find peace and freedom."

18 After centuries of suffering, they are praying that America will be the place where they will finally belong. The United Nations has been trying to find a home for the Bantu for more than a decade because it is painfully clear they cannot return to Somalia.

19 In Somalia, the lighter-skinned majority rejected the Bantu, for their slave origins and dark skin and wide features. Even after they were freed from bondage, the Bantu were denied meaningful political representation and rights to land ownership. During the Somali civil war, they were disproportionately victims of rapes and killings.

20 The discrimination and violence continues in the barren camps today—even here—where the Bantu are often attacked and dismissed as Mushungulis, which means slave people.

21 But finding a new home for the Bantu refugees here has not been easy. First Tanzania and then Mozambique, the Bantu's ancestral homelands, agreed to take the tribe. Both impoverished countries ultimately reneged, saying they could not afford to resettle the group.

22 In 1999, the United States determined that the Somali Bantu tribe was a per-secuted group eligible for resettlement. The number of African refugees approved

for admission in the United States surged from 3,318 in 1990 to 20,084 a decade later as the cold war ended and American officials focused on assisting refugees beyond those fleeing Communist countries.

"I don't think Somalia is my country because we Somali Bantus have seen our   23
people treated like donkeys there," said Fatuma Abdekadir, 20, who was waiting for her class to start. "I think my country is where I am going.

"There, there is peace. Nobody can treat you badly. Nobody can come into   24
your house and beat you."

The refugees watch snippets of American life on videos in class, and they   25
marvel at the images of supermarkets filled with peppers and tomatoes and of tall buildings that reach for the clouds. But they know little about racism, poverty, the bone-chilling cold or the cities that will be chosen for them by refugee resettlement agencies.

What they know is this flat, parched corner of Africa, a place of thorn trees   26
and numbing hunger where water comes from wells when it comes at all—a place of fierce heat and wind that whips the sand into biting and blinding storms.

In the classes, the teachers try to prepare the Bantu for a modern world.   27
Issack Adan carefully guides his students through the lessons, taking questions from older men with graying beards, teenage girls with ballpoint pens tucked into their head scarves and young mothers with babies tied to their backs.

The lesson of the day: a white flush toilet. "Come close, come close," Mr. Adan   28
said as the women approached the strange object doubtfully. "Mothers, you sit on it, you don't stand on it."

The women nodded, although they seemed uncertain. Mr. Adan showed   29
them how to flush the toilet and how to clean it. "You wash with this thing and you will have a good smell," he said.

"A very nice smell," the students agreed.   30

Then Abubakar Saidali, a 30-year-old student, looked closely at the odd con-   31
traption and asked, "But where does that water go?" For an answer, Mr. Adan took the refugees outside to show them the pipes that carry the sewage.

Back in the classroom, the students spent the next few hours learning about   32
the refrigerator, ice cubes and strawberry jam. They watched eagerly as Mr. Adan washed dishes in a sink and admired the bathtub and shower. One woman demurred, however, when he invited her to step into the tub.

"It is so clean," she said shyly. "Can I really step in it?"   33

Some students grumbled that the American appliances seemed more com-   34
plicated than their ordinary ways of living. Why worry about cleaning a toilet, some refugees said aloud, when the bushes never need to be cleaned?

But Mr. Saidali said he was thrilled to learn about modern toilets after years   35
of relying on smelly pit latrines.

"This latrine is inside the house," marveled Mr. Saidali, a lean man in tat-   36
tered sneakers. "It's better than what we are now using. It has a seat for sitting and the water goes down.

37   "Even this sink—it's my first time," he said. "This sink is for washing. It cleans things very nicely."

38   Even with the lessons, some Bantu are worried about how they will cope in America. They know that blacks and Muslims are minorities there. Will Americans be welcoming? Will they learn English quickly enough? Will they find jobs and housing and friends? Some officials here worry, too.

39   "These people are from rural areas," Mr. Adan said. "They don't know much about modern life."

40   But the refugees who arrived on the plane here said they were eager for the challenge.

41   Uncertain of what might be needed in the United States, they carried most of their precious possessions—broken brooms, chipped mugs, metal plates—as they boarded a rattling bus that roared deep into the camp as the sun sank beyond the horizon.

42   The refugees knew they would be sleeping on the ground again and going hungry as they have often done. But they also knew that this was only the first phase of an incredible journey.

43   First stop, Kakuma. Next stop, America.

Vocabulary

Directions: Locate each of the key words in the reading selection. Try to figure out each word's meaning by using the context. Confirm your guess by checking the dictionary or thesaurus. Write the meanings of the words in the margin of the text. Then record the meanings in the following chart.

Key Word	Paragraph	Meaning
1. desolate	1	
2. harbinger	3	
3. ambivalence	10	
4. disproportionately	19	
5. snippets	25	
6. contraption	31	
Others?		

Guide Questions

Directions: These questions will guide your understanding of what you have read. Write your answers in your notebook, or on a separate sheet of paper if your instructor wishes to collect it. Your answers to these questions will be the basis of class discussion.

1. Who are the people referred to as "Africa's lost tribe"? Identify them and tell a bit about their history.
2. The people in the article are currently living in a refugee camp. What is their final destination?
3. Based on what you learned from reading the article, contrast the life the Somali Bantu have lived up until now with the life they will find in the United States.
4. Assume you are in charge of teaching the Somali Bantu all about America. What would you teach them? Make a list of all the things they'll need to learn if they are to successfully adapt to their new culture. Include ordinary things like riding in an elevator and more complicated things like driving a car.
5. If you could talk with the Somali Bantu people in the refugee camp, what advice would you give them about America?

Application

Use the Internet or the library to find a map of Africa. Locate the countries mentioned in the article: (1) the people's home countries of Mozambique, Malawi, and Tanzania; (2) the country that enslaved them, Somalia; (3) Kenya, where the refugee camp is located.

To find out more about the Somali Bantu people, check the website <http://www.somalibantu.com>.

Making Connections

Read the following selection, "Africa's Lost Tribe Discovers Its American Dream."

The previous reading selection, "Africa's Lost Tribe Hopes to Discover America," was written in March 2003. It reported on the Somali Bantu people living in refugee camps after escaping from wretched conditions in their homeland. They were eagerly anticipating and training for their new lives in America. In this article, which appeared in July 2004, we get an update on their amazing story.

AFRICA'S LOST TRIBE DISCOVERS ITS AMERICAN DREAM

William L. Hamilton

1   For Abkow Edow, a Bantu refugee from Somalia who now lives in Tucson, the Fourth of July was just another day. Though fireworks on the mountain and a reggae concert were scheduled, Mr. Edow was washing dishes at the Westin La Paloma Resort and Spa, wearing a baseball cap and thick rubber gloves that came up to his elbows. His wife, Madina Idle, was folding sheets and towels several corridors away in the vast underground complex below the desert views, the fountains and the valet golf carts.

2   But work is good. If the Fourth was just another day, it was a day in an extraordinary year for the couple, their two children and a grandson.

3   Mr. Edow, 57, and Ms. Idle, 42, have found themselves, after 12 years in refugee camps, at the end of the rainbow: America.

4   "In Somalia, I dreamed of the United States, even though I didn't know anything about it," Mr. Edow said, speaking through a translator like the other Bantu adults interviewed. America represents opportunity, Bantu refugees say, which involves hard work, struggles with English, discarding cultural ways— like the physical disciplining of children and arranged marriages—and a wary assimilation with Americans and other refugee groups in Tucson.

5   For them, independence is not a holiday but a daily engagement.

6   Mr. Edow (pronounced EE-doh) and Ms. Idle (pronounced EE-dalay) are part of a continuing resettlement of 13,000 Bantu people from Somalia, descendants of people kidnapped from southern Africa by Arab slave traders two centuries ago. As part of one of the most ambitious relocations of political refugees by the United States in recent history, the Bantu couple arrived in Tucson in May 2003 from a Kenyan camp. They were uneducated, unemployed and unfamiliar with basic facts of American life like electrical appliances and indoor plumbing.

7   Now Mr. Edow and Ms. Idle drive themselves to work in their own car, a Ford Escort they bought in September. They shop at 99-cent stores. They pay the $635 rent for their three-bedroom apartment. The children, a 15-year-old and two 8-year-olds, are in school, earning good grades and, like other Bantu children, school officials say, outperforming the general student population. Mr. Edow is saving money to buy a house.

8   "Every month I pay rent," he said, sitting in his kitchen with a bare foot propped on his seat, a cellphone in his hand and a videotape of "Shrek" entertaining his children in the next room. "It's good to own a house. It belongs to you."

Mr. Edow, who could not read numbers a year ago, knows what a down pay- 9
ment is. In May, he applied for a green card, celebrating his application with a
red, white and blue cake.

The availability of entry-level jobs in the hospitality industry has made 10
Tucson a popular destination for the resettlement of Bosnians, Afghans and
Liberians. There are 71 Bantu people, and more than 100 are expected by the
end of the year.

Mr. Edow and Ms. Idle escaped from Somalia to Kenya on foot, a 10-day 11
walk without food. In Somalia, Mr. Edow said, he watched as his father was exe-
cuted with a hammer and nails.

Now, in life-skill classes that supplement daily English classes, Bantu parents 12
learn that hitting their children is discouraged, though that was how they were
disciplined in Africa. They make a wary peace with African-Americans at home
and at school who consider them foreign. They learn that Fourth of July fireworks
are exploded to entertain, not kill, and that being hit by a water balloon, as Bantu
children were in one incident at school, is a game and not a hateful fight.

At work, the Bantu refugees learn how to prepare hotel amenities, like plac- 13
ing courtesy soaps and folding the tips of the toilet tissue, though they used pit
latrines in Kenya and Somalia and had never seen a toilet.

But caseworkers, school officials and employers say the Bantus are making the 14
most remarkable progress of the refugee groups in Tucson, given that they arrived
with the most remarkable disadvantages: the trauma of tribal war in Somalia,
where the Bantus were considered low-caste and denied opportunities for education and employment, and a rural ignorance of Western culture and modern life.

The Bantu refugees had to be taught to tell time, an accomplishment that 15
fills them with pride.

Wall clocks and calendars decorate many Bantu homes in Mission Vista, an 16
80-unit apartment complex where many, including Mr. Edow and Ms. Idle, live.

"I adjusted to time," said Makai Osman, 38, a Bantu friend of Ms. Idle's who 17
lives in Mission Vista with her husband, Mudey Libange, 36, and their five children. "I was scared, but I'm punctual now."

Though job training required professional coaches, Karen Vallecillo, the direc- 18
tor of human resources at the Westin La Paloma, gave the Bantu refugees high
marks.

"They were a group that had been through pretty atrocious things, probably 19
more than any other group," Ms. Vallecillo said. "Learning to trust authority
again probably took them a little longer."

Twelve languages, including four Somali dialects, are spoken at the hotel, 20
which has 500 employees, 25 percent of whom are refugees.

"We'd be lost without our partnerships with refugee agencies," Ms. Vallecillo 21
said. "We don't seem to be able to raise American citizens to want to take these
kinds of jobs."

The federal government organized the relocation effort but contracted with 22
agencies, like the International Rescue Committee in Tucson, to provide financial support and social services to the refugees in each city.

23   At Mission Vista one Friday, Ms. Osman's son, Abdullahi Osman, 15, sat at home at the dining table, homework assignments and an English-Somali dictionary in his lap.

24   Several Bantu friends have taken jobs when they turned 16 to help their parents. Older children like Abdullahi's sister, Halima Osman, who is 13, run the home while their parents work, taking care of younger brothers and sisters and the children of other families as well.

25   "Until I finish my education, I don't want to do anything else," said Abdullahi, who dreams of becoming a doctor. He said that books were his most valued possessions, though he checks them out of the public library. Abdullahi's girl-friend, a Bantu he met in Kenya, was relocated to Salt Lake City. They speak on the telephone.

26   "If I stay for a long time and I have money, I want to go and meet, and see how she is," he said.

27   As Abdullahi spoke, children from other families entered or left the apartment, or opened the door to peek. Each Bantu family has its own apartment, but as is most familiar to them as villagers and camp internees, they visit frequently and without formality.

28   "I know in American culture, if someone is going to visit you, he's going to call, 'What time are you going to visit?'" said Ms. Osman, sitting forward with determination, legs apart, elbows on her knees, her sandaled feet embellished by designs in henna. "For us, it's not a big deal. People can visit us anytime."

29   Ms. Osman gave a brief tour of her apartment.

30   "I have a lot of stuff," she said, with a small laugh. "I don't want to move it somewhere."

31   Ever present is the memory, still as strong as reality, of the long relocation route. With arrival in America has come miles and miles of documentation, regulation, offices and appointments. In speaking with the Bantu refugees, in the patient looks in their faces and in the acceptance in their attitudes toward case-workers, teachers, employers and even strangers, there is a palpable sense that the stop in Tucson could be a stage in an unending journey if they do not acquiesce to the bewildering bureaucracy.

32   "With most refugees, until they've gotten their citizenship, there's always that feeling that it's just not real," said Karen Bailey, the community resource coordinator with the International Rescue Committee.

33   Ms. Osman, who became eligible for a green card in July, said forcefully: "I want to be Tucsonian. I don't want to go back, no way. I don't dream at all of going back to Somalia."

34   But forgetting can be hard.

35   Outside, as the cool of the evening descended and the clouds above the desert blossomed in the sunset, four Bantu girls sat in a circle on the sidewalk playing shabko, a traditional game of tossing stones. Ms. Osman's daughter, Halima, who was shepherding the children, chased Mr. Abkow's son, Ahmed, 8, with a stick when he angered her by disobeying. Ahmed, crying, disappeared into the shadow of a building corridor, then returned silently to the group, like a shy dog, and sat behind a bush.

"In Somalia, we didn't know America," said Hamadi Musse, 16, whose best   36
friend in Tucson is Hakim Rahimi, a 14-year-old Afghan boy.

Hakim and his family lived in Pakistan before being resettled here six   37
months ago. Hakim worked from 4 a.m. until 8 p.m. laying floors in Pakistan.

"We saw on TV, the American people," he said.   38

Hamadi, who goes to school and helps his brother at his job at a Boston   39
Market restaurant, said of his new life, "I don't have time for watching TV."

Vocabulary

Directions: Locate each of the key words in the reading selection. Try to figure out each word's meaning by using the context. Confirm your guess by checking the dictionary or thesaurus. Write the meanings of the words in the margin of the text. Then record the meanings in the following chart.

Key Word	Paragraph	Meaning
1. wary	4	
2. assimilation	4	
3. trauma	14	
4. atrocious	19	
Others?		

Guide Questions

Directions: These questions will guide your understanding of what you have read. Write your answers in your notebook, or on a separate sheet of paper if your instructor wishes to collect it. Your answers to these questions will be the basis of class discussion.

1. When the Bantu refugees say, "America represents opportunity," what do they mean?
2. The article describes some of the accomplishments of the former refugees. What things have they learned?
3. What lessons about America have the Bantu refugees learned in their life-skill classes?
4. Explain why caseworkers say the Bantu refugees have made "remarkable progress."

Writing

Write 1–2 paragraphs reacting to the story of the Bantu Somali refugees.

Most Americans (if they think about it at all) think of monogamy as "natural" and are sur-prised to learn that many other societies practice different forms of marriage. Problems can arise when people leave their home countries and immigrate to new lands with different values and norms. Should immigrants be allowed to bring their customs with them? What if those customs are illegal in their new countries? This article appeared in the interna-tional section of The New York Times *in January 1996.*

AFRICAN WOMEN IN FRANCE BATTLE POLYGAMY

Marlise Simons

1   Khadi Keita shifted in her chair in a Paris cafe as she described the day she became a stranger in her own home. That was the day in 1985 when her husband suddenly arrived here with a new wife.

2   He hung a curtain in the middle of the cramped bedroom and announced that, from now on, the two women would have to share him, the kitchen, the closets, everything.

3   The next four years became a nightmare of pregnancies, babies, nasty fights, and long, hostile silences, Mrs. Keita said. Then her husband, a Muslim, went home to his African village, married again and brought wife no. 3.

4   Mrs. Keita, who has since divorced—a rarity in polygamous marriages—and become a social worker, is an immigrant from Senegal. She is one of the African women in France who are now willing to speak openly about the secrets of polygamy and about the strains, the anger, and the humiliations of their marriages.

5   Long overshadowed by other immigrant problems of poverty and discrimi-nation, the widespread practice of polygamy in France is coming to light because African women here are fighting the tradition. In the current anti-immigrant mood, the government has also decided to take a stand.

6   After quietly tolerating the Muslim male right to have up to four wives, the government has said France will recognize only one spouse and consider other marriages annulled.

7   The discussion of polygamy has raised anew the question of how a society should deal with immigrant customs that are unacceptable or against the law in a new land. There have already been heated debates about whether girls may wear Muslim headscarves, a religious symbol, in France's secular schools, and French prosecutors have gone to court to forbid the tradition of sexually mutilating Muslim girls.

A Custom Tolerated in the Homeland Turns Sour Abroad

8   "Polygamy may be as old as Africa, but it doesn't work in France," said Mrs. Keita, whose former husband could not be located.

9   "It's unbearable because there is no room for two or three wives and fifteen children in one small place. The women are rivals. The husband is never fair. He has a favorite, so there are horrible fights."

There is the wrenching lack of privacy. "You hear everything, your husband   10
and the other wives," she said. "You hear how he behaves with his favorite,
usually the new one. The women end up hating the man. Everyone feels bad
inside."

The politics of polygamy is no less charged. Ivry, a Paris suburb, has some   11
fifteen hundred African immigrants, and two out of three families are polygamous. "Consider the costs," a town official said. "One husband with three wives
and a team of children may need government health care, education, and subsi-
dies for up to twenty people. Is this fair?"

He said this question weighs heavily at a time when France's social welfare   12
system is in the midst of an enormous debt crisis. In December, government
plans to cut benefits caused three weeks of strikes and protests.

Polygamy has come to France with the tens of thousands of African immi-   13
grants from countries like Senegal, Mali, and Mauritania. The French Interior
Ministry says there are no firm statistics because foreign wives are often in the
country clandestinely and immigrants keep other wives back in Africa.

In the United States, the law bars polygamous immigrants and the authori-   14
ties say they believe that such cases are rare.

In the Paris area alone, it is estimated that 200,000 people live in polyga-   15
mous families. They live in the rickety neighborhoods behind Montmartre and
in glum suburbs like Bobigny, St. Denis, and Creteil.

Moustafa Djaara, a construction worker from Mali, lives in Bobigny with   16
his two wives and nine children. Both wives are pregnant. He wants to bring his
young, third wife to France. His modest income is more than doubled by the
generous benefits the French state pays to children and pregnant women,
regardless of their status.

Mr. Djaara asserts that polygamy is hardest for the husband because his wives   17
fight a lot, he has his job, and does all the shopping. He shops because he must
control all the money, he said.

Given his complaints, why does he want more than one wife? "My father did,   18
my grandfather did, so why shouldn't I?" Mr. Djaara said.

"When my wife is sick and I don't have another, who will care for me?"   19
Besides, he said, "one wife on her own is trouble. When there are several, they are
forced to be polite and well behaved. If they misbehave, you threaten that you'll
take another wife."

Ruling at home may be one thing, but living with the neighbors is   20
another.

Town officials and building owners have refused large tribal families on their   21
premises. In St. Denis last year, a welfare office allocated a small apartment to a
Mauritanian family of six. Two months later, thirty members of the same family
had moved in. The French neighbors, outraged at the noise, pressed the town hall
until the group was moved.

It was mainly the Socialist government in the 1980s that quietly admitted   22
more than one wife per husband as part of its family-reunification policy. The
argument was that immigrants had the right to a "normal" family life.

23   As a result, many immigrants brought not just their wives but, as their income improved, they went home to buy new, young brides, often still teenagers. Once the women gave birth in France, mother and child were allowed to stay.

24   "We've been telling the French for ten years that this was wrong, that polygamy couldn't work here because we saw the problems," said Madine Diallo, who was born in Mali and now heads an African women's health and family-planning group.

25   "In Africa there is space. Even if co-wives live around the same courtyard, at least each wife has her own room or her house. The man visits her there, in her own bed. Here two, three families are packed into two rooms."

26   It is a myth that African women like polygamy, she continued. "Our mothers and grandmothers and every woman before them would go to the witch doctor to get a potion or cast a spell if she knew her husband was going to take another wife. Many still do. And women do it even here."

27   Fatima Traoré, who came from Mali, said she sometimes feels she will lose her mind. Sometimes she and her two co-wives do not talk to each other for days. She and her husband had been in Paris for four years when he went "on holiday" and came back with another wife.

28   "From one day to the next, another wife comes and does what you do," Mrs. Traoré said. "She meddles in the house. She gets pregnant. You still get your turn with your husband, your nights with him. But he pays no attention to you. Just two, three minutes to satisfy himself. That's it. Whatever you do makes no difference. You can cry all you want. He doesn't care."

29   Women in polygamous marriages describe the marital routine like this: The husband spends two nights with one wife, then two nights with the next. The wife who has her turn in the marital bed does the cooking for the family. "If a woman says 'It's my turn in the kitchen,' then you know," Mrs. Traoré said.

30   Health workers say the feelings boiling in close quarters can make the women ill or violent.

31   "Sometimes the women go crazy, they attack each other," said Catherine Rixain, a family counselor who works in the suburbs. "Or they take it out on each other's children. We have seen children beaten by a desperate co-wife."

32   Hawa Koulibali is one of the women who feel trapped. She came as a young bride from Mali twenty years ago and now lives with her two co-wives and their fourteen children in Marne-la-Vallée, half an hour's train ride east of Paris. But she and the co-wives have never seen Paris. They cannot read. They speak no French.

33   Although their husband goes home every two years, he says a trip for all of them would be too expensive. Cut off from France and cut off from Mali, Mrs. Koulibali feels lost. She and the co-wives try to get along. But being friends is too difficult, she said.

34   Beyond the strains and rivalry at home, immigrant women can find moments of solidarity in the support groups formed by French and African social workers. One group met recently in a day-care center at Emerainville, east of Paris.

The center is a cheerful, airy place, festooned with toys and drawings. But in   35
a back room, sixteen women, all in polygamous marriages, met around a small
table. Ostensibly they met to discuss child care. But other questions seemed
more haunting.

They denied that anyone liked polygamy. "We have no choice!" a woman in   36
her thirties shouted. The consensus was that the immigrant women here had lost
their dignity.

"If you don't get along with your co-wife in Africa, you do not pass by her   37
door and she does not pass yours," a woman from Mauritania said. Another par-
ticipant whispered: "An African woman will not sleep with her husband in a bed
that another woman uses. Here we must take turns."

The anger quickly focused on the men. The women complained of injustices: 38
husbands gave money to their favorite wife, usually the new one; husbands had
used money a wife had earned in France in order to go to Africa and buy another
wife. As humiliating, the women said, was when a husband took the wife's identity card to Africa and used it to bring in a new wife.

In the support groups, counselors have been prodding women to warn their   39
husbands that they will denounce them if they beat their wives or if they seize
their cards.

"We try to stop some of the dirty tricks," said Kani Sidibe, who used to work   40
for Air Afrique and is now a social worker. "Some women are losing their fear.
They come and talk to us. But we have a long way to go."

Some signs of change have appeared; for example, in the life of Moustafa   41
Diop, an immigrant from Senegal who lives near Charles de Gaulle Airport. He
does odd jobs driving a truck. One wife works as a part-time cleaner and one as
a seamstress. The third does the home work. At night they look after the eighteen children.

He concedes that "the women are not content," but now outright rebellion   42
looms. Two years ago Mr. Diop went back to Senegal and used the family savings
to buy another bride. He paid for a dowry and a big wedding. "It gives a man
great standing," he said.

While he prepared to bring his young bride from Dakar, his three wives in   43
Paris banded together. They are furious because he wasted their hard-earned
money on another wife.

"They say if the new one comes, they will all leave," Mr. Diop said. With   44
three wives in France and one in Dakar, Mr. Diop said he has great prestige in his
village, but he is unsure how to deal with the rebellion at home. The French government may settle that. The Interior Ministry has already said it will not give a
residence permit to more than one wife.

Vocabulary

Directions: Locate each of the key words in the article. Try to figure out each word's
meaning by using the context. Confirm your guess by checking the dictionary or thesaurus. Write the meanings of the words in the margin of the text. Then record the meanings in the following chart.

Key Word	Paragraph	Meaning
1. annulled	6	
2. wrenching	10	
3. clandestinely	13	
4. rickety	15	
5. meddles	28	
6. prodding	39	
Others?		

Guide Questions

Directions: These questions will guide your understanding of what you have read. Write your answers in your notebook or on a separate sheet of paper if your instructor wishes to collect it. Your answers to these questions will be the basis of class discussion.

1. Define the word *polygamy* and try to recall anything you may know about it.
2. According to the author, why is the practice of polygamy in France coming to the attention of the public at this time?
3. Cite some of the statistics on polygamy in France (and the difficulty of acquiring good statistics).
4. Beginning in paragraph 16, Moustafa Djaara gives the polygamous man's side of the story. What are the pros and cons of polygamy for Mr. Djaara?
5. Why do town officials, landlords, and neighbors oppose having polygamous families in their neighborhoods?
6. Describe some of the complaints voiced by the women in polygamous marriages in the article.
7. What are some strategies that African women in France are using to combat polygamy?
8. Explain the relationship between the practice of polygamy and the question of how a society should deal with immigrant customs that are unacceptable or illegal in a new land.

Application

1. We learned in the article that polygamy is practiced in Senegal, Mali, and Mauritania. Use the library or the Internet to research the issue further.

In what other countries is polygamy practiced? Is it legal or is it practiced illegally? Was polygamy ever practiced in the United States? Use the information you gather as a basis for a class discussion.

2. For an interesting look at polygamy from the perspective of a woman who favors it, read "In Defense of Polygamy" on page 300.

Writing

Imagine you are the husband of one of the women in the article "African Women in France Battle Polygamy." Write a letter to *The New York Times* reacting to the information in the article.

Making Connections

How did the information in the preceding chapters ("Culture," "Norms," "Values," "Unity in Diversity") affect your reading of this article?

Marking Text

Mark the article "African Women in France Battle Polygamy." (Directions for marking text are on page 413.)

SHORT TAKE

Marriage Takes Many Different Forms throughout the World

The number of spouses that are allowed varies from culture to culture. North Americans are most familiar with **monogamy** (from the Greek word part *mono,* meaning "one," and *gamy,* meaning "marriage")—one man married to one woman. In reality, though, with the divorce rate in the United States hovering at around 50 percent, a system of **serial monogamy,** marriage to multiple spouses—but one at a time—is becoming the norm. Contrast this with the system in some Greek villages, where women have traditionally been socially prohibited from marrying again after the death of their husbands. Widows take on a sexually neutral status and are therefore free for the first time in their lives to go into male places such as coffeehouses. However, for the rest of their lives they must wear black clothes to indicate their widow status. In contrast, Greek men who become widowers are not similarly restricted, nor are they stigmatized as being gender neutral.

Polygamy (from the Greek word parts *poly,* meaning "many," and *gamy,* meaning "marriage") means any combination of multiple spouses. When most people think of polygamy, they assume a structure in which two or more women share one husband. Strictly speaking, though, this form of marriage is **polygyny** (from the Greek word part *poly,* meaning "many," and *gyny,* meaning "female"). In this form of marriage there is one husband and two or more wives. Polygyny is most common today in Muslim nations, among traditional cattle-herding societies in East Africa, and in remnants of the old kingdoms of West Africa.

Among the polygamous Turkana of East Africa, a wife generally considers it an economic advantage for her family to have co-wives, because the women help each other with domestic chores and caring for the animals. They may even help their husband find a new bride. They interview prospective wives to find one who will be compatible and hard working. Usually the husband must have his current wives' approval before he can marry again.

Most Westerners view polygyny as advantageous for the husband only—more sexual partners, more children, and above all more prestige in society. However, multiple wives can be a disadvantage as well: the co-wives may gang up on him and force him to do things he may not want to do.

There is also a rarer structure called **polyandry** (from the Greek word part *poly,* meaning "many," and *andr,* meaning "male"). This form of marriage includes one wife and two or more husbands. Polyandry is very rare, found in less than 1 percent of societies. Polyandry is most often found in economically depressed societies. Since a woman can have only one child per year, this form of marriage keeps the birth rate down. Polyandry is found in some rural regions of India, Sri Lanka, Nepal, and Tibet. Usually it is *fraternal polyandry,* that is, two brothers married to the same woman. This reduces the problem of determining what family their children belong to, since both potential fathers have the same parents. The younger brother usually marries the shared wife when he is in his early teens but often does not have sexual relations with her for years.

Polyandry has definite economic advantages for small-scale agricultural societies. It keeps the family farm in one piece. It allows one of the husbands to be away from the farm, working for years at a time without disrupting the family. It provides economic security for the wife when one of her husbands dies. However, it also places an extra workload on her.

Over the past decade or so, the notion of romantic love has disrupted the tradition of polyandry, as men and women have begun to demand exclusive bonds with their spouse.

In the 1970s, as its population soared toward 1 billion, China began the implementation of strict family-planning measures. Over the next two decades the average number of babies per woman dropped from five or six to two or three. Without the controls, officials say, 240 million more babies would have been born. The goal of one child per family is now accepted in the cities and, even in the countryside, most people are having fewer children than their parents did. But an unforeseen problem has arisen: millions of children are growing up without siblings and are the sole object of their parents' affection. As a result, many Chinese say the children are growing up spoiled, selfish, and lazy. This article appeared in The New York Times *in 1996.*

AS A PAMPERED GENERATION
GROWS UP, CHINESE WORRY

Patrick E. Tyler

It was just another school day for Liu Huamin when the father of one of her students burst through the classroom door and said his teen-age son was threatening to commit suicide by jumping off the fourth-floor balcony of the family's apartment building.   1

Why? asked Mrs. Liu, a chemistry teacher at Waluji Middle School here.   2

Because, the man replied, the boy's mother would not cook his favorite meat dumplings for breakfast.   3

He did not jump, but the story of his breathtaking display of willfulness incites a look of instant recognition across the faces of many Chinese teachers today.   4

Indeed, it seems at times as if the willfulness of China's generation of "little emperors"—children growing up without siblings under China's one-child population control policy—knows no bounds.   5

In Guangdong Province a power failure prevented a housewife from cooking dinner for her fourteen-year-old son, who flew into a rage and went out to watch television with a friend. When the boy returned, there was still no dinner, so he seized a meat cleaver and killed his mother with ten blows to the head. Then he hanged himself.   6

An extreme case, but the fact that China's government-run news organization gave it prominent display last year also illustrates the concern of many Chinese that its first generation of only children is rapidly maturing into a generation of spoiled, self-absorbed tyrants.   7

After decades of famine and political turmoil in China, parents who grew up in troubled and often violent times under Mao, suffering long periods of deprivation in the countryside and interrupted schooling, are now rearing—in many cases doting on—a generation of only children.   8

And these new parents are filled with anxiety about whether they are doing it right.   9

"This is a fixation," said James L. Watson, an anthropologist at Harvard University who has studied the Chinese family. "I would call it kind of a compensation complex. The generation of parents that we are dealing with now, many of   10 them are Cultural Revolution veterans who themselves did not have much of a childhood, and I think that many of them are trying hard to make sure that their own children get all the benefits and more that they missed out on."

11   But they are doing it with little cultural guidance. The current generation of parents has been cut adrift from both the traditional Confucian values emphasizing reverence for elders that were once the foundation of China's extended families and from the Communist values imposed for three decades under Mao.

12   Neither has much credibility in China today.

13   Specialists say it is too early to say whether China's "little emperors" are growing up to be a generation of self-centered autocrats, whose politics may be more aggressive than the generation that grew up under Mao, or whether they are so over-indulged at home that they will be ill prepared for the competitive pressures and harsh realities of China's market economy.

Off to Bad Start, Teachers Say

14   "Seems like it could go either way," said David Y. H. Wu, an anthropologist at Chinese University of Hong Kong. "You could either raise a generation of rebels against the controls of the Communist party or you could raise a generation that would feel more nationalistic and assertive as Chinese.

15   "Talking about personality traits and trying to project to the whole nation is very difficult, but I can see a whole generation perhaps more independent and willing to challenge authority, or simply more authoritative because of their intensified relationships with their parents, and the symbol of parents is government."

16   Either way, if today's teachers are any judge, the "little emperor" generation is off to an inauspicious start.

17   "As life and economic conditions get better and better, the moral principles of students and their sense of responsibility to society and family get worse and worse," said Mrs. Liu, the chemistry teacher, who has an eighteen-year-old son. "We teachers often wonder how these students can take up their social responsibility when they get older."

18   Teachers around the world have long complained about the quality of the next generation. But in China, a generation of children is growing up in the midst of a profound economic revolution, where social and political values seem suspended in time as the country waits for the death of Deng Xiaoping,[*] the ninety-one-year-old paramount leader, not knowing whether that event will usher in a new era with a new value system.

19   "My most terrifying concern," said Zhang Xiaoyun, thirty-three, who teaches literature at the China Youth Political College in Beijing, a former Communist party school, "is that you must raise a child within some system of beliefs, but our generation has no beliefs, so how can we educate our children?"

---

[*] Deng Xiaoping died on February 19, 1997.

The demographic shift from multi-child families under strong patriarchs to   20
small, nuclear families centered on only children "is going to have a profound effect"
on Chinese society, Professor Watson said.

Increased Spending on Toys and Books

One of the ways that Chinese are overcompensating in bringing up the country's   21
only children is by spending the greatest portion of family income ever on toys,
books, educational materials, personal computers, and food.

The national obsession with children is fostering multibillion-dollar oppor-   22
tunities for business.

Baby food, which barely existed in China a decade ago, is now a staple of   23
family life and a major item in family budgets.

China's "little emperors" are the single greatest force in determining con-   24
sumer decisions today, experts say.

"I met a woman who took her daughter to McDonald's in Beijing twice a   25
week to give her modern nutrition," said Yan Yunxiang, a Chinese-born anthropologist at Johns Hopkins University, who frequently returns to examine the culture he grew up in.

When he asked the woman why she was spending as much as half a normal   26
worker's income each month on McDonald's, she replied: "I want my daughter to
learn more about American culture. She is taking English typing classes now, and
next year I will buy her a computer."

Professor Watson said: "It turns out that most Chinese don't even like the   27
food, but what they are buying is culture. They are buying connectedness to the
world system.

"The idea is that if these kids can connect with McDonald's, they are going   28
to end up at Harvard Law School."

One of China's most popular amusement parks, Window on the World in   29
Shenzhen, has no rides and no arcades. Chinese come from all over the country to
pay, in some cases a week's wages, to show their children miniatures of Manhattan
Island, the Statue of Liberty, the Eiffel Tower, and the Taj Mahal.

A Generation Driven by Rewards

"Most of our time and money are spent on this child," said Wen Geli, the mother   30
of a two-year-old boy who seems less attentive to the park's attractions than to
gorging himself on ice cream. "We want to give him an introduction to the world
and expand his outlook."

"My generation grew up with hardship," said her husband, Zhang Xinwen,   31
a communications officer in the Chinese Army. "We were born in the 1960s, and
that was a period of bitter shortage, but this generation is growing up in richer
times and we want to take advantage of this better environment."

Not far away, a retired sports teacher, Cai Kunling, fifty-nine, was squiring   32
his five-year-old granddaughter, Fu Hua, past the wonders of the world. "She
should be in kindergarten today," he said, "but she wanted to take me to this
place," he added in a tone that reflected who was in charge.

33   The two of them sat for their photo in front of a miniature of Niagara Falls and then strolled over to the little Manhattan.

34   To Mr. Cai, who lived through the Mao period, it was like a dream world.

35   "My generation made a lot of sacrifices and had a lot of devotion to the country," he said. "But this generation needs a reward if you want them to do something. If there is no compensation, they don't want to do it."

Free-for-All Future Worries the Parents

36   Sitting around a dinner of baked carp with three other teachers one evening, Mrs. Liu and some of her colleagues vented their anxieties.

37   Li Shunmei, thirty-one, a high-school teacher with a three-year-old daughter, said: "I worry a lot about my daughter's future, because I have doubts about whether she can survive under the harsher and harsher competition of Chinese society.

38   "Nowadays, there are many children who commit suicide. I think it is because parents obey their children's every demand, so they are not able to endure any reversals or hard times."

39   This strain of anxiety is very prominent in Chinese families.

40   The old "iron rice bowl" society of cradle-to-grave social welfare protection is giving way year by year to the new market economy, where life is beginning to look like a terrifying free-for-all to many Chinese used to something more secure.

41   "The home can be very sweet and gentle for these toddlers, but the world out there is a cruel world," said Jing Jun, a Beijing native who now teaches anthropology at City College in New York. "When we were growing up, the state arranged everything for you, but now parents know the state is not going to do anything for them and the job market is pretty grim."

42   Mr. Jing said he believed that China's "little emperors" would have to pass through a tough period of adjustment. "They are under so much pressure," he said, "and their parents have such great expectations for them. Whether they are psychologically prepared for that, I cannot say."

43   Professor Watson said, "A lot of people, including Chinese psychologists, are concerned whether the next generation is going to be able to 'eat bitterness,' whether they are going to be able to work hard or whether they will be willing to sacrifice themselves as was true under socialism."

44   Some Chinese feel that the "little emperors" will adjust.

45   "I'm optimistic," said Wang Xujin, a teacher at Beijing Business College with a nine-year-old son.

46   But, he confessed, "although the students each year are smarter and smarter, I like them less and less."

Vocabulary

Directions: Locate each of the key words in the article. Try to figure out each word's meaning by using the context. Confirm your guess by checking the dictionary or thesaurus. Write the meanings of the words in the margin of the text. Then record the meanings in the following chart.

Key Word	Paragraph	Meaning
1. willfulness	4, 5	
2. fixation	10	
3. autocrats	13	
4. traits	15	
5. inauspicious	16	
6. overcompensating	21	
7. staple	23	
8. gorging	30	
Others?		

Guide Questions

Directions: These questions will guide your understanding of what you have read. Write your answers in your notebook or on a separate sheet of paper if your instructor wishes to collect it. Your answers to these questions will be the basis of class discussion.

1. Here, as in many news feature stories, the author begins with an example to illustrate his main point. Summarize the example and the point it illustrates.
2. Why are the children in the article described as "little emperors"?
3. Describe the differences in living conditions now and during the childhood of the parents of the "little emperors."
4. According to anthropologist James Watson, why are Chinese parents "doting on" their children now?
5. Explain the author's point in paragraph 11: "But they are doing it with little cultural guidance."
6. Anthropologist David Y. H. Wu says, "Seems like it could go either way." What does he mean?
7. Adults throughout history have complained about "the next generation." Judging from the information in this article and anything else you may know about the topic, do you think the next generation of Chinese children will have special problems? Explain.

8. React to the comments of the mother described in paragraph 25 who, among other things, took her child to McDonald's to give her "modern nutrition."

9. Do you see similarities between the treatment of Chinese children as described in the article and treatment of American children?

10. a. Explain what is meant by the old "iron rice bowl" society of China.
   b. Contrast the "iron rice bowl" society with the situation in China today.

Application

1. China's one-child policy was established in the 1970s. Use the Internet or the library to investigate the reasons for the policy and what the results have been.

2. If you read the selections "Norms" (page 66) and "Values" (page 72), try to make connections between what you learned from those selections and the problems facing the parents of China's current generation of children. Be sure to consider the information in paragraphs 10 through 12 of "As a Pampered Generation Grows Up, Chinese Worry."

Marking Text

Review how to mark your text on page 413. Then mark the article, "As a Pampered Generation Grows Up, Chinese Worry."

SHORT TAKE

Bare Branches

In China today, 117 boys are born for each 100 girls. These are the official figures, but unofficial observations have turned up ratios as high as 150 to 100. What is causing this imbalance? In China, boys have traditionally been more desired than girls. Boys are expected to care for their parents when they grow old, while a girl is expected to marry and become part of her husband's family. Thus boys are economically essential for the average Chinese family, particularly those in the countryside. Amniocentesis and ultrasound can easily identify the sex of a fetus, and sex-selective abortion has become an everyday practice even though it is illegal. In the 1980s portable ultrasound machines became readily available. Doctors began to do prenatal exams—ostensibly to test for birth defects and other ailments, but inevitably also to determine gender. In her book, *Bare Branches: The Security Implications of Asia's Surplus Male Population,* Valerie Hudson says that while the practitioner may not *say* anything, he may make some special gesture to signal the woman that she is carrying a boy. Daughters who are born are frequently given up, and thousands are adopted out of the country every year.

Hudson and her co-author, Andrea den Boer, say the imbalance of boys versus girls may lead to increased turmoil in society. With a surplus of boys, a large segment of the male population will not have the chance to marry and settle into a traditional role in society. If the abnormal sex ratio at birth continues to increase, Chinese males will have to fight to find a wife in the near future, and about 50 million men will be unable to find a partner. "The marriage crisis will have a great impact on family structures, on the way we provide for the aged, on social ethics and the economy," said Tiam Xueyuan, vice-president of the Chinese Population Association. Males will have more difficulties finding employment, and crimes such as kidnapping women could become more widespread, he added.

The authors of *Bare Branches* claim that men without wives tend to be more aggressive and that studies have shown a link between the "bare branches" (a Chinese term for men who cannot find spouses) and increased criminal activity. Some experts argue that history, biology, and sociology all suggest that these "surplus males" will generate high levels of crime and social disorder, the authors say. Even worse, they continue, is the possibility that the governments will build up huge armies as a way to channel the energy of angry, frustrated young men.

Thirty years have passed since China implemented its one-child policy. While it has been enormously successful in limiting the country's population growth, the policy has also had some unexpected and worrisome results.

This article was written for Radio Free Europe/Radio Liberty in January 2005.

CHINA: A FUTURE WITH A SHORTAGE OF BRIDES, AN ABUNDANCE OF ELDERLY

Daisy Sindelar

1   PRAGUE, 6 January 2005 — China today officially passed a population milestone — the birth of its 1.3 billionth baby.

2   A Chinese government official announced the news in Beijing after awarding a certificate to the infant's mother: "The 1.3 billionth citizen was born at 00:02 on January 6, 2005."

3   And the gender of the history-making baby? A boy.

4   That fact might not surprise China-watchers, who say the country's true population story is not its size, but its composition.

5   China's one-child family planning policy has largely succeeded in curbing the country's population growth over the past 25 years.

6   But Chinese officials are now faced with two resulting complications: dwindling numbers of marriageable women — and larger numbers of elderly born during a post–World War II baby boom.

7   The international programs division of the United States Census Bureau estimates that roughly seven out of 100 Chinese are currently over the age of 65. Within the next 30 years, that number is set to more than double.

8   By 2030, elderly Chinese will number some 240 million — slightly higher than the entire population of Indonesia.

9   The so-called "graying" trend is an issue facing many countries to varying degrees, including the United States and many in Western Europe. But unlike much of the West, the aging of China's population is taking place at a rapid rate — leaving the government little time to prepare.

10   Chinese society has traditionally depended on the family, rather than the state, to care for its elderly. In the past, couples would have as many as six children to ensure a comfortable old age.

11   But the one-child policy has dramatically reduced the number of offspring parents can count on to provide for them as they grow older. This has forced the state to begin experimenting with pension systems and other reforms.

12   Loraine West, an economist with the U.S. Census Bureau, says the real challenge will be changing the mindset of rural Chinese, who make up some two-thirds of the population: "The pension program still is largely an urban-based program. And that's where I think you see the change first. An increasing proportion of the elderly are no longer solely dependent on their children; they have a pension to rely on. The rural areas are still, I would say, relatively dependent on their children.

But that's where it will be critical to see if the government can successfully expand this program, or put in place something comparable for the rural population. They're going to have fewer dependents. As time passes, they'll be relying on one or two children and it will be increasingly important that they have some other resources available to them."

For young Chinese, an even more worrying trend is the prospect of a future with too many men and too few women.   13

The one-child policy, a traditional preference for sons, and accessibility to selective abortions have combined to leave China with a strongly skewed gender ratio. The underreporting of girls by families hoping to reserve their "official" spot for a boy is also cited as a cause for the imbalance—as are, to a lesser degree, adoption and infanticide.   14

Male babies naturally outnumber female babies throughout much of the world. But in China, the gap has grown unusually large.   15

In most societies, there are between 102 and 106 male births for every 100 female births. In China, that number is estimated to be as high as 117.   16

Census Bureau demographer Daniel Goodkind says surplus grooms will eventually number in the millions—a trend with significant social implications: "The most common one that demographers talk about is called 'marriage squeeze'—that is, when you have an imbalance in either potential husbands or wives. So that can affect the marital chances of the sex that's in greater supply—in this case, males. So if you're female in China over the next 20 years, in terms of the number of potential partners, you'll be doing pretty well, assuming it's a free market."   17

With the one-child policy hitting the quarter-century mark, the sex-ratio crisis is already being felt.   18

Chinese media increasingly cover cases of "bride stealing"—the kidnapping and trafficking of young single women for marriage. One recent television documentary profiled a police officer responsible for recovering more than 100 "stolen brides" over the past several years.   19

Chinese officials are attempting to counter the problem by relaxing some restrictions on the number of children a family can have—meaning less pressure on mothers to produce a son, and fewer selective abortions. They are also taking steps to criminalize abortions based on gender.   20

Other social trends may help balance the sex ratio as well. David Osterhout, a journalist living in Shanghai, says China's dramatic economic growth is slowly changing the way some Chinese look at their daughters.   21

He says with more and more women entering the workforce, daughters are no longer seen as a financial handicap: "The other thing is that I think girls are becoming more prized as society changes, and women are getting into jobs traditionally reserved for men, and are making salary levels comparable with the levels of men."   22

Not all Chinese men may be pleased with the idea of a future world inhabited by powerful working women and a shortage of wives. Chinese women, however, may see it in a different way.   23

Vocabulary

Directions: Locate each of the key words in the reading selection. Try to figure out each word's meaning by using the context. Confirm your guess by checking the dictionary or thesaurus. Write the meanings of the words in the margin of the text. Then record the meanings in the following chart.

Key Word	Paragraph	Meaning
1. milestone	1	
2. curbing	5	
3. dwindling	6	
4. skewed	14	
5. demographer	17	
Others?		

Guide Questions

Directions: These questions will guide your understanding of what you have read. Write your answers in your notebook, or on a separate sheet of paper if your instructor wishes to collect it. Your answers to these questions will be the basis of class discussion.

1. Explain the point of paragraph 4: "… the country's true population story is not its size, but its composition."
2. Explain the problem that results from a "graying" population in China.
3. What "worrying trend" concerns young Chinese?
4. Are the potential results of China's one-child policy all bad? Are there any positive aspects?

Application

Directions: Compare China's population with that of the United States, India, and Indonesia. If you are from another country, include your native country. Use the Internet or the library to get the population statistics.

Making Connections

Directions: Reread the article "As a Pampered Generation Grows Up, Chinese Worry." Draw connections between that story, written in 1996, and this article written in 2005.

Writing

Directions: React to what you've read about Chinese population problems and policies. In your reaction, comment on the Chinese government's decision to enforce a one-child policy. If you were in charge of China's government, what would you do? Write two or more paragraphs.

After 20 years of negotiation, the Inuit people of the Arctic have finally achieved their long-desired dream: a territory of their own. Carved out of northern Canada, it is home to the largest population of Inuit people in the world. But the past 20 years have seen enormous changes in the lives of these northern inhabitants. This article was researched and written by Yva Momatiuk and John Eastcott, a freelance photojournalist team. It appeared in The World and I *in July 2000 and focuses on the women of Nunavut, their sudden entry into the modern world, and their newfound independence.*

OUR LAND: NUNAVUT'S INUIT WOMEN

Yva Momatiuk and John Eastcott

1   Mabel Angulalik ties the dead bird's feet to the top of a makeshift post. She spreads its wings to warn other seagulls patrolling the beach: leave my drying fish alone. Around the post, wooden racks bend under slabs of Arctic char curing in the weak July sun. Its warmth has only just begun to melt the sea ice around Victoria Island in Canada's new territory of Nunavut, *Our Land* in Inktitut, the language of the Inuit.

2   Angulalik watches the shifting ice, and the lines in her old face deepen. After she was born, her mother—paralyzed from the waist down—put her baby daughter in the snow to freeze. "My mother was crawling on her hands and knew she couldn't look after me," Angulalik says quietly. "But another family camping nearby found me and took me in. And here I am."

3   Indeed she is. Yet her memories of the nomadic life following animals across tundra and ice are full of hardship: Hardly any food. No oil for lamps. A husband chosen for her, as required by custom. Babies born in snow houses. Caribou hides to sew, fish to dry, seal blubber to preserve.

4   Today Angulalik lives in a warm house in the nearby town of Ikaluktitiak, which means Good Fishing Place. She spends her summers in a cabin by the sea, tending to fish racks and smelling the salty air. But when a young relative arrives to collect her, she hikes up her wolverine-trimmed parka, climbs aboard the all-terrain vehicle, and holds tight as they bump back to Ikaluktitiak.

5   The town, like most Arctic settlements, has an airport, a nurses' station, several stores, schools, hotels, and churches. The political entity of Nunavut was created on April 1, 1999, and constitutes about one-fifth of Canada's landmass. Eighty-five percent of its inhabitants, some 17,500 people, are Inuit. It took them twenty years to negotiate independence, and now the Inuit want to plan the future on their terms. Yet things have changed in twenty years.

6   Change has brought forth a new Inuit woman. Today she is more likely to drive a truck than a dogsled, visit a tanning salon than her fishing net, and worry about her children's grades rather than food for them. If she is forty-five or older, she may be fluent in her ancestors' tongue as well as in English; if she is younger, her Inuktitut may be limited to a few phrases. She holds a job, travels south for holidays, and prefers Big Macs to blubber. She is a bridge between her traditional parents and the thoroughly modern youngsters. She is the glue of her family and at times the sole wage earner.

One of the earliest debates in Nunavut was over equal representation of women and men in the new government. It failed, but today the Pauktuutit Inuit Women's Association funds job-training programs, helps women fighting custody battles, and builds shelters for abused wives.   7

Eva Otokiak is the manager of Ikaluktitiak's seven-bed shelter and a former victim of domestic violence. "I endured because of my five children," she says, stroking her short hair. She explains that as families left the open land for settlements, many became troubled. The men discovered that their legendary survival and hunting skills were useless. Unless they attended school, learned English, and joined the market economy, they had to survive on government handouts. Welfare covered necessities but killed pride; alcohol and drugs obliterated pain but destroyed whole families. Nunavut's suicide rate is seven times that of southern Canada.   8

In some families, men who once hunted take care of the children while the women work. Women aren't just chasing better jobs, however; they have also emerged as a healing force. Most Inuit women try to ensure the kind of robust family life, communal ties, and connection to the land that social researchers say are necessary for emotional health.   9

"I have to say no to my children more often than if we still lived on the land," Otokiak says. "I say no to big parties, no to getting pregnant early." To cope with the new life, she learned to be more assertive than her ancestors, a difficult task if you come from an intrinsically cooperative culture.   10

Nunavut women credit the men with much of their strength. Brenda Jencke decided to return north from her husband's home province of Ontario, so their three children would grow up close to her Inuit roots. He supported her all the way, and today she heads their construction company in Ikaluktitiak.   11

A slender woman with a dazzling smile, Margo Kadlun works for a caribou research project. She remembers how much she wanted to go hunting when she was small. "My father warned me: 'You cannot go if you are whining, and I won't bring you back if you get tired,'" she recalls. "We walked miles and miles across the tundra until we got a couple caribou. Brought back several leg bones and cached the rest. But my father never told me I couldn't go because I was a girl. And he taught me not to whine but to stick to what I want to do. He gave me that."   12

Vocabulary

Directions: Locate each of the key words in the reading selection. Try to figure out each word's meaning by using the context. Confirm your guess by checking the dictionary or thesaurus. Write the meanings of the words in the margin of the text. Then record the meanings in the following chart.

Key Word	Paragraph	Meaning
1. makeshift	1	
2. tundra	3	
3. blubber	3	

Key Word	Paragraph	Meaning
4. robust	9	
5. intrinsically	10	
Others?		

Guide Questions

Directions: These questions will guide your understanding of what you have read. Write your answers in your notebook or on a separate sheet of paper if your instructor wishes to collect it. Your answers to these questions will be the basis of class discussion.

1. Compare and contrast the life of Inuit women today and their life of 20 years ago. Include information on where they live, the food they eat, the comforts of their homes, and their worries, marriage, work, transportation, and language.
2. Describe the problems that resulted as families left the open land for settlements.
3. What have Inuit women learned in order to cope with their new life?
4. Explain what Margo Kadlun means when she speaks of her father: "He gave me that."

Application

Use the library or the Internet to do some research on this brand-new territory of Nunavut. One excellent source is www.facts.com, which is available through many libraries. Major newspapers and magazines are also excellent sources of information.

Marking Text

Review how to mark text on page 413. Mark this article, "Our Land," and then compare your marked text to the model on page 115.

Writing

Directions: Now use your marked text to write a concise summary of this article. Summary writing is explained on page 417.

Example of Marked Text

* *After twenty years of negotiation, the Inuit people of the Arctic have finally achieved their long-desired dream: a territory of their own.* Carved out of northern Canada, it is home to the largest population of Inuit people in the world. But the past twenty years have seen enormous changes in the lives of these northern inhabitants. This article was researched and written by Yva Momatiuk and John Eastcott, a freelance photojournalist team. It appeared in The World and I *in July 2000 and focuses on the women of Nunavut, their sudden entry into the modern world, and their newfound independence.*

OUR LAND: NUNAVUT'S INUIT WOMEN

Yva Momatiuk and John Eastcott

Intro

Mabel Angulalik ties the dead bird's feet to the top of a makeshift post. She spreads its wings to warn other seagulls patrolling the beach: leave my drying fish alone. Around the post, wooden racks bend under slabs of Arctic char curing in the weak July sun. Its warmth has only just begun to melt the sea ice around Victoria Island in Canada's new territory of Nunavut, *Our Land* in Inktitut, the language of the Inuit. 1

Angulalik watches the shifting ice, and the lines in her old face deepen. After she was born, her mother—paralyzed from the waist down—put her baby daughter in the snow to freeze. "My mother was crawling on her hands and knew she couldn't look after me," Angulalik says quietly. "But another family camping nearby found me and took me in. And here I am." 2

Contrast past:

Indeed she is. Yet <u>her memories of the nomadic life following animals across tundra and ice are full of hardship: Hardly any food. No oil for lamps. A husband chosen for her, as required by custom. Babies born in snow houses.</u> Caribou hides to sew, fish to dry; seal blubber to preserve. 3

present:

<u>Today Angulalik lives in a warm house in the nearby town of Ikaluktitiak, which means Good Fishing Place. She spends her summers in a cabin by the sea,</u> tending to fish racks and smelling the salty air. But when a young relative arrives to collect her, she hikes up her wolverine-trimmed parka, climbs aboard the all-terrain vehicle, and holds tight as they bump back to Ikaluktitiak. 4

a new nation
→Nunavut

<u>The town, like most Arctic settlements, has an airport, a nurses station, several stores, schools, hotels, and churches. The political entity of Nunavut was created on April 1, 1999, and constitutes about one-fifth of Canada's landmass. Eighty-five percent of its inhabitants, some 17,500 people, are Inuit. It took them twenty years to negotiate independence, and now the Inuit want to plan the future on their terms.</u> Yet <u>things have changed</u> in twenty years. 5   *Inuit*

MI → **
    *

New roles for women

<u>Change has brought forth a new Inuit woman. Today she is more likely</u> to drive a truck than a dogsled, visit a tanning salon than her fishing net, and worry about her children's grades rather than food for them. If she is forty-five or older, she may be fluent in her ancestors' tongue as well as in English; if she is younger, her Inuktitut may be limited to a few phrases. She holds a job, travels south for holidays, and prefers Big Macs to blubber. <u>She is a bridge between her traditional</u> 6

parents and the thoroughly modern youngsters. She is the glue of her family and at times the sole wage earner.

7   One of the earliest debates in Nunavut was over equal representation of women and men in the new government. It failed, but today the Pauktuutit Inuit Women's Association funds job-training programs, helps women fighting custody battles, and builds shelters for abused wives.

8   Eva Otokiak is the manager of Ikaluktitiak's seven-bed shelter and a former victim of domestic violence. "I endured because of my five children," she says, stroking her short hair. She explains that as families left the open land for settlements, many became troubled. The men discovered that their legendary survival and hunting skills were useless. Unless they attended school, learned English, and joined the market economy, they had to survive on government handouts. Welfare covered necessities but killed pride; alcohol and drugs obliterated pain but destroyed whole families. Nunavut's suicide rate is seven times that of southern Canada.

men lost their power ∴ problems

9   In some families, men who once hunted take care of the children while the women work. Women aren't just chasing better jobs, however; they have also emerged as a healing force. Most Inuit women try to ensure the kind of robust family life, communal ties, and connection to the land that social researchers say are necessary for emotional health.

ex of "culture change"

women support families + try to heal society

10   "I have to say no to my children more often than if we still lived on the land," Otokiak says. "I say no to big parties, no to getting pregnant early." To cope with the new life, she learned to be more assertive than her ancestors, a difficult task if you come from an intrinsically cooperative culture.

11   Nunavut women credit the men with much of their strength. Brenda Jencke decided to return north from her husband's home province of Ontario, so their three children would grow up close to her Inuit roots. He supported her all the way, and today she heads their construction company in Ikaluktitiak.

men support women emotionally

12   A slender woman with a dazzling smile, Margo Kadlun works for a caribou research project. She remembers how much she wanted to go hunting when she was small. "My father warned me: 'You cannot go if you are whining, and I won't bring you back if you get tired,'" she recalls. "We walked miles and miles across the tundra until we got a couple caribou. Brought back several leg bones and cached the rest. But my father never told me I couldn't go because I was a girl. And he taught me not to whine but to stick to what I want to do. He gave me that."

ex of man supporting woman's independence

Writer Esmeralda Santiago was 13 when her mother decided to move from Puerto Rico to Brooklyn with her eight children. Santiago found the move frightening: New York was cold, dark, its language and customs incomprehensible. In her 1993 memoir, When I Was Puerto Rican, *Santiago describes the difficult transition between two cultures. The following is an excerpt from that book.*

A PUERTO RICAN STEW

Esmeralda Santiago

To Mami, the trip north made me "Americana."
But I found my own recipe for identity.

I'm in my kitchen, browsing through Puerto Rican cookbooks, when it hits me.   1
These books are in English, written for people who don't know a *sofrito* from a *sombrero.* Then I remember the afternoon I returned to Puerto Rico for the summer after 15 years of living in the United States. The family gathered for dinner in my mother's house. The men settled in a corner of the living room, while Mami and my sisters chopped, washed, seasoned: I stood on the other side of the kitchen island, enjoying their Dance of the Stove with Pots and Pans—the flat metal sounds, the thud of the refrigerator door opening and closing, the swish of running water—a percussive accompaniment enhancing the fragrant sizzle of garlic and onions in hot oil.

"Do you cook Puerto Rican?" Norma asked as she cored a red pepper.   2

"No," I answered, "I never got the hang of it."   3

"How can you be Puerto Rican without your rice and beans?" joked Alicia.   4

"Easy," said Mami. "She's no longer Puerto Rican."   5

If she had stabbed me with the chicken-gutting knife in her hand it would   6
have hurt less. I swallowed the pain. "Si, Mami," I said, "I have become Americana."

I parried with "Wasn't that what you wanted when you first brought us to   7
New York?"

As Mami split the chicken, her voice rose, indignant: "I only wanted the best   8
for you."

The dance was over, a knife suspended above tomato halves, rinse water run-   9
ning through rice clear as sunshine. I walked away, pushed by their silence—my mother, my sisters, my brothers-in law. No one followed me, or challenged her assessment of me as a turncoat who had abandoned her culture. I stood in the gravelly yard, the soles of my sandals separating me from the ground as if I were on stilts, unable to touch my native soil, unable to feel a connection. I wanted to cry, but would not give them nor myself the satisfaction of tears. Instead, I leaned against a fence and wondered if her words hurt so much because they were true.

Whatever I was, Puerto Rican or not, had been orchestrated by Mami. When   10
I was 13, she moved us from rural Puerto Rico to Brooklyn. We were to learn English, to graduate from high school, to find jobs in clean offices not factories. We were to assimilate into American society to put an end to the poverty she was forced to endure for lack of an education.

11   I, the oldest, took up the challenge. I learned English so well that people told me I didn't "speak like a Puerto Rican." I gave up the bright, form-fitting clothes of my friends and relatives for drab loose garments that would not brand me as a "hot tomato." I developed a formal evasive manner when asked about my background. I would not admit to being poor, to living with my mother and 10 sisters and brothers in a three-room apartment. I would tremble with shame if newspapers identified a criminal as Puerto Rican.

12   Mami beamed when I got a job as a typist in Manhattan. She reminded me that I was to show my sisters and brothers the path to success without becoming "Americanized," a status that was never clearly defined but to be avoided at all costs.

13   That afternoon in her kitchen was the first time we had spoken in seven years. The grudge we held was so deep, neither could bridge it without losing *dignidad,* an imperative of Puerto Rican self-esteem. The break had come when I stopped being a "good" Puerto Rican girl and behaved like an American one.

14   At 21, I assumed I was old enough to live my life as I pleased. And what I pleased was a man a year older than Mami. I ran away with him, leaving a letter telling Mami I wouldn't be home after work because I was eloping. "Don't worry," I signed off, "I still love you."

15   She tracked me down to an apartment in Fort Lauderdale more luxurious than any we'd ever lived in, to say that if I returned home all would be forgiven. I refused. During those seven years, the man for whom I'd left my mother turned out to be as old-fashioned, possessive and domineering as she had seemed. From him, too, I ran away.

16   To question my Puerto Rican identity that afternoon in her kitchen was Mami's perfect comeback to what had surely been seven years of worry. It was also her way of recognizing her own folly. She had expected me to thrive in American culture, but I was to remain 100 percent Puerto Rican.

17   Mami came to realize the impossibility of such a demand, how difficult it is for someone from a "traditional" culture to achieve success in the United States without becoming something other than the person she set out to be. My one act of rebellion forced her to face what she had never expected. In the United States, her children would challenge her authority based on different rules of conduct. Within a year of my leaving home, she packed up the family and returned to Puerto Rico, where, she hoped, her children would be what they couldn't be in the United States: real Puerto Ricans.

18   I stayed behind, immersed in the American culture she feared. But I never considered myself any less Puerto Rican. I was born there, spoke its language, identified with its culture. But to Puerto Ricans on the island during my summer there, I was a different creature altogether. Employers complained that I was too assertive, men said I was too feminist, my cousin suggested I had no manners and everyone accused me of being too independent. Those, I was made to understand, were Americanisms.

19   Back in the United States, I was constantly asked where I was from, the comments about my not looking, behaving or talking like a Puerto Rican followed

me into the era of political correctness, when it's no longer polite to say things like that.

I've learned to insist on my peculiar brand of Puerto Rican identity. One not bound by geographical, linguistic or behavioral boundaries, but rather, by a deep identification with a place, a people and a culture which, in spite of appearances, define my behavior and determine the rhythms of my days. An identity in which I've forgiven myself for having to look up a recipe for *arroz con pollo* in a Puerto Rican cookbook meant for people who don't know a *sombrero* from a *sofrito*.

20

Vocabulary

Directions: Locate each of the key words in the story. Try to figure out each word's meaning by using the context. Confirm your guess by checking the dictionary or thesaurus. Write the meanings of the words in the margin of the text. Then record the meanings in the following chart.

Key Word	Paragraph	Meaning
1. parried	7	
2. indignant	8	
3. turncoat	9	
4. assimilate	10	
5. evasive	11	
6. folly	16	
7. thrive	16	
Others?		

Guide Questions

Directions: These questions will guide your understanding of what you have read. Write your answers in your notebook or on a separate sheet of paper if your instructor wishes to collect it. Your answers to these questions will be the basis of class discussion.

1. Describe the scene at the beginning of the story: the setting, the characters, their actions.
2. Why did Santiago become upset and leave the kitchen?

3. Why did Santiago's mother decide to leave Puerto Rico and move to New York?
4. Describe Santiago's experiences after the move to New York.
5. What was Santiago's mother's impossible "demand"?
6. Describe Santiago's "peculiar brand of Puerto Rican identity."
7. Why do you think the author titled her story "A Puerto Rican Stew"?

Making Connections

Relate this story to what you learned in earlier parts of this unit. Give some examples of how the values and norms of Puerto Rico were different from those of the United States. Why did these differences cause Santiago to suffer? Have you ever experienced a culture conflict like this?

SHORT TAKE

Watch Your Language!

The world is becoming more homogeneous each day: American fast-food restaurants appear in the heart of Paris and the center of Beijing; teenagers in the farthest corners of the earth wear T-shirts by the same "hot" designers; pop music is heard blasting from shortwave radios in the middle of the Gobi desert and in ice-shrouded research stations in Greenland. But that doesn't mean there still aren't a few problems, a few misunderstandings along the way. Consider the messages on these signs found in businesses all over Europe and Asia.

"Please leave your values at the front desk," requests a Paris hotel. "Because of the impropriety of entertaining guests of the opposite sex in the bedroom, it is suggested that the lobby be used for this purpose," advises a hotel in Zurich. A Japanese hotel sign says, "You are invited to take advantage of the chambermaid."

If all these moral dilemmas make you hungry, head for the restaurant in Poland whose menu features "roasted duck let loose" and "beef rashers beaten up in the country people's fashion." Or try the inn in Spain that offers "swerd cherde with anals."

Or try sightseeing. In Moscow, you might follow the suggestion of a hotel sign that reads, "You are welcome to visit the cemetery, where famous Russian and Soviet composers, artists, and writers are buried daily except Thursday."

But be careful if you are visiting a Bucharest zoo. A sign there reads: "Please do not feed the animals. If you have any suitable food, give it to the guard on duty."

If shopping in Sweden, by all means avoid the furrier who advertises "Fur coats made for ladies from their own skin." Or the Paris shop that sells "dresses for street walking."

But who needs clothes? Go to Bangkok, where a dry cleaner says, "Drop your trousers here for best results."

Sandra Cisneros writes about Mexican and Mexican American women. Born in Chicago in 1954, she often writes about women who fight to rise above poverty and discrimination. Her first book, The House on Mango Street, *was published in 1984 and received wide acclaim. Her next book,* Woman Hollering Creek and Other Stories, *was published in 1991 and marked Cisneros as the first Chicana (Mexican-American woman) to receive a major publishing contract for a work about Chicanas. The book, a series of short stories about strong Mexican American women, received praise from critics across the nation. In this article, Cisneros reflects on her life as the only girl in a family of seven children—six boys and "the only daughter."*

ONLY DAUGHTER

Sandra Cisneros

1   Once, several years ago, when I was just starting out my writing career, I was asked to write my own contributor's note for an anthology I was part of. I wrote: "I am the only daughter in a family of six sons. That explains everything."

2   Well, I've thought about that ever since, and yes, it explains a lot to me, but for the reader's sake I should have written: "I am the only daughter in a *Mexican* family of six sons." Or even: "I am the only daughter of a Mexican father and a Mexican-American mother." Or: "I am the only daughter of a working-class family of nine." All of these had everything to do with who I am today.

3   I was/am the only daughter and *only* a daughter. Being an only daughter in a family of six sons forced me by circumstance to spend a lot of time by myself because my brothers felt it beneath them to play with a *girl* in public. But that aloneness, that loneliness, was good for a would-be writer. It allowed me time to think and think, to imagine, to read and prepare myself.

4   Being only a daughter for my father meant my destiny would lead me to become someone's wife. That's what he believed. But when I was in the fifth grade and shared my plans for college with him, I was sure he understood. I remember my father saying. *"Que bueno, mi hi'ja**, that's good." That meant a lot to me, especially since my brothers thought the idea hilarious. What I didn't realize was that my father thought college was good for girls—good for finding a husband. After four years in college and two more in graduate school, and still no husband, my father shakes his head even now and says I wasted all that education.

5   In retrospect, I'm lucky my father believed daughters were meant for husbands. It meant it didn't matter if I majored in something silly like English. After all, I'd find a nice professional eventually, right? This allowed me the liberty to putter about embroidering my little poems and stories without my father interrupting with so much as a "What's that you're writing?"

6   But the truth is, I wanted him to interrupt. I wanted my father to understand what it was I was scribbling, to introduce me as "My only daughter, the writer." Not as "This is only my daughter. She teaches." *Es maestra*—teacher. Not even *profesora.*

---

* mi'ja or mi hi'ja—my daughter

7   In a sense, everything I have ever written has been for him, to win his approval even though I know my father can't read English words, even though my father's only reading includes the brown-ink *Esto* sports magazines from Mexico City and the bloody *¡Alarma!* magazines that feature yet another sighting of *La Virgen de Guadalupe* on a tortilla or a wife's revenge on her philandering husband by bashing his skull in with a *molcajete* (a kitchen mortar made of volcanic rock), Or the *fotonovelas,* the little picture paperbacks with tragedy and trauma erupting from the characters' mouths in bubbles.

8   My father represents, then, the public majority. A public who is disinterested in reading, and yet one whom I am writing about and for, and privately trying to woo.

9   When we were growing up in Chicago, we moved a lot because of my father. He suffered bouts of nostalgia. Then we'd have to let go of our flat, store the furniture with mother's relatives, load the station wagon with baggage and bologna sandwiches and head south. To Mexico City.

10   We came back, of course. To yet another Chicago flat, another Chicago neighborhood, another Catholic school. Each time, my father would seek out the parish priest in order to get a tuition break, and complain or boast: "I have seven sons."

11   He meant *siete hijos*, seven children, but he translated it as "sons." "I have seven sons." To anyone who would listen. The Sears Roebuck employee who sold us the washing machine. The short-order cook where my father ate his ham-and-eggs breakfasts. "I have seven sons." As if he deserved a medal from the state.

12   My papa. He didn't mean anything by that mistranslation, I'm sure. But somehow I could feel myself being erased. I'd tug my father's sleeve and whisper: "Not seven sons. Six! and *one daughter.*"

13   When my oldest brother graduated from medical school, he fulfilled my father's dream that we study hard and use this—our heads, instead of this—our hands. Even now my father's hands are thick and yellow, stubbed by a history of hammer and nails and twine and coils and springs. "Use this," my father said, tapping his head, "and not this," showing us those hands. He always looked tired when he said it.

14   Wasn't college an investment? And hadn't I spent all those years in college? And if I didn't marry, what was it all for? Why would anyone go to college and then choose to be poor? Especially someone who had always been poor.

15   Last year, after ten years of writing professionally, the financial rewards started to trickle in. My second National Endowment for the Arts Fellowship. A guest professorship at the University of California, Berkeley. My book, which sold to a major New York publishing house.

16   At Christmas, I flew home to Chicago. The house was throbbing, same as always: hot tamales and sweet tamales hissing in my mother's pressure cooker, and everybody—my mother, six brothers, wives, babies, aunts, cousins—talking too loud and at the same time. Like in a Fellini film because that's just how we are.

17   I went upstairs to my father's room. One of my stories had just been translated into Spanish and published in an anthology of Chicano writing and I wanted to show it to him. Ever since he recovered from a stroke two years ago, my father

likes to spend his leisure hours horizontally. And that's how I found him, watching a Pedro Infante movie on Galavisión and eating rice pudding.

There was a glass filled with milk on the bedside table. There were several   18
vials of pills and balled Kleenex. And on the floor, one black sock and a plastic urinal that I didn't want to look at but looked at anyway. Pedro Infante was about to burst into song, and my father was laughing.

I'm not sure if it was because my story was translated into Spanish, or because   19
it was published in Mexico, or perhaps because the story dealt with Tepeyac, the *colonia* my father was raised in and the house he grew up in, but at any rate, my father punched the mute button on his remote control and read my story.

I sat on the bed next to my father and waited. He read it very slowly. As if   20
he were reading each line over and over. He laughed at all the right places and read lines he liked out loud. He pointed and asked questions: "Is this So-and-so?" "Yes," I said. He kept reading.

When he was finally finished, after what seemed like hours, my father looked   21
up and asked: "Where can we get more copies of this for the relatives?"

Of all the wonderful things that happened to me last year, that was the most   22
wonderful.

Vocabulary

Directions: Locate each of the key words in the story. Try to figure out each word's meaning by using the context. Confirm your guess by checking the dictionary or thesaurus. Write the meanings of the words in the margin of the text. Then record the meanings in the following chart.

Key Word	Paragraph	Meaning
1. anthology	1	
2. retrospect	5	
3. embroidering	5	
4. philandering	7	
5. trauma	7	
6. woo	8	
7. nostalgia	9	
Others?		

Guide Questions

Directions: These questions will guide your understanding of what you have read. Write your answers in your notebook or on a separate sheet of paper if your instructor wishes to collect it. Your answers to these questions will be the basis of class discussion.

1. Cisneros calls herself both an *only* daughter and *only a daughter*. What are the differences between the two?
2. Cisneros says she was alone much of the time during her childhood, because her brothers didn't want to include a girl in their play. Why does she say her loneliness, her aloneness, was a good thing?
3. a. What was Cisneros's "destiny" in her father's mind? Why would he think she had "wasted" her education?

    b. In what way was her father's attitude a benefit for her?
4. Why does Cisneros say that her father represents "the public majority"?
5. Explain the father's use of the phrase "seven sons" to describe his six boys and one girl.
6. What was the "most wonderful thing" that happened to Cisneros that year?

Writing

Was your experience growing up similar to that of Cisneros? Compare and contrast your experiences with hers. Write two paragraphs, the first describing the similarities, the second the differences.

Deborah Rodriguez is an American woman with a can-do attitude. Hoping to help the Afghan people recover from years of Taliban oppression, she went to Kabul in 2002. What resulted was one of the strangest foreign aid projects ever imagined. Rodriguez's book, Kabul Beauty School, *tells her story of founding an academy to train Afghan beauticians— training that would give them cash and personal independence—a radical idea in a country where women have, in the words of William Grimes of* The New York Times, *"the approximate status of dirt."*

SHEAR INSANITY IN *KABUL BEAUTY SCHOOL*

A hairdresser from Michigan uses her profession to improve the lot of Afghan women

Marjorie Kehe

Here's a wild idea for a truly madcap sitcom: Uproot a hairdresser named Deb from Holland, Mich., and ship her to Kabul, Afghanistan.   1

Make sure, of course, that she's enough of a character—an ex-prison guard with spiky red hair and long fingernails who's often seen pulling hard on a cigarette— to offend even those Afghans who don't support the Taliban. But don't forget that she'll also need a heart of gold and a soft-as-mush interior in order to interact feelingly with a different traumatized Afghan woman each week.   2

Too implausible, you say? Not at all. This is Deborah Rodriguez's actual life.   3

In *Kabul Beauty School,* Rodriguez (with the help of coauthor Kristin Ohlson) tells the utterly improbable but also genuinely moving story of how she traveled to Afghanistan to help after 9/11 and ended up with an Afghan husband (Sam, an Afghan businessman with another wife and eight children in Saudi Arabia) and a commitment to live in Kabul and train Afghan women to become beauty salon operators.   4

Somehow Rodriguez, who certainly has the hairdresser's gift for entertaining and confidential gab, manages to make it all seem almost reasonable.   5

Although planted firmly in Michigan for most of her life, Rodriguez had a yearning for both a larger world and a higher purpose that led her to take disaster relief training two months before 9/11. Shortly thereafter she hears that aid workers are needed in Afghanistan and quickly signs up.   6

She imagines, she tells us, that she will spend a month "bandaging wounds, splinting broken limbs, clambering over rubble, and helping people who were still hiding from the Taliban climb into daylight."   7

The reality is that, once in Kabul, no one really knows what to do with her. Unlike the medics, engineers, and nutritionists with whom she had traveled, her skills serve no clear purpose in Kabul. Even worse, Rodriguez suspects, her colleagues, many of whom are affiliated with Christian churches, are uncomfortable with her appearance. Perhaps, they suggest, she had best stay indoors and pray for them.   8

But Rodriguez doesn't have a stay-at-home personality. Before long she is out walking where she's been told not to walk and making all sorts of Afghan friends.   9

10   As she learns more of Kabul (a city she describes as "dense with sadness") and its residents it becomes clear to her that her profession—hairdressing—is one of the few truly viable options for would-be female Afghan entrepreneurs. There's a huge demand for such services, as many Afghan women sport elaborate hair and makeup styles under their burqas. At the same time, it's work that can be done entirely in female company—a necessity in a segregated society.

11   Soon, Rodriguez decides to open a school to teach Afghan women the skills they'd need to open their own salons. No shrinking violet, she petitions U.S. beauty supply manufacturers for help, and easily raises a half-million dollars in donations.

12   Of course, nothing about implementing Rodriguez's plan is easy, and this is where Sam proves indispensable. As unlikely a match as they are, he at least admires and supports her goals. (When they first meet and she explains to him that as a wife she would be a partner and not a servant, he insists, "I see this kind of wife on television and I want one.")

13   But most of the credit for coping falls to Rodriguez herself. Ever inventive, she engages Afghan women in hair dying by asking them to see unwanted hair pigment as Satan, who must be vanquished. She comes to find it normal to direct people to her home by telling them to turn right at the bombed-out movie theater and then continue along the street with all the dead cows. She accepts—and even romanticizes—a husband so exhausted by her emotional needs that he pays a proxy to talk to her. (Of course, compared with Rodriguez's ex back in the U.S. and the husbands of many of her students, Sam is a gem.)

14   But perhaps best about Rodriguez is her refusal to either patronize her beloved Afghan students (whose heartrending stories are woven throughout the book) or to drape herself in too much of a hero's mantle. "Sometimes I wonder if I'm doing much good here at all," she writes, acknowledging the limited degree to which any Westerner can fully grasp the complexities of Afghan life.

15   What she does know for sure, she says, is that the courage and strength she has seen in Afghan women have become her inspiration. They are moving toward the light, she tells us, and that makes it all the more poignant when, at the book's uncertain ending, Rodriguez begs the rest of us to "look, watch, and make sure nothing puts out that light again."

Vocabulary

Directions: Find each of the key words in the essay. Try to figure out each word's meaning by using the context. Confirm your guess by checking the dictionary. Write the meanings of the words in the margin of the text, near the word. Then record the meanings in the following chart.

Key Word	Paragraph	Meaning
1. madcap	1	
2. implausible	3	

Key Word	Paragraph	Meaning
3. gab	5	
4. clambering	7	
5. viable	10	
6. vanquished	13	
7. proxy	13	
8. patronize	14	
Others?		

More Vocabulary

The author of this story uses a great deal of figurative language (see page 427 for an explanation of figurative language) and plays on words. Let's look at a few of her colorful uses of language. In paragraph 2, she describes Rodriguez as having a "heart of gold" and a "soft-as-mush interior." What does she mean by this? In paragraph 11, Rodriguez is described as "no shrinking violet." What is a shrinking violet? In paragraph 13, Sam is described as a "gem." (at least compared to the other husbands); in what way is Sam a "gem"? Finally, Rodriguez describes the Afghan women as having "heartrending" stories (paragraph 14) and as "moving toward the light" (paragraph 15). Explain the meanings of these words and phrases.

Guide Questions

Directions: Answer these questions to ensure that you understand what you've read. Write your answers in your notebook or on a separate sheet of paper if your instructor will collect it. Your answers will be the basis of class discussion.

1. Kehe begins the article by comparing Deborah Rodriguez's trip to Afghanistan to a "madcap sitcom." Why do you think she does this? Do you think it is a good comparison?
2. What prompted Rodriguez to go to Afghanistan?
3. In a few sentences, summarize Rodriguez's experience in Kabul.
4. Why does she decide that hairdressing is "one of the few truly viable options" for the Afghan women?
5. Who is Sam? What do we learn about him?
6. What is your opinion of Rodriguez? Do you think her work in Kabul was valuable?

Writing

Directions: Write a paragraph reacting to the story. What do you think of Rodriguez and her efforts in Kabul?

Application

Directions: Find out how Rodriguez's story ends. Go to the Internet to learn what happened— did Rodriguez stay in Kabul? Did she and Sam stay married? What can you find out about the women who attended the beauty school?

In this excerpt from the textbook Sociology, *we learn about one of the great distinguishing features of the United States—immigration. Few other nations have been so welcoming and at the same time so conflicted by the flow of immigrants from every corner of the world. They may not always be welcomed by those who preceded them (former immigrants themselves), but new arrivals have shaped this country and will continue to change it.*

THE UNITED STATES: LAND OF IMMIGRANTS

Henry Tischler

Since the settlement of Jamestown in 1607, well over 45 million people have immigrated to the United States. Up until 1882, the policy of the United States was almost one of free and unrestricted admittance. The country was regarded as the land of the free, a haven for those oppressed by tyrants, and a place of opportunity. The words of Emma Lazarus, inscribed on the Statue of Liberty, were indeed appropriate: 1

> Give me your tired, your poor,
> Your huddled masses yearning to breathe free,
> The wretched refuse of your teeming shore.
> Send these, the homeless, tempest-tost to me,
> I lift my lamp beside the golden door!

To be sure, there were those who had misgivings about the immigrants. George Washington wrote to John Adams in 1794, "My opinion with respect to immigration is that except for useful mechanics and some particular descriptions of men or professions, there is no need for encouragement." Thomas Jefferson was even more emphatic in expressing the wish that there might be "an ocean of fire between this country and Europe, so that it would be impossible for any more immigrants to come hither." Such fears, however, were not widely felt. There was the West to be opened, railroads to be built, and canals to be dug; there was land for the asking. People poured across the mountains, and the young nation was eager for population.   2

Immigration of white ethnics to the United States can be viewed from the perspective of old migration and new migration. The old migration consisted of people from northern Europe who came before the 1880s. The new migration was much larger in numbers and consisted of people from southern and eastern Europe who came between 1880 and 1920. The ethnic groups that made up the old migration included the English, Dutch, French, Germans, Irish, Scandinavians, Scots, and Welsh. The new migration included Poles, Hungarians, Ukrainians, Russians, Italians, Greeks, Portuguese, and Armenians.   3

Figure 1 on page 130 shows the number of immigrants who came to the United States in each decade from 1820 to 2000. The new migration sent far more immigrants to the United States than the old migration. The earlier immigrants felt threatened by the waves of unskilled and uneducated newcomers, whose   4 appearance and culture were so different from their own. Public pressure for immigration restriction increased. After 1921, quotas were established limiting the number of people who could arrive from any particular country. The quotas were designed specifically to discriminate against potential immigrants from the southern and eastern European countries. The discriminatory immigration policy remained in effect until 1965, when a new policy was established.

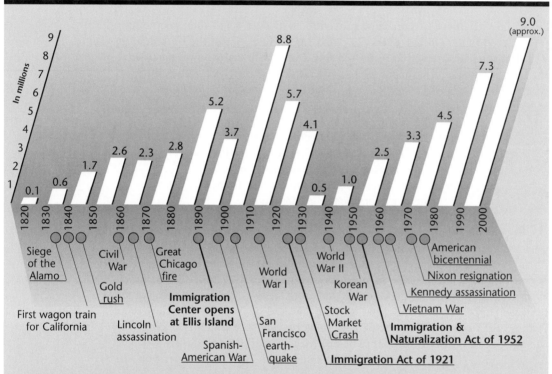

1882: Chinese immigration prohibited, more restrictions placed on immigration.

Immigration reached a peak between 1901 and 1910, when 8.8 million newcomers (8 million of them white Europeans) arrived in the United States.

1921: First immigration quotas (by country) announced.

1948: Refugee Relief Act brings in homeless Europeans and Soviets. Will be used later for Hungarians, Chinese, and Cubans.

1965: Quotas by hemisphere replaced limits by country.

Four out of five immigrants in the 1980s came from Asia, Latin America, and the Caribbean. Counting approximately 500,000 undocumented immigrants, there will be more newcomers in the United States in the 1990s than in any previous decade.

1986: Immigration and Refugee Control Act created means for immigrants in U.S. since 1962 to become citizens; led to legalization of many agricultural workers. Major beneficiaries: Mexicans (3 million have become legal residents since 1987), Cubans, Haitians.

Figure 1   Immigration to the United States, 1820–2000

TABLE 1   United States Immigration Restrictions

1769–1875	No restrictions; open-door policy
1875	No convicts; no prostitutes
1882	No idiots; no lunatics; no people likely to need public care Start of head tax
1882–1943	No Chinese
1885	No gangs of cheap contract laborers
1891	No immigrants with dangerous contagious diseases; no paupers; no polygamists Start of medical inspections
1903	No epileptics; no insane people; no betters; no anarchists
1907	No feeble-minded; no children under 16 unaccompanied by parents; no immigrants unable to support themselves because of physical or mental defects
1917	No immigrants from most of Asia or the Pacific islands; no adults unable to read or write Start of literacy tests
1921	No more than 3% of foreign-born of each nationality in U.S. in 1910; total about 350,000 annually
1924–1927	National Origins Quota Law; no more than 2% of foreign-born of each nationality already in U.S. in 1890; total about 150,000 annually
1940	Alien Registration Act; all aliens must register and be fingerprinted
1950	Exclusion and deportation of aliens dangerous to national security
1952	Codification, nationalization, and minor alterations of previous immigration laws
1965	National Origins Quota system abolished; no more than 20,000 from any one country outside the Western Hemisphere; total about 170,000 annually Start of restrictions on immigrants from other Western Hemisphere countries; no more than 120,000 annually Preference to refugees, aliens with relatives here, and workers with skills needed in the United States
1980	Congress passes the Refugee Act of 1980, repealing ideological and geographical preferences that had favored refugees fleeing communism and Middle Eastern countries
1986	The Immigration Reform and Control Act (IRCA) takes effect; grants amnesty to illegal immigrants residing in the United States since 1982; increases sanctions against employers for hiring illegal immigrants
1990	President George Bush increases immigration quotas

Source: Smithsonian Institution exhibit, Washington, DC.

In Table 1 you will see a list of the various peoples who were excluded from   5
immigrating to the United States during each of the periods in its history. As
you can see, we were much more lenient during the early days of our history.
However, even with our periods of restrictive immigration, the United States has
had one of the most open immigration policies in the world, and we continue to
take in more legal immigrants than the rest of the world combined.

Immigration Today Compared with the Past

6 The past 30 years have seen a marked shift in United States immigration patterns. From the beginning of the country's birth until the 1960s, most immigrants were from European countries. Mexico, the Philippines, China, Korea, and Vietnam were the top five countries of origin for immigrants during the 1980s.

7 A huge wave of immigrants entered the United States in the late 1980s and early 1990s, peaking in 1991 with 1.8 million legal immigrants. Many of these "immigrants" had lived in the country for many years before becoming part of the government's statistics.

8 Today's immigrants are unique in their ethnic origins, education, and skills. The waves of immigration during earlier periods in our history were mostly from European countries. Today's immigrants are primarily from Latin American and Asian countries. Their education levels are at two extremes. While most native-born people have completed high school, immigrants are only half as likely to have done so. At the same time, many other immigrants are highly educated, and some immigrants are more likely than [the] native born to have advanced college degrees.

9 The Census Bureau projects that 880,000 legal immigrants per year will enter the country between 1997 and 2050. Thirty-seven percent of the immigrants will be Hispanic, 35% will be from Asian countries, approximately 23% will be white non-Hispanics, and 7% are expected to be black. With this type of immigration, non-Hispanic whites will account for barely half of the total U.S. population, while Asians and Hispanics will form nearly one-third. The African-American share of the population is expected to rise to 14% (see Figure 2 on page 133).

10 With the large number of people immigrating to the United States, nearly 1 in 10 U.S. residents (9.6%) was foreign born in 1997. This is the highest percentage of foreign-born residents since World War II and nearly double the 1970 level of 4.8%. Many of these people are recent arrivals. Of the 25.8 million foreign-born people living in the United States in March of 1997, 7.5 million had arrived during the previous 7 years. Nearly one-third of these new immigrants live in California, with New York and Florida attracting another 25% (U.S. Bureau of the Census, Current Population Survey, March 1997).

Illegal Immigration

11 Since 1970, illegal immigration has figured prominently in the ethnic makeup of certain regions of the United States. The U.S. Immigration and Naturalization Service (INS) estimates that currently, 3.5 million to 4 million people are residing in the country illegally and that the number is growing by 200,000 a year. There are two types of illegal immigrants: those who enter the United States legally but overstay their visa limits, and those who enter illegally to begin with. Those who migrate over the border each day to work must also be figured into the total.

12 Mexico, El Salvador, and Guatemala account for 44% of the total number of illegal immigrants (see Table 2 on page 134). Illegal immigrants tend to settle in certain states. California is home to 40% of the total, with New York, Florida, Texas, and

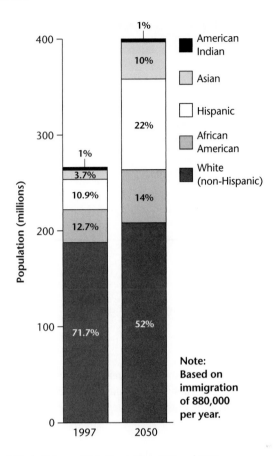

Figure 2   Racial and Ethnic Makeup of U.S. Population, 1997 and 2050

Illinois accounting for most of the rest. The vast majority (71%) of the illegal immigrants are between ages 15 and 39; very few are over 65.

In 1986, the Immigration Reform and Control Act (IRCA) was passed, a law designed to control the flow of illegal immigrants into the United States. The law makes it a crime for employers, even individuals hiring household help, to knowingly employ an illegal immigrant. Stiff fines and criminal penalties can be imposed if they do so. The law also provided legal status to illegal immigrants who entered the United States before 1982 and who have lived here continuously since then. Between 1989 and 1993, 2.7 million people were granted legal resident status under special provisions of the IRCA. These people had lived and worked in the country illegally during the 1980s. Interestingly, only 4% of those who applied for amnesty under the 1986 act worked in farming, fishing, or forestry, running counter to the perception that most illegal immigrants are migrant farm workers.

What is America's racial and ethnic composition today? As you can see in Figure 2, the United States is perhaps the most racially and ethnically diverse

13

14

TABLE 2   Top Ten Countries of Origin of Illegal Immigrants

Country	Percent of Total
Mexico	31
El Salvador	9
Guatemala	4
Canada	3
Poland	3
Philippines	3
Haiti	3
Nicaragua	2
Colombia	2
Bahamas	2

Source: Immigration and Naturalization Service.

country in the world. Unlike many other countries, it has no ethnic group that makes up a numerical majority of the population.

Vocabulary

Directions: Locate each of the key words in the reading selection. Try to figure out each word's meaning by its context. Confirm your guess by checking the dictionary or thesaurus. Write the meanings of the words in the margin of the text. Then record the meanings in the following chart.

Key Word	Paragraph	Meaning
1. haven	1	
2. misgivings	2	
3. lenient	5	
Others?		

Guide Questions

Directions: These questions will guide your understanding of what you have read. Write your answers in your notebook or on a separate sheet of paper if your instructor wishes to collect it. Your answers to these questions will be the basis of class discussion.

1. a. Describe the attitudes toward immigration of two of America's Founding Fathers, George Washington and Thomas Jefferson.
   b. Were you surprised when you read their opinions?
2. Explain why the author says Washington's and Jefferson's fears "were not widely felt."
3. Contrast the "old immigration" with the "new immigration."
4. According to the text, why were quotas limiting immigration imposed after 1921?
5. Describe the change in immigration patterns that began in the 1960s. (Include information on ethnic origins, education, and skills.)
6. Summarize the Census Bureau's predictions of future immigration.
7. State the current estimates of the number of illegal residents in the United States today.
8. What are the "two types" of illegal immigration?
9. Summarize the key elements of the 1986 Immigration Reform and Control Act.

Working with Graphs

Directions: Answer the following questions based on the information in Figure 1 on page 130.

1. Which decade of the 20th century experienced the greatest influx of immigrants?
2. Which decade of the 20th century had the fewest immigrants?
3. Why do think there was so little immigration from approximately 1930 to the mid-1950s?

Use the information in Figure 2 on page 133 to answer these questions.

1. In 1997, what percentage of the U.S. population was the following:
   American Indian?
   Hispanic?
   African American?
2. Which group is expected to increase the most by the year 2050?
3. Is any group expected to decline in number?
4. What was the total population (approximately) of the United States in 1997?
5. What is the total population expected to be in 2050?

Application/Writing

1. Use the Internet or your library to research the current immigration situation in your state. Use the same racial/ethnic categories given in Figure 2 on page 133.
2. Prepare a graph, a list, or a brief essay summarizing the racial/ethnic makeup of your state according to the latest census figures.

   Suggested website: <www.census.gov>

SHORT TAKE

Questions from the U.S. Citizenship Test

The government recently restructured the exam that immigrants must pass before they can become U.S. citizens. Chances are, you'll never take it; but if you did, would you pass? Here are a few sample questions from the test. See how well you do.

1. How many amendments does the Constitution have?
   A. 10
   B. 27
   C. 29

2. When was the Declaration of Independence adopted?
   A. 1776
   B. 1777
   C. 1786

3. How many justices are on the Supreme Court?
   A. 9
   B. 12
   C. 15

4. When is the last day you can send in federal income tax forms?
   A. April 15
   B. May 20
   C. Jan. 16

5. Who did the United States fight in World War II?
   A. Germany, Italy and Russia
   B. Japan, Germany and Italy
   C. Japan, Germany and Russia

6. What do we call the first 10 amendments to the Constitution?
   A. Preamble
   B. Bill of Rights
   C. Declaration of Independence

7. What territory did the United States buy from France in 1803?
   A. Alaska
   B. Florida
   C. Louisiana

8. How many U.S. senators are there?
   A. 50
   B. 100
   C. 435

9. Who wrote the Declaration of Independence?
   A. John Adams
   B. Thomas Jefferson
   C. George Washington

10. If both the president and the vice president can no longer serve, who becomes president?
    A. Senate majority leader
    B. Secretary of State
    C. Speaker of the House

11. What is the name of the national anthem?
    A. "The Star-Spangled Banner"
    B. "Stars and Stripes Forever"
    C. "This Land is Our Land"

12. The House of Representatives has how many voting members?
    A. 50
    B. 100
    C. 435

[Answers: 1. b 2. a 3. a 4. a 5. b 6. b 7. c 8. b 9. b 10. c 11. a 12. c]

An appreciation for cultural diversity is a good thing, right? What could be wrong with learning about other cultures, other ways of living, of looking? Well, maybe plenty. Read this witty story in which a mother describes the "celebration" of Cultural Diversity Month at her daughter's preschool.

This story first appeared in the National Review *in 1997.*

THEY'VE GOT TO BE CAREFULLY TAUGHT

Susan Brady Konig

1   At my daughter's preschool it's time for all the children to learn that they are different from one another. Even though these kids are at that remarkable age when they are thoroughly color blind, their teachers are spending a month emphasizing race, color, and background. The little tots are being taught in no uncertain terms that their hair is different, their skin is different, and their parents come from different places. It's Cultural Diversity Month.

2   I hadn't really given much thought to the ethnic and national backgrounds of Sarah's classmates. I can guarantee that Sarah, being two and a half, gave the subject absolutely no thought. Her teachers, however, had apparently given it quite a lot of thought. They sent a letter asking each parent to contribute to the cultural-awareness effort by "providing any information and/or material regarding your family's cultural background. For example: favorite recipe or song." All well and good, unless your culture isn't *diverse* enough.

3   The next day I take Sarah to school and her teacher, Miss Laura, anxious to get this Cultural Diversity show on the road, begins the interrogation.

4   "Where are you and your husband from?" she cheerily demands.

5   "We're Americans," I reply—less, I must confess, out of patriotism than from sheer lack of coffee. It was barely 9:00 a.m.

6   "Yes, of course, but where are you *from?*" I'm beginning to feel like a night-club patron being badgered by a no-talent stand-up comic.

7   "We're native New Yorkers."

8   "But where are your *people* from?"

9   "Well," I dive in with a sigh, "my family is originally Irish on both sides. My husband's father was from Czechoslovakia and his mother is from the Bronx, but her grandparents were from Ukraine."

10   "Can you cook Irish?"

11   "I could bring in potatoes and beer for the whole class."

12   Miss Laura doesn't get it.

13   "Look," I say, "we're Americans. Our kids are Americans. We tell them about American history and George Washington and apple pie and all that stuff. If you want me to do something American, I can do that."

14   She is decidedly unexcited.

15   A few days later, she tells me that she was trying to explain to Sarah that her dad is from Ireland.

"Wrong," I say, "but go on."   16

"He's *not* from Ireland?"   17

No, I sigh. He's from Queens. I'm from Ireland. I mean I'm Irish—that   18
is my great-grandparents were. Don't get me wrong. I'm proud of my heritage—but that's entirely beside the point. I told you we tell Sarah she's American.

"Well, anyway," she smiles, "Sarah thinks her Daddy's from *Iceland!* Isn't that   19
cute?"

Later in the month, Miss Laura admits that her class is not quite getting the   20
whole skin-color thing. "I tried to show them how we all have different skin," she chuckled. Apparently, little Henry is the only one who successfully grasped the concept. He now runs around the classroom announcing to anyone who'll listen, "I'm white!" Miss Laura asked the children what color her own skin was. (She is a light-skinned Hispanic, which would make her skin color . . . what? Caramel? Mochaccino?). The kids opted for purple or orange. "They looked at me like I was crazy!" Miss Laura said. I just smile.

The culmination of Cultural Diversity Month, the day when the parents   21
come into class and join their children in a glorious celebration of multicultural disparity, has arrived. As I arrive I see a large collage on the wall depicting the earth, with all the children's names placed next to the country they are from. Next to my daughter's name it says "Ireland." I politely remind Miss Laura that Sarah is, in fact, from America and suggest that, by insisting otherwise, she is confusing my daughter. She reluctantly changes Sarah's affiliation to USA. It will be the only one of its kind on the wall.

The mom from Brazil brings in a bunch of great music, and the whole class   22
is doing the samba and running around in a conga line. It's very cute. Then I get up to teach the children an indigenous folk tune from the culture of Sarah's people, passed down through the generations from her grandparents to her parents and now to Sarah—a song called "Take Me Out to the Ballgame." First I explain to the kids that Sarah was born right here in New York—and that's in what country, Sarah? Sarah looks at me and says, "France." I look at Miss Laura, who just shrugs.

I stand there in my baseball cap and sing my song. The teacher tries to rush   23
me off. I say, "Don't you want them to learn it?" They took long enough learning to samba! I am granted permission to sing it one more time. The kids join in on the "root, root, root" and the "1, 2, 3 strikes you're out," but they can see their teacher isn't enthusiastic.

So now these sweet, innocent babies who thought they were all the same are   24
becoming culturally aware. Two little girls are touching each other's hair and saying, "Your hair is blonde, just like mine." Off to one side a little dark-haired girl stands alone, excluded. She looks confused as to what to do next. She knows she's not blonde. Sure, all children notice these things eventually, but, thanks to the concerted efforts of their teachers, these two- and three-year-olds are talking about things that separate rather than connect.

25   And Sarah only knows what she has been taught: Little Henry is white, her daddy's from Iceland, and New York's in France.

Vocabulary

Directions: Locate each of the key words in the reading selection. Try to figure out each word's meaning by using the context. Confirm your guess by checking the dictionary or thesaurus. Write the meanings of the words in the margin of the text. Then record the meanings in the following chart.

Key Word	Paragraph	Meaning
1. badgered	6	
2. opted	20	
3. culmination	21	
4. disparity	21	
5. indigenous	22	
6. concerted	24	
Others?		

Guide Questions

Directions: These questions will guide your understanding of what you have read. Write your answers in your notebook, or on a separate sheet of paper if your instructor wishes to collect it. Your answers to these questions will be the basis of class discussion.

1. Ms. Konig and Miss Laura are obviously engaged in a disagreement about Cultural Diversity Month.
   a. What do you think are the school and teacher's goals in promoting Cultural Diversity Month?
   b. Why is Ms. Konig bothered by the Cultural Diversity Month activities?
2. What do you think Sarah learned from the activities during Cultural Diversity Month?
3. Your reaction? Write three or four sentences.

Application/Writing
Directions: Choose one of the following questions.

1. The title of this story is an allusion (a reference) to a well-known song from the musical *South Pacific,* written by Rodgers and Hammerstein in 1949 and presented thousands of times over the years. The name of the song is "You've Got to Be Carefully Taught." Go to the Internet and find the lyrics of the song (one site is <http://www.lyricskeeper.com/south_pacific_soundtrack-lyrics.htm>). Read the lyrics and think about this question: Do you agree with the ideas in the song? Write one or two paragraphs expressing your opinion.

2. Write a letter from Miss Laura to the mother in the story. In your letter, explain the reasons for Cultural Diversity Month and why Miss Laura thinks it is a good idea.

COLLABORATIVE LEARNING

Working in Groups to Guide Your Own Reading

All of the reading selections so far in this unit have been accompanied by questions and exercises that are meant to help you understand and use what you've read. However, in much of your college reading (not to mention in your real life), you will be expected to master the material on your own.

Research has shown that one of the most effective ways to learn is in *groups*. In college, working with classmates can help you to master the material of a college course. The give-and-take that comes naturally when working with other people helps us to avoid falling into bad habits like *passive reading*. (We have all had the awful experience of reading a whole chapter, then realizing that we don't remember one single thing we've read.) Working with other students will help you to avoid such problems. For this assignment, form groups of approximately four students. In your group, read and think about the two following reading selections: "Indian Companies are Adding Western Flavor" by Saritha Rai and "Muslim American Teens Search for Identity" by Robin Riccitiello and Karen Breslav. Then, create your own vocabulary chart, guide questions, and application and writing assignments.

Follow these steps to complete this assignment:

1. Preview the selection before you read—look at and think about the title, any headings or subheadings, the first paragraph, the last paragraph, and the first sentence of each paragraph.
2. Read through the selection one time quickly.
3. Read the selection a second time, more carefully. This time mark the text. Review how to do this by turning to page 413, "Learning Strategy III—Marking Text."
4. Brainstorm with your group. Ask yourselves: What important issues is the author discussing? What new information did you learn? Can the issues discussed in the selection be connected to those you have already studied? Can any of the information here be applied to situations in your own life?
5. Now, create a set of exercises similar to those you have completed in previous chapters of this book:
   a. **Vocabulary**. Make a list of key words from the text. Set them up in chart format as on page 61.
   b. **Guide Questions**. Write questions that will guide understanding of the major ideas in the reading.
   c. **Application**. Prepare an application exercise that takes one or more of the important ideas in the reading and relates it to real life.
   d. **Writing**. Create a writing assignment to conclude the chapter.

Before you begin, it would be a good idea to review the questions and exercises in the previous reading selections in this book for reference.

When you are finished, submit your work to your instructor. Your instructor may review and combine the work of all the groups and return the exercise to the class. You will then have the opportunity to answer the questions you and your classmates have developed.

Now, use your skills as an active, independent reader to tackle the following reading selections. Good luck!

As more and more technology jobs move to India, China, and other countries, foreign employees are realizing it is not enough to be well-trained in the job and to be fluent in English. It is essential to "speak" the culture as well.

This article appeared in The New York Times *in 2003.*

INDIAN COMPANIES ARE ADDING WESTERN FLAVOR

Saritha Rai

Arun Kumar had never shaken hands with a foreigner nor needed to wear a necktie. He vaguely thought that raising a toast had something to do with eating bread. If it was dark outside, he greeted people with a "good night."   1

But Mr. Kumar, 27, and six other engineers graduating from the local university with master's degrees in computer applications, were recently recruited by the Hyderabad offices of Sierra Atlantic, a software company based in Fremont, California. And before they came face to face with one of Sierra's 200 or so American customers, the new employees went through a grueling four-week training session aimed at providing them with global-employee skills like learning how to speak on a conference call, how to address colleagues (as Mr. or Ms.) and how to sip wine properly. "Teetotalers practice by sipping Coke out of their wine glasses," Mr. Kumar said at the session in early July.   2

As more and more service- and knowledge-intensive jobs migrate to India, such training programs, covering some substance as well as style, are increasingly common at companies with large numbers of Indian employees. It is particularly imperative for employees of software companies to appear culturally seamless with Americans. American clients account for more than two-thirds of India's software and services export revenues.   3

Sierra Atlantic, a midsize software services company, says that one-fourth of its 400 employees, all but a handful of them Indian and most of them working out of the Hyderabad offices, are constantly interacting with foreigners. For Sierra and others, the training in Western ways is intended not only to help employees perform daily business interactions with American or European colleagues and customers but to help the companies transcend their image as cheap labor.   4

Mr. Kumar is typical of the thousands of eager young engineering graduates. Though he and his peers are technologically adept and fluent in English, most lack the sophistication needed to flourish in a global business setting. "It is not always understood that speaking a common language, English, is rarely a guarantee of communicating the same way," said Partha Iyengar, vice president for research at Gartner India Research and Advisory Services.   5

"Your interaction with people of alien cultures will only increase," Col. Gowri Shankar, a 30-year veteran of the Indian Army and Sierra's trainer, told   6

Mr. Kumar and half a dozen other young engineers that morning in July, "and you should be equally at ease whether in Hyderabad or Houston."

7   The Sierra programmers listened raptly as Colonel Shankar listed common complaints: speaking one of India's many languages in front of foreigners, questioning colleagues about their compensation and cracking ethnic jokes. Some things he covers are not acceptable in any corporate setting and some are particular sore points with foreigners. He is fiendish about punctuality and a stickler for protocol.

8   "Americans are friendly, but do not slap an American on his back or call him by his first name in the first meeting," said Colonel Shankar, whose training materials are fine-tuned by information from programmers returning from trips abroad.

9   Across the world, Global Savvy, a consulting company in Palo Alto, California, trains high-tech employees to work together in projects around the world. "The training in American culture is not to make Indian software professionals less Indian," said Lu Ellen Schafer, the executive director. "It is to make them more globally competent."

10   "As an aggregate, Indian software professionals have not changed in the way they present themselves," said Peter Nag, vice president and global program management officer for Lehman Brothers in New York, which is a client of Wipro. "We find that Indians hesitate to say no even though we ask them all the time to speak their minds. Then there are small things, like getting up from the seat when a senior colleague enters the room. This feels strange."

11   Still, some companies training their employees say they are already seeing the benefits. Sierra said that in February its Indian unit won a bid against a technically able Indian competitor because the Sierra employees were seen as a better fit. "It all adds up to better rates and bigger projects," said the project leader, Kalyani Manda.

12   Ms. Manda said she noticed a difference when she herself conformed, even in a seemingly minor way. On her first trip to the United States three years ago, she wore a salwar kameez, a loose-fitting Indian garment, and felt totally out of place. "On the next trip," she said, "I wore pants, fitted in better and delivered more."

Vocabulary

Directions: Mark any important words in the reading selection that you don't know. Then list them in the chart below along with their paragraph numbers. Try to figure out each word's meaning by reading over the context carefully for clues to help you guess the meaning of the unfamiliar word. Check your dictionary to confirm your guess. After discussing the word with your group members, write the meanings in the margin of the text, near the word. Then enter them in the following chart as well.

Key Word	Paragraph	Meaning

Guide Questions

Directions: Create a list of questions that elicit the important ideas in the reading selection. Start at the beginning and work your way sequentially through the text until you have dealt with all of the author's major ideas.

Application

Directions: When you have a list of guide questions, read through the reading selection again. This time, write one or more questions that require application of the information in the text to a new situation or perhaps to your own life.

Writing

Directions: Your last task is to create a writing assignment. For example, you might ask for a reaction to one or more of the ideas in the reading selection—but be sure to write directions that are related specifically to the ideas in this article.

A generation of Muslim American children is facing the challenge of navigating between the demands of their faith and their desire to fit into the broader culture. This essay, which appeared on Newsweek's MSNBC.com Website describes how they cope.

MUSLIM AMERICAN TEENS SEARCH FOR IDENTITY
Robin Riccitiello and Karen Breslau

1   Saba Anees fits her observance of Islam seamlessly into her jam-packed teenage schedule. The 16-year-old high-school junior from Sunnyvale, Calif.—an aspiring fashion editor—has tailored her headscarf for tennis practice. She chats with friends online, under the watchful eye of her Pakistani immigrant parents. Anees makes time for her mosque youth group, despite the pressures of classes, homework and social pursuits—in part to please her parents, who work in Silicon Valley's high-tech industry. Confident and outspoken, she has learned that being Muslim in America often means being an ambassador for the faith, even when the questions are anything but diplomatic. "When I started high school a boy asked, 'Do you wear that scarf to hide your bruises?'" she says. "People expect you to be abused or something."

2   It fell to Anees, then 14, to explain that adhering to Islam's modest dress code for women "doesn't mean you're kept back by men." Her mother, after all, works as an analytical chemist for a pharmaceutical company and would like to see her daughter become a lawyer someday. But dealing with misconceptions is only part of the challenge for observant Muslim teens. Navigating the risks and temptations of American pop culture—whether racy music, dating or having an account on Facebook—can be far trickier. "Parents who didn't grow up here aren't used to teenagers who have their own lives," says Sarah Azad, a volunteer youth group leader at the Muslim Community Center Association (MCA) of Silicon Valley, where Anees and her family attend. "The No. 1 complaint I hear from parents is not that their children aren't religious, but that they spend too much time on the computer."

3   The lament is hardly unique to Muslim parents. But for a generation of Muslim children, learning to walk the line between the demands of their faith and their desire to fit into the local culture is part of a broader identity search. Each Friday evening, Anees and a group of teenage girls meet at the MCA mosque with Azad, who squeezes time from her grueling schedule as a first-year medical resident, and another counselor to vent—and to give each other support. For the younger generation, Azad says the main complaint is that immigrant parents can't understand what it means to grow up as a minority in a culture where values are far different from those their parents experienced growing up in India, Pakistan, Syria or Morocco. It's a dilemma Azad understands well. The daughter of Afghan immigrants, she grew up in St. Louis, answering the same questions about Islam—having the same struggles with her parents, that the girls do now.

4   Sometimes, the accommodations are easy. Yousur Alhlou, 17, a high-school senior, who was born in Oklahoma, says it's not hard to find music that won't offend her—or her Syrian-born parents. She likes Coldplay and sometimes just switches to

news radio when she can't find music she considers appropriate. "Anees convinced her parents to lighten up by downloading a Carrie Underwood song from iTunes. Country music, with its clean lyrics, seems to be a safe middle ground.

But dating, or even mingling unsupervised with boys, is an entirely different matter. Courtship and marriage are considered by many Muslims to be a social negotiation involving families, not just a would-be couple themselves. During high school and college, Muslim girls are expected to socialize with other girls. Alhlou, a 17-year-old senior, has many non-Muslim friends who organize all-girl movie outings so she can join them. The public high school Alhlou attends in San Jose has so many Muslim students that on prom night, the organizers rented an extra room so that Muslim girls could have their own dance space—a compromise that allows them to both have fun and remain observant. Alhlou cracks up the group with her story of a classmate who asked if he would have to marry her because he saw her hair come loose from her hijab. "I told him, 'Yeah.' The poor guy got so scared." 5

Fitting into American jock culture has proven surprisingly easy. Mounia O'Neal, the daughter of a Moroccan mother and an American father, plays tennis and runs track in her hijab. Others play volleyball and basketball and field hockey in long pants instead of shorts, often laughing at the distraction their headscarves can provoke among opposing players. Saadia Hameed, one of the youth-group leaders, tells the girls how she snorkels and goes scuba-diving wearing a hijab and a modest swim outfit specially designed for Muslim women. Every now and then, someone at her local health club will ask about her getup. "If I'm not running on the treadmill, I'll explain things—that it's a sign of modesty," says Hameed, who plans to become a school psychologist. 6

The defining moment of their young Muslim lives continues to be 9/11. O'Neal, then a fourth-grader, cried along with her classmates on the day of the attacks. Soon though, she remembers that other children started echoing their parents' fears and a young Muslim boy running for student council found the word "terrorist"—spelled wrong—written in green crayon all over his campaign posters. Saba Anees says her Muslim elementary school had to shut down for a week because it received so many threats. But, as it did for their parents, the attacks spurred many young people to deepen their commitment to Islam. After 9/11, says O'Neal, 14, "I felt I have more of a duty to be myself and wear a hijab and become more of a Muslim, so I can represent Islam the right way." 7

Despite the challenges, for the girls at the MCA mosque, identifying as both Muslim and American has proven easier than for their parents. Saba Anees has spent nearly her whole life in America and worries that she'd feel like a stranger in Pakistan. "I feel like sometimes I can't connect to the Pakistani culture as much anymore. If I were to go back and try to speak Urdu, they'd be like, 'What are you doing?'" Visiting their parents' countries can bring up interesting conflicts, especially when relatives in the home country are not as observant as the American teens. Some of Yousour Alhlou's relatives in Syria don't wear a hijab, and they smoke. The relatives assume that the American girls don't strictly follow Islam. "I get the occasional, 'So, do you wear a scarf? How many boyfriends do you have?'" 8

Alhlou says. "Some things I do more religiously than they even do. But even if you tell them that, I get doubtful looks and 'Yeah, right.' They think we worship Britney Spears!"

9   As if.

Vocabulary

Directions: Mark any important words in the reading selection that you don't know. Then list them in the chart below along with their paragraph numbers. Try to figure out each word's meaning by reading over the context carefully for clues to help you guess the meaning of the unfamiliar word. Check your dictionary to confirm your guess. After discussing the word with your group members, write the meanings in the margin of the text, near the word. Then enter them in the following chart as well.

Key Word	Paragraph	Meaning

Guide Questions

Directions: Create a list of questions that elicit the important ideas in the reading selection. Start at the beginning and work your way sequentially through the text until you have dealt with all of the author's major ideas.

Application

Directions: When you have a list of guide questions, read through the reading selection again. This time, write one or more questions that require application of the information in the text to a new situation or perhaps to your own life.

Writing

Directions: Your last task is to create a writing assignment. For example, you might ask your classmates to write a paragraph commenting on the ideas in the reading selection—but be sure to write directions that are specific to the ideas in the reading selection. Make sure your classmates know what to do.

SPECIAL PROJECT

Exploring Your Own Culture

How much do you know about your own culture? As you have seen in the readings in this unit of the text, every culture has its own set of traditions and beliefs. Investigate your roots by interviewing older family members and friends and by reading about your culture in the library.

Describe the rituals and traditions associated with

1. the birth of a child
2. a wedding
3. a funeral
4. a special holiday or event

Visit the library and use the Internet to find materials describing the traditions of your culture. List the books, periodicals, and other references you find at the end of your report.

Your report should consist of four sections. Give a title to each section; for example, you might name your first section "The Birth of a Child in Mexico." Then describe the rituals surrounding this event. For example, you may answer questions such as the following: Is it customary to have a party to celebrate the birth of a baby? Do friends and family bring gifts? Is a special type of gift traditional? Are special foods prepared? How long does the celebration last? Is the baby given a name at this time? How is the name chosen? Is special clothing worn? If there are other features to your culture's celebration, include them. Does your own family have any special customs?

Do the same with the other three sections of your report: a wedding, a funeral, a special holiday or event.

At the end of your report, include a list of references. Think of this list as a resource for someone who would like to learn more about your culture and its traditions.

UNIT THREE

READING AND THINKING ABOUT LANGUAGE

All words are pegs to hang ideas on.

—Henry Ward Beecher

{It} is only through language that we enter fully into our human estate and culture, communicate freely with our fellows, acquire and share information. If we cannot do this, we will be bizarrely disabled and cut off—whatever our desires, or endeavors, or native capacities.

—Oliver Sacks

Thinking about Language

Before you begin this part of the text, think about and answer these questions.

1. What is language? Write your own definition.
2. Do animals have language? If so, is it the same as human language? In what ways is it the same? In what ways is it different?
3. Many linguists, the people who study language, believe humans began using language about 50,000 years ago. Before then, they relied on crude gestures and sounds for what communication did go on. Try to imagine that you are a "cave man" or a "cave woman." What are some gestures, signs, or sounds you would use to communicate?
4. How would your life be different if humans had never developed language? Imagine some of the events of a typical day and describe how you would communicate what you need to say, without words.

Everyone has a very personal interest in language. Because it is all around us and within us, too, we all feel that language belongs to us. And all of us, bank presidents, farmers, secretaries, and traffic cops, are language experts even though we don't often stop to think about it.

Before you read this selection, take a moment to think about language—its definition and its meaning in your life.

LANGUAGE

Mary Fjeldstad

Defining Language

1   What is language? If you asked five different people, you would probably get five different answers. So, before we can talk about language, we need to agree on its definition. Let's construct a definition by listing the *characteristics* of language. First, the most basic characteristic of language is that it is a means of *communication*. Language is what we use to get through the day, to buy a newspaper, order a cup of coffee, ask for directions on the street, or decide on a movie. Language lets us think about our desire for a better life, the love we feel for our family, the vacation we plan to take, and the sadness at the death of a friend. Language lets us dream about things that never were, and perhaps never will be. You can imagine a werewolf or a vampire because you have the language for it, even though such a thing never existed. If you see a picture of a handsome or beautiful person, you can imagine or talk about meeting such a person in your future because you have language. The past and the future can be just as great a part of your reality as the present—because of language.

2   Without language we would be isolated from our fellow humans. Human societies as we know them never would have formed without language; cultures never would have developed. Language is essentially what made human civilization possible. It is language that has allowed us to produce literature, music, mathematics, and science. Language has allowed us to transmit knowledge, the sum of our stored experience in spoken or written form, from one generation to the next. Without language, life as we know it would not be possible.

Language Consists of Symbols

3   A second major characteristic of language is that it consists of *symbols.* A symbol is something that represents something else. A person can be a symbol. For example, Martin Luther King Jr. stood for nonviolent opposition to racial discrimination. The Pope is a symbol of the Catholic church. *Gestures,* like the clenched fist, or a facial expression like a smile or a frown, can be symbols of attitudes or moods. *Objects* can be symbols. In the United States a woman may wear a diamond ring on her left hand as a symbol of her engagement to a man; in the Fiji Islands young women wore hibiscus flowers behind their ears to symbolize the fact they were in love.

But *words* are also symbols. The word *hamburger* is a symbol for that item of food Americans so love to eat, and while the word may set our mouths to watering, we do not start chewing on the word—we must wait until the thing it symbolizes is cooked and on the plate.   4

We live in two worlds at the same time: the real (or physical) world—the world we can see and touch and smell and taste—and the verbal (or symbolic) world—where we use language to name and talk about and think about all the things we experience in the physical world.   5

Imagine what it would be like if you did not have the ease of words or symbols to communicate with other people. Your conversation would be limited to the objects, or persons, or events actually present in your physical world at that moment in the conversation. People have long been fascinated by this notion of language as symbols. The writer Jonathan Swift, in his famous satire, *Gulliver's Travels,* plays with the possibility of nonsymbolic words: 6

> [This] was urged as a great advantage in point of health as well as brevity. For it is plain that every word we speak is, in some degree, a diminution of our lungs by corrosion, and consequently contributes to the shortening of our lives. An expedient was therefore offered that since words are only names for things it would be more convenient for all men to carry about with them such things as were necessary to express a particular business they are to discourse [speak] on. . . . Many of the most learned and wise adhere to the new scheme of expressing themselves by things, which has only this inconvenience attending it, that, if a man's business be very great, and of various kinds, he must be obliged, in proportion, to carry a greater bundle of things upon his back unless he can afford one or two strong servants to attend him. I have often beheld two of these sages [wise men] almost sinking under the weight of their packs, like peddlers among us; who, when they meet in the street, would lay down their loads, open their packs, hold conversation for an hour, and then put up their implements, help each other to resume their burdens, and take their leave.

Swift's comical description makes the importance of symbols in language clear—just imagine if the people in his story wished to talk about an elephant or the Empire State Building!   7

Is Language Unique to Humans?

People have long speculated that animals have their own languages, and of course many animals do communicate with one another. Birds use sounds to warn other birds of danger or to announce "ownership" of a particular tree. Bees "dance" to inform other bees of food sources. Velvet monkeys make sounds that signal the proximity of predators. Certainly many pet owners swear that their dog or cat "talks" to them and understands them when they talk. But none of these examples of communication will fit our definition of language, because they are not *symbolic;* that is, none has a one-to-one correlation to a specific object or concept.   8

9   Several years ago there was great excitement among language researchers when it was shown that the great apes (especially chimpanzees) could learn language to some extent. While they do not have the physical apparatus necessary for speech, apes do have the ability to understand the meanings of words as symbols for things and relationships. Apes have been taught a limited number of words through sign language and through the use of typewriters and other devices. A gorilla named Koko was taught more than 300 words in American Sign Language. To the surprise of most scientists, she also was able to "invent" new words and phrases, a skill that was previously believed to be uniquely human. For example, she invented sign words for *ring* ("finger bracelet") and *mask* ("eye hat"). She was even able to use sign words to refer to abstract ideas, such as pain and fear. Although the success of Koko and other apes encouraged many scientists to believe that these animals are capable of sophisticated human language, it soon became apparent that the apes' abilities are severely limited. No ape has ever progressed beyond the level of that of a two-and-a-half-year-old child. Nor can apes produce sentences of more than two words. Human language, on the other hand, allows us to communicate an infinite number of thoughts and to preserve these thoughts over long periods of time and distance.

10   Language allows us to step out beyond the confinement of the immediate present. It means that people can, for example, talk about food to eat at the present time as well as food tomorrow and food yesterday. If you believe that your dog has a humanlike language ability to communicate, try to talk to Spot about "dog food tomorrow." Another example is the important symbol of the personal name. While it seems clear that dogs understand names—their own, their masters', and others—they do not understand them in the same way humans do. If you say to Spot, "Sam is at work," how does Spot react? He will look for Sam, understanding *Sam* only as an immediate sign, exactly as he would react to his master's voice or the sound of his footsteps at the door. A human, on the other hand, will probably ask you something like, "When is Sam coming home?" or "How does he like his job?" or any of thousands of other thoughts that were stimulated by the symbol *Sam.* All of these thoughts are forever beyond the capabilities of the dog.

Symbols Are Not the Events They Symbolize

11   When you communicate with another person, you use symbols—words. However, the words you use to refer to objects, persons, events, situations, sensations, and feelings are not those *actual* objects, persons, events, situations, sensations, or feelings. For example, it is one thing to experience a toothache and quite another to comment, "I have a toothache." Those words merely refer to your pain, but there is no way the other person can experience your toothache.

12   Have you ever tried to think about something—anything—without using its name? As Peter Farb says, "Try to think about the stars, a grasshopper, love or hate, pain, anything at all—and it must be done in terms of language. There is no other way; thinking is language spoken to oneself. Until language has made sense of

experience, that experience is meaningless." Our ability to use the symbol system of language is the main thing that makes us different from other animals.

Language Is Systematic

A third characteristic of language is that it is a *system*. That system is called *gram-*   13
mar. Grammar is a set of rules that defines how words may be combined. For example, because we know the grammar system of English, we understand the sentence *The man bit the dog* to mean one thing and *The dog bit the man* to mean something quite different. In both examples, the meanings of the five words are exactly the same. But the way they are combined changes the meaning of the sentence completely. Similarly, *The bit dog man the,* although using the same, easy-to-understand words, is meaningless—because it does not follow the rules of grammar we all carry around in our heads.

Language Is Limitless

The final characteristic of language is that it is infinitely creative. In fact, most   14
of the sentences we utter are original; that is, we have never heard or read them before in exactly the same form. As Steven Pinker says in his book, *The Language Instinct,* "Go into the Library of Congress and pick a sentence at random from any volume, and chances are you would fail to find an exact repetition no matter how long you continued to search. Estimates of the number of sentences that an ordinary person is capable of producing are breathtaking."

Definition of Language

To conclude, let's review the characteristics of language we have discussed: Lan-   15
guage is communication. Language is symbolic. Language is systematic. Language is infinitely creative.

Now we can write our definition: *Language is an infinitely creative system of com-*   16
munication, consisting of symbols. Compare this definition to the one you wrote at the beginning of this selection, and think about what you've learned as you study the rest of this unit.

Vocabulary

Directions: Find each of the key words in the reading selection. Study each word in its context and try to determine its meaning. Write what you think it means in the margin of the text, near the word. Then read over the sentence, mentally substituting your guess for the key word. Does the sentence still make sense? Does it retain its original meaning? If it does, you've probably figured out the meaning of the key word correctly. In any case, confirm your guess by checking a dictionary or thesaurus.

If you take your meaning from a dictionary or thesaurus, be sure the definition includes words you already know and feel comfortable using. If it doesn't, you will be worse off than when you started—you will have begun with one word you didn't know and ended with *two* words you don't know!

Record the new words you've learned in the following chart.

Key Word	Paragraph	Meaning
1. satire	6	
2. adhere	6	
3. speculated	8	
4. predators	8	
5. infinitely	14	
Others?		

Guide Questions

Directions: These questions will guide your understanding of what you have read. Your thoughtful answers will ensure that you have understood the main ideas the author wanted to convey. Some of the questions require you simply to find the stated facts in the reading selection; others will ask you to do more difficult tasks, such as paraphrasing information (putting the author's ideas into your own words), synthesizing several ideas into one complex thought, evaluating (making judgments about) an idea, or taking information from the reading and applying it to a new situation or to your own life.

Write answers to the questions in your notebook or on a separate sheet of paper if your instructor wishes to collect them. Your answers will form the basis of class discussion.

1. Define *symbol* and give some examples of symbols.
2. In the excerpt from Jonathan Swift's classic novel *Gulliver's Travels,* people supposedly believed speaking corroded their lungs and shortened their lives. So they decided it would be better for their health to stop using words, the symbols of things, and carry around the things themselves. Assume you did this in school tomorrow. What things would you have to carry with you? Imagine your participation in class, or a conversation with a friend in the cafeteria. What things would you pull out of your bag? How would you communicate your thoughts about those things without using any words? How would you feel about communicating like this? How does Swift's story reinforce the idea that words are symbols?
3. Do you agree with the statement made by the linguist Peter Farb in paragraph 12? Please explain.

4. Consider a famous example of two headlines of two different news stories:

Dog Bites Man
Man Bites Dog

Each headline contains exactly the same words. Why, then, do the sentences have two very different meanings? Can you invent a similar example?

5. Following are some strings of words that, while containing easily comprehensible English words, are in some way "not quite right." Consider each example, and explain why it does not make sense; that is, explain how it violates the rules of grammar.

This sentence no verb.
This book has contains six units.
Is raining.
The car was put in the.
Where did he put it the car?
Please say those little three words.

Can you invent some examples? Make up a "not quite right sentence" and show it to your classmates. See if they can figure out what is wrong.

Application

Work in groups to complete this exercise. Think of a simple everyday message you would like to convey to the members of another group in the class. Then try to communicate your message without using words.

Writing

Think about the exercise you did in the Application section. What difficulties did you have with communicating your message and understanding the messages of other groups? In a paragraph, describe your experience and how you felt about it. Relate your experience to what you learned when you read the selection "Language."

Marking Text

Turn to page 413, "Learning Strategy III—Marking Text." Read and study the information on how to mark your text. Then mark the selection "Language" using what you've learned. To get you started, here is a model of how you might mark the first few paragraphs of the selection. Finish marking it on your own.

LANGUAGE

Mary Fjeldstad

Defining Language

1 What is language? If you asked five different people, you would probably get five different answers. So, before we can talk about language, we need to agree on its definition. Let's construct a definition by listing the *characteristics* of language. First the most basic characteristic of language is that it is a means of *communication.* Language is what we use to get through the day, to buy a newspaper, order a cup of coffee, ask for directions on the street, or decide on a movie. Language lets us think about our desire for a better life, the love we feel for our family, the vacation we plan to take, and the sadness at the death of a friend. Language lets us dream about things that never were, and perhaps never will be. You can imagine a werewolf or a vampire because you have a name for it, even though such a thing never existed. If you see a picture of a handsome or beautiful person, you can imagine or talk about meeting such a person in your future because you have language. The past and the future can be just as great a part of your reality as the present—because of language.

1st characteristic of L: means of communication

2 Without language we would be isolated from our fellow humans. Human societies never would have formed without language; cultures never would have developed. Language is essentially what made human civilization possible. It is language that has allowed us to produce literature, music, mathematics, and science. Language has allowed us to transmit knowledge, the sum of our stored experience in spoken or written form, from one generation to the next. Without language, life as we know it would not be possible.

Importance of language to humans

Language Consists of Symbols

3 A second major characteristic of language is that it consists of *symbols*. A symbol is something that represents something else. A person can be a symbol. For example, Martin Luther King Jr. stood for nonviolent opposition to racial discrimination. The Pope is a symbol of the Catholic church. *Gestures,* like the clenched fist, or a facial expression like a smile or a frown, can be symbols of attitudes or moods. *Objects* can be symbols. In the United States a woman may wear a diamond ring on her left hand as a symbol of her engagement to a man; in the Fiji Islands young women wore hibiscus flowers behind their ears to symbolize the fact they were in love.

2nd characteristic: symbolic

Symbols can be
1—person
2—gesture
3—object
＊4—words

4 But *words* are also symbols. The word *hamburger* is a symbol for that item of food Americans so love to eat, and while the word may set our mouths to watering, we do not start chewing on the word—we must wait until the thing it symbolizes is cooked and on the plate.

Now finish marking the essay on your own.

SHORT TAKE

Most Widely Spoken Languages in the World

Language	Approximate number of speakers
1. Chinese (Mandarin)	1,075,000,000
2. English	514,000,000
3. Hindustani[1]	496,000,000
4. Spanish	425,000,000
5. Russian	275,000,000
6. Arabic	256,000,000
7. Bengali	215,000,000
8. Portuguese	194,000,000
9. Malay–Indonesian	176,000,000
10. French	129,000,000

Source: *Ethnologue,* 13th ed., and other sources.

[1]Encompasses multiple dialects, including Hindi and Urdu.

Helen Keller was born in 1880. At the age of 19 months, she suffered an illness that left her both blind and deaf. Later she also became unable to speak. Her young years were indeed difficult as she raged against her forced isolation from the world, unable to communicate except by means of gestures and direct physical contact. Nevertheless, by age 24, she had graduated cum laude *from Radcliffe College, where, in addition to mastering all her other subjects, she learned many different languages, including Latin and Greek. She went on to write many books and travel the country giving inspirational speeches, many on behalf of the handicapped—all with the help of her dedicated teacher, Anne Sullivan, who came to her when Keller was seven. In this excerpt from her autobiography, Keller takes the first indispensable step to thought and to learning—realizing that words are symbols.*

In the Beginning was the Word.

—St. John

THE KEY TO LANGUAGE

Helen Keller

1 The morning after my teacher came she led me into her room and gave me a doll. The little blind children at the Perkins Institution had sent it and Laura Bridgman had dressed it; but I did not know this until afterward.

2 When I had played with it a little while, Miss Sullivan slowly spelled into my hand the word "d-o-l-l." I was at once interested in this finger play and tried to imitate it. When I finally succeeded in making the letters correctly I was flushed with childish pleasure and pride. Running downstairs to my mother I held up my hands and made the letters for doll. I did not know that I was spelling a word or even that words existed; I was simply making my fingers go in monkey-like imitation. In the days that followed I learned to spell in this uncomprehending way a great many words, among them *pin, hat, cup,* and a few verbs like *sit, stand,* and *walk.* But my teacher had been with me several weeks before I understood that everything has a name.

3 One day, while I was playing with my new doll, Miss Sullivan put my big rag doll into my lap also, spelled "d-o-l-l" and tried to make me understand that "d-o-l-l" applied to both. Earlier in the day we had had a tussle over the words "m-u-g" and "w-a-t-e-r." Miss Sullivan had tried to impress it upon me that "m-u-g" is *mug* and "w-a-t-e-r" is *water,* but I persisted in confounding the two. In despair she had dropped the subject for the time only to renew it at the first opportunity. I became impatient at her repeated attempts and, seizing the new doll, I dashed it upon the floor. . . .

4 We walked down the path to the well-house, attracted by the fragrance of the honeysuckle with which it was covered. Someone was drawing water and my teacher placed my hand under the spout. As the cool stream gushed over one

hand she spelled into the other the word *water,* first slowly, then rapidly. I stood still, my whole attention fixed upon the motions of her fingers. Suddenly I felt a misty consciousness, as of something forgotten—a thrill of returning thought; and somehow the mystery of language was revealed to me. I knew then that "w-a-t-e-r" meant the wonderful cool something that was flowing over my hand. That living word awakened my soul, gave it light, hope, joy, set it free. There were barriers still, it is true, but barriers that could, in time, be swept away.

I left the well-house eager to learn. Everything had a name and each name   5 gave birth to a new thought. As we returned to the house every object which I touched seemed to quiver with life. That was because I saw everything with the strange, new sight that had come to me. On entering the door I remembered the doll I had broken. I felt my way to the hearth and picked up the pieces. I vainly tried to put them together. Then my eyes filled with tears; for I realized what I had done, and for the first time I felt repentance and sorrow.

I learned a great many new words that day. I do not remember what they all   6 were; but I do know that *mother, father, sister, teacher* were among them—words that were to make the world blossom for me, "like Aaron's rod, with flowers." It would have been difficult to find a happier child than I was as I lay in my crib at the close of that eventful day and lived over the joys it had brought me, and, for the first time, longed for a new day to come. . . .

I had now the key to all language and I was eager to learn to use it. Children   7 who hear acquire language without any particular effort; the words that fall from others' lips they catch on the wing, as it were, delightedly, while the little deaf child must trap them by a slow and often painful process. But whatever the process, the result is wonderful. Gradually, from naming an object we advance step by step until we have traversed the vast distance between our first stammered syllable and the sweep of thought in a line of Shakespeare.

At first, when my teacher told me about a new thing I asked very few ques-   8 tions. My ideas were vague, and my vocabulary was inadequate, but as my knowledge of things grew, and I learned more and more words, my field of inquiry broadened, and I would return again and again to the same subject, eager for further information. Sometimes a new word revived an image that some earlier experiences had engraved on my brain.

I remember the morning that I first asked the meaning of the word *love.* This   9 was before I knew many words. I had found a few early violets in the garden and brought them to my teacher. She tried to kiss me; but at that time I did not like to have anyone kiss me except my mother. Miss Sullivan put her arm gently around me and spelled into my hand "I love Helen."

"What is love?" I asked.   10

She drew me closer to her and said, "It is here," pointing to my heart, whose   11 beats I was conscious of for the first time. Her words puzzled me very much because I did not then understand anything unless I touched it.

I smelt the violets in her hand and asked, half in words, half in signs, a ques-   12 tion which means, "Is love the sweetness of flowers?"

"No," said my teacher.   13

14   Again I thought. The warm sun was shining on us.

15   "Is this not love?" I asked, pointing in the direction from which the heat came, "Is this not love?"

16   It seemed to me that there could be nothing more beautiful than the sun, whose warmth makes all things grow. But Miss Sullivan shook her head, and I was greatly puzzled and disappointed. I thought it strange that my teacher could not show me love.

17   A day or two afterward I was stringing beads of different sizes in symmetrical groups—two large beads, three small ones, and so on. I had made many mistakes, and Miss Sullivan had pointed them out again and again with gentle patience. Finally I noticed a very obvious error in the sequence and, for an instant, I concentrated my attention on the lesson and tried to think how I should have arranged the beads. Miss Sullivan touched my forehead and spelled with decided emphasis, "Think."

18   In a flash, I knew that the word was the name of the process that was going on in my head. This was my first conscious perception of an abstract idea.

Vocabulary

Directions: Locate each of the key words in the reading selection. Then read and study each word in its context and try to determine its meaning. Use a dictionary or thesaurus to check your guess. Write the meanings of the words in the margin of the text.

Record the new words you've learned in the following chart.

Key Word	Paragraph	Meaning
1. quiver	5	
2. hearth	5	
3. vainly	5	
4. repentance	5	
5. symmetrical	17	
Others?		

Guide Questions

Directions: These questions will guide your understanding of what you have read. They also will help you to analyze and evaluate the author's ideas and apply them to the real world and your own life.

Write answers to the questions in your notebook or on a separate sheet of paper if your instructor wishes to collect them. Your answers will form the basis of class discussion.

1. Because most of us learned language at a very early age, we do not remember, nor were we old enough to comprehend, the power that the use of language gave to us. Describe the process that brought Keller to her exciting discovery that words are symbols.
2. Contrast the way hearing children learn language with the way deaf children learn it, according to Keller.
3. To Keller, was there a difference in learning that the word *doll* was a symbol for a doll and that the word *love* was a symbol for love? Explain why these are different concepts.

Application

Keller's discovery of the "key to language" was obviously a turning point in her life. Think about the turning points in your own life. What were they? What were their results? Describe one or more of the turning points in your life in a paragraph or two.

Writing

React to the fact that, despite her enormous handicaps, Keller managed to graduate from Radcliffe College and become a world-famous lecturer and scholar. Write a paragraph or two.

Making Connections

Return to the selection titled "Language" on page 152. What connections can you make between the information in "Language" and the story of Helen Keller's discovery of "The Key to Language"?

Amy Tan, the daughter of Chinese immigrants, was born and raised in California. Her first novel, The Joy Luck Club, *became an international favorite. Much of her writing focuses on the clash of Chinese and American cultures and on Tan's intense and complicated relationship with her mother. This essay first appeared in the* Threepenny Review *in 1989.*

MOTHER TONGUE

Amy Tan

1   I am not a scholar of English or literature. I cannot give you much more than personal opinions on the English language and its variations in this country or others.

2   I am a writer. And by that definition, I am someone who has always loved language. I am fascinated by language in daily life. I spend a great deal of my time thinking about the power of language—the way it can evoke an emotion, a visual image, a complex idea, or a simple truth. Language is the tool of my trade. And I use them all—all the Englishes I grew up with.

3   Recently, I was made keenly aware of the different Englishes I do use. I was giving a talk to a large group of people, the same talk I had already given to half a dozen other groups. The nature of the talk was about my writing, my life, and my book, *The Joy Luck Club.* The talk was going along well enough, until I remembered one major difference that made the whole talk sound wrong. My mother was in the room. And it was perhaps the first time she had heard me give a lengthy speech, using the kind of English I have never used with her. I was saying things like, "The intersection of memory upon imagination" and "There is an aspect of my fiction that relates to thus-and-thus"—a speech filled with carefully wrought grammatical phrases, burdened, it suddenly seemed to me, with nominalized forms, past perfect tenses, conditional phrases, all the forms of standard English that I had learned in school and through books, the forms of English I did not use at home with my mother.

4   Just last week, I was walking down the street with my mother, and I again found myself conscious of the English I was using, the English I do use with her. We were talking about the price of new and used furniture and I heard myself saying this: "Not waste money that way." My husband was with us as well, and he didn't notice any switch in my English. And then I realized why. It's because over the twenty years we've been together I've often used that same kind of English with him, and sometimes he even uses it with me. It has become our language of intimacy, a different sort of English that relates to family talk, the language I grew up with.

5   So you'll have some idea of what this family talk I heard sounds like, I'll quote what my mother said during a recent conversation which I videotaped and then transcribed. During this conversation, my mother was talking about a political gangster in Shanghai who had the same last name as her family's, Du, and how the gangster in his early years wanted to be adopted by her family, which

was rich by comparison. Later, the gangster became more powerful, far richer than my mother's family, and one day showed up at my mother's wedding to pay his respects. Here's what she said in part:

"Du Yusong having business like fruit stand. Like off the street kind. He is Du like Du Zong—but not Tsung-ming Island people. The local people call putong, the river east side, he belong to that side local people. That man want to ask Du Zong father take him in like become own family. Du Zong father wasn't look down on him, but didn't take seriously, until that man big like become a mafia. Now important person, very hard to inviting him. Chinese way, came only to show respect, don't stay for dinner. Respect for making big celebration, he shows up. Mean gives lots of respect. Chinese custom. Chinese social life that way. If too important won't have to stay too long. He come to my wedding. I didn't see, I heard it. I gone to boy's side, they have YMCA dinner. Chinese age I was nineteen."

You should know that my mother's expressive command of English belies how much she actually understands. She reads the *Forbes* report, listens to *Wall Street Week*, converses daily with her stockbroker, reads all of Shirley MacLaine's books with ease—all kinds of things I can't begin to understand. Yet some of my friends tell me they understand 50 percent of what my mother says. Some say they understand 80 to 90 percent. Some say they understand none of it, as if she were speaking pure Chinese. But to me, my mother's English is perfectly clear, perfectly natural. It's my mother tongue. Her language, as I hear it, is vivid, direct, full of observation and imagery. That was the language that helped shape the way I saw things, expressed things, made sense of the world.

Lately, I've been giving more thought to the kind of English my mother speaks. Like others, I have described it to people as "broken" or "fractured" English. But I wince when I say that. It has always bothered me that I can think of no way to describe it other than "broken," as if it were damaged and needed to be fixed, as if it lacked a certain wholeness and soundness. I've heard other terms used, "limited English," for example. But they seem just as bad, as if everything is limited, including people's perceptions of the limited English speaker.

I know this for a fact, because when I was growing up, my mother's "limited" English limited *my* perception of her. I was ashamed of her English. I believed that her English reflected the quality of what she had to say. That is, because she expressed them imperfectly her thoughts were imperfect. And I had plenty of empirical evidence to support me: the fact that people in department stores, at banks, and at restaurants did not take her seriously, did not give her good service, pretended not to understand her, or even acted as if they did not hear her.

My mother has long realized the limitations of her English as well. When I was fifteen, she used to have me call people on the phone to pretend I was she. In this guise, I was forced to ask for information or even to complain and yell at people who had been rude to her. One time it was a call to her stockbroker in New York. She had cashed out her small portfolio and it just so happened we were going to go to New York the next week, our very first trip outside California. I had to get on the phone and say in an adolescent voice that was not very convincing, "This is Mrs. Tan."

11   And my mother was standing in the back whispering loudly, "Why he don't send me check, already two weeks late. So mad he lie to me, losing me money."

12   And then I said in perfect English, "Yes, I'm getting rather concerned. You had agreed to send the check two weeks ago, but it hasn't arrived."

13   Then she began to talk more loudly. "What he want, I come to New York tell him front of his boss, you cheating me?" And I was trying to calm her down, make her be quiet, while telling the stockbroker, "I can't tolerate any more excuses. If I don't receive the check immediately, I am going to have to speak to your manager when I'm in New York next week." And sure enough, the following week there we were in front of this astonished stockbroker, and I was sitting there redfaced and quiet, and my mother, the real Mrs. Tan, was shouting at his boss in her impeccable broken English.

14   We used a similar routine just five days ago, for a situation that was far less humorous. My mother had gone to the hospital for an appointment, to find out about a benign brain tumor a CAT scan had revealed a month ago. She said she had spoken very good English, her best English, no mistakes. Still, she said, the hospital did not apologize when they said they had lost the CAT scan and she had come for nothing. She said they did not seem to have any sympathy when she told them she was anxious to know the exact diagnosis, since her husband and son had both died of brain tumors. She said they would not give her any more information until the next time and she would have to make another appointment for that. So she said she would not leave until the doctor called her daughter. She wouldn't budge. And when the doctor finally called her daughter, me, who spoke in perfect English—lo and behold—we had assurances the CAT scan would be found, promise that a conference call on Monday would be held, and apologies for any suffering my mother had gone through for a most regrettable mistake.

15   I think my mother's English almost had an effect on limiting my possibilities in life as well. Sociologists and linguists probably will tell you that a person's developing language skills are more influenced by peers. But I do think that the language spoken in the family, especially in immigrant families which are more insular, plays a large role in shaping the language of the child. And I believe that it affected my results on achievement tests, IQ tests, and the SAT. While my English skills were never judged as poor, compared to math, English could not be considered my strong suit. In grade school I did moderately well, getting perhaps B's, sometimes B-pluses, in English and scoring perhaps in the sixtieth or seventieth percentile on achievement tests. But those scores were not good enough to override the opinion that my true abilities lay in math and science, because in those areas I achieved A's and scored in the ninetieth percentile or higher.

16   This was understandable. Math is precise; there is only one correct answer. Whereas, for me at least, the answers on English tests were always a judgment

call, a matter of opinion and personal experience. Those tests were constructed around items like fill-in-the-blank sentence completion, such as, "Even though Tom was————, Mary thought he was————." And the correct answer always seemed to be the most bland combinations of thoughts, for example, "Even though Tom was shy, Mary thought he was charming," with the grammatical structure "even though" limiting the correct answer to some sort of semantic opposites, so you wouldn't get answers like, "Even though Tom was foolish, Mary thought he was ridiculous." Well, according to my mother, there were very few limitations as to what Tom could have been and what Mary might have thought of him. So I never did well on tests like that.

The same was true with word analogies, pairs of words in which you were supposed to find some sort of logical, semantic relationship—for example, "*Sunset* is to *nightfall* as ————is to————." And here you would be presented with a list of four possible pairs, one of which showed the same kind of relationship: *red* is to *stoplight, bus* is to *arrival, chills* is to *fever, yawn* is to *boring*. Well, I could never think that way. I knew what the tests were asking, but I could not block out of my mind the images already created by the first pair, "*sunset* is to *nightfall*"—and I would see a burst of color against a darkening sky, the moon rising, the lowering of a curtain of stars. And all the other pairs of words—red, bus, stoplight, boring—just threw up a mass of confusing images, making it impossible for me to sort out something as logical as saying: "A sunset precedes nightfall" is the same as "a chill precedes a fever." The only way I would have gotten that answer right would have been to imagine an associative situation, for example, by being disobedient and staying out past sunset, catching a chill at night which turns into feverish pneumonia as punishment, which indeed did happen to me.

I have been thinking about all this lately, about my mother's English, about achievement tests. Because lately I've been asked, as a writer, why there are not more Asian Americans represented in American literature. Why are there few Asian Americans enrolled in creative writing programs? Why do so many Chinese students go into engineering? Well, these are broad sociological questions I can't begin to answer. But I have noticed in surveys—in fact, just last week—that Asian students, as a whole, always do significantly better on math achievement tests than in English. And this makes me think that there are other Asian-American students whose English spoken in the home might also be described as "broken" or "limited." And perhaps they also have teachers who are steering them away from writing and into math and science, which is what happened to me.

Fortunately, I happen to be rebellious in nature and enjoy the challenge of disproving assumptions made about me. I became an English major my first year in college, after being enrolled as pre-med. I started writing nonfiction as a freelancer the week after I was told by my former boss that writing was my worst skill and I should hone my talents toward account management.

20   But it wasn't until 1985 that I finally began to write fiction. And at first I wrote using what I thought to be wittily crafted sentences, sentences that would finally prove I had mastery over the English language. Here's an example from the first draft of a story that later made its way into *The Joy Luck Club,* but without this line: "That was my mental quandary in its nascent state." A terrible line, which I can hardly pronounce.

21   Fortunately, for reasons I won't get into today, I later decided I should envision a reader for the stories I would write. And the reader I decided upon was my mother, because these were stories about mothers. So with this reader in mind— and in fact she did read my early drafts—I began to write stories using all the Englishes I grew up with: the English I spoke to my mother, which for lack of a better term might be described as "simple"; the English she used with me, which for lack of a better term might be described as "broken"; my translation of her Chinese, which could certainly be described as "watered down"; and what I imagine to be her translation of her Chinese if she could speak in perfect English, her internal language, and for that I sought to preserve the essence, but neither an English nor a Chinese structure. I wanted to capture what language ability tests can never reveal: her intent, her passion, her imagery, the rhythms of her speech and the nature of her thoughts.

22   Apart from what any critic had to say about my writing, I knew I had succeeded where it counted when my mother finished reading my book and gave me her verdict: "So easy to read."

Vocabulary

Directions: Locate each of the key words in the reading selection. Try to figure out each word's meaning by using the context. Confirm your guess by checking the dictionary or thesaurus. Write the meanings of the words in the margin of the text. Then record the meanings in the following chart.

Key Word	Paragraph	Meaning
1. evoke	2	
2. belies	7	
3. vivid	7	
4. wince	8	
5. empirical	9	
6. guise	10	
7. insular	15	

Key Word	Paragraph	Meaning
8. bland	16	
9. hone	19	
Others?		

Guide Questions

Directions: These questions will guide your understanding of what you have read. Write your answers in your notebook or on a separate sheet of paper if your instructor wishes to collect it. Your answers to these questions will be the basis of class discussion.

1. From reading the introduction and the first few paragraphs of the essay, what do we learn about Amy Tan? Who is she? What does she do? How does she describe herself? Have you read any of her novels?
2. In paragraph 3, Tan describes giving a speech she'd given many times successfully. What went wrong this time?
3. There seems to be a big difference in Tan's mother's ability to read/understand English and her ability to speak "standard" English. Describe this difference.
4. What words does Tan use to describe her mother's English? Which of these words make her wince? Why?
5. Why was Tan ashamed of her mother's English when she was growing up?
6. What did Tan's mother think of her own English language skills?
7. Explain why Tan says she had trouble with analogies.
8. How does all this relate to Tan's questions about why there are not more Asian Americans represented in American literature?
9. When Tan first decided to write fiction, she wrote some lines she calls "terrible." How did she solve this problem?
10. Amy Tan speaks about "different Englishes." What does she mean by this? How many "different Englishes" does she talk about?
11. There are at least two ways you could define the term *mother tongue*. What would these two definitions be?

Writing

What is your mother tongue? Do you have more than one? Think about the way Amy Tan's world was affected by her mother tongue. How has your mother tongue affected you and the way you view yourself and your world? Have you had to struggle with or reject anything about your mother tongue?

SHORT TAKE

Is English Broken Here?

Consider the following English sentences, written by persons with, to say the least, an imperfect command of the language. Can you "translate" these fractured sentences into comprehensible English?

A warning to motorists by a Tokyo car rental agency: "When a passenger of the foot heave in sight, tootle the horn. Trumpet at him melodiously at first, but if he still obstacles your passage, then tootle him with vigor."

A sign at an Austrian ski resort: "Do not preambulate the corridors in the hours of repose in the boots of ascension."

A hotel in Acapulco boasted: "The manager has personally passed all the water served here."

A notice in a Norwegian cocktail lounge reads: "Ladies are requested not to have children in the bar."

An airline in Copenhagen promises to "take your bags and send them in all directions."

Instructions on a package of convenience food from Italy: "Besmear a backing pan, previously buttered with a good tomato sauce, and after, dispose the cannelloni, lightly distanced between them in a only couch."

A sign in a Tokyo hotel: "It is forbidden to steal hotel towels please. If you are not a person to do such thing please not to read notice."

A dentist in Hong Kong advertised tooth extractions: "using the latest Methodists."

In the brochure of an Italian hotel: "We can offer you a commodious chamber, with balcony imminent to a romantic gorge. We hope you want to drop in. In the close village you can buy jolly memorials for when you pass away."

What a joy it is to know English! To be able to express your thoughts in such a rich variety of ways—and words! If required, an English speaker may help, aid, or assist another. If he is looking for an answer, the English speaker may ask (question, interrogate) someone. If he wants to describe a fashion model, the English speaker has numerous words at his disposal: slender, thin, skinny, spare, emaciated, or pretty, lovely, fair, attractive, beautiful, gorgeous. . . . To end (finish, conclude) this point, let us just say that English's vocabulary surpasses that of all other languages—it is huge (big, large, immense, gigantic, capacious, massive, whopping, vast, humungous, . . . well, we could go on).

One reason for its richness is that English is the product of two mother tongues—the Anglo-Saxon of England plus the Latin-French spoken by the Norman conquerors. Over many years, these languages mixed and evolved to eventually become the English we speak today. Perhaps because of its mixed heritage, English has always been open to expansion. In fact, English is a great sponge, soaking up words from every language. Just look at these few examples: typhoon *comes from Cantonese,* kindergarten *from German,* camel *from Hebrew,* safari *and* alcohol *from Arabic,* vodka *from Russian,* boondocks *from Tagalog,* igloo *and* kayak *from Eskimo languages,* sugar *from Sanskrit,* tattoo *from Tahitian, and* zebra *from the Bantu languages. But in addition to stealing—oops,* borrowing—*words from other nations, English speakers are constantly* inventing *new words to add to its already huge vocabulary. Where do all these words come from?*

WHERE DO NEW WORDS COME FROM?

Mary Fjeldstad

Etymology

Etymology is the study of the history of words. If a word is borrowed from another language, its etymology will trace its origins, its mother language and its travel and changes through time. For example, *opera* was borrowed from Italian, which inherited it from Latin; *plumber* came from the Middle English, which got it from the Middle French, which inherited it from Latin (where it meant a person who works with lead).   1

But new words come from many other sources, too. Here are a few of them.   2

Coinage

Many words are simply coined, or invented. One rich source of coined words is product names and advertising. *Kleenex, Xerox, Jell-O, Band-Aid, Pampers, Vaseline,* and *nylon* are all examples of words that were invented as product names and that eventually came to mean a category of things—any brand of tissue is now routinely called kleenex, and you may very well xerox your papers using a Hewlett-Packard or Dell copier. Many companies now sell their own version of "Vaseline," even though strictly speaking, the name refers only to products of that brand. Notice that some of these words were created using existing words as a base—Kleenex came from *clean* and Jell-o came from the word *gel*. One interesting example of coinage is the Jeep, which was developed by the U.S. military for use in World War II and called simply a "general purpose" (or g.p.) vehicle. Say the letters *g.p.* fast, and you'll discover the origin of the word *jeep*.   3

Shortening or Clipping

4   Americans tend to like their words short and sweet. Thus, many long words are "clipped" and their shortened versions have made us forget about their longer ancestors. Thus, *gym* is short for *gymnasium, phone* is short for *telephone, ad* comes from *advertising, bike* from *bicycle, fax* from *facsimile, gas* from *gasoline,* and many more.

Personal and Place Names

5   Names of persons and places often become common words. *Sandwich,* for example, was named after the Earl of Sandwich, a man who loved gambling so much he did not want to stop for food. He asked his servants to put meat between two slices of bread so he could eat while he played! *Jumbo,* a word meaning "very huge," comes from the name of an elephant that performed in P.T. Barnum's circus. *Bedlam,* a word that means "chaos," comes from the mispronunciation of the word *Bethlehem,* the name of a notorious insane asylum in England.

Acronyms

6   Some new words come from using the initials of a group of words. One of the most recent inventions is AIDS (acquired immune deficiency syndrome). Older creations include radar (radio detecting and ranging), scuba (self-contained underwater breathing apparatus), and RAM (random-access memory).

7   While not strictly words, many unpronounceable *initials* have achieved near-word status: NFL (National Football League), FBI (Federal Bureau of Investigation), CIA (Central Intelligence Agency), MRI (magnetic resonance imaging), STD (sexually transmitted disease) and PDA (personal digital assistant) are a few examples.

Blending

8   Blending is the combining of two words into one new word. For example, *motel* is a blend of *motor* and *hotel. Smog* is a blend of *smoke* and *fog, brunch* a blend of *breakfast* and *lunch. Aquacise* is a form of exercise in the water. A new blended word is *infomercial*—a combination of *information* and *commercial. Work* plus *alcoholic* combine to make a *workaholic.*

9   One new blend (for a less than delightful development) is *McJob*—a word that describes low-level minimum wage work typical of McDonald's. Another less than delightful activity has given birth to the term *narcoterrorism.*

Technology

10 Many new words have emerged because of technology. The word *retail* means "buying at a store," but *e-tail* means "buying online." An *e-zine* is an online magazine. And an *emoticon* is a way to express emotions while texting ☺.

11   Old words have become new in the context of technology—*boot, bug, cookie, zombie,* and many others have taken on new meanings. And many words are a result of a combination of technology and blending. *Netiquette* is a blend of *net* (the Internet) and *etiquette* (proper behavior in social situations). A *podcast* is a blend of *pod* (from iPod) and *broadcast. Blog* is a word formed by blending *web* and

log (a *log* is a diary or chronicle of events). And to take the blending a step further, *blogosphere* results from blending *web, log,* and *atmosphere.*

Merriam-Webster announced the inclusion of nearly 100 new words into its dictionary in July 2007. Their number one pick? *Ginormous*—a blend of *giant* and *enormous.* Other additions were *Bollywood, smackdown, speed dating, sudoku,* and *telenovela.*   12

It is always risky to predict the future, but one thing seems certain. English, which some have called "this glorious mongrel," will continue to change and grow.   13

Vocabulary

Directions: Find each of the key words in the essay. Try to figure out each word's meaning by using the context. Confirm your guess by checking the dictionary. Write the meanings of the words in the margin of the text, near the word. Then record the meanings in the following chart.

Key Word	Paragraph	Meaning
1. notorious	5	
2. mongrel	13	
Others?		

Guide Questions

Directions: These questions will guide your understanding of what you have read. Write your answers in your notebook or on a separate sheet of paper if your instructor will collect it. Your answers will be the basis of class discussion.

1. Look up the word *etymology* in the dictionary. (You'll need a full-size dictionary, not a pocket size.) What is the etymology of *etymology*? What language does it come from? In what year was the word first used?

2. Language experts in France and Spain established "academies" to oversee their language. These experts believe it is important to keep the language as "pure" as possible. They resist the inclusion of new words—especially from English—into the vocabulary. In France, for example, the Académie française discourages the use of the words *walkman* and *software.* Instead, French speakers are encouraged to use the invented French words *baladeur* and *logiciel.* After much discussion the academy decided to resist the use of the word *e-mail,* instead choosing a Canadian French word—*courriel.* (By the way, the word *blog* in French is *un blogue,* at least for now.)

Based on what you've read and your knowledge of English, why do you think the United States doesn't have a similar language academy?

Marking Text/Summary Writing

Mark the text of this article (if you need to review how to mark text, turn to page 413). Then write a summary of "Where Do New Words Come From?" Hint: In your marking and your summary you should include all the categories listed in the article. (To review summary writing, turn to Learning Strategy IV on page 417.)

Application

From the reading selection, choose at least two of the categories of new words. Brainstorm in a small group to find other words that would fit that category. Combine the examples you think of with those of your classmates to create a class list of words.

And, for more than you ever wanted to know about words, go to Merriam-Webster's web site: <www.m-w.com>. There you will find words, definitions, etymologies, word games, a word of the day, a language learner's guide, and much more.

Santha Rama Rau has written widely: novels, essays, and travel articles. Often her work focuses on the clash of cultures that resulted from Britain's long economic and political control over India, which did not end until 1947. This excerpt from her 1951 novel, Gifts of Passage, *first appeared in the* New Yorker *magazine. In it, Rama Rau describes the first experience of an Indian child sent to attend a British-run school.*

BY ANY OTHER NAME

Santha Rama Rau

At the Anglo-Indian day school in Zorinabad to which my sister and I were sent   1
when she was eight and I was five and a half, they changed our names. On the
first day of school, a hot, windless morning of a north Indian September, we stood
in the headmistress's study and she said, "Now you're the *new* girls. What are your
names?"

My sister answered for us. "I am Premila, and she"—nodding in my direction—   2
"is Santha."

The headmistress had been in India, I suppose, fifteen years or so, but she   3
still smiled at her helpless inability to cope with Indian names. Her rimless half-
glasses glittered, and the precarious bun on top of her head trembled as she shook
her head. "Oh, my dears, those are much too hard for me. Suppose we give you
pretty English names. Wouldn't that be more jolly? Let's see, now—Pamela for
you, I think." She shrugged in a baffled way at my sister. "That's as close as I can
get. And for *you,*" she said to me, "how about Cynthia? Isn't that nice?"

My sister was always less easily intimidated than I was, and while she kept a   4
stubborn silence, I said, "Thank you," in a very tiny voice.

We had been sent to that school because my father, among his responsibili-   5
ties as an officer of the civil service, had a tour of duty to perform in the villages
around that steamy little provincial town, where he had his headquarters at that
time. He used to make his shorter inspection tours on horseback, and a week
before, in the stale heat of a typically postmonsoon day, we had waved good-by
to him and a little procession—an assistant, a secretary, two bearers, and the man
to look after the bedding rolls and luggage. They rode away through our large
garden, still bright green from the rains, and we turned back into the twilight of
the house and the sound of fans whispering in every room.

Up to then, my mother had refused to send Premila to school in the British-   6
run establishments of that time, because, she used to say, "you can bury a dog's
tail for seven years and it still comes out curly, and you can take a Britisher away
from his home for a lifetime, and he still remains insular." The examinations and
degrees from entirely Indian schools were not, in those days, considered valid. In
my case, the question had never come up, and probably never would have come
up if Mother's extraordinary good health had not broken down. For the first time
in my life, she was not able to continue the lessons she had been giving us every
morning. So our Hindi books were put away, the stories of the Lord Krishna as a
little boy were left in midair, and we were sent to the Anglo-Indian school.

7   That first day at school is still, when I think of it, a remarkable one. At that age, if one's name is changed, one develops a curious form of dual personality. I remember having a certain detached and disbelieving concern in the actions of "Cynthia," but certainly no responsibility. Accordingly, I followed the thin, erect back of the headmistress down the veranda to my classroom feeling, at most, a passing interest in what was going to happen to me in this strange, new atmosphere of School.

8   The building was Indian in design, with wide verandas opening onto a central courtyard, but Indian verandas are usually whitewashed, with stone floors. These, in the tradition of British schools, were painted dark brown and had matting on the floors. It gave a feeling of extra intensity to the heat.

9   I suppose there were about a dozen Indian children in the school—which contained perhaps forty children in all—and four of them were in my class. They were all sitting at the back of the room and I went to join them. I sat next to a small, solemn girl who didn't smile at me. She had long, glossy-black braids and wore a cotton dress, but she still kept on her Indian jewelry—a gold chain around her neck, thin gold bracelets, and tiny ruby studs in her ears. Like most Indian children, she had a rim of black kohl around her eyes. The cotton dress should have looked strange, but all I could think of was that I should ask my mother if I couldn't wear a dress to school, too, instead of my Indian clothes.

10   I can't remember too much about the proceedings in class that day, except for the beginning. The teacher pointed to me and asked me to stand up "Now, dear, tell the class your name."

11   I said nothing.

12   "Come along," she said frowning slightly. "What's your name, dear?"

13   "I don't know," I said, finally.

14   The English children in the front of the class—there were about eight or ten of them—giggled and twisted around in their chairs to look at me. I sat down quickly and opened my eyes very wide, hoping in that way to dry them off. The little girl with the braids put out her hand and very lightly touched my arm. She still didn't smile.

15   Most of that morning I was rather bored. I looked briefly at the children's drawings pinned to the wall, and then concentrated on a lizard clinging to the ledge of the high, barred window behind the teacher's head. Occasionally it would shoot out its long yellow tongue for a fly, and then it would rest, with its eyes closed and its belly palpitating, as though it were swallowing several times quickly. The lessons were mostly concerned with reading and writing and simple numbers—things that my mother had already taught me—and I paid very little attention. The teacher wrote on the easel blackboard words like "bat" and "cat," which seemed babyish to me; only "apple" was new and incomprehensible.

16   When it was time for the lunch recess, I followed the girl with braids out onto the veranda. There the children from the other classes were assembled. I saw Premila at once and ran over to her, as she had charge of our lunchbox. The children were all opening packages and sitting down to eat sandwiches. Premila and I were the only ones who had Indian food—thin wheat chapatties, some vegetable curry,

and a bottle of buttermilk. Premila thrust half of it into my hand and whispered fiercely that I should go and sit with my class, because that was what the others seemed to be doing.

The enormous black eyes of the little Indian girl from my class looked at my   17
food longingly, so I offered her some. But she only shook her head and plowed her way solemnly through her sandwiches.

I was very sleepy after lunch, because at home we always took a siesta. It was   18
usually a pleasant time of day, with the bedroom darkened against the harsh afternoon sun, the drifting off into sleep with the sound of Mother's voice reading a story in one's mind, and, finally, the shrill, fussy voice of the ayah waking one for tea.

At school, we rested for a short time on low, folding cots on the veranda, and   19
then we were expected to play games. During the hot part of the afternoon we played indoors, and after the shadows had begun to lengthen and the slight breeze of the evening had come up we moved outside to the wide courtyard.

I had never really grasped the system of competitive games. At home, when-   20
ever we played tag or guessing games, I was always allowed to "win"—"because," Mother used to tell Premila, "she is the youngest, and we have to allow for that." I had often heard her say it, and it seemed quite reasonable to me, but the result was that I had no clear idea of what "winning" meant.

When we played twos-and-threes that afternoon at school, in accordance   21
with my training, I let one of the small English boys catch me, but was naturally rather puzzled when the other children did not return the courtesy. I ran about for what seemed like hours without ever catching anyone, until it was time for school to close. Much later I learned that my attitude was called "not being a good sport," and I stopped allowing myself to be caught, but it was not for years that I really learned the spirit of the thing.

When I saw our car come up to the school gate, I broke away from my class-   22
mates and rushed toward it yelling, "Ayah! Ayah!" It seemed like an eternity since I had seen her that morning—a wizened, affectionate figure in her white cotton sari, giving me dozens of urgent and useless instructions on how to be a good girl at school. Premila followed more sedately, and she told me on the way home never to do that again in front of the other children.

When we got home we went straight to Mother's high, white room to have   23
tea with her, and I immediately climbed onto the bed and bounced gently up and down on the springs. Mother asked how we had liked our first day in school. I was so pleased to be home and to have left that peculiar Cynthia behind that I had nothing whatever to say about school, except to ask what "apple" meant. But Premila told Mother about the classes, and added that in her class they had weekly tests to see if they learned their lessons well.

I asked, "What's a test?"   24

Premila said, "You're too small to have them. You won't have them in your   25
class for donkey's years." She had learned the expression that day and was using it for the first time. We all laughed enormously at her wit. She also told Mother, in an aside, that we should take sandwiches to school the next day. Not, she said, that *she* minded. But they would be simpler for me to handle.

26   That whole lovely evening I didn't think about school at all. I sprinted barefoot across the lawn with my favorite playmate, the cook's son, to the stream at the end of the garden. We quarreled in our usual way, waded in the tepid water under the lime trees, and waited for the night to bring out the smell of the jasmine. I listened with fascination to his stories of ghosts and demons, until I was too frightened to cross the garden alone in the semidarkness. The ayah found me, shouted at the cook's son, scolded me, hurried me into supper—it was an entirely usual, wonderful evening.

27   It was a week later, the day of Premila's first test, that our lives changed rather abruptly. I was sitting at the back of my class, in my usual inattentive way, only half listening to the teacher. I had started a rather guarded friendship with the girl with the braids, whose name turned out to be Nalini (Nancy, in school). The three other Indian children were already fast friends. Even at that age it was apparent to all of us that friendship with the English or Anglo-Indian children was out of the question. Occasionally, during the class, my new friend and I would draw pictures and show them to each other secretly.

28   The door opened sharply and Premila marched in. At first, the teacher smiled at her in a kindly and encouraging way and said, "Now, you're little Cynthia's sister?"

29   Premila didn't even look at her. She stood with her feet planted firmly apart and her shoulders rigid, and addressed herself directly to me. "Get up," she said. "We're going home."

30   I didn't know what had happened, but I was aware that it was a crisis of some sort. I rose obediently and started to walk toward my sister.

31   "Bring your pencils and your notebook," she said.

32   I went back for them, and together we left the room. The teacher started to say something just as Premila closed the door, but we didn't wait to hear what it was.

33   In complete silence we left the school grounds and started to walk home. Then I asked Premila what the matter was. All she would say was "We're going home for good."

34   It was a very tiring walk for a child of five and a half, and I dragged along behind Premila with my pencils growing sticky in my hand. I can still remember looking at the dusty hedges, and the tangles of thorns in the ditches by the side of the road, smelling the faint fragrance from the eucalyptus trees and wondering whether we would ever reach home. Occasionally a horse-drawn tonga passed us, and the women, in their pink or green silks, stared at Premila and me trudging along on the side of the road. A few coolies and a line of women carrying baskets of vegetables on their heads smiled at us. But it was nearing the hottest time of day, and the road was almost deserted. I walked more and more slowly, and shouted to Premila, from time to time, "Wait for me!" with increasing peevishness. She spoke to me only once, and that was to tell me to carry my notebook on my head, because of the sun.

When we got to our house the ayah was just taking a tray of lunch into   35
Mother's room. She immediately started a long, worried questioning about what
are you children doing back here at this hour of the day.

Mother looked very startled and very concerned, and asked Premila what had   36
happened.

Premila said, "We had our test today, and she made me and the other Indians   37
sit at the back of the room, with a desk between each one."

Mother said, "Why was that, darling?"   38

"She said it was because Indians cheat," Premila added. "So I don't think we   39
should go back to that school."

Mother looked very distant, and was silent a long time. At last she said, "Of   40
course not, darling." She sounded displeased.

We all shared the curry she was having for lunch, and afterward I was sent   41
off to the beautifully familiar bedroom for my siesta. I could hear Mother and
Premila talking through the open door.

Mother said, "Do you suppose she understood all that?"   42

Premila said, "I shouldn't think so. She's a baby."   43

Mother said, "Well, I hope it won't bother her."   44

Of course, they were both wrong. I understood it perfectly, and I remember   45
it all very clearly. But I put it happily away, because it had all happened to a girl
called Cynthia, and I never was really particularly interested in her.

Vocabulary

Directions: Locate each of the key words in the reading selection. Try to figure out each
word's meaning by its context. Confirm your guess by checking the dictionary or thesaurus. Write the meanings of the words in the margin of the text. Then record the meanings in the following chart.

Key Word	Paragraph	Meaning
1. precarious	3	
2. insular	6	
3. detached	7	
4. veranda	7	
5. palpitating	15	
6. wizened	22	
7. tepid	26	

Key Word	Paragraph	Meaning
Others?		

Guide Questions

Directions: These questions will guide your understanding of what you have read. Write your answers in your notebook or on a separate sheet of paper if your instructor wishes to collect it. Your answers to these questions will be the basis of class discussion.

1. Summarize what we learn in the story about Rau and her family; for example, where does the story take place? why is the Rau family there? and so on. Identify the major characters in the story.
2. Interpret Rau's mother's comment in paragraph 6: "you can bury a dog's tail for seven years and it still comes out curly, and you can take a Britisher away from his home for a lifetime, and he still remains insular."
3. Contrast the life and status of the girls at home and at school.
4. a. Describe the day of Premila's test, the day the sisters' lives changed. What caused the change?
   b. What effect did this crisis have on Santha?

Application/Writing

1. The old saying goes, "Sticks and stones can break my bones, but words can never hurt me." Do you agree?
2. Have you ever been called a derogatory name? What effect did it have on you?
3. Have you ever changed your name? Why? What was the result?
4. Do you think a person's name establishes his or her identity (or a part of it)? Why?

Making Connections

The title of the story, "By Any Other Name," is an allusion (a reference) to Shakespeare's play, *Romeo and Juliet*. Read the following excerpt from Act II: Scene II. Can you paraphrase what Juliet means? Compare the idea about names in Romeo and Juliet to the selection "By Any Other Name." Are the ideas the same?

Juliet: O Romeo, Romeo! Wherefore art thou Romeo?
Deny thy father and refuse thy name;
Or, if thou wilt not, be but sworn, my love,
And I'll no longer be a Capulet.
    . . .

'Tis but thy name that is my enemy;
Thou art thyself, though not a Montague.
What's a Montague? It is nor hand, nor foot,
Nor arm, nor face, nor any other part
Belonging to a man. O, be some other name!
What's in a name? that which we call a rose
By any other name would smell as sweet;
So Romeo would, were he not Romeo call'd,
Retain that dear perfection which he owes
Without that title. Romeo, doff thy name,
And for that name which is no part of thee
take all myself.

Romeo: I take thee at thy word:
Call me but love, and I'll be new baptized;
Henceforth I never will be Romeo.

SHORT TAKE

Phraseology

Henry Alford

Actual Selections from Phrase Books and Language Primers for Travelers

You're a tourist in Yemen. Upon awakening one morning, you stumble down to the lobby of your hotel, where the proprietor asks you in Yemeni Arabic how you slept. Unsure how best to articulate your response, you open a copy of "Spoken Yemeni Arabic." You turn to the appropriate section and recite the first thing that catches your eye, from page 148:

> *I did not sleep all night. The next time I want a drug.*

You're visiting Japan, where you have befriended a native. He invites you to his home; you go, looking over his house with more than a little interest. Eager to make a good impression, you pull out your trusty "Complete Japanese Expression Guide," cast a glance at Example 4 on page 38 and say:

> *There is a big difference in our income levels.*

You're in a cafe in Albania, talking in Albanian with a waitress. Casting about for something to say during a lull in the conversation, you glance at your copy of "Spoken Albanian" on the table in front of you. You read from Unit 17:

> *I wanted you to explain to me your customs concerning blood vengeance.*

Language primers and phrase books for travelers can be an odd introduction to a foreign country. Blithely insensitive to the subtleties of polite conversation, these tiny manuals re-enforce the xenophobic notion that all foreign travel is rife with unpleasure and mishap. Sometimes the source of this unpleasure and mishap is unspecified—the reader of "Teach Yourself Catalan," for instance, can only wonder what dire circumstances will require the use of the phrase

I am prepared to raffle the goat.

Other times the source of unpleasure and mishap is all too clear, as in the phrase book from the Imperial Russia era that is mentioned in James Thurber's essay "There's No Place Like Home." There, the reader is supplied with the Russian for

Oh, dear, our postilion has been struck by lightning!

Indeed, vehicular calamity (a postilion is a person who rides the left-hand leading horse of a four- or two-horse carriage) is a veritable staple of the language guide for travelers. These books imply that when not crawling out of a Citröen that has skidded off the autobahn, you will probably be watching *others* crawling out of Citröens that have skidded off the autobahn. As a rather dispassionate exchange between two bystanders to a car crash in "Spoken Turkish" runs:

The poor people are covered with blood. I wonder if they're suffering much?
I don't think so, since they've fainted.

A less delicate reference to a car crash appears in the "Fanagalo Dictionary," which translates a crude lingua franca used mostly in the mines of South Africa:

One European is dead; another has a broken arm, and a baby is bleeding from the mouth and ears.

Of course, automobiles are not the only source of conflict in phrase book land. Each manual seems to tap a new vein of potential misfortune. The "Introductory Course in Spoken Hindi" cites weather conditions:

You seem to be off mood today, what happened?
It seems that I got fever and bad cold.
How did it happen all of a sudden?
I got wet in the rain yesterday.
Perhaps you got flu.
Oh! What a hell!

And "2001 French and English Idioms" invokes modern medicine:

After the injection, I felt funny.

As is only to be expected, however, the lion's share of phrase book opprobrium is directed at fellow humans. In phrase books, as in the work of Jean-Paul

Sartre, hell is other people. An exchange from "German Chit-Chat" puts it most succinctly:

Why did you not play with Willibald?
Because I don't like him.

When we are dealing with servants, clerks or waiters, phrase books would have us adopt a brisk, businesslike tone. Consider the "Tailor" section of the Baedeker "Traveler's Manual of Conversation," which deals in four languages:

Good morning to you; you have kept me waiting long enough.

A later episode in that book has us inform a merchant:

That is very dear. Such a price frightens me.

The appalling "Spoken Hawaiian" advocates outright hostility:

Slave, bring fish, taro and a squid. If you don't do this fast, you'll be a live sacrifice.

Whatever their deficiencies, however, phrase books cannot be accused of countenancing boredom. Blood vengeance, goat raffles, live sacrifice—this is a colorful and decisive, if somewhat mysterious, world. Those who fail to capture this sense of drama will have to answer to "The Complete Japanese Expression Guide":

Every comment you make is just so innocuous!

Do you ever go to the restroom to rest? Or to the powder room to powder? And just how often do you take a bath when you make a trip to the bathroom? Did you know that in many parts of the southern United States, people don't die? No, they "pass away." Some even "go to their reward." In other parts of the country, people just "buy the farm" or experience the "end of the ball game." Shakespeare never said "die;" instead, his characters "shuffled off this mortal coil." People who would be mortally ashamed to discuss being naked feel free to discuss their "birthday suit," or "being in the altogether." Aware of it or not, we all use euphemisms. Here, the author of A Dictionary of Euphemisms and Other Doubletalk *introduces us to these "linguistic fig leaves and verbal flourishes for artful users of the English language."*

EUPHEMISMS

Hugh Rawson

1   Mr. Milquetoast gets up from the table, explaining that he has to go to the *little boys' room* or to *see a man about a dog;* a young woman announces that she is *enceinte.* A secretary complains that her boss is a pain in the *derriere;* an undertaker or *mortician* asks delicately where to ship the *loved one.* These are euphemisms—mild, agreeable, or roundabout words used in place of coarse, painful, or offensive ones. The term comes from the Greek *eu,* meaning "well" or "sounding good," and *pheme,* "speech."

2   Many euphemisms are so delightfully ridiculous that everyone laughs at them. (Well, almost everyone: The people who call themselves the National Selected Morticians usually manage to keep from smiling.) Yet euphemisms have very serious reasons for being. They conceal the things people fear the most—death, the dead, the supernatural. They cover up the facts of life—of sex and reproduction and excretion—which inevitably remind even the most refined people that they are made of clay, or worse. They are beloved by individuals and institutions (governments, especially) who are anxious to present only the handsomest possible images of themselves to the world. And they are embedded so deeply in our language that few of us, even those who pride themselves on being plain-spoken, ever get through a day without using them.

3   The same sophisticates who look down their noses at *little boys' room* and other euphemisms of that ilk will nevertheless say that they are going to the *bathroom* when no bath is intended; that Mary has been *sleeping around* even though she has been getting precious little shut-eye; that John has *passed away* or even *departed* (as if he'd just made the last train to Darien); and that Sam and Janet are *friends,* which sounds a lot better than "illicit lovers."

4   Thus, euphemisms are society's basic *lingua franca.* As such, they are outward and visible signs of our inward anxieties, conflicts, fears, and shames. They are like radioactive isotopes. By tracing them, it is possible to see what has been (and is) going on in our language, our minds, and our culture.

5   Euphemisms can be divided into two general types—positive and negative. The positive ones inflate and magnify, making the euphemized items seem

altogether grander and more important than they really are. The negative euphemisms deflate and diminish. They are defensive in nature, off-setting the power of tabooed terms and otherwise eradicating from the language everything that people prefer not to deal with directly.

Positive euphemisms include the many occupational titles, which salve the   6
egos of workers by elevating their job status: *custodian* for janitor (itself a euphemism for caretaker), *counsel* for lawyer, the many kinds of *engineer* (*exterminating engineer, mattress engineer, publicity engineer,* ad infinitum), *help* for servant (itself an old euphemism for slave), *hooker* and *working girl* for whore, and so forth. A common approach is to try to turn one's trade into a profession, usually in imitation of the medical profession. *Beautician* and the aforementioned *mortician* are the classic examples, but the same imitative instinct is responsible for social workers calling welfare recipients *clients,* for football coaches conducting *clinics,* and for undertakers referring to corpses as *cases* or even *patients.*

Other kinds of positive euphemisms include personal honorifics such as   7
colonel, the *honorable,* and *major,* and the many institutional euphemisms, which convert madhouses into *mental hospitals,* colleges into *universities,* and small business establishments into *emporiums, parlors, salons,* and *shoppes.* The desire to improve one's surroundings also is evident in geographical place names, most prominently in the case of the distinctly non-green *Greenland* (attributed to an early real-estate developer named Eric the Red), but also in the designation of many small burgs as *cities,* and in the names of some cities, such as *Troy,* New York (née Vanderheyden's Ferry, its name-change in 1789 began a fad for adopting classical place names in the United States).

Negative, defensive euphemisms are extremely ancient. It was the Greeks, for   8
example, who transformed the Furies into the Eumenides (the "kindly ones"). In many cultures, it is forbidden to pronounce the name of God (hence, pious Jews say Adonai) or of Satan (giving rise to the *deuce,* the *good man,* the *great fellow,* the generalized *Devil,* and many other roundabouts). The names of the dead, and of animals that are hunted or feared, may also be euphemized this way. The bear is called *grandfather* by many peoples and the tiger is alluded to as the *striped one.* The common motivation seems to be a confusion between the names of things and the things themselves: The name is viewed as an extension of the thing. Thus, to know the name is to give one power over the thing (as in the Rumpelstiltskin story). But such power may be dangerous: "Speak of the Devil and he appears." For mere mortals, then, the safest policy is to use another name, usually a flattering, euphemistic one, in place of the supernatural being's true name.

As strong as—or stronger than—the taboos against names are the taboos   9
against particular words, especially the infamous *four-letter words.* (According to a recent Supreme Court decision, the set of *four-letter words* actually contains some words with as few as three and as many as twelve letters, but the logic of Supreme Court decisions is not always immediately apparent). These words form part of the vocabulary of everyone above the age of six or seven. They are not slang terms, but legitimate Standard English of the oldest stock, and they are euphemized in many ways, typically by conversion into pseudo-Latin (e.g., *copulation, defecation,*

urination) into slang (*make love, number two, pee*), or into socially acceptable dashes (f——, s——, p——, etc.). In the electronic media, the function of the dash is fulfilled by the *bleep* (sometimes pronounced *blip*), which has completed the circle and found its way into print.

10   The taboo against words frequently degenerates into mere prudery. At least—though the defensive principle is the same—the primitive (or *preliterate*) hunter's use of *grandfather* seems to operate on a more elemental level than the excessive modesty that has produced *abdomen* for belly, *afterpart* for ass, *bosom* for breast, *limb* for leg, *white meat* for breast (of a chicken), and so on.

11   When carried too far, which is what always seems to happen, positive and negative euphemisms tend finally to coalesce into an unappetizing mush of elegancies and genteelism, in which the underlying terms are hardly worth the trouble of euphemizing, i.e., *ablutions* for washing, *bender* for knee, *dentures* for false teeth, *expectorate* for spit, *home* for house, *honorarium* for fee, *ill* for sick, *libation* for drink, *perspire* for sweat, *position* for job, etc., etc., etc.

Vocabulary

Directions: Locate each of the key words in the reading selection. Then read and study each word in its context and try to determine its meaning. Use a dictionary or thesaurus to check your guess. Write the meanings of the words in the margin of the text.

Record the new words you've learned.

Key Word	Paragraph	Meaning
1. enceinte	1	
2. ilk	3	
3. eradicating	5	
4. honorifics	7	
5. née	7	
6. infamous	9	
7. prudery	10	
8. coalesce	11	
Others?		

Guide Questions

Directions: These questions will guide your understanding of what you have read. They also will help you to analyze and evaluate the author's ideas and apply them to the real world and your own life.

Write answers to the questions in your notebook or on a separate sheet of paper if your instructor wishes to collect them. Your answers will form the basis of class discussion.

1. Explain and give two examples of euphemisms.
2. Contrast the two types of euphemisms Rawson describes.
3. According to Rawson, what happens when the use of euphemisms is "carried too far"?
4. If you read the selection "Language" (page 152), relate the use of euphemisms to the notion of confusing symbols (in this case, words) with the actual things they symbolize.
5. Rawson gives many examples of euphemisms, but he does not exhaust the subject. Money is one of the subjects we tend to disguise with euphemisms. In many cases it is considered poor taste to ask people about their financial affairs; we don't usually ask casual acquaintances, "How much is your salary?" Bill collectors often use indirect ways of asking for payment: "We beg to call your attention to what might be an oversight on your part," or "We would appreciate your early attention to this matter," instead of "Send us the money you owe!" Can you think of any other topics that we discuss using euphemisms?

Application

Directions: Working in pairs or in small groups, collect euphemisms. You will find ads from magazines, newspapers, radio, and TV especially rich sources of euphemisms, but you can easily find them in magazine and newspaper articles as well as in day-to-day conversations. Fill in the following chart with your collection of euphemisms.

Cite the source for each euphemism (for example, a real estate ad or a television commercial). Copy the euphemism into the appropriate column. Then write the word(s) you think the euphemism replaces in the last column. An example is done for you.

Source	The Euphemism	The Word(s) the Euphemism Replaces
A memo from the CEO of my company.	It said: "We are forced by a downturn in the economy to downsize our work force."	It meant that they are going to fire a lot of us.

Writing

Directions: Write a summary of the selection "Euphemisms." (To review summary writing, turn to page 417.) To make the summary clear and complete, include one or two examples of each of the key ideas.

SHORT TAKE

More Broken English

Here are a few more examples of how English takes a beating as it travels the world. Can you repair these sentences?

A doctor in Rome advertised his specialties as: "women and other diseases."

A hotel in Yugoslavia announced heartily: "The flattening of underwear with pleasure is the job of the chambermaid. Turn to her straightaway."

Beware of a tailor on the Greek island of Rhodes who couldn't guarantee he could finish summer suits ordered by tourists: "Because is big rush we will execute customers in strict rotation."

A laundry in Rome invites: "Ladies, leave your clothes here and spend the afternoon having a good time."

Good news for pregnant tourists: a Czech tourist agency advertises, "Take one of our horse-drawn city tours. We guarantee no miscarriages."

A note on a Swiss menu: "Our wines leave you nothing to hope for."

After that wine, maybe it's for the best: A Swiss inn advises, "Special today—no ice cream."

And a bottle of the Swiss wine, please. A Polish menu tempts us with "Salad a firm's own make; limpid red beet soup with cheesy dumplings in the form of a finger; roasted duck let loose; beef rashers beaten up in the country people's fashion."

Finally, be very careful at the gas station in Italy that displayed these instructions:

- To insert the notes aligned to the right in any verse
- To wait the accreditation in the display
- To select the wanted bomb
- Out to the spy of the select bomb, to take the supplier

(Be extra careful with that "bomb," please.)

Writing is written language. The earliest writing we know of is called cuneiform, which dates back to about 3500 B.C. in the valley of the Tigris and Euphrates Rivers. Within the next 500 years or so, the Egyptians developed a picture-writing system called hieroglyphics. Somewhere around 1800 B.C. it is believed the Phoenicians developed a phonetic alphabet— one based on sounds. All the phonetic alphabets of history, including that of English, are based on this great invention. In the following essay, the author helps us imagine the beginnings of writing.

Before you read "Symbols of Humankind," try to think of what prompted humans to invent writing.

1. *Why was spoken language insufficient for human needs? Think about the advantages that written language has over spoken language.*
2. *Nonliterate societies (people who do not have a written language) still exist. Why do you suppose they have not developed writing?*
3. *Imagine how daily life would be if written language had never been developed. List some of the things you do each day that are completely dependent on writing.*

SYMBOLS OF HUMANKIND

Don Lago

Many thousands of years ago, a man quietly resting on a log reached down and picked up a stick and with it began scratching upon the sand at his feet. He moved the stick slowly back and forth and up and down, carefully guiding it through curves and straight lines. He gazed upon what he had made, and a gentle satisfaction lighted his face.   1

Other people noticed this man drawing on the sand. They gazed upon the figures he had made, and though they at once recognized the shapes of familiar things such as fish or birds or humans, they took a bit longer to realize what the man had meant to say by arranging these familiar shapes in this particular way. Understanding what he had done, they nodded or smiled in recognition.   2

This small band of humans didn't realize what they were beginning. The images these people left in the sand would soon be swept away by the wind, but their new idea would slowly grow until it had remade the human species. These people had discovered writing.   3

Writing, early people would learn, could contain much more information than human memory could and contain it more accurately. It could carry thoughts much farther than mere sounds could—farther in distance and in time. Profound thoughts born in a single mind could spread and endure.   4

The first written messages were simply pictures relating familiar objects in some meaningful way—pictographs. Yet there were no images for much that was important in human life. What, for instance, was the image for sorrow or bravery? So from pictographs humans developed ideograms to represent more abstract ideas. An eye flowing with tears could represent sorrow, and a man with the head of a lion might be bravery.   5

6   The next leap occurred when the figures became independent of things or ideas and came to stand for spoken sounds. Written figures were free to lose all resemblance to actual objects. Some societies developed syllabic systems of writing in which several hundred signs corresponded to several hundred spoken sounds. Others discovered the much simpler alphabetic system, in which a handful of signs represented the basic sounds the human voice can make.

7   At first, ideas flowed only slightly faster when written than they had through speech. But as technologies evolved, humans embodied their thoughts in new ways: through the printing press, in Morse code, in electromagnetic waves bouncing through the atmosphere, and in the binary language of computers.

8   Today, when the earth is covered with a swarming interchange of ideas, we are even trying to send our thoughts beyond our planet to other minds in the universe. Our first efforts at sending our thoughts beyond earth have taken a very ancient form: pictographs. The first message, on plaques aboard the *Pioneer* spacecraft launched in 1972 and 1973, featured a simple line drawing of two humans, one male and one female, the male holding up his hand in greeting. Behind them was an outline of the *Pioneer* spacecraft, from which the size of the humans could be judged. The plaque also included the "address" of the two human figures: a picture of the solar system, with a spacecraft emerging from the third planet. Most exobiologists believe that when other civilizations attempt to communicate with us they too will use pictures.

9   All the accomplishments since humans first scribbled in the sand have led us back to where we began. Written language only works when two individuals know what the symbols mean. We can only return to the simplest form of symbol available and work from there. In interstellar communication, we are at the same stage our ancestors were when they used sticks to trace a few simple images in the sand.

10   We still hold their sticks in our hands and draw pictures with them. But the stick is no longer made of wood; over the ages that piece of wood has been transformed into a massive radio telescope. And we no longer scratch on sand; now we write our thoughts onto the emptiness of space itself.

Vocabulary

Directions: Locate each of the key words in the reading selection. Then read and study each word in its context and try to determine its meaning. Use a dictionary or thesaurus to check your guess. Write the meanings of the words in the margin of the text.

Record the new words you've learned in the following chart.

Key Word	Paragraph	Meaning
1. profound	4	
2. pictographs	5	

Key Word	Paragraph	Meaning
3. ideograms	5	
4. plaques	8	
5. interstellar	9	
Others?		

Guide Questions

Directions: These questions will guide your understanding of what you have read. They also will help you to analyze and evaluate the author's ideas and apply them to the real world and your own life.

Write answers to the questions in your notebook or on a separate sheet of paper if your instructor wishes to collect them. Your answers will form the basis of class discussion.

1. Until humans invented writing, human societies relied upon an oral tradition to pass on their culture from one generation to the next. Older people told stories that explained their world and history to the children. What are some advantages that a system of writing has for humans?
2. Explain what Lago means when he says that the first systems of writing used *pictographs,* whereas more sophisticated writing systems developed *ideograms.* Be sure to explain the distinction the author makes between pictographs and ideograms.
3. Explain the next "leap" that occurred in the development of writing.
4. What kind of alphabetic system does English use: pictograph, ideogram, syllabic, or phonetic?
5. What new systems of writing have developed as technology has advanced?
6. Explain what the author means when he says, "All the accomplishments since humans first scribbled in the sand have led us back to where we began."

Application

1. Imagine you are the first person to use writing to communicate your thoughts. What would be the first ideas you would try to communicate to your fellow humans? Write the symbols you would use. Then write the same ideas in the writing system you use now.

2. Imagine again that you are one of the first people to use writing to communicate. What would you write to communicate the following ideas?

a. fire
b. stars
c. snow
d. happy
e. fear
f. Run! Danger!
g. I'm hungry.
h. I love my children.
i. Meet me tomorrow at sunset.

Did you find the last six ideas more difficult to represent than the first three? Explain why it is easier to write about a star than about love.

Marking Text

Mark (underline and annotate) this selection. If you need to review how to mark your text, turn to page 413.

Making Connections

Return to guide question 2 of "Language" (page 156). Compare your experience answering that question to your experience in answering Application questions 1 and 2 in this selection.

Writing

Directions: Return to the questions in the introduction to "Symbols of Humankind" on page 189. Think again about your answers. Then choose one of the questions and write one or two paragraphs in response.

SHORT TAKE

Break It to Me Gently . . .

Writers know that when they submit their work to publishers it is very likely to be rejected. Most American publishers simply return the manuscript along with a brief letter saying effectively, "Thanks, but no thanks." A Chinese journal of economics, however, found a way to say NO in an entirely new and marvelous way:

> *We have read your manuscript with boundless delight. If we were to publish your paper it would be impossible for us to publish any work of a lower standard. As it is unthinkable that, in the next thousand years, we shall see its equal, we are, to our regret, compelled to return your divine composition, and to beg you a thousand times to overlook our short sight and timidity.*

Can you remember an experience that affected you so strongly that it changed the entire direction of your life? Here a writer describes a turning point in his life, when, he says "at the eleventh hour as it were, I had discovered a calling."

LEARNING TO WRITE

Russell Baker

When our class was assigned to Mr. Fleagle for third-year English I anticipated another grim year in that dreariest of subjects. Mr. Fleagle was notorious among City students for dullness and inability to inspire. He was said to be stuffy, dull, and hopelessly out of date. To me he looked to be sixty or seventy and prim to a fault. He wore primly severe eyeglasses, his wavy hair was primly cut and primly combed. He wore prim vested suits with neckties blocked primly against the collar buttons of his primly starched white shirts. He had a primly pointed jaw, a primly straight nose, and a prim manner of speaking that was so correct, so gentlemanly, that he seemed a comic antique.   1

I anticipated a listless, unfruitful year with Mr. Fleagle and for a long time was not disappointed. We read *Macbeth.* Mr. Fleagle loved *Macbeth* and wanted us to love it too, but he lacked the gift of infecting others with his own passion. He tried to convey the murderous ferocity of Lady Macbeth one day by reading aloud the passage that concludes   2

> . . . I have given suck, and know
> How tender 'tis to love the babe that milks me.
> I would, while it was smiling in my face,
> Have plucked my nipple from his boneless gums . . .

The idea of prim Mr. Fleagle plucking his nipple from boneless gums was too much for the class. We burst into gasps of irrepressible snickering. Mr. Fleagle stopped.   3

"There is nothing funny, boys, about giving suck to a babe. It is the very essence of motherhood, don't you see."   4

He constantly sprinkled his sentences with "don't you see." It wasn't a question but an exclamation of mild surprise at our ignorance. "Your pronoun needs an antecedent, don't you see," he would say, very primly. "The purpose of the Porter's scene, boys, is to provide comic relief from the horror, don't you see."   5

Late in the year we tackled the informal essay. "The essay, don't you see, is the. . . ." My mind went numb. Of all forms of writing, none seemed so boring as the essay. Naturally we would have to write informal essays. Mr. Fleagle distributed a homework sheet offering us a choice of topics. None was quite so simpleminded as "What I Did on My Summer Vacation," but most seemed to be almost as dull. I took the list home and dawdled until the night before the essay was due. Sprawled on the sofa, I finally faced up to the grim task, took the list out of   6 my notebook, and scanned it. The topic on which my eye stopped was "The Art of Eating Spaghetti."

7   This title produced an extraordinary sequence of mental images. Surging up out of the depths of memory came a vivid recollection of a night in Belleville when all of us were seated around the supper table—Uncle Allen, my mother, Uncle Charlie, Doris, Uncle Hal—and Aunt Pat served spaghetti for supper. Spaghetti was an exotic treat in those days. Neither Doris nor I had ever eaten spaghetti, and none of the adults had enough experience to be good at it. All the good humor of Uncle Allen's house reawoke in my mind as I recalled the laughing arguments we had that night about the socially respectable method for moving spaghetti from plate to mouth.

8   Suddenly I wanted to write about that, about the warmth and good feeling of it, but I wanted to put it down simply for my own joy, not for Mr. Fleagle. It was a moment I wanted to recapture and hold for myself. I wanted to relive the pleasure of an evening at New Street. To write it as I wanted, however, would violate all the rules of formal composition I'd learned in school, and Mr. Fleagle would surely give it a failing grade. Never mind. I would write something else for Mr. Fleagle after I had written this thing for myself.

9   When I finished it the night was half gone and there was no time left to compose a proper, respectable essay for Mr. Fleagle. There was no choice next morning but to turn in my private reminiscence of Belleville. Two days passed before Mr. Fleagle returned the graded papers, and he returned everyone's but mine. I was bracing myself for a command to report to Mr. Fleagle immediately after school for discipline when I saw him lift my paper from his desk and rap for the class's attention.

10   "Now, boys," he said, "I want to read you an essay. This is titled 'The Art of Eating Spaghetti.'"

11   And he started to read. My words! He was reading my words out loud to the entire class. What's more, the entire class was listening. Listening attentively. Then somebody laughed, then the entire class was laughing, and not in contempt and ridicule, but with openhearted enjoyment. Even Mr. Fleagle stopped two or three times to repress a small prim smile.

12   I did my best to avoid showing pleasure, but what I was feeling was pure ecstasy at this startling demonstration that my words had the power to make people laugh. In the eleventh grade, at the eleventh hour as it were, I had discovered a calling. It was the happiest moment of my entire school career. When Mr. Fleagle finished he put the final seal on my happiness by saying, "Now that, boys, is an essay, don't you see. It's—don't you see—it's the very essence of the essay, don't you see. Congratulations, Mr. Baker."

Vocabulary

Directions: Locate each of the key words in the reading selection. Then read and study each word in its context and try to determine its meaning. Use a dictionary or thesaurus to check your guess. Write the meanings of the words in the margin of the text.

Record the new words you've learned in the following chart.

Key Word	Paragraph	Meaning
1. grim	1	
2. prim	1	
3. listless	2	
4. dawdled	6	
5. reminiscence	9	
6. ecstasy	12	
7. calling	12	
Others?		

Guide Questions

Directions: These questions will guide your understanding of what you have read. They also will help you to analyze and evaluate the author's ideas and apply them to the real world and your own life.

Write answers to the questions in your notebook or on a separate sheet of paper if your instructor wishes to collect them. Your answers will form the basis of class discussion.

1. a. In describing Mr. Fleagle, Baker uses the word *prim* again and again. Surely you have been taught by your writing teachers not to constantly repeat words in your essays. Why does Baker do it here? What effect does it have on the reader?
   b. What other words or phrases are repeated in the story?
2. Describe your impression of Mr. Fleagle at the beginning of the story. Does your opinion of him change by the end? Explain.
3. When Mr. Fleagle first assigns the informal essay, Baker dreads having to write it. What makes him change his mind and get excited about writing an essay?
4. What does Baker mean when he says in the last paragraph, "In the eleventh grade, at the eleventh hour as it were, I had discovered a calling"? Have you experienced a similar moment?

Application

Directions: Read this story about the great Russian writer Anton Chekhov.

Chekhov told the story of a kitten that was given to his uncle. Wanting to make a champion mouse-killer of the kitten, the uncle set out to train it when it was still very young. First he showed the kitten a live mouse in a cage. The kitten inspected the mouse curiously but without any hostility. The uncle, wanting the kitten to know the mouse was its enemy, slapped and scolded the kitten and sent it away in disgrace. The next day the uncle again showed the mouse to the kitten. This time the kitten looked at the mouse fearfully, but still did not show any signs of attack. Again the uncle slapped and scolded the kitten and sent it away. Day after day, the training went on until the kitten would begin to scream and cry the moment it saw the mouse. The uncle became furious and gave away the kitten, saying it would never learn. He did not realize that the kitten had indeed learned exactly what it had been taught. "I can sympathize with that kitten," said Chekhov, "because that same uncle tried to teach me Latin."

Describe your experience learning to write in elementary and high school. Was it similar to Russell Baker's experience? Or more like the experience of the kitten in Chekhov's story? Write one paragraph.

Writing

Directions: Write one or two paragraphs describing, as Baker does in his story, "the happiest moment of my entire school career."

Do you groan aloud when faced with the prospect of writing a personal letter? Does it seem like a burden and a chore? Or is it a pleasant opportunity to express yourself to a friend in a relaxed way? Why write a letter these days when it's so easy to pick up the telephone? How are letters and phone calls different? Would you rather have a call from an old friend or receive a letter? Garrison Keillor, the popular radio show host and writer, gives us some delightful insights on the value of letter writing and some practical hints on how to write a good letter—"to be our own sweet selves and express the music of our souls."

HOW TO WRITE A PERSONAL LETTER

Garrison Keillor

We shy persons need to write a letter now and then, or else we'll dry up and blow   1
away. It's true. And I speak as one who loves to reach for the phone, dial the
number, and talk. I say "Big Bopper here—what's shakin', babes?" The telephone is to shyness what Hawaii is to February, it's a way out of the woods, and yet:
a letter is better.

Such a sweet gift—a piece of handmade writing, in an envelope that is not   2
a bill, sitting in our friend's path when she trudges home from a long day spent
among wahoos and savages, a day our words will help repair. They don't need to
be immortal, just sincere. She can read them twice and again tomorrow: *You're
someone I care about, Corinne, and think of often and every time I do you make me smile.*

We need to write, otherwise nobody will know who we are. They will have   3
only a vague impression of us as A Nice Person, because frankly, we don't shine
at conversation, we lack the confidence to thrust our faces forward and say, "Hi,
I'm Heather Hooten, let me tell you about my week." Mostly we say "Uh-huh"
and "Oh really." People smile and look over our shoulder, looking for someone
else to talk to.

So a shy person sits down and writes a letter. To be known by another person—   4
to meet and talk freely on the page—to be close despite distance. To escape
from anonymity and be our own sweet selves and express the music of our souls.

Same thing that moves a giant rock star to sing his heart out in front of   5
123,000 people moves us to take ballpoint pen in hand and write a few lines to
our dear Aunt Eleanor. *We want to be known.* We want her to know that we have
fallen in love, that we quit our job, that we're moving to New York, and we want
to say a few things that might not get said in casual conversation: *thank you for
what you've meant to me, I am very happy right now.*

Skip the Guilt

The first step in writing letters is to get over the guilt of *not* writing. You don't   6
"owe" anybody a letter. Letters are a gift. The burning shame you feel when you
see unanswered mail makes it harder to pick up a pen and makes for a cheerless
letter when you finally do. *I feel bad about not writing, but I've been so busy,* etc. Skip
this. Few letters are obligatory, and they are *Thanks for the wonderful gift* and *I am*

terribly sorry to hear about George's death, and *Yes, you're welcome to stay with us next month,* and not many more than that. Write those promptly if you want to keep your friends. Don't worry about the others, except love letters, of course. When your true love writes *Dear Light of My Life, Joy of My Heart, O Lovely Pulsating Core of My Sensate Life,* some response is called for.

7   Some of the best letters are tossed off in a burst of inspiration, so keep your writing stuff in one place where you can sit down for a few minutes and *Dear Ray, I am in the middle of an essay for* International Paper *but thought I'd drop you a line. Hi to your sweetie too;* dash off a note to a pal. Envelopes, stamps, address book, everything in a drawer so you can write fast when the pen is hot.

8   A blank white 8″ by 11″ sheet can look as big as Montana if the pen's not so hot—try a smaller page and write boldly. Or use a note card with a piece of fine art on the front; if your letter ain't good, at least they get the Matisse. Get a pen that makes a sensuous line, get a comfortable typewriter, a friendly word processor—whichever feels easy to the hand.

9   Sit for a few minutes with the blank sheet in front of you, and meditate on the person you will write to, let your friend come to mind until you can almost see her or him in the room with you. Remember the last time you saw each other and how your friend looked and what you said and what perhaps was unsaid between you, and when your friend becomes real to you, start to write.

Tell Us What You're Doing

10   Write the salutation—*Dear You*—and take a deep breath and plunge in. A simple declarative sentence will do, followed by another and another and another. Tell us what you're doing and tell it like you were talking to us. Don't think about grammar, don't think about lit'ry style, don't try to write dramatically, just give us your news. Where did you go? who did you see, what did they say, what do you think?

11   If you don't know where to begin, start with the present moment: *I'm sitting at the kitchen table on a rainy Saturday morning. Everyone is gone and the house is quiet.* Let your simple description of the present moment lead to something else, let the letter drift gently along.

Take It Easy

12   The toughest letter to crank out is one that is meant to impress, as we all know from writing job applications; if it's hard work to slip off a letter to a friend, maybe you're trying too hard to be terrific. A letter is only a report to someone who already likes you for reasons other than your brilliance. Take it easy.

13   Don't worry about form. It's not a term paper. When you come to the end of one episode, just start a new paragraph. You can go from a few lines about the sad state of rock 'n' roll to the fight with your mother to your fond memories of Mexico to your cat's urinary-tract infection to a few thoughts on personal indebtedness to the kitchen sink and what's in it. The more you write, the easier it gets, and when you have a True True Friend to write to, a *compadre,* a soul sibling, then it's

like driving a car down a country road, you just get behind the keyboard and press on the gas.

Don't tear up the page and start over when you write a bad line—try to write   14
your way out of it. Make mistakes and plunge on. Let the letter cook along and let yourself be bold. Outrage, confusion, love—whatever is in your mind, let it find a way to the page. Writing is a means of discovery, always, and when you come to the end and write *Yours ever* or *Hugs and Kisses,* you'll know something you didn't when you wrote *Dear Pal.*

An Object of Art

Probably your friend will put your letter away, and it'll be read again a few years   15
from now—and it will improve with age.

And forty years from now, your friend's grandkids will dig it out of the attic   16
and read it, a sweet and precious relic of the ancient Nineties that gives them a sudden clear glimpse of you and her and the world we old-timers knew. You will then have created an object of art. Your simple lines about where you went, who you saw, what they said, will speak to those children and they will feel in their hearts the humanity of our times.

You can't pick up a phone and call the future and tell them about our times.   17
You have to pick up a piece of paper.

Vocabulary

Directions: Locate each of the key words in the reading selection. Then read and study each word in its context and try to determine its meaning. Use a dictionary or thesaurus to check your guess. Write the meanings of the words in the margin of the text.

Record the new words you've learned.

Key Word	Paragraph	Meaning
1. trudges	2	
2. anonymity	4	
3. sensuous	8	
4. relic	16	
Others?		

Guide Questions

Directions: These questions will guide your understanding of what you have read. Write your answers in your notebook or on a separate sheet of paper if your instructor wishes to collect it. Your answers to these questions will be the basis of class discussion.

1. Garrison Keillor is probably America's best-known "shy person." Yet it seems that making a phone call or writing a letter is a pleasure for him. Why do you think that is true? If you are also a shy person, do you feel the same way that Keillor does about phoning and writing?
2. What does Keillor mean when he says in paragraph 8, "if your letter ain't good, at least they get the Matisse." Your answer must, of course, identify Matisse.
3. Summarize the hints Keillor gives for writing a good letter.
4. Look back over the selection. Note the many words that are printed in italic type. Italics are often used for emphasis, as in paragraph 5, where Keillor says with feeling, *"We want to be known."* But why are italics used in other places, for example in paragraph 11, *"I'm sitting at the kitchen table . . ."?*

Application

Directions: In a small group, compare and contrast writing a letter to making a phone call. Discuss the advantages and disadvantages of each. Use the following chart to organize your ideas.

	Letters	Phone Calls
Advantages		
Disadvantages		

Writing

Directions: Choose one of the following assignments.

1. Write a letter to a friend you haven't seen for a long time. Use the advice Keillor gives you in this selection. At the end of the letter, write a paragraph describing how the advice helped you.
2. Using the advice Keillor gives in this essay, write a letter to one of your instructors. In your letter, ask any questions you may have about any of

the topics in the course, the course itself, or school in general. You may have some comments for the instructor that you would prefer to make in writing rather than in person—use this letter as your opportunity to speak your mind. Your letter should be at least one page, preferably typewritten.

Marking Text

Mark this selection "How to Write a Personal Letter." Remember, marking text is explained on page 413.

Who would believe that a black South African boy so poor his family often had nothing to eat, who did not learn English until he was ten, who attended schools under the poorest possible conditions, would go on to graduate from an American university and write a best-selling autobiography? Here, Mark Mathabane, the author of Kaffir Boy, *tells how writing helped him to survive and to heal himself.*

KAFFIR BOY AT THE TYPEWRITER

Determination and a Creative Gift Offer a Rescue from Hell

Mark Mathabane

1   I was born and raised in Alexandra township, a squalid one-square-mile ghetto just outside Johannesburg, South Africa, with a population of more than 150,000 blacks. The eldest of seven children—two boys and five girls—I lived with my parents and siblings in a shack made of crumbling bricks and rusted sheets of metal zinks. The shack measured roughly 15 × 15 feet. Till I was ten, my siblings and I slept on pieces of cardboard under the kitchen table. During the bitterly cold months of June and July my mother reinforced our flimsy blanket with pieces of old newspapers. My father, whose self-taught skills as a carpenter the Job Discrimination Act (an apartheid law) refused to recognize, earned about $10 a week as a menial laborer. He was often arrested for the "crime" of being unemployed.

2   Whenever my father was carted away to prison, the family, to stay alive, scavenged for half-eaten sandwiches thrown away by whites at the garbage dump. Sometimes we ate leech-like worms called *sonjas* or begged at the local abattoir for cattle blood, which we boiled as soup. During good times, our diet consisted mostly of cornmeal, chicken feet and heads, cattle intestines and greens. There were many days when nothing was available to eat, and we would simply stare at each other, at the empty pots, and at the sun going down.

3   My mother attempted to still our pangs of hunger with her mesmerizing storytelling. Her stories about black culture, traditions, magic, and heroes and heroines were the only books we had. By sharpening my sensibilities and firing my curiosity and imagination, these stories, almost Homeric in their vividness, drama, and invention, became the seeds of my own creativity.

4   To force blacks to leave Alexandra and move to their respective homelands— arid and impoverished reservations run by ruthless and corrupt tribal leaders— the government ordered the local *Peri-Urban* police to raid the ghetto frequently, making random arrests for Influx Control infractions. Under these Kafkaesque laws, my parents had to have a permit allowing them to live together as husband and wife under the same roof. They couldn't get it. So as a child I was awakened almost daily by brutal midnight police raids, which were launched amid a pandemonium of blaring sirens, barking dogs, and thumping feet. I would watch in horror as my parents were marched naked out of bed and interrogated in the middle of the shack.

Though illiterate, my mother, a woman of indomitable faith, courage, and   5
love, believed that an education might rescue me from the pit of poverty, suffering, and degradation into which I was born, and for all intents and purposes, into
which I was expected to die. The black educational system, known as *Bantu
Education,* was designed in the '50s by Dr. H. Verwoerd, a fanatical believer in
apartheid. It was meant to reconcile us black children to our subjection and the
status quo, to keep us ignorant of our fundamental rights as human beings, and
to make us better servants of whites. That is why, on June 16, 1976, black students revolted against it.

My father was vehemently opposed to *Bantu Education*—partly because he   6
felt that it strained his meager wages at a time when survival was first priority;
partly because he saw many educated blacks working at menial jobs. It was left
to my mother to struggle almost singlehandedly to have me educated. Since
black education was not free or compulsory, it took her nearly six months to
obtain the birth certificate and permits necessary to enroll me in the local tribal
school, which I refused to attend. On my first day of school, she and my grandmother had to literally bind me and drag me to school for the boys on the streets
had told me horror stories about teachers beating pupils for lacking books, uniforms, or school fees. My mother used food money to purchase me a slate and uniform, and to pay my school fees. This infuriated my father, who then beat my
mother. Witnessing my mother's abuse made me pledge to her that I would go to
school for as long as she wanted me to, despite the hardships of black education.
Through discipline, drive, and respect for teachers, I soon became the top student.

I began learning English, my fifth language, when I was about ten. When I   7
was eleven, my grandmother—who worked for a white family that didn't believe
in apartheid—took me to the white world for the first time in my life. I remember gaping with amazement at the large, beautiful homes with neat lawns and
beds of flowers, the many stores, the paved roads, the many cars, the neatly
dressed and happy-looking white schoolchildren, the tennis courts and swim-
ming pools. *Why is life for whites paradisiacal and for blacks hellish?* I began asking.
Granny's employer began giving me books that were only read in white schools.
These "revolutionary" books—*Treasure Island, David Copperfield,* and other
classics—changed my life. They convinced me that there was a world beyond
that of the violence, poverty, and suffering in which I was steeped. They helped
emancipate me from mental slavery and taught me to believe in my own worth
and abilities, despite apartheid's attempts to limit my aspirations and prescribe
my place in life.

When I was around thirteen, I began working for Granny's employer on   8
weekends. I mowed the lawn, washed cars, cleaned the pool, polished brass and
silver and shoes, and swept the driveway. One day I was given a slightly warped
tennis racket as extra payment for a day's work well done.

I took the racket back to the ghetto and began pounding balls against the   9
wall at the local stadium where there were a couple sand courts. In November
1973, nearly a year after I took up tennis, Arthur Ashe was finally allowed to set
foot on South African soil. Before that he had been *persona non grata* because of his

harsh criticism of apartheid. Like all black children in South Africa, I idolized black American athletes and entertainers, who, we assumed, were typical of blacks in America. I went to see Ashe play in Johannesburg, and he became my first positive role model. He was the first free black man I had ever seen. His intelligence, brilliant tennis skills, and confidence before whites filled me with a desire to come to America.

10   I realized that dream in 1977 when I met 1972 Wimbledon champion Stan Smith and his wife, Margie, during a tournament in which I was the only black playing. After listening to my life story, and my desire to attend college in America, Stan and Margie agreed to help. Upon returning to the States, Stan contacted college tennis coaches on my behalf. In the fall of 1978, I finally left South Africa on a full tennis scholarship to Limestone College in South Carolina.

11   Once in America, I realized how unrealistic my dream of becoming a professional athlete was. I began emphasizing my education. Culture shock, my refusal to allow coaches to exploit my athletic abilities at the expense of my education, and my desire to express my individuality rather than conform and blindly follow custom and authority, all combined to force me to transfer colleges three times, during which time I lost my scholarship and was supported by Stan Smith.

12   Shortly after transferring to Dowling College, my fourth school, I volunteered to become the first black editor of the college paper, even though I couldn't yet type properly. In life I have always taken risks. Working on the paper convinced me that, as my favorite novelist, Joseph Conrad, said, "The right accent and the right word can move the world." And his incredible story of not learning English until he was in his twenties, and of not writing a word until he was in his late thirties, inspired me to begin *Kaffir Boy,* especially since, a year earlier, I had become infected by the fiery eloquence of Richard Wright, and longed to write about black life in South Africa the way he wrote about black life in the South.

13   When I began writing *Kaffir Boy* one snowy winter morning during my junior year, when I was twenty-one, I hardly dreamed that my story would become a nationwide bestseller, reaching #1 on *The Washington Post* bestseller list and #3 on *The New York Times* list. I did not even think it would get published.

14   Many who heard that I was writing a book dismissed my attempt as futile. Some thought I was crazy. But I was undeterred. I was determined to prove them wrong. Though there were times when I despaired, when I thought of giving up, writing down the experiences that had once haunted me—the night I witnessed a grisly murder, the day I attempted suicide at age ten, the morning my mother and I discovered a dead baby while scavenging for food at the garbage dump (black mothers were sometimes driven to kill their babies so they would not lose their jobs)—gave me a feeling of being purged. I was finally able to fully accept who I was and where I came from. In short, I wrote to heal myself as well as inform others.

15   After graduating from Dowling College with a degree in economics, I wanted nothing more than to complete writing *Kaffir Boy.* I approached Stan Smith with the idea and he agreed to support me for a year while I completed the

book (under immigration laws, I wasn't allowed to work at the time). During this year of writing continuously, I was occasionally asked to speak publicly about my years in South Africa.

One day Oprah Winfrey saw the paperback version of *Kaffir Boy* prominently displayed in a bookstore. She bought a copy. She was so moved by the story that she tracked me down and offered me an appearance on her show. When she learned that I had been separated from my family for nearly nine years, she helped bring several members to America. Our reunion on *Oprah* made nationwide headlines. Shortly thereafter the book became a bestseller in paperback, with more than 200,000 copies in print. It is required reading in many high schools across the nation. Most readers of *Kaffir Boy* wanted to know what happened to me and my family after I left South Africa in 1978. The results of those requests is *Kaffir Boy in America,* which was published in June [1989].

My advice to aspiring writers is never lose hope—keep writing and believing in yourself despite the rejection slips, despite what others may say. Something within compelled me to begin writing my book—an inner voice yearning to be heard; a need to understand myself and come to terms with my past; a longing to show the rest of the world the deplorable truths, in human terms, about the system of legalized segregation and racial discrimination in my homeland. Above all, I wanted to record how, through the support of my family, through clinging to the positive values I was taught when a child, through believing that education was a powerful weapon of hope, and through a determination never to give up the struggle to influence my own destiny, I was able to survive the raging hell of the ghetto with my soul and dignity largely intact.

Vocabulary

Directions: Locate each of the key words in the reading selection. Then read and study each word in its context and try to determine its meaning. Use a dictionary or thesaurus to check your guess. Write the meanings of the words in the margin of the text.

Record the new words you've learned in the following chart.

Key Word	Paragraph	Meaning
1. squalid	1	
2. scavenged	2	
3. mesmerizing	3	
4. pandemonium	4	
5. indomitable	5	
6. vehemently	6	

Key Word	Paragraph	Meaning
7. emancipate	7	
8. warped	8	
9. *persona non grata*	9	
10. eloquence	12	
11. deplorable	17	
Others?		

Guide Questions

Directions: These questions will guide your understanding of what you have read. They also will help you to analyze and evaluate the author's ideas and apply them to the real world and your own life.

Write answers to the questions in your notebook or on a separate sheet of paper if your instructor wishes to collect them. Your answers will form the basis of class discussion.

1. Synthesize the information in the story with what you already know about South Africa and its system of apartheid. Paint a picture in words of life in South Africa for black people in the 1970s when Mathabane was growing up.
2. Describe the factors that helped Mathabane rise above what he describes as the "hell" of life in South Africa to become a success.
3. Mathabane describes such books as *Treasure Island* and *David Copperfield* as "revolutionary." Are these books considered revolutionary in the United States? Why do you think South Africa considered them revolutionary?
4. Mathabane tells us that entertainers and athletes like tennis star Arthur Ashe were assumed to be "typical of blacks in America." Why do you think he believed this? Was it true? Explain.
5. Mathabane says he wrote "to heal myself as well as to inform others." What does he mean by this?

Application

Directions: Mathabane makes allusions to several important writers in his story: Homer (in paragraph 3); Franz Kafka (in paragraph 4); Joseph Conrad (in paragraph 12); and Richard Wright (in paragraph 12). If you are not familiar with these men and their work, visit the library or use the Internet to learn about them. In small groups, discuss who they were and the importance of their work.

Writing

Directions: Does Mathabane's notion of the value of writing ring true to you? Can you imagine using writing to help yourself feel better? One study showed that college students who spent time writing about their thoughts and experiences had more positive feelings about school and fewer visits to the infirmary. Other studies found that writing can help people recover from personal tragedy. James Pennebaker, a professor of psychology at Southern Methodist University, says that "The act of writing helps label and organize stressful events, making them seem more manageable." Have you ever tried it? If you have, write a paragraph or two describing the experience and how you benefited from it.

If you have never tried it, try it now. Think about a problem you are currently struggling with. Write it down, describing it in detail. Then write as many possible solutions as you can to the problem. In your last few sentences, state whether this exercise helped you begin to solve the problem or made you feel better.

SHORT TAKE

Speaking Different Languages

Deborah Tannen

An American woman set out for a vacation cruise and landed in a Turkish prison. Reading her book *Never Pass This Way Again,* I could see that Gene LePere's ordeal was an extreme example of the disastrous consequences that can result from cross-cultural differences in what I term conversational style—ways of framing how you mean what you say, and what you think you are doing when you say it. LePere's experience also illustrates, in an unusually dramatic way, the dangers of trying to avoid conflict and say "no" in a polite way.

LePere left her cruise ship for a brief tour of ancient ruins in Turkey. At an archeological site, she fell behind her group as she became absorbed in admiring the ruins. Suddenly, her path was blocked by a man selling artifacts she had no interest in buying. Yet she found herself holding a stone head, and when she told him politely that she did not want it, he would not take it back. Instead, he thrust forward another one, which she also automatically accepted. Since the man would not take either head back, the only path to escape she could envision was offering to buy them. She cut his price in half and hoped he'd refuse so she could move on. Instead he agreed to drop the price, and she dropped the two heads into her tote. But as she handed him the money, he handed her a third head. Once more she insisted she did not want it, but he just stepped back to avoid repossessing it. Seeing no alternative, she paid for the third head and stalked off—shaken and angry.

When LePere tried to reboard her cruise ship, she showed her purchases to customs officials, who had her arrested and thrown into jail for trying to smuggle out a national treasure. The third head was a genuine antiquity.

Having lived in Greece and observed the verbal art of bargaining, I could see that talking to the vendor and saying she did not want the artifacts would mean to him that she might want them if the price were lower. If she really had no intention of buying, she would not have talked to him at all. She would have pushed her way past him and walked on, never establishing eye contact—and surely not taking possession of any heads, no matter how insistently he proffered them. Each time she accepted a head, he received evidence of her interest and encouragement to offer another. Each step in his increasingly aggressive sales pitch was a response to what likely appeared to him as her bargaining maneuvers. Refusing to look at or talk to him, or, as a last resort, placing the heads on the ground—these were unthinkable alternatives for a polite American woman.

COLLABORATIVE LEARNING

Working in Groups to Guide Your Own Reading

All of the reading selections so far in this unit have been accompanied by questions and exercises that are meant to help you understand and use what you've read. However, in much of your college reading (not to mention in your real life), you will be expected to master the material on your own.

Research has shown that one of the most effective ways to learn is in *groups*. In college, working with classmates can help you to master the material of a college course. The give-and-take that comes naturally when working with other people helps us to avoid falling into bad habits like *passive reading*. (We have all had the awful experience of reading a whole chapter, then realizing that we don't remember one single thing we've read.) Working with other students will help you to avoid such problems. For this assignment, form groups of approximately four students. In your group, read and think about the two following reading selections: "Rx: Translation, Please?" by Perri Klass and "Translating America" by Chris Hedges. Then, create your own vocabulary chart, guide questions, and application and writing assignments.

Follow these steps to complete the assignment:

1. Preview the selection before you read—look at and think about the title, any headings or subheadings, the first paragraph, the last paragraph, and the first sentence of each paragraph.
2. Read through the selection one time quickly.
3. Read the selection a second time, more carefully. This time mark the text. Review how to do this by reading "Learning Strategy III—Marking Text" beginning on page 413.
4. Brainstorm with your group. Ask yourselves: What important issues is the author discussing? What new information did you learn? Can the issues discussed in the selection be connected to those you have already studied? Can any of the information here be applied to situations in your own life?
5. Now, create a set of exercises similar to those you have completed in previous chapters of this book:
   a. **Vocabulary.** Make a list of key words from the text. Set them up in chart format as on page 156.
   b. **Guide Questions.** Write questions that will guide understanding of the major ideas in the reading.
   c. **Application.** Prepare an application exercise that takes one or more of the important ideas in the reading and relates it to real life.
   d. **Writing.** Create a writing assignment to conclude the chapter.

Before you begin, it would be a good idea to review the questions and exercises in the previous reading selections in this book.

When you are finished, submit your work to your instructor. Your instructor may review and combine the work of all the groups and return the exercise to the class. You will then have the opportunity to *answer* the questions you and your classmates have developed.

Now, use your skills as an active, independent reader to tackle the following reading selections. Good luck!

Perri Klass is both a doctor and a writer, so it is only natural she would take an interest in the special language of medicine. Many professions have their own jargon (if you have ever spent an evening with a group of computer specialists, you know what true loneliness is), but Klass illustrates that the special idiom of medicine is especially fascinating—as well as confusing, frightening, useful, and . . . seductive.

RX: TRANSLATION, PLEASE?

Perri Klass

"Mrs. Tolstoy is your basic L.O.L. in N.A.D., admitted for a soft rule-out M.I.," the intern announces. I scribble that on my patient list. In other words Mrs. Tolstoy is a Little Old Lady in No Apparent Distress who is in the hospital to make sure she hasn't had a heart attack (rule out a myocardial infarction). And we think it's unlikely that she has had a heart attack (a *soft* rule-out).

If I learned nothing else during my first three months of working in the hospital as a medical student, I learned endless jargon and abbreviations. I started out in a state of primeval innocence, in which I didn't even know that "s̄ C.P., S.O.B., N/V" meant "without chest pain, shortness of breath, or nausea and vomiting." By the end I took the abbreviations so for granted that I would complain to my mother the English professor, "And can you believe I had to put down *three* NG tubes last night?"

"You'll have to tell me what an NG tube is if you want me to sympathize properly," my mother said. NG, nasogastric—isn't it obvious?

I picked up not only the specific expressions but also the patterns of speech and the grammatical conventions; for example, you never say that a patient's blood pressure fell or that his cardiac enzymes rose. Instead, the patient is always the subject of the verb: "He dropped his pressure." "He bumped his enzymes." This sort of construction probably reflects that profound irritation of the intern when the nurses come in the middle of the night to say that Mr. Dickinson has disturbingly low blood pressure. "Oh, he's gonna hurt me bad tonight," the intern may say, inevitably angry at Mr. Dickinson for dropping his pressure and creating a problem.

When chemotherapy fails to cure Mrs. Bacon's cancer, what we say is, "Mrs. Bacon failed chemotherapy."

"Well, we've already had one hit today, and we're up next, but at least we've got mostly stable players on our team." This means that our team (group of doctors and medical students) has already gotten one new admission today, and it is our turn again, so we'll get whoever is next admitted in emergency, but at least most of the patients we already have are fairly stable, that is, unlikely to drop their pressures or in any other way get suddenly sicker and hurt us bad. Baseball metaphor is pervasive: a no-hitter is a night without any new admissions. A player is always a patient—a nitrate player is a patient on nitrates, a unit player is a patient in the intensive-care unit, and so on, until you reach the terminal player.

It is interesting to consider what it means to be winning, or doing well, in this perennial baseball game. When the intern hangs up the phone and announces,

"I got a hit," that is not cause for congratulations. The team is not scoring points; rather, it is getting hit, being bombarded with new patients. The object of the game from the point of view of the doctors, considering the players for whom they are already responsible, is to get as few new hits as possible.

8   These special languages contribute to a sense of closeness and professional spirit among people who are under a great deal of stress. As a medical student, it was exciting for me to discover that I'd finally cracked the code, that I could understand what doctors said and wrote and could use the same formulations myself. Some people seem to become enamored of the jargon for its own sake, perhaps because they are so deeply thrilled with the idea of medicine, with the idea of themselves as doctors.

9   I knew a medical student who was referred to by the interns on the team as Mr. Eponym because he was so infatuated with eponymous terminology,* the more obscure the better. He never said "capillary pulsation" if he could say "Quincke's pulses." He would lovingly tell over the multinamed syndromes— Wolff–Parkinson–White, Lown–Ganong–Levine, Henoch–Schonlein—until the temptation to suggest Schleswig–Holstein or Stevenson–Kefauver or Baskin–Robbins became irresistible to his less reverent colleagues.

10   And there is the jargon that you don't ever want to hear yourself using. You know that your training is changing you, but there are certain changes you think would be going a little too far.

11   The resident was describing a man with devastating terminal pancreatic cancer. "Basically he's C.T.D.," the resident concluded. I reminded myself that I had resolved not to be shy about asking when I didn't understand things. "C.T.D.?" I asked timidly.

12   The resident smirked at me. "Circling The Drain."

13   The images are vivid and terrible. "What happened to Mrs. Melville?"

14   "Oh, she boxed last night." To box is to die, of course.

15   Then there are the more pompous locutions that can make the beginning medical student nervous about the effects of medical training. A friend of mine was told by his resident, "A pregnant woman with sickle-cell represents a failure of genetic counseling."

16   Mr. Eponym, who tried hard to talk like the doctors, once explained to me, "An infant is basically a brainstem preparation." A brainstem preparation, as used in neurological research, is an animal whose higher brain functions have been destroyed so that only the most primitive reflexes remain, like the sucking reflex, the startle reflex, and the rooting reflex.

17   The more extreme forms aside, one most important function of medical jargon is to help doctors maintain some distance from their patients. By reformulating a patient's pain and problems into a language that the patient doesn't even speak, I suppose we are in some sense taking those pains and problems under our jurisdiction and also reducing their emotional impact. This linguistic separation

---

* *Eponymous* means "named after"—in this case, diseases or syndromes are named after the scientists who discovered them.

between doctors and patients allows conversations to go on at the bedside that are unintelligible to the patient. "Naturally, we're worried about adeno-C.A.," the intern can say to the medical student, and lung cancer need never be mentioned.

I learned a new language this past summer. At times it thrills me to hear myself using it. It enables me to understand my colleagues, to communicate effectively in the hospital. Yet I am uncomfortably aware that I will never again notice the peculiarities and even atrocities of medical language as keenly as I did this summer. There may be specific expressions I manage to avoid, but even as I remark on them, promising myself I will never use them, I find that this language is becoming my professional speech. It no longer sounds strange in my ears—or coming from my mouth. And I am afraid that, as with any new language, to use it properly you must absorb not only the vocabulary but also the structure, the logic, the attitudes. At first you may notice these new alien assumptions every time you put together a sentence, but with time and increased fluency you stop being aware of them at all. And as you lose that awareness, for better or for worse, you move closer and closer to being a doctor instead of just talking like one.

18

Vocabulary

Directions: Mark any important words in the reading selection that you don't know. Then list them in the following chart along with their paragraph numbers. Try to figure out each word's meaning by reading over the context carefully for clues to help you guess the meaning of the unfamiliar word. Check your dictionary or thesaurus to confirm your guess. After discussing the words with your group members, write the meanings in the margin of the text, near the word. Then enter them in the chart.

Key Word	Paragraph	Meaning

Guide Questions

Directions: Develop a list of questions that elicit the important ideas in the reading selection. Start at the beginning and work your way sequentially through the text until you have addressed all of the author's major ideas.

Application

Directions: When you have a list of guide questions, read through the selection again. This time, write one or more questions that require the information in the text to be applied to a situation in the real world.

Writing

Directions: Your last task is to prepare a writing assignment. For example, you might ask for a paragraph in which the writer comments on the ideas in the reading selection. You might also ask for a summary of the selection.

This article, which appeared in The New York Times, *points out one of the less-noted features of immigration: the newcomers often do not speak English. As most grown-ups are painfully aware, it is very difficult to learn a new language as an adult. On the other hand, children soak up their new language like a sponge, leaving them to assume the difficult role of translator in their families. This story focuses on an elementary school in Queens, New York.*

TRANSLATING AMERICA

Chris Hedges

It was an elementary school summit meeting. Crammed around the low table in the first-grade classroom sat the parents (fidgeting nervously), the principal, the first-grade teacher, the speech therapist and the 11-year-old translator, who had been hauled out of her sixth-grade class for the meeting. 1

The news was not unexpected. Eduardo Barros, who like nearly 80 percent of the incoming students in Public School 139 arrived speaking no English, needed to spend another year in first grade to improve his language and comprehension skills. 2

"Mommy," said Edda Barros, who translated the news about her brother to her parents, "they are saying that Eduardo has too much trouble reading and understanding. They do not want to put him in second grade and then move him back down. It is better if he does another year." 3

Edda's was not an unfamiliar role. She accompanies her parents, who were born in Ecuador, to the bank, to the doctor and on shopping trips, as well as to all school functions. It is her job to make sure her brother understands and completes his homework and to riffle through electric and gas bills, business letters, rent notices and school and community announcements. Edda's cousins, some in their 20's, often call with questions about English phrasing. One, who is 30, has used her help to get through a computer course. After learning about American traditions for holidays like Thanksgiving and Easter, Edda explained the customs to her family and insisted that her mother stuff and bake a turkey in November and hide candy eggs around the apartment in April. 4

Like millions of young children in immigrant families, Edda is much more than a translator for first-generation parents who speak little English. She interprets American culture, customs and mores for her parents, at times gently correcting and advising them. She plays a vital and at times nerve-racking role, navigating the complex and intimidating world of hospitals, law offices and officialdom. One slip, she knows, could mean disaster. 5

She assumes, as do more than half the students in her class, responsibilities and duties usually left to parents in English-speaking families. Along the way, she must listen to unvarnished and unsettling accounts of her father's illnesses and looming financial difficulties. It can be, she says, overwhelming. 6

"There are times, especially with doctors, when I have no idea what they are talking about," Edda said in English, seated in her Queens apartment with her parents. 7

"But I have to translate something. My parents rely on me. I have to keep asking and asking what it means, what they are talking about. And sometimes I have my own life, my own work to do, but I have to stop to help my brother or leave to go with mother or father. It is tiring."

8   Teachers and administrators in schools like P.S. 139, where 36 different languages are spoken and 77 of the 100 children in kindergarten come from homes in which the parents speak a foreign language, say young children must often mediate with parents to get them to conform to American society. And each new hurdle loads more onto the children.

9   "It is often too much for their fragile nervous systems," said Khanna Borukhov, a teacher in the English as a Second Language program at P.S. 139.

10   "They want to be leaders, but they do not have the capacity. They struggle to validate themselves, going from family appointment to family appointment. It leads to a kind of role reversal. Parents can begin to resent the power the child assumes. The parent wants to be a parent and the child wants to be a child, but because of the circumstances they cannot. With all that pressure it is hard for the child to function academically."

11   Dr. Gary D. Goldenback, the supervisor of the E.S.L. program for District 28, which includes P.S. 139, says that when children are taken out of school to accompany parents to appointments or on routine chores, the missed classes can affect homework and test scores.

12   "When this is done excessively, it can even harm chances for promotion," he said. "One should remember that some of these parents do not even have the English facility to buy a subway token or ask directions, so they must take the child along."

13   Conflict often comes in later years, when parents try to reclaim the authority they have ceded.

14   "This has contributed to the gang culture," said Frayda Sharaby, an E.S.L. teacher at P.S. 139. "These older children look for other avenues where they can again exercise authority."

15   Conflict also often erupts around benign and simple tasks. Many immigrant parents will not sign school permission slips or allow their children to go on overnight trips.

16   "A lot of these families live in fear of deportation," said Dr. Goldenback. "They fear that something could happen to the child if they sign anything, even a report card. At school, a child may be told every day to get his parents to sign a slip, and at home, his parents may be steadfastly refusing to cooperate. It is a lot of pressure."

17   And there is pressure on these students to Americanize their parents. "Bangladeshi women will typically not leave their homes, day or night, unescorted," said Dr. Goldenback. "The school can call, say a child is sick, but it does not mean the mother can come. She may have to wait for her husband. What looks like negligence is not."

18   Just as parents fight to grasp the new world, teachers fight to comprehend the old. Discussions about summer camps, for example, have disturbed children

from the former Yugoslavia, where families were held in detention centers. Simple rituals, such as fire drills, have sent some children into hysterics.

"We had a child who thought we were being bombed," said Steven C. Rosenberg, the principal of P.S. 139.   19

And school officials, as well as parents, can become perplexed by it all.   20

Cristina Chin, the co-president of the P.S. 139 parents' association, said she resorted at one point to speaking with a parent in an improvised sign language. And Mr. Rosenberg's best efforts to bridge the language gap have sometimes backfired. "I brought a boy in the office to help translate for a couple that did not speak English," he said. "He listened and told me, 'That's not my kind of Chinese.'"   21

Classrooms must also adjust to new traditions, such as allowing Muslims to skip lunch during Ramadan, and new cultural sensitivities.   22

BREAKDOWN

Melting Pot

Primary home language of students attending
Public School 139 in Queens

	Number of Students		Number of Students
Russian	200	Ukrainian	5
English	189	Bengali	4
Spanish	174	Polish	4
Mandarin	53	Portuguese	4
Cantonese	44	Georgian	3
Korean	40	Serbo-Croatian	3
Hindi	30	French	2
Chinese, other or unidentified dialects	21	Japanese	2
Pilipino	10	Khoisan	2
Hebrew	8	Czech	1
Indonesian	8	French-Khmer	1
Romanian	8	Greek	1
Urdu	8	Hungarian	1
Dari/Farsi/Persian	7	Malayalam	1
Albanian	6	Sinhalese	1
Arabic	6	Slovenian	1
Bulgarian	6	Tamil	1
Gujarati	5	Yonba	1

Source: P.S. 139 Queens

23   "I had a child from Iran in my class," said Ms. Sharaby, the E.S.L. teacher. "One day Mitre did something I perceived as brilliant. I said it was not just one thumb up, but two thumbs up. She fell to the floor laughing." The thumbs up sign, it turns out, is a foul insult in Iran.

24   The new wave of immigrants is so diverse that it is also impossible to keep up with the plethora of languages, even in schools such as P.S. 139, where teachers or administsrators speak Spanish, Korean and Russian.

25   The parents-night meetings are broken down into clusters, so children can translate what is being discussed. Newsletters go out in Russian, Spanish, Korean and Chinese, in an effort to reach at least some of the community in their own tongue. And teachers, dizzy with the infusion of cultures, customs and languages, look for ways to make the American experience relevant.

26   "How are the Pilgrims like Russians?" Jackie A. Neuwirt, the first grade teacher in classroom 1-229, asked her pupils one morning last week.

27   Mrs. Neuwirt, whose parents did not speak English when they arrived in Queens in 1959 from Israel, explained to her pupils that the Russians came to the United States to escape religious persecution and find freedom. She pointed to a bulletin board in her classroom labeled "We are the children of the world" that had 15 figures, labeled with names of countries like Peru, Azerbaijan, Nepal and Taiwan, that represented the cultural backgrounds of her 20 students.

28   "How many other people came for this reason?" she asked.

29   The music teacher at P.S. 139, Fern Nash, has the school choral group do songs in Spanish, Portuguese, Russian, Yiddish, French, Korean, German and Mandarin.

30   "We incorporate the school's diversity into the program," she said. "I have Chinese kids who know songs in Yiddish and have danced in Indian costumes. It is all here."

31   Years later, some who assumed the role of interlocutors say it was not only burdensome but uncomfortable.

32   Mrs. Neuwirt's sister, Zeporah Brecker-Gonzalez, a fifth-grade teacher at John I. Smith Elementary in Miami, remembers what it felt like to be the family translator.

33   "I was often embarrassed that my parents could not speak English or assimiliate," she said. "I wanted to be just like the other kids. I wanted to be an American."

34   One way she rebelled was by refusing to respond in Hebrew when her parents spoke to her. Despite the family tensions, she said she believed she was a stronger person for the experience.

35   "They could not help me with my homework," she said of her parents. "I had to do it myself. I could not depend on them to help me as much as other parents that spoke English. It made me more self-reliant than other children."

Vocabulary

Directions: Mark any important words in the reading selection that you don't know. Then list them in the following chart along with their paragraph numbers. Try to figure out each word's meaning by reading over the context carefully for clues to help you guess the meaning of the unfamiliar word. Check your dictionary or thesaurus to confirm your guess. After you discuss the words with your group members, write the meanings in the margin of the text, near the word. Then enter them in the following chart.

Key Word	Paragraph	Meaning

Guide Questions

Directions: Develop a list of questions that elicit the important ideas in the reading selection. Start at the beginning and work your way sequentially through the text until you have addressed all of the author's major ideas.

Application

Directions: When you have a list of guide questions, read through the selection again. This time write one or more questions that require the information in the text to be applied to a situation in the real world.

Writing

Directions: Your last task is to prepare a writing assignment. For example, you might ask for a paragraph in which the writer comments on the ideas in the reading selection. You might also ask for a summary of the selection.

SPECIAL PROJECT

LANGUAGE

A Personal Mini-Dictionary

Many of the new words you will encounter in your college reading will not be words used in everyday speaking and writing. Rather, they will be specific to your major field of study, to your future career. For example, terms such as *double-entry system, trial balance*, and *amortization* are generally used in the accounting field and not by the general public. Science and technology abound with vocabulary unique to their fields. For example, *hardware, software, boot*, and *byte* are words used in the computer field.

For this project you will create a mini-dictionary of words you need to know in your major field. Find the words in newspapers or magazines, not in your textbooks or dictionaries. For example, if you are a business major, you should be reading a periodical such as *The Wall Street Journal* and one of the major business journals. When you come across a technical term you don't know, enter it in your mini-dictionary according to the following format:

WORD:

DEFINITION:

CONTEXT SENTENCE:

SOURCE:

1. Enter the word.
2. Write the definition of the word. Try to figure out the definition by using the context. If you can't, use a dictionary. If the word is not in the dictionary, you will have to consult a professional dictionary or ask a teacher or someone in the field.
3. Copy the context sentence from the newspaper, periodical, or other source.
4. Name the source of the word—that is, the name of the magazine or newspaper where you found the word.

Follow this procedure for at least ten words each week.

UNIT FOUR

READING AND THINKING ABOUT WORK AND THE WORLD OF BUSINESS

Working hours are never long enough. Each day is a holiday and ordinary holidays . . . are grudged as enforced interruptions in an absorbing vacation.

—Winston Churchill

Thinking about Working

Before you begin to read about the world of work, take a few minutes to consider your own attitudes toward working. Read the following questions, think about them, and then write down answers. Write freely—there are no "right" or "wrong" answers.

1. Consider former British Prime Minister Winston Churchill's attitude toward work (in the opening quotation). Write a sentence or two summarizing how you feel about working.
2. What factors about a job can make you feel happy and satisfied?
3. What factors will enable you to achieve success in your career?
4. If you are unhappy or dissatisfied with your job, what can you do to change things (besides quit)?
5. If you had enough money so that you did not need to work, would you work anyway? Why or why not?
6. Imagine it is your retirement day. What would be the one thing you would want to be able to say about your job? About yourself?

The first day on the job can be terrifying, but imagine how very terrifying it would be if another person's life depended on you doing that job, and doing it right, the first time! In this frightening, comical, and touching chapter from his book The Making of a Surgeon, *doctor and writer William Nolen tells of his first day on the job—as a surgeon.*

THE FIRST APPENDECTOMY

William A. Nolen, M.D.

1   The patient, or better, victim, of my first major surgical venture was a man I'll call Mr. Polansky. He was fat, he weighed one hundred and ninety pounds and was five feet eight inches tall. He spoke only broken English. He had had a sore abdomen with all the classical signs and symptoms of appendicitis for twenty-four hours before he came to Bellevue.

2   After two months of my internship, though I had yet to do anything that could be decently called an "operation," I had had what I thought was a fair amount of operating time. I'd watched the assistant residents work, I'd tied knots, cut sutures, and even, in order to remove a skin lesion, made an occasional incision. Frankly, I didn't think that surgery was going to be too damn difficult. I figured I was ready, and I was chomping at the bit to go, so when Mr. Polansky arrived I greeted him like a long-lost friend. He was overwhelmed at the interest I showed in his case. He probably couldn't understand why any doctor should be so fascinated by a case of appendicitis: wasn't it a common disease? It was just as well that he didn't realize my interest in him was so personal. He might have been frightened, and with good reason.

3   At any rate, I set some sort of record in preparing Mr. Polansky for surgery. He had arrived on the ward at four o'clock. By six I had examined him, checked his blood and urine, taken his chest x-ray and had him ready for the operating room.

4   George Walters, the senior resident on call that night, was to "assist" me during the operation. George was older than the rest of us. I was twenty-five at this time and he was thirty-two. He had taken his surgical training in Europe and was spending one year as a senior resident in an American hospital to establish eligibility for the American College of Surgeons. He had had more experience than the other residents and it took a lot to disturb his equanimity in the operating room. As it turned out, this made him the ideal assistant for me.

5   It was ten o'clock when we wheeled Mr. Polansky to the operating room. At Bellevue, at night, only two operating rooms were kept open—there were six or more going all day—so we had to wait our turn. In the time I had to myself before the operation I had reread the section on appendectomy in the *Atlas of Operative Technique* in our surgical library, and had spent half an hour tying knots on the bedpost in my room. I was, I felt, "ready."

6   I delivered Mr. Polansky to the operating room and started an intravenous going in his arm. Then I left him to the care of the anesthetist. I had ordered a

sedative prior to surgery, so Mr. Polansky was drowsy. The anesthetist, after checking his chart, soon had him sleeping.

Once he was asleep I scrubbed the enormous expanse of Mr. Polansky's abdomen for ten minutes. Then, while George placed the sterile drapes, I scrubbed my own hands for another five, mentally reviewing each step of the operation as I did so. Donning gown and gloves I took my place on the right side of the operating-room table. The nurse handed me the scalpel. I was ready to begin.   7

Suddenly my entire attitude changed. A split second earlier I had been supremely confident; now, with the knife finally in my hand, I stared down at Mr. Polansky's abdomen and for the life of me could not decide where to make the incision. The "landmarks" had disappeared. There was too much belly.   8

George waited a few seconds, then looked up at me and said, "'Go ahead."   9

"What?" I asked.   10

"Make the incision," said George.   11

"Where?" I asked.   12

"Where?"   13

"Yes," I answered, "where?"   14

"Why, here, of course," said George and drew an imaginary line on the abdomen with his fingers.   15

I took the scalpel and followed where he had directed. I barely scratched Mr. Polansky.   16

"Press a little harder," George directed. I did. The blade went through the skin to a depth of perhaps one-sixteenth of an inch.   17

"Deeper," said George.   18

There are five layers of tissue in the abdominal wall: skin, fat, fascia (a tough membranous tissue), muscle, and peritoneum (the smooth, glistening, transparent inner lining of the abdomen). I cut down into the fat. Another sixteenth of an inch.   19

"Bill," said George, looking up at me, "this patient is big. There's at least three inches of fat to get through before we even reach the fascia. At the rate you're going we won't be into the abdomen for another four hours. For God's sake, will you cut?"   20

I made up my mind not to be hesitant. I pressed down hard on the knife, and suddenly we were not only through the fat but through the fascia as well.   21

"Not that hard," George shouted, grabbing my right wrist with his left hand while with his other hand he plunged a gauze pack into the wound to stop the bleeding. "Start clamping," he told me.   22

The nurse handed us hemostats and we applied them to the numerous vessels I had so hastily opened. "All right," George said, "start tying."   23

I took the ligature material from the nurse and began to tie off the vessels. Or rather, I tried to tie off the vessels, because suddenly my knot-tying proficiency had melted away. The casual dexterity I had displayed on the bedpost a short hour ago was nowhere in evidence. My fingers, greasy with fat, simply would not perform. My ties slipped off the vessels, the sutures snapped in my   24 fingers, at one point I even managed to tie the end of my rubber glove into the wound. It was, to put it bluntly, a performance in fumbling that would have made Robert Benchley blush.

25   Here I must give my first paean of praise to George. His patience during the entire performance was nothing short of miraculous. The temptation to pick up the catgut and do the tying himself must have been strong. He could have tied off all the vessels in two minutes. It took me twenty.

26   Finally we were ready to proceed. "Now," George directed, "split the muscle. But gently, please."

27   I reverted to my earlier tack. Fiber by fiber I spread the muscle which was the last layer but one that kept us from the inside of the abdomen. Each time I separated the fibers and withdrew my clamp, the fibers rolled together again. After five minutes I was no nearer the appendix than I had been at the start.

28   George could stand it no longer. But he was apparently afraid to suggest I take a more aggressive approach, fearing I would stick the clamp into, or possibly through, the entire abdomen. Instead he suggested that he help me by spreading the muscle in one direction while I spread it in the other. I made my usual infinitesimal attack on the muscle. In one fell swoop George spread the rest.

29   "Very well done," he complimented me. "Now let's get in."

30   We each took a clamp and picked up the tissue-paper-thin peritoneum. After two or three hesitant attacks with the scalpel I finally opened it. We were in the abdomen.

31   "Now," said George, "put your fingers in, feel the cecum (the portion of the bowel to which the appendix is attached) and bring it into the wound."

32   I stuck my right hand into the abdomen. I felt around—but what was I feeling? I had no idea.

33   It had always looked so simple when the senior resident did it. Open the abdomen, reach inside, pull up the appendix. Nothing to it. But apparently there was.

34   Everything felt the same to me. The small intestine, the large intestine, the cecum—how did one tell them apart without seeing them? I grabbed something and pulled it into the wound. Small intestine. No good. Put it back. I grabbed again. This time it was the sigmoid colon. Put it back. On my third try I had the small intestine again.

35   "The appendix must be in an abnormal position," I said to George. "I can't seem to find it."

36   "Mind if I try?" he asked.

37   "Not at all," I answered. "I wish you would."

38   Two of his fingers disappeared into the wound. Five seconds later they emerged, cecum between them, with the appendix flopping from it.

39   "Stuck down a little," he said kindly. "That's probably why you didn't feel it. It's a hot one," he added. "Let's get at it."

40   The nurse handed me the hemostats, and one by one I applied them to the mesentery of the appendix—the veil of tissue in which the blood vessels run. With George holding the veil between his fingers I had no trouble; I took the

ligatures and tied the vessels without a single error. My confidence was coming back.

"Now," George directed, "put in your purse string." (The cecum is a portion of the bowel which has the shape of half a hemisphere. The appendix projects from its surface like a finger. In an appendectomy the routine procedure is to tie the appendix at its base and cut it off a little beyond the tie. Then the remaining stump is inverted into the cecum and kept there by tying the purse-string stitch. This was the stitch I was now going to sew.)   41

It went horribly. The wall of the cecum is not very thick—perhaps one-eighth of an inch. The suture must be placed deeply enough in the wall so that it won't cut through when tied, but not so deep as to pass all the way through the wall. My sutures were alternately too superficial or too deep, but eventually I got the job done.   42

"All right," said George, "let's get the appendix out of here. Tie off the base."   43

I did.   44

"Now cut off the appendix."   45

At least in this, the definitive act of the operation, I would be decisive. I took the knife and with one quick slash cut through the appendix—too close to the ligature.   46

"Oh oh, watch it," said George. "That tie is going to slip."   47

It did. The appendiceal stump lay there, open. I felt faint.   48

"Don't panic," said George. "We've still got the purse string. I'll push the stump in—you pull up the stitch and tie. That will take care of it."   49

I picked up the two ends of the suture and put in the first stitch. George shoved the open stump into the cecum. It disappeared as I snugged my tie. Beautiful.   50

"Two more knots," said George. "Just to be safe."   51

I tied the first knot and breathed a sigh of relief. The appendiceal stump remained out of sight. On the third knot—for the sake of security—I pulled a little tighter. The stitch broke; the open stump popped up; the cecum disappeared into the abdomen. I broke out in a cold sweat and my knees started to crumble.   52

Even George momentarily lost his composure. "For Christ's sake, Bill," he said, grasping desperately for the bowel, "what did you have to do that for?" The low point of the operation had been reached.   53

By the time we had retrieved the cecum, Mr. Polansky's peritoneal cavity had been contaminated. My self-confidence was shattered. And still George let me continue. True, he all but held my hand as we retied and resutured, but the instruments were in my hand.   54

The closure was anticlimactic. Once I had the peritoneum sutured, things went reasonably smoothly. Two hours after we began, the operation was over. "Nice job," George said, doing his best to sound sincere.   55

"Thanks," I answered, lamely.   56

The scrub nurse laughed.   57

Mr. Polansky recovered, I am happy to report, though not without a long and complicated convalescence. His bowel refused to function normally for two   58 weeks and he became enormously distended. He was referred to at our nightly conferences as "Dr. Nolen's pregnant man." Each time the reference was made, it elicited a shudder from me.

59   During his convalescence I spent every spare moment I could at Mr. Polansky's bedside. My feelings of guilt and responsibility were overwhelming. If he had died I think I would have given up surgery for good.

Vocabulary

Directions: Find each of the key words in the reading selection. Study each word in its context and try to determine its meaning. Write what you think it means in the margin of the text, near the word. Then read over the sentence, mentally substituting your guess for the key word. Does the sentence still make sense? Does it retain its original meaning? If it does, you've probably figured out the meaning of the key word correctly. In any case, confirm your guess by checking a dictionary or thesaurus.

If you take your meaning from the dictionary or thesaurus, be sure the definition contains words you already know and feel comfortable using. If it doesn't, you will be worse off than when you started—you will have begun with one word you didn't know and ended with *two* words you don't know!

Record the new words you've learned in the following chart.

Key Word	Paragraph	Meaning
1. chomping at the bit	2	
2. equanimity	4	
3. donning	7	
4. dexterity	24	
5. infinitesimal	28	
6. contaminated	54	
7. distended	58	
8. convalescence	59	
Others?		

Guide Questions

Directions: These questions will guide your analysis of the text. Your thoughtful answers will ensure that you have understood the main ideas the author wanted to convey. Some of the questions require you simply to find the stated facts in the reading selection; others will ask you to do more difficult tasks, such as paraphrasing information (putting the author's ideas into your own words), synthesizing several ideas into one complex thought, evaluating (making judgments about) an idea, or taking information from the reading and applying it to a new situation or to your own life.

Write answers to the questions in your notebook or on a separate sheet of paper if your instructor wishes to collect them. Your answers will form the basis of class discussion.

1. Dr. Nolen had studied hard and prepared abundantly for the appendectomy. Why do you think he had so much trouble when the time came to actually do the job?
2. Why do you think George (Dr. Walters) allowed Nolen to continue when he was making such a mess of things?
3. The story of the operation has many elements of humor despite the tone of nervousness, even terror. Cite a few points in the narrative that are funny.
4. How do you think Nolen's next operation went?

Application

Directions: In small groups, discuss a point in your life when you did something for a terrifying "first time"—your first day on a job, or perhaps the first time you drove a car, or gave a speech.

Writing

Directions: Choose one of the following writing assignments.

1. Using the ideas you generated in the Application exercise above, write a story describing your first time, using "The First Appendectomy" as a model. Write at least 250 words.
2. Rewrite the story "The First Appendectomy" from the perspective of either the scrub nurse or George. Write at least 250 words.

K. C. Cole is a writer who devotes herself mainly to science and women's issues. In this essay, which first appeared in The New York Times *in 1981, she explores the reasons that very few women choose science as a career.*

WOMEN IN SCIENCE

K. C. Cole

1   I know few other women who do what I do. What I do is write about science, mainly physics. And to do that, I spend a lot of time reading about science, talking to scientists, and struggling to understand physics. In fact, most of the women (and men) I know think me quite queer for actually liking physics. "How can you write about that stuff?" they ask, always somewhat askance. "I could never understand that in a million years." Or more simply, "I hate science."

2   I didn't realize what an odd creature a woman interested in physics was until a few years ago when a science magazine sent me to Johns Hopkins University in Baltimore for a conference on an electrical phenomenon known as the Hall effect. We sat in a huge lecture hall and listened as physicists talked about things engineers didn't understand, and engineers talked about things physicists didn't understand. What *I* didn't understand was why, out of several hundred young students of physics and engineering in the room, less than a handful were women.

3   Sometime later, I found myself at the California Institute of Technology reporting on the search for the origins of the universe. I interviewed physicist after physicist, man after man. I asked one young administrator why none of the physicists were women. And he answered: "I don't know, but I suppose it must be something innate. My seven-year-old daughter doesn't seem to be much interested in science."

4   It was with that experience fresh in my mind that I attended a conference in Cambridge, Massachusetts, on science literacy, or rather the worrisome lack of it in this country today. We three women—a science teacher, a young chemist, and myself—sat surrounded by a company of august men. The chemist, I think, first tentatively raised the issue of science illiteracy in women. It seemed like an obvious point. After all, everyone had agreed over and over again that scientific knowledge these days was a key factor in economic power. But as soon as she made the point, it became clear that we women had committed a grievous social error. Our genders were suddenly showing; we had interrupted the serious talk with a subject unforgivably silly.

5   For the first time, I stopped being puzzled about why there weren't any women in science and began to be angry. Because if science is a search for answers to fundamental questions then it hardly seems frivolous to find out why women are excluded. Never mind the economic consequences.

6   A lot of the reasons women are excluded are spelled out by the Massachusetts Institute of Technology experimental physicist Vera Kistiakowsky in a recent article in *Physics Today* called "Women in Physics: Unnecessary, Injurious, and Out of Place?" The title was taken from a nineteenth-century essay written in

opposition to the appointment of a female mathematician to a professorship at the University of Stockholm. "As decidedly as two and two make four," a woman in mathematics is a "monstrosity," concluded the writer of the essay.

Dr. Kistiakowsky went on to discuss the factors that make women in science today, if not monstrosities, at least oddities. Contrary to much popular opinion, one of those is *not* an innate difference in the scientific ability of boys and girls. But early conditioning does play a stubborn and subtle role. A recent *Nova* program, "The Pinks and the Blues," documented how girls and boys are treated differently from birth—the boys always encouraged in more physical kinds of play, more active explorations of their environments. Sheila Tobias, in her book *Math Anxiety,* showed how the games boys play help them to develop an intuitive understanding of speed, motion, and mass.   7

The main sorting out of the girls from the boys in science seems to happen in junior high school. As a friend who teaches in a science museum said, "By the time we get to electricity, the boys already have had some experience with it. But it's unfamiliar to the girls." Science books draw on boys' experiences. "The examples are all about throwing a baseball at such and such a speed," said my stepdaughter, who barely escaped being a science drop-out.   8

The most obvious reason there are not many more women in science is that women are discriminated against as a class, in promotions, salaries, and hirings, a conclusion reached by a recent analysis by the National Academy of Sciences.   9

Finally, said Dr. Kistiakowsky, women are simply made to feel out of place in science. Her conclusion was supported by a Ford Foundation study by Lynn H. Fox on the problems of women in mathematics. When students were asked to choose among six reasons accounting for girls' lack of interest in math, the girls rated this statement second: "Men do not want girls in the mathematical occupations."   10

A friend of mine remembers winning a Bronxwide mathematics competition in the second grade. Her friends—both boys and girls—warned her that she shouldn't be good at math: "You'll never find a boy who likes you." My friend continued nevertheless to excel in math and science, won many awards during her years at the Bronx High School of Science, and then earned a full scholarship to Harvard. After one year of Harvard science, she decided to major in English.   11

When I asked her why, she mentioned what she called the "macho mores" of science. "It would have been O.K. if I'd had someone to talk to," she said. "But the rules of comportment were such that you never admitted you didn't understand. I later realized that even the boys didn't get everything clearly right away. You had to stick with it until it had time to sink in. But for the boys, there was a payoff in suffering through the hard times, and a kind of punishment—a shame—if they didn't. For the girls it was O.K. not to get it, and the only payoff for sticking it out was that you'd be considered a freak."   12

Science is undeniably hard. Often, it can seem quite boring. It is unfortunately too often presented as laws to be memorized instead of mysteries to be explored.   13

It is too often kept a secret that science, like art, takes a well-developed esthetic sense. Women aren't the only ones who say, "I hate science."

14   That's why everyone who goes into science needs a little help from friends. For the past ten years, I have been getting more than a little help from a friend who is a physicist. But my stepdaughter—who earned the highest grades ever recorded in her California high school on the math Scholastic Aptitude Test—flunked calculus in her first year at Harvard. When my friend the physicist heard about it, he said, "Harvard should be ashamed of itself."

15   What he meant was that she needed that little extra encouragement that makes all the difference. Instead, she got that little extra discouragement that makes all the difference.

16   "In the first place, all the math teachers are men," she explained. "In the second place, when I met a boy I liked and told him I was taking chemistry, he immediately said: 'Oh, you're one of those science types.' In the third place, it's just a kind of a social thing. The math clubs are full of boys and you don't feel comfortable joining."

17   In other words, she was made to feel unnecessary, injurious, and out of place.

18   A few months ago, I accompanied a male colleague from the science museum where I sometimes work to a lunch of the history of science faculty at the University of California. I was the only woman there, and my presence for the most part was obviously and rudely ignored. I was so surprised and hurt by this that I made an extra effort to speak knowledgeably and well. At the end of the lunch, one of the professors turned to me in all seriousness and said: "Well, K. C., what do the women think of Carl Sagan?" I replied that I had no idea what "the women" thought about anything. But now I know what I should have said: I should have told him that his comment was unnecessary, injurious, and out of place.

Vocabulary

Directions: Locate each of the key words in the reading selection. Try to figure out each word's meaning by using the context. Confirm your guess by checking the dictionary or thesaurus. Write the meanings of the words in the margin of the text. Then record the meanings in the following chart.

Key Word	Paragraph	Meaning
1. askance	1	
2. innate	3	
3. august	4	
4. frivolous	5	
5. esthetic (often spelled aesthetic)	13	

Key Word	Paragraph	Meaning
Others?		

Guide Questions

Directions: These questions will guide your understanding of what you have read. Write your answers in your notebook or on a separate sheet of paper if your instructor wishes to collect it. Your answers to these questions will be the basis of class discussion.

1. What do you think prompted the author to write this article? Would you be surprised to find an article titled "Men in Science" in a magazine or newspaper? Why?
2. According to the essay, what are some of the reasons women are excluded from the field of science?
3. Cole describes a friend who excelled in science but, after studying at Harvard for a year, changed her major to English. What reason does Cole's friend give for dropping science?
4. Cole states that "science is undeniably hard" (paragraph 13) and that men also say "I hate science." If these things are true, what explains the fact that women tend to drop out of science while men are much more likely to continue?

Application

Directions: Interview four adults. Try to find one person working in the field of science, one in math, and two from other fields. Ask them if their gender made a difference in which profession they chose and, if so, why. Compare their answers to the ideas in the essay. Use your interviews as a basis for a class discussion.

Writing

Directions: Describe your own experience studying science and math. Were boys and girls treated equally? Were there equal opportunities and encouragement for both boys and girls? Think about why you did or did not continue studying science. Are your experiences similar to those you read about in "Women in Science"? Write at least two paragraphs.

Making Connections

Directions: Read the following selection, "Sex and Science."

In January 2005, the president of Harvard University, Lawrence Summers, created a furor when he stated that genetic differences between men and women might explain why fewer women succeed in science and math careers. When a firestorm of angry reaction resulted, Summers quickly apologized, evidently hoping that would end the brouhaha. But reactions to his comments continued to appear in the media and be discussed in universities, boardrooms, and around kitchen tables. In his speech, Summers offered at least two explanations for the shortage of women in senior posts in science and engineering: first, their reluctance to work long hours because of child care responsibilities; and second, genetic difference. As an example, Dr. Summers cited his daughter, who had received two trucks as gifts. She treated them like dolls, and named them "mummy" and "daddy" trucks.

Hundreds, perhaps thousands, of news stories appeared about the controversy over the following several weeks. This article appeared on the MSNBC website and in Newsweek *magazine in January 2005.*

SEX AND SCIENCE

Barbara Kantrowitz

1   When Amber Post started grad school in physics at Princeton, her goal was the same as her male colleagues': a tenure-track job at a major university. Now with her Ph.D. just a year away, Post is thinking instead about working for a policy-making agency in Washington. Even though Princeton is generally welcoming to female scientists (the president, Shirley Tilghman, is a molecular biologist), Post, 25, senses that her reception in the larger academic world might be chillier. At elite universities, the percentage of women earning doctorates in science and engineering is considerably higher than the percentage of women professors—which means that a lot of talented women Ph.D.s like Post leave campus for jobs in government or industry instead of climbing the faculty ladder.

2   Stopping this female brain drain has been a challenge for years, and universities from MIT to Stanford are pushing hard with mentoring programs and stepped-up recruitment efforts. But Harvard president Lawrence Summers inadvertently threw the issue into the national spotlight when he suggested, at a recent academic conference, that women aren't succeeding because they lack "innate ability" in math and science. Scientists have uncovered some subtle differences in male and female brains, but it's unclear how these differences affect aptitude, and it certainly doesn't explain why there were only four women among 32 Harvard faculty members offered tenure last year. Around the country, women account for nearly half the bachelor's degrees in chemistry and math but only about 10 percent of the faculty. Summers's comments drew immediate criticism from women scientists at Harvard and elsewhere, and he issued a quick apology. "The human potential to excel in science is not somehow the province of one gender or another," he said in a statement.

3   But for many women scientists, the damage was done. "We all know that when we walk into a classroom or present research at a conference, there will be people who will think we are only there because we were given a break somewhere

along the line,' says Post. "But when the president of Harvard University appears to support the theory of innate differences, that pushes the stereotype into the realm of fact and makes it acceptable to think that women are just a little dumber by nature." MIT biology professor Nancy Hopkins, a Harvard alum who attended the Jan. 14 conference, walked out on Summers because, she says, his comments made her "sick." A few hours later, she told a reporter from *The Boston Globe* about Summers's remarks, which were made during a private session on women in science hosted by the National Bureau of Economics. After the *Globe*'s story, Hopkins ended up on the "Today" show. That attention, she says, may be the only good to come out of the media firestorm. "People will realize what these women face," she says. "They must deal with men like Larry Summers. They'll tell you they have no bias, but in their head they are thinking, 'Can women really do math?'"

In his talk, Summers proposed two other possible barriers for women: the 4 conflict between tenure clocks and biological clocks, and outright bias against women (which he seemed to dismiss). Many women scientists blame these problems—not a lack of ability—for the dearth of women professors. Junior faculty need to spend their 20s and 30s on research and publication. Those are the same years when women have children. Time is an enemy for women in other professions, especially law and medicine. But while women doctors and lawyers benefit from lots of successful role models, academic science continues to be dominated by men. Harvard physics professor Melissa Franklin says that even though she has many talented women physics majors whom she tries to encourage, relatively few consider graduate school. "The atmosphere isn't compelling or welcoming to them," she says. "It's a very subtle thing."

And sometimes not so subtle. Lillian Pierce was Princeton's valedictorian 5 when she graduated in 2002 and received her master's in math from Oxford as a Rhodes scholar. Now back at Princeton, she's studying for her Ph.D. Even with that sterling resume, she says, "I myself have experienced behavior that is hard to explain in terms of anything but discrimination: senior male mathematicians ignoring my presence when I'm introduced to them or suggesting point-blank that I pursue another career, such as medicine." She says too many of her female friends "drop out of graduate programs simply because they're disillusioned with the environment, not because they can't handle the math."

Even against this background, there has been some progress. Kristina 6 Johnson, dean of engineering at Duke, says that more universities are making efforts to assist male and female faculty members with young families. "I've got 18 women on my faculty and the majority are raising children under 12," she says. "Yes, it's a challenge to raise kids and go through the tenure process, but it's one that both men and women face. Men don't want to miss out on raising their kids, either." But ultimately, the best remedy against bias would be more women on top, like Princeton's Tilghman, Susan Hockfield of MIT or Shirley Ann Jackson of Rensselaer Polytechnic Institute. "People need to see a career trajectory of someone who looks like them," says Jackson, "a trajectory that shows them that, with talent, a real career is possible." Although maybe not at Harvard—for now.

Vocabulary

Directions: Locate each of the key words in the reading selection. Try to figure out each word's meaning by using the context. Confirm your guess by checking the dictionary or thesaurus. Write the meanings of the words in the margin of the text. Then record the meanings in the following chart.

Key Word	Paragraph	Meaning
1. brouhaha	Introduction	
2. tenure-track	1	
3. elite	1	
4. inadvertently	2	
5. dearth	4	
6. point-blank	5	
7. trajectory	6	
Others?		

Guide Questions

Directions: These questions will guide your understanding of what you have read. Write your answers in your notebook, or on a separate sheet of paper if your instructor wishes to collect it. Your answers to these questions will be the basis of class discussion.

1. In paragraph 2, we learn that President Lawrence Summers "threw the issue into the national spotlight." Explain what the issue is and how it came under the national spotlight.
2. In the article we learn that at Harvard in 2004, 32 Harvard faulty members were offered tenure. Of these 32, four were women. We also learn that around the country, women earn nearly half the bachelor's degrees in chemistry and math, but make up 10 percent of the faculty. How are these facts relevant?
3. As you know from reading this article and the previous one, "Women in Science," Summers is not the only person to question women's innate abilities in science. Why did *his* remarks spark so much reaction?
4. Explain the two possible barriers for women mentioned in paragraph 4.
5. How does Lillian Pierce describe her experience as a woman in science?
6. Summarize the information in the last paragraph.

Making Connections

1. Return to "Women in Science." K. C. Cole cites several factors that make women in science "oddities." List them. Then do the same for "Sex and Science." Compare and contrast the lists. What are the similarities? What are the differences?

2. Remember, the article "Women in Science" was written in 1981. Imagine K. C. Cole were to read this 2005 article, "Sex and Science." How do you think she would react? Write a paragraph or two.

Application

Directions: Return to paragraph 2. Compare the number of female graduates from your college with the number of tenured women on the faculty. This information should be on your school's website or available through the school's institutional research office. How do the numbers compare to those cited in paragraph 2?

Writing

Directions: Following are a few of the letters that appeared in *The New York Times* reacting to Summers' statements. Choose one of the letters and respond to it in a letter of your own.

To the Editor:

Re "Harvard President Apologizes Again for Remarks on Gender" (news article, Jan. 20):

When Lawrence H. Summers, the president of Harvard University, suggested that women's underrepresentation in science may be attributed to innate factors related to gender, he created a "teachable moment" for greater public awareness of the need to advance women in science.

Considerable research and experience refute the notion that the status quo for women in science is natural, inevitable and unrelated to social factors. Research also shows that expectations heavily influence learning and performance.

If society and individuals anticipate that women will not perform as well as men, there is a good chance that those expectations will be met.

We must continue to address the many ways people are discouraged from pursuing an interest in science and engineering. Society benefits most when we take full advantage of all the talent among us.

It is time to create a broader awareness that enables women and other underrepresented groups to step beyond historical barriers in science and engineering.

Carol B. Muller
Sally K. Ride
Palo Alto, Calif., Jan. 20, 2005

The writers are, respectively, chief executive of MentorNet (the E-Mentoring Network for Women in Engineering and Science) and a professor of space science, University of California, San Diego. The letter was also signed by 98 other academics and scientists.

To the Editor:

I am saddened that the president of Harvard is under attack for suggesting some possible causes for the relative scarcity of senior women in science. As a woman with a talent for science, I have a personal interest in understanding why I have met so few like me.

We have ample evidence that there are differences in the ways men's and women's brains process information and in the ways their bodies process medications. Why shouldn't science question whether some differences, unrelated to social conditioning, might make the genders more or less competent at science?

While the academic community may have faith that scientific talent is gender-neutral, some of us would still like to know the truth of the matter so that we may one day understand, predict and control it.

Elizabeth Bryson
San Diego, Jan. 20, 2005

To the Editor:

I do not understand the public outcry regarding Lawrence H. Summers's suggestion that innate differences between the sexes may explain why fewer women succeed in science and math careers.

Is Harvard, a bastion of excellence in higher education, not allowed to touch that question? I hope not.

For critical and free-thinking ideas to flourish, it needs to be addressed.

There is a procedure in evaluating hypotheses within the scientific method. If Mr. Summers's statement falls on its merits, it will be because it will be thoroughly investigated and then summarily rejected. This, in turn, will attract more women into the various scientific fields and foster a greater understanding.

Isn't that, after all, the point of science?

Tony McGovern
Broomfield, Colo., Jan. 20, 2005

To the Editor:

Women are a rarity in mathematics and engineering. As a female engineering student, I see this every day. That said, the idea that this fact is representative of the different biological programming between men and women is utter nonsense.

In recent years, the number of women entering these fields has increased significantly, as has the range of female understanding. It is thus not inability that limits numbers, but perhaps the stubborn refusal to let go of ignorant hypotheses.

Kelsey Burrell
La Jolla, Calif., Jan. 20, 2005

Think back to your elementary school days. If your experience is like most people's, all of your teachers were women. Why do you think this was so? Why don't men go into this profession? Has this situation changed in recent years? In the essay that follows, a male elementary school teacher describes his work days and some of the problems he faces as a man doing "woman's work."

ONE MAN'S KIDS

Daniel Meier

I teach first graders. I live in a world of skinned knees, double-knotted shoelaces, riddles that I've heard a dozen times, stale birthday cakes, hurt feelings, wandering stories, and one lost shoe ("and if you don't find it my mother'll kill me"). My work is dominated by six-year-olds.   1

It's 10:45, the middle of snack, and I'm helping Emily open her milk carton. She has already tried the other end without success, and now there's so much paint and ink on the carton from her fingers that I'm not sure she should drink it at all. But I open it. Then I turn to help Scott clean up some milk he has just spilled onto Rebecca's whale crossword puzzle.   2

While I wipe my milk- and paint-covered hands, Jenny wants to know if I've seen that funny book about penguins that I read in class. As I hunt for it in a messy pile of books, Jason wants to know if there is a new seating arrangement for lunch tables. I find the book, turn to answer Jason, then face Maya, who is fast approaching with a new knock-knock joke. After what seems like the tenth "Who's there?" I laugh and Maya is pleased.   3

Then Andrew wants to know how to spell "flukes" for his crossword. As I get to "u," I give a hand signal for Sarah to take away the snack. But just as Sarah is almost out the door, two children complain that "we haven't even had ours yet." I stop the snack mid-flight, complying with their request for graham crackers. I then return to Andrew, noticing that he has put "flu" for 9 Down, rather than 9 Across. It's now 10:50.   4

My work is not traditional male work. It's not a singular pursuit. There is not a large pile of paper to get through or one deal to transact. I don't have one area of expertise or knowledge. I don't have the singular power over language of a lawyer, the physical force of a construction worker, the command over fellow workers of a surgeon, the wheeling and dealing transactions of a businessman. My energy is not spent in pursuing, climbing, achieving, conquering, or cornering some goal or object.   5

My energy is spent in encouraging, supporting, consoling, and praising my children. In teaching, the inner rewards come from without. On any given day, quite apart from teaching reading and spelling, I bandage a cut, dry a tear, erase a frown, tape a torn doll, and locate a long-lost boot. The day is really won through matters of the heart. As my students groan, laugh, shudder, cry, exult, and wonder, I do too. I have to be soft around the edges.   6

7   A few years ago, when I was interviewing for an elementary school teaching position, every principal told me with confidence that, as a male, I had an advantage over female applicants because of the lack of male teachers. But in the next breath, they asked with a hint of suspicion why I chose to work with young children. I told them that I wanted to observe and contribute to the intellectual growth of a maturing mind. What I really felt like saying, but didn't, was that I loved helping a child learn to write his name for the first time, finding someone a new friend, or sharing in the hilarity of reading about Winnie the Pooh getting so stuck in a hole that only his head and rear show.

8   I gave that answer to those principals, who were mostly male, because I thought they wanted a "male" response. This meant talking about intellectual matters. If I had taken a different course and talked about my interest in helping children in their emotional development, it would have been seen as closer to a "female" answer. I even altered my language, not once mentioning the word *love* to describe what I do indeed love about teaching. My answer worked; every principal nodded approvingly.

9   Some of the principals also asked what I saw myself doing later in my career. They wanted to know if I eventually wanted to go into educational administration. Becoming a dean of students or a principal has never been one of my goals, but they seemed to expect me, as a male, to want to climb higher on the career stepladder. So I mentioned that, at some point, I would be interested in working with teachers as a curriculum coordinator. Again, they nodded approvingly.

10   If those principals had been female instead of male, I wonder whether their questions, and my answers, would have been different. My guess is that they would have been.

11   At other times, when I'm at a party or a dinner and tell someone that I teach young children, I've found that men and women respond differently. Most men ask about the subjects I teach and the courses I took in my training. Then, unless they bring up an issue such as merit pay, the conversation stops. Most women, on the other hand, begin the conversation on a more immediate and personal level. They say things like "those kids must love having a male teacher" or "that age is just wonderful, you must love it." Then, more often than not, they'll talk about their own kids or ask me specific questions about what I do. We're then off and talking shop.

12   Possibly, men would have more to say to me, and I to them, if my job had more of the trappings and benefits of more traditional male jobs. But my job has no bonuses or promotions. No complimentary box seats at the ball park. No cab fare home. No drinking buddies after work. No briefcase. No suit. (Ties get stuck in paint jars.) No power lunches. (I eat peanut butter and jelly, chips, milk, and cookies with the kids.) No taking clients out for cocktails. The only place I take my kids is to the playground.

13   Although I could have pursued a career in law or business, as several of my friends did, I chose teaching instead. My job has benefits all its own. I'm able to bake cookies without getting them stuck together as they cool, buy cheap sewing

materials, take out splinters, and search just the right trash cans for useful odds and ends. I'm sometimes called "Daddy" and even "Mommy" by my students, and if there's ever a lull in the conversation at a dinner party, I can always ask those assembled if they've heard the latest riddle about why the turkey crossed the road. (He thought he was a chicken.)

Vocabulary

Directions: Locate each of the key words in the reading selection. Try to figure out each word's meaning by using the context. Confirm your guess by checking the dictionary or thesaurus. Write the meanings of the words in the margin of the text. Then record the meanings in the following chart.

Key Word	Paragraph	Meaning
1. exult	6	
2. hilarity	7	
3. trappings	12	
4. lull	13	
Others?		

Guide Questions

Directions: These questions will guide your understanding of what you have read. Write your answers in your notebook or on a separate sheet of paper if your instructor wishes to collect it. Your answers to these questions will be the basis of class discussion.

1. Describe what the author does for a living. Then describe your reaction to his profession when you first read the article.
2. What does Meier mean when he says in paragraph 5 that his work is not a "singular pursuit"?
3. Why did Meier think he could not give truly honest answers to the principals who interviewed him for jobs as a teacher?
4. Contrast the types of conversations Meier has with women and with men at social occasions.
5. If you know someone who has held a job typically performed by the opposite sex, describe their experience. Would they recommend such a job to you?

Application

Directions: Think back to the essay, "Women in Science" (page 228). In small groups, discuss the similarities and differences between Daniel Meier's and K. C. Cole's experiences in careers dominated by the opposite sex.

Writing

Directions: Reflect on what you have read and on the discussion you had in the Application exercise. Now, think about and answer this question: Would you take a job in a field dominated by the opposite sex? For example, if you are a woman, would you work as a truck driver, construction worker, or firefighter? If you are a man, would you work as a nurse, elementary school teacher, or secretary? Consider the advantages and disadvantages of such a job. Write your response and supporting reasons for your response in two or three paragraphs.

Do you dread placing your order at a fast-food restaurant? Fear the sneers of the super-market clerk? Spend hours looking for what you want at the store rather than risk the hos-tility of the clerk lounging in the corner? You are not alone. Customers are expressing more and more frustration at the bad attitudes and incompetent service of workers. Bosses are, too, and they're looking for answers. But a shrug is often the only option. This article appeared in the March 6, 2000, issue of Newsweek.

TIRED OF SMILE-FREE SERVICE?

Keith Naughton

Hustling off to work one morning recently, Ann Andraska pulled into her neigh-borhood gas station in Ann Arbor, Mich., for a fill-up. On her way to the checkout counter, the elementary-school speech therapist grabbed a Coke and a five-pound bag of ice. As she fumbled with the ice while trying to pull money from her purse, the cashier barked, "Would you put that stuff down! I need the money." Andraska did as she was told, and the clerk flung her change across the counter. Shocked by such rudeness, Andraska sighed. "If you want better service," the clerk growled, "go across the street."

The problem is, it's not likely to be much better across the street. It's no secret that service is abysmal, a fact confirmed last week by a new University of Michigan survey of customer satisfaction that puts an exclamation point on an unfortunate Econ 101 lesson: as unemployment has fallen to its lowest level in 30 years, it's tough to find good workers. And that's why customer satisfaction at fast-food restaurants, retailers, gas stations and banks has fallen to its lowest level since the consumer survey began in 1994. The real burden, though, falls on the frontline managers who not only have to recruit and train workers who aren't exactly the creamiest of the crop, but also have to tolerate the bad service of their employees or else resume the hunt for new workers. In this overheated business climate, entire staffs can turn over three times in a year, despite $10-an-hour wages. Employees who stick around more than 90 days are often considered old hands. Terry Guth, director of staffing for 7-Eleven convenience stores, has started combing welfare rolls for applicants. Store owners offer new hires up to $12 an hour to serve Slurpees. The war for workers is more fierce than the battle for customers. "We're all fighting it out for people," he says.

Recruiters desperately seeking applicants are coming up with new strategies. Target, the big discount chain, installed kiosks in the front of its stores where prospects can fill out a computerized application and be on the job in 24 hours. "Applicants are so scarce, you have to be able to respond quickly," says vice presi-dent Betty Kimbrough. "If we don't get to your application for a week, you're probably already working for someone else." In addition to offering fat paychecks that make a mockery of the $5.15 minimum wage, retailers like Wal-Mart are now extending medical benefits and 401(k) savings plans to part-timers. Home Depot is so anxious to recruit workers it spent millions to launch its first national television help-wanted ad. The commercial, filled with smiling employees who promise that "great careers are built" at Home Depot, got the green light after executives calculated that having too few staffers cost them tens of millions in lost sales. "If you don't have enough people, that represents lost revenue," says Cindy Durning, Home Depot's recruitment vice president. The ad seemed to work. Since it debuted, Home Depot says, applications have quadrupled at some stores.

4   The luxury of leisurely classroom training for new recruits has all but vanished. Fresh hires at Wal-Mart and McDonald's no longer spend days locked in the back room watching training videos. Most training comes on the job, and if the rookie needs more he can log on to the computer in the break room. "We used to teach them the history of the potato, but they don't need all that to make fries," says Barry Mehrman, McDonald's director of human resources. Critics say this rush to get inexperienced workers behind the counter explains why service is declining. "You see a lot of trainees these days fumbling at the cash register," says economist Russ Thibeault of Applied Economic Research in New Hampshire. As quality hires grow scarce, bosses find they must teach the most rudimentary manners. "Some people just don't want to smile," says Charles Valluzzo, a McDonald's franchisee in Baton Rouge, La., who is hiring more workers off welfare. "It's a challenge to motivate these people. You've got to sit there and work with them daily."

5   And be awfully forgiving if you want them to stick around. With help-wanted signs papering the windows of stores everywhere, workers hold the power and managers hesitate to reprimand. Arrive late for work or don't show up at all? Don't worry, the boss will give you another chance. "If someone was late three times in a row in the past, I might let them go," says Bill Tarpey, who manages Sunset Foods in Lake Forest, Ill. "Now I think twice. Without bodies, you can't give good service." Even dressing down a customer is a forgivable offense. When a cashier at a 7-Eleven in Farmington Hills, Mich., recently snapped at a young woman who balked when asked to show ID to buy alcohol, owner Jim Chatham sent the worker to the back room to cool off. But he never considered firing her. "I'm not going to dump a good employee just because two or three customers had a bad reaction," says Chatham. "I always back my employees."

6   So much for the days when the customer was always right. These days customers had better just bite their tongues. Mary Beltrian discovered that when she complained to the manager of her car wash in Chicago after a worker sprayed bleach on her dashboard. "The manager told me he didn't get paid enough to deal with it," says the 36-year-old nurse. A Detroit couple who filed a $100 million lawsuit against McDonald's last week claim they received even rougher treatment. They allege they were beaten by three Detroit McDonald's employees after they tried to return a watery milkshake. McDonald's Detroit marketing manager Vicky Free responded: "This matter is under investigation and litigation, and it's inappropriate to discuss it further."

7   As workers have grown more frustrated with customers, they've begun to vent their hostility online. The customerssuck.com site gets 1,200 hits a day. In the anonymity of cyberspace, workers rail about customers' dumbest questions ("How much is a 99-cent cheeseburger?") and give their finicky shoppers pet

names ("Return Rita," "Mr. SlowMotion Man"). Quincy, Mass., liquor-store manager George Duncan, 25, started the customerssuck.com site two years ago, giving it the slogan "The customer is never right." Duncan argues that the booming economy has made consumers arrogant and corporate owners even more greedy. Workers, he contends, are caught in the middle. "Companies still want more profits, even though they are relying on fewer people to do the work," says Duncan. "It can be a nightmare for the clerk."

Predictably, not many customers are sympathetic. Los Angeles vending-machine salesman Ruben Nogales fumes about the inept service he's been getting lately from the trainees running the drive-throughs he frequents for lunch. When Nogales pulled up to the window at a taco joint recently, he was handed the wrong order and his debit card was charged $450 for the lunch. The manager had to get involved to unravel the mess. Nogales vows he'll never return to that restaurant. "I don't care how hungry I am," he huffs. "It's not worth the aggravation." With service suffering everywhere, Nogales's chances of having a happy meal are growing slim. But hey, at least the economy is still booming. So have a nice day.

Vocabulary

Directions: Locate each of the key words in the reading selection. Try to figure out each word's meaning by using the context. Confirm your guess by checking the dictionary or thesaurus. Write the meanings of the words in the margin of the text. Then record the meanings in the following chart.

Key Word	Paragraph	Meaning
1. abysmal	2	
2. combing	2	
3. kiosks	3	
4. reprimand	5	
5. dressing down	5	
6. allege	6	
7. unravel	8	
Others?		

Guide Questions

Directions: These questions will guide your understanding of what you have read. Write your answers in your notebook or on a separate sheet of paper if your instructor wishes to collect it. Your answers to these questions will be the basis of class discussion.

1. According to the article, why is it difficult to find good workers these days?
2. Why does the author say "the real burden . . . falls on the frontline managers"?
3. Cite some of the statistics from the article regarding pay, other incentives, and worker turnover.
4. According to the article, what is the effect of low unemployment on the following?
   a. training for workers
   b. attitudes of workers
   c. the service that workers provide to customers
5. Cite one of the examples of poor service mentioned in the article. Does the description of poor or hostile service ring true to you? Have you had similar experiences? Do you think service is worse than it was in the past?
6. According to the article, is the problem all one-sided? Or are some customers at fault, too?
7. If you have ever worked in a service job, did you encounter difficult customers? How did you handle those situations?

Application/Writing

1. Who do you think is more at fault: the customers or the workers? Why? Can you think of any solution to the problem of poor or hostile service? Discuss your ideas with your classmates. Then write a letter to *Newsweek* explaining your solution.
2. Describe an experience you've had as a customer with a surly clerk (or alternatively, your experience trying to serve a hostile customer). Write a paragraph or two.

Millions of Americans work full-time but do not earn enough to escape poverty. In 1998 Barbara Ehrenreich embarked on a year-long journey to find out how people manage to survive when they are living on the minimum wage. Beginning in Florida, where she worked in restaurants, she moved on to Maine, where she cleaned houses with the "Merry Maids" and worked in a nursing home. Then it was on to Minnesota, where she took a job, as so many people have, with Wal-Mart. Fearful at first that her Ph.D. in biology and long career as a writer would mark her as somehow "overqualified" for these low-income jobs, she found instead that even the "lowliest" of occupations require exhausting mental and physical efforts. She also discovered that one job was usually not enough to live on—unless you were willing to live in your car, as many of her colleagues did.

At the end of her year Ehrenreich returned to her middle-class life in Key West to write the book Nickel and Dimed, *which chronicled her experiences and those of America's working poor. This article was written in 2006.*

THE HIGH COST OF BEING POOR
Barbara Ehrenreich

There are people, concentrated in the Hamptons and Beverly Hills, who still confuse poverty with the simple life. No cable TV, no altercations with the maid, no summer home maintenance issues—just the basics like family, sunsets, and walks in the park. What they don't know is that it's expensive to be poor.   1

In fact, you, the reader of middling income, could probably not afford it. A new study from the Brookings Institute documents the "ghetto tax," or higher cost of living in low-income urban neighborhoods. It comes at you from every direction, from food prices to auto insurance. A few examples from this study, by Matt Fellowes, that covered 12 American cities: 2

- Poor people are less likely to have bank accounts, which can be expensive for those with low balances, and so they tend to cash their pay checks at check-cashing businesses, which in the cities surveyed, charged $5 to $50 for a $500 check.   3
- Nationwide, low-income car buyers, defined as people earning less than $30,000 a year, pay two percentage points more for a car loan than more affluent buyers.   4
- Low-income drivers pay more for car insurance. In New York, Baltimore and Hartford, they pay an average $400 more a year to insure the exact same car and driver risk than wealthier drivers.   5
- Poorer people pay an average of one percentage point more in mortgage interest.   6
- They are more likely to buy their furniture and appliances through pricey rent-to-own businesses. In Wisconsin, the study reports, a $200 rent-to-own TV set can cost $700 with the interest included.   7
- They are less likely to have access to large supermarkets and hence to rely on the far more expensive, and lower quality offerings, of small grocery and convenience stores.   8

9   I didn't live in any ghettoes when I worked on *Nickel and Dimed*—a trailer park, yes, but no ghetto—and on my average wage of $7 an hour, or about $14,400 a year, I wasn't in the market for furniture, a house or a car. But the high cost of poverty was brought home to me within a few days of my entry into the low-wage life, when, slipping into social-worker mode, I chastised a co-worker for living in a motel room when it would be so much cheaper to rent an apartment. Her response: Where would she get the first month's rent and security deposit it takes to pin down an apartment? The lack of that amount of capital—probably well over $1,000—condemned her to paying $40 a night at the Day's Inn.

10   Then there was the problem of sustenance. I had gone into the project imagining myself preparing vast quantities of cheap, nutritious soups and stews, which I would freeze and heat for dinner each day. But surprise: I didn't have the proverbial pot to pee in, not to mention spices or Tupperware. A scouting trip to K-Mart established that it would take about a $40 capital investment to get my kitchenette up to speed for the low-wage way of life.

11   The food situation got only more challenging when I, too, found myself living in a motel. Lacking a fridge and microwave, all my food had to come from the nearest convenience store (hardboiled eggs and banana for breakfast) or, for the big meal of the day, Wendy's or KFC. I have no nutritional complaints; after all, there is a veggie, or flecks of one, in Wendy's broccoli and cheese baked potato. The problem was financial. A double cheeseburger and fries is lot more expensive than that hypothetical homemade lentil stew.

12   There are other tolls along the road well-traveled by the working poor. If your credit is lousy, which it is likely to be, you'll pay a higher deposit for a phone. If you don't have health insurance, you may end taking that feverish child to an emergency room, and please don't think of ER's as socialized medicine for the poor. The average cost of a visit is over $1,000, which is over ten times more than what a clinic pediatrician would charge. Or you neglect that hypertension, diabetes or mystery lump until you end up with a $100,000 problem on your hands.

13   So let's have a little less talk about how the poor should learn to manage their money, and a little more attention to all the ways that money is being systematically siphoned off. Yes, certain kinds of advice would be helpful: skip the pay-day loans and rent-to-pay furniture, for example. But we need laws in more states to stop predatory practices like $50 charges for check cashing. Also, think what some microcredit could do to move families from motels and shelters to apartments. And did I mention a living wage?

14   If you're rich, you might want to stay that way. It's a whole lot cheaper than being poor.

Vocabulary

Directions: Find each of the key words in the essay. Try to figure out each word's meaning by using the context. Confirm your guess by checking the dictionary. Write the meanings of the words in the margin of the text, near the word. Then record the meanings in the following chart.

Key Word	Paragraph	Meaning
1. altercations	1	
2. middling	2	
3. chastised	9	
4. sustenance	10	
5. hypothetical	11	
6. siphoned	13	
7. predatory	13	
Others		

Guide Questions

Directions: These questions will guide your understanding of what you've read. Write your answers in your notebook or on a separate sheet of paper if your instructor will collect it. Your answers will be the basis of class discussion.

1. a. Ehrenreich discusses what she calls the "ghetto tax." Explain what she means by this term.
   b. List some of the findings of the Brookings Institute study.
2. Why did Ehrenreich's co-worker choose to live in a (relatively) expensive motel room rather than rent an apartment, which would be cheaper?
3. What was Ehrenreich's problem with "sustenance?"
4. Ehrenreich lists several other "tolls along the road" that the working poor must pay. List a few of them.
5. What advice does Ehrenreich give to people who criticize poor people? What advice does she give to poor people?

Application

When the author began her project, the national minimum wage was $5.15 per hour. Some states had a slightly higher minimum. Go to the Internet to find the current minimum wage at both the federal level and in your state.

Compute how much you would earn each month if you worked full-time at minimum wage. Then compute how much your monthly expenses are. Would your earnings be enough to live on?

Marking Text/Summary Writing

Mark the text of this article (if you need to review how to mark text, turn to page 413). Then write a summary of "The High Cost of Being Poor."

Writing

What is your reaction to the information in Ehrenreich's article? Write one paragraph.

Millions of Americans work at low-wage jobs, struggling to earn enough money to feed themselves and their families. This story, which appeared in The New York Times *in 2007, tells the story of one young mother in Texas—but it is really the story of many.*

DREAMS IN THE DARK
AT THE DRIVE-THROUGH WINDOW

Charlie LeDuff

DALLAS— Off a bleak and empty interchange midway through the Dallas sprawl stands a Burger King. It's past midnight, the rain sizzles on the parking lot blacktop like frying bacon. A young woman is working the lobster shift at the drive-through window. She is overweight and wears pink lipstick. 1

"Nothing special," she says of herself. "Nothing much." 2

Gloria Castillo is 22, married, a mother of two, a Latina from the rough side of Dallas. She is on the low side of making it. 3

The night is busy, and a mustache of perspiration breaks across her lip. She is alone with the fry cook. 4

The customers are rude tonight, drunk and bellicose. One guy doesn't want to pay for his food, figuring it ought to be free. If he had wanted to rob the place, Ms. Castillo says with a tight smile, it would have been easy enough; the window doesn't lock here like it does at the McDonald's. 5

From the car window, the whole fast-food experience is a numbing routine. Pull up. Order from the billboard. Idle. Pay. Drive away. Fast food has become a $120 billion motorized American experience. 6

But consider the life inside that window on Loop 12 in West Dallas. There is a woman with children and no health insurance, undereducated, a foot soldier in the army of the working poor. The fry cook sneezes on the meat patties. Cigarettes go half smoked. Cameras spy on the employees. Customers throw their fries and soft drinks sometimes because they think it's funny. 7

"I hate this job," Ms. Castillo says with a smile. "I hate it." It is her third drive-through job. First it was Whataburger. Then McDonald's. Now here. It is becoming a career. 8

"Burger King pays better," she says. Even so, she has taken a second job: "It's a bar. There's a lot of white guys in there. I go and clean the restrooms. There's three restrooms I clean for $150, and I do it in one hour and 30 minutes. One hour and a half." 9

Ms. Castillo is the daughter of an illegal immigrant who came to America from Honduras by bus 22 years ago, with Ms. Castillo gestating inside her. Her mother lives on a disability check now, and Ms. Castillo is the American who sees herself competing with illegal labor, labor that drives down her wage, she says. 10

"I never worked with white people," she says while putting a cup of soda and ice together. "Everywhere I go and apply, it's always Mexicans, black or Chinese." 11

12   She surmises that the entire morning staff at her Burger King is illegal. "I can tell you everyone who works here in the morning works fake papers. No English. Nobody in the morning knows English.

13   "Somebody takes the order and then we tell them in Spanish."

14   Ernesto Hernandez, her manager, says that he does not know if he employs people who work with false Social Security numbers and that it is not his job to know if the numbers are real. "Call corporate," he says in a thick accent. "They have that information."

15   Corporate did not return calls.

16   Whatever the truth of the matter, there's a lot of ethnic friction behind the drive-through glass, Ms. Castillo says: "There's a lot of hate."

17   She hands the soda and a sack of 10 tacos to a guy in a Chevy who looks stoned. He doesn't count his change. He drives away with one hand on the wheel, one in the sack of tacos.

18   A sign on the window says: "Burgers for breakfast beginning at 8 a.m."

19   Ms. Castillo works from 10:30 p.m. to 6:30 a.m. She earns $252 a week before taxes. There is no chance of overtime, because the boss doesn't allow it. To make ends meet, she and her husband work split shifts, he at an auto parts place during the day and she at the Burger King at night. And so the children, ages 7 and 8, are alone for a half-hour in the morning, left to wash and dress themselves.

20   Ms. Castillo arrives at her two-bedroom rental house on a tough street at 7. She takes the boys to McDonald's for breakfast at 7:15 — the same place she used to work — before dropping them off at school at 7:45. A man named Carlos works the window there. They used to work there together.

21   Every morning, the boys' order is the same: one sausage, egg and cheese biscuit; one bacon biscuit; two hash browns; and two orange juices. Ms. Castillo could take free food home from Burger King, but the boys like McDonald's better.

22   She returns home, sleeps until 2 and collects the boys from school. She cooks them supper prepared from frozen packages, and sometimes they eat it in front of the television. It takes time and money to eat healthy, she says.

23   At 7 she puts the kids to bed. She spends a few hours with her husband, dresses in her purple polyester uniform with the yellow piping and drives to work. On Saturdays she attends community college, hoping that in a few years she will be a paralegal going to work in a downtown office tower, wearing a pantsuit. She is hoping for $20 an hour and a lunch break.

24   "Regrets, yes, I got some," she says. She wishes she would have worked harder in school. Not gotten pregnant at 13. Again at 14. She wishes she would have thought about life instead of letting it come at her, one dead end job at a time.

25   Around 2 a.m. work begins to slow down. This is the unpredictable hour. It could be filled with only the fry cook's music, or it could be the hour that gunmen rob the place and lock them in the freezer. It's happened before, she says. It happens dozens of times a month at fast food restaurants across the country.

26   Tonight, it's music. Gloria Castillo stares out the open window, allowing the wet air to blow inside. "I got dreams," she says. "I'm a human being."

27   She looks at the crummy little house across the parking lot with peeling paint. "That would be good too, a little house. I don't want much."

Vocabulary

Directions: Locate each of the key words in the reading selection. Try to figure out each word's meaning by using the context. Confirm your guess by checking the dictionary or thesaurus. Write the meanings of the words in the margin of the text. Then record the meanings in the following chart.

Key Word	Paragraph	Meaning
1. lobster shift	1	
2. bellicose	5	
3. numbing	6	
4. surmises	12	
Others?		

Guide Questions

Directions: These questions will guide your understanding of what you have read. Write your answers in your notebook or on a separate sheet of paper if your instructor wishes to collect it. Your answers to these questions will be the basis of class discussion.

1. This newspaper feature article tells us the story of a young mother in Dallas. In a few sentences, summarize her situation.
2. Do you think there are many others like Gloria Castillo out there?
3. What can you infer about Ms. Castillo's attitude toward illegal immigrants? Cite a paragraph in the story to back up your answer.
4. What tone do you hear in the story? Do you think the writer wants us to *feel* something, or is he just giving us the facts? Give a few examples to support your answer.

Making Connections

1. Compute Gloria Castillo's hourly wage. How much does she earn per hour? Compare that figure to the minimum wage in your state.
2. If you read the previous selection, "The High Cost of Being Poor," answer the following question:

    In paragraph 22, Ms. Castillo says, "It takes time and money to eat healthy." Relate this to Barbara Ehrenreich's comments on the "problem of sustenance" (paragraph 10 in "The High Cost of Being Poor") where she explains how difficult it is to eat healthfully while living on minimum wage.
3. Imagine a conversation between Gloria Castillo and Barbara Ehrenreich. What would they say to one another? Write a paragraph or two.

Application/Writing

Directions: If you can, watch the video interview with Gloria Castillo (www.nytimes.com/national. Search "Gloria Castillo.") before answering the following questions.

1. If you could speak to Ms. Castillo, what advice would you give her?
2. Have you ever worked at a job like Gloria Castillo's? Discuss your experience with your classmates. Then write a paragraph or two summarizing your experience.

This article reports on the findings of a survey of the readers of the magazine Working Woman. *Before you read, try your hand at answering some questions from the same survey.*

For each of the following situations, state whether you think it is an ethical problem or not an ethical problem.

1. *Unethical or no problem: Your boss treats clients to cocaine.*
2. *Unethical or no problem: A real estate agent showing a house doesn't say that the basement floods.*
3. *Unethical or no problem: An executive learns that his company is about to be sold, which will send its stock price soaring. He leaks this information to two clients as well as to several friends.*
4. *Unethical or no problem: An administrative assistant routinely makes up excuses for her boss when he takes long lunches with his secretary.*
5. *Unethical or no problem: After a year of poor sales, a sales representative convinces her boss to let her give expensive gifts to prospective clients. The tactic works and sales increase.*
6. *Unethical or no problem: A publisher gives his college-age niece a highly sought-after unpaid summer internship at his company.*
7. *Unethical or no problem: Company policy forbids employees to discuss salaries with each other, but two people trade information to negotiate better with their boss.*
8. *Unethical or no problem: A manager has accumulated sick days. She calls in sick even though she isn't and takes a few days off.*
9. *Unethical or no problem: A job applicant finds out the morning before her job interview that she is pregnant. She decides not to say anything rather than jeopardize her chances.*

HOW ETHICAL IS AMERICAN BUSINESS?

Ronni Sandroff

Would you work for a company that was polluting the environment . . . or a boss who lied to customers? Do you think it's unethical to flirt to make a sale? Or to call in sick when you need a "mental health" day? More than fourteen hundred *Working Woman* readers examined their scruples—and those of their colleagues—by responding to "Business Ethics: What Are Your Personal Standards?" published in the February issue. Hundreds went beyond the survey to enclose heartfelt letters. Their conclusion? Fair play is disappearing from the American business scene—and it hurts.

The majority of respondents said they personally have witnessed such foul play as lying to employees; expense-account abuses at the highest levels; and in-office jockeying involving favoritism, nepotism, and taking credit for other people's work. Almost half have seen discrimination based on sex and color, more than a third, sexual harassment; and just under a third, lying to make a sale. And they charge that this apparent erosion of the fair-play ethic is not only disheartening but is also harmful to productivity, job stability, and profits in American business.

3   "I worked for a medical-device manufacturer that released a product for humans without implant studies," wrote one reader. Her protests went unheeded and the product failed in some cases, causing unnecessary surgery in already weakened patients. The same company was sued for sending a maintenance man on an industrial espionage mission to sift through a competitor's garbage and collect information. Are tales like this symptomatic of a decline in American business ethics, or are they just a reflection of business as usual? Fifty-six percent of the respondents in the *Working Woman* ethics survey believe that American business ethics have deteriorated in the past ten years.

4   Contributing to employees' dismay, perhaps, is the fact that bad deeds seem to go unpunished: The companies or institutions that most respondents have worked for have not gotten into trouble over ethical violations. Part of the reason may be that the violations readers have seen most often, such as lying to employees, expense-account abuses, and so on, are difficult to prosecute.

5   And where is this wrongdoing taking place? When asked which industries were hotbeds of unethical behavior, a startlingly high number of readers — 66 percent — pointed the finger at the government. We might dismiss this as simply good old American government-bashing if it weren't for the fact that women who work for the government are among those most likely to bash it: 62 percent of government workers feel the government is most unethical. "The government is the most unethical institution I've ever been associated with," wrote one reader. In contrast, other occupation groups think their ethics are better than the popular perception. For example, only 9 percent of lawyers — compared with 40 percent of all respondents — rated law as the most unethical.

6   How will a concern for ethics affect future career patterns? Ethics-wise, most respondents are willing to put their money where their mouths are: A strong majority of those polled said they would not work for a company with a history of environmental accidents, insider trading or worker accidents, or a law firm that defends known racketeers. Women in the helping professions were most scrupulous about where they'd work. However, more lawyers said they would work for any of these companies. "If all attorneys decided that they were too 'ethical' to defend 'known criminals,'" one reader reminded us, "accused persons would have no rights."

Where Do You Draw the Line?

7   Umpiring the ethics of the workplace is not merely a spectator sport. Every worker is a player. What personal decisions do people make — and why do they make them? When it comes to personal scruples, the issues seem less clear-cut. Readers consider stealing time (in the form of phony sick days or personal phone calls) and supplies (computer software, office staples) or sharing company discounts with outsiders only minor violations. And trading competitive information with friends in the same industry is OK with almost half the respondents. More than 60 percent would use a stolen secret report from a competitor's company.

"Unethical behavior is quickly becoming acceptable behavior," wrote an
information-systems director from St. Louis. "Some of us do little things like
[putting] an occasional lunch with a friend on the old expense account. Without
proper controls, the occasional lunch becomes the occasional trip or vacation. The
result is still the same: Someone else pays for the ride." 8

The majority of respondents (53 percent) agreed that most successful business people occasionally have to compromise their principles. In fact, in a number
of areas, women who rated themselves as highly successful (and generally had the
highest incomes and education levels) were more willing to bend and break rules
than less successful women. "Had I taken this survey five years ago while in
middle management, my answers would have been much more black-and-white.
The more exposed to business I become, the more aware I am of the gray areas. Is
this because there are gray areas, or because justification has begun to set in?" one
reader wondered. 9

The Reasons—and Excuses?

When asked if it's sometimes necessary to break the rules to get ahead, 42 percent 10
of the respondents said yes and 44 percent said no. Some readers blamed the
decline in ethics on the atmosphere created in the executive suite. "A fearful,
angry employee will steal to get even for the emotional beating she feels she is
taking," wrote one respondent. Another asked: "How ethical is it for large
corporations to deny workers a pay raise while upper management still receives
ridiculously large bonuses? This type of entrenched corruption at high levels
eventually creates dishonest behaviors at the lower levels."

Unfair treatment of women managers and workers sometimes is used as a 11
justification for not being completely aboveboard with employers. Take the possibility of pregnancy's having a negative impact on a woman's career. Seventy-six
percent of respondents did not have ethical difficulty with a job applicant who
doesn't tell a prospective employer that she's pregnant. Women with high
incomes and education levels were more likely than others to think this way.

Standing Your Ground—and Yielding It

Petty thievery and lies aside, what do people do when confronted with a truly 12
grievous wrong, such as the release of a dangerous product, or theft that is
likely to bankrupt a company? About two out of three women over thirty years
of age have had some experience in taking an ethical stand at work (though
fewer than half of those in the eighteen-to-twenty-five-year-old group have yet
been tested).

Did their stand get results? Respondents were split. "My attempts at 'correcting' 13
ethical wrongs never engendered lasting change," wrote one discouraged reader
who has worked for years in both the public and private sectors and ended up
with a "great feeling of futility."

Another reader learned the hard way that fighting the good fight is worthwhile. 14
"I had a good job that I quit rather than make the tough decision," she wrote.
Six months later a male co-worker took the risk and informed one owner that the

owner's partner was a cheat. The partner was forced out and the co-worker was rewarded with his job. "I would have been in line for the position if I had stayed and tattled," she wrote. She's since learned to speak out. "I have found that you can usually get the ethical point across and still get the job done."

15   Of women who have taken an ethical stand that has affected their careers, 37 percent said it had a positive effect and 30 percent said it had a negative effect. Some of the women who took a stand with negative results—like getting fired—have learned, with bitterness, to keep their mouths and eyes shut. "In the two years I have worked full-time, I have seen numerous unethical situations. More often than not, I have decided to make it 'someone else's problem' so as not to jeopardize my career or my peace of mind."

16   This sort of detached cynicism can be painful for the individual. "While working on this survey I faced a very unsettling fact about myself," wrote one reader. "I find that I choose the path of least resistance more often than not [even though] I believe in honesty. It is scary to see how easily and subtly unethical behavior has become a pattern in my working life, as though one can be one person at work and a totally different creature at home."

17   What's the answer? Do written codes of ethics help? Should the government step in? Overwhelmingly respondents said the ethical decisions they make on the job were learned at their parents' knees, and those values continue to be the most influential, along with religious teachings and the influences of friends, business colleagues, superiors, and books. Eleven percent had taken a special course in ethics, but only a few of these (1 percent) found that it made a difference.

18   Since many areas of confusion—such as pirating computer software and accepting gifts from suppliers—are not covered in the Ten Commandments, business ethics specific to the contemporary scene are clearly needed. Yet according to our respondents, these issues tend to be discussed only when a problem arises. Of readers whose workplaces do not have a formal code of ethics, almost 60 percent think it would be helpful. However, fewer than a third want government regulation of ethics.

19   The traditional American idea put forth by James Madison that free institutions should not depend on virtue but be fueled by selfish impulses, properly balanced—is echoed by one reader: "There must be a way to teach ethics as self-interest rather than sacrifice: to emphasize that right action is the best way to build community values, trust, and long-term business relationships."

20   Is this possible in the real world? "I work for a corporation in which the company's standards of conduct are an everyday topic of conversation," wrote one reader. Her company insists on honest business dealings with customers and will not allow stealing confidential information from competitors. "My guess is that we are considered too principled for our own good. But when organizations within the company stray from company values, the results are always bad: low profits, high turnover, poor product quality—and hell to pay with the executive committee." This reader is thrilled to be out of the ethical mire of her previous jobs and to find that, at least in some places, fair play can be a winning strategy.

Vocabulary

Directions: Locate each of the key words in the reading selection. Then read and study each word in its context and try to determine its meaning. Use a dictionary or thesaurus to check your guess. Write the meanings of the words in the margin of the text.

Record the new words you've learned in the following chart.

Key Word	Paragraph	Meaning
1. scruples	1	
2. nepotism	2	
3. erosion	2	
4. unheeded	3	
5. deteriorated	3	
6. hotbeds	5	
7. entrenched	10	
8. engendered	13	
9. cynicism	16	
Others?		

Guide Questions

Directions: These questions will guide your understanding of what you have read. They also will help you to analyze and evaluate the author's ideas and apply them to the real world and your own life.

Write answers to the questions in your notebook or on a separate sheet of paper if your instructor wishes to collect them. Your answers will form the basis of class discussion.

1. Describe the survey, its source, and its purpose.
2. The author of the article states her conclusion at the very beginning of the article; paraphrase it here.
3. Summarize some of the most important findings of the survey.

4. The author asks if the personal stories told by respondents to the survey are "symptomatic of a decline in American business ethics, or are they just a reflection of business as usual?" What does she mean by this question? What answer does she give?

5. According to the selection, where is the "hotbed" of unethical behavior? Does the answer surprise you? Why or why not?

6. Which group listed its own profession as the least unethical?

7. How did most people respond when asked if they would work for a company that allowed unethical situations to persist?

8. The author makes it clear that making ethical decisions is something that every worker must do. Give a few examples from your own knowledge and experience of the personal decisions employees have to make.

9. True or false: According to the article, the more successful and highly paid an employee is, the more likely he or she is to bend and break ethical rules.

10. a. Answer this question from your own perspective: Is it sometimes necessary to break the rules to get ahead?
    b. How did the respondents to the survey answer that same question?

11. Paragraph 16 begins, "This sort of detached cynicism can be painful for the individual." What is the author referring to here?

12. According to the respondents to the survey, where did they learn the values they used in making ethical decisions at work?

13. List some possible solutions to the problems of making ethical decisions at work.

Application

Here are some further results of the survey. A list of ethical violations is followed by the percentage of respondents who have personally observed them.

Violations	Percent who have witnessed violation
Fairness violations	
Favoritism or nepotism	70%
Taking credit for others' work	67%
Doing business with sexist clients	52%
Discrimination	47%
Sexual harassment	41%
Dishonesty	
Lying to employees	62%
Violating confidentiality	64%
Lying to make a sale	31%
Stealing	
Expense-account abuses	52%
Bribery	5%
Sexual trading	
Flirting to make a sale	43%
Sexual intimacy with boss	29%
Sex with co-worker on company time	19%
Sex with client to make a sale	10%

Have you personally observed any of these violations? Which ones? What did you do about it? Why? Discuss these questions with your classmates.

Writing

Directions: Return to the answers you gave to the survey questions in the introduction to the selection. Following are the actual results of the survey. Compare your answers to the ones respondents gave.

1. Your boss treats clients to cocaine.
   Unethical   99%
   No problem   1%
2. A real estate agent showing a house doesn't say that the basement floods.
   Unethical   92%
   No problem   8%
3. An executive learns that his company is about to be sold, which will send its stock price soaring. He leaks this information to two clients as well as to several friends.
   Unethical   91%
   No problem   9%
4. An administrative assistant routinely makes up excuses for her boss when he takes long lunches with his secretary.
   Unethical   56%
   No problem   44%
5. After a year of poor sales, a sales representative convinces her boss to let her give expensive gifts to prospective clients. The tactic works and sales increase.
   Unethical   46%
   No problem   54%
6. A publisher gives his college-age niece a highly sought-after unpaid summer internship at his company.
   Unethical   42%
   No problem   58%
7. Company policy forbids employees to discuss salaries with each other, but two people trade information to negotiate better with their boss.
   Unethical   40%
   No problem   60%
8. A manager has accumulated sick days. She calls in sick even though she isn't and takes a few days off.
   Unethical   34%
   No problem   66%
9. A job applicant finds out the morning before her job interview that she is pregnant. She decides not to say anything rather than jeopardize her chances.
   Unethical   24%
   No problem   76%

Choose one of the questions from this list. State your answer and then explain why you answered it the way you did. Write one paragraph.

Harold Krents studied at Harvard and Oxford, was a partner in a Washington, D.C., law firm, was the inspiration for a long-running Broadway show, Butterflies Are Free, *and wrote a popular TV movie,* To Race the Wind. *Throughout his life, Krents worked to ensure equal opportunity for the handicapped. He died in 1987 at the age of 43 of a brain tumor.*

In this selection, Krents describes his frustrating search for work and his rejection by employers—not because he lacked ability but because he had a disability.

DARKNESS AT NOON

Harold Krents

1 Blind from birth, I have never had the opportunity to see myself and have been completely dependent on the image I create in the eye of the observer. To date it has not been narcissistic.

2 There are those who assume that since I can't see, I obviously also cannot hear. Very often people will converse with me at the top of their lungs, enunciating each word very carefully. Conversely, people will also often whisper, assuming that since my eyes don't work, my ears don't either.

3 For example, when I go to the airport and ask the ticket agent for assistance to the plane, he or she will invariably pick up the phone, call a ground hostess and whisper: "Hi, Jane, we've got a seventy here." I have concluded that the word *blind* is not used for one of two reasons: Either they fear that if the dread word is spoken, the ticket agent's retina will immediately detach, or they are reluctant to inform me of my condition of which I may not have been previously aware.

4 On the other hand, others know that, of course, I can hear, but believe that I can't talk. Often, therefore, when my wife and I go out to dinner, a waiter or waitress will ask Kit if "he would like a drink" to which I respond that "indeed he would."

5 This point was graphically driven home to me while we were in England. I had been given a year's leave of absence from my Washington law firm to study for a diploma in law degree at Oxford University. During the year I became ill and was hospitalized. Immediately after admission, I was wheeled down to the X-ray room. Just at the door sat an elderly woman—elderly I would judge from the sound of her voice. "What is his name?" the woman asked the orderly who had been wheeling me.

6 "What's your name?" the orderly repeated to me.

7 "Harold Krents," I replied.

8 "Harold Krents," he repeated.

9 "When was he born?"

10 "When were you born?"

11 "November 5, 1944," I responded.

12 "November 5, 1944," the orderly intoned.

13 This procedure continued for approximately five minutes, at which point even my saint-like disposition deserted me. "Look," I finally blurted out, "this is

absolutely ridiculous. Okay, granted I can't see, but it's got to have become pretty clear to both of you that I don't need an interpreter."

"He says he doesn't need an interpreter," the orderly reported to the woman.   14

The toughest misconception of all is the view that because I can't see, I can't   15
work. I was turned down by over forty law firms because of my blindness, even though my qualifications included a cum laude degree from Harvard College and a good ranking in my Harvard Law School class.

The attempt to find employment, the continuous frustration of being told   16
that it was impossible for a blind person to practice law, the rejection letters, not based on my lack of ability but rather on my disability, will always remain one of the most disillusioning experiences of my life.

Fortunately, this view of limitation and exclusion is beginning to change.   17
On April 16, 1976 the Department of Labor issued regulations that mandate equal-employment opportunities for the handicapped. By and large, the business community's response to offering employment to the disabled has been enthusiastic.

I therefore look forward to the day, with the expectation that it is certain to   18
come, when employers will view their handicapped workers as a little child did me years ago when my family still lived in Scarsdale.

I was playing basketball with my father in our backyard according to proce-   19
dures we had developed. My father would stand beneath the hoop, shout, and I would shoot over his head at the basket attached to our garage. Our next-door neighbor, aged five, wandered over into our yard with a playmate. "He's blind," our neighbor whispered to her friend in a voice that could be heard distinctly by Dad and me. Dad shot and missed; I did the same. Dad hit the rim; I missed entirely; Dad shot and missed the garage entirely. "Which one is blind?" whispered back the little friend.

I would hope that, in the near future, when a plant manager is touring   20
the factory with the foreman and comes upon a handicapped and nonhandi-capped person working together, his comment after watching them work will be, "Which one is disabled?"

Vocabulary

Directions: Locate each of the key words in the reading selection. Then read and study each word in its context and try to determine its meaning. Use a dictionary or thesaurus to check your guess. Write the meanings of the words in the margin of the text.

Record the new words you've learned in the following chart.

Key Word	Paragraph	Meaning
1. narcissistic	1	
2. enunciating	2	
3. invariably	3	

Key Word	Paragraph	Meaning
4. retina	3	
5. disillusioning	16	
Others?		

Guide Questions

Directions: These questions will guide your understanding of what you have read. They will also help you to analyze and evaluate the author's ideas and apply them to the real world and your own life.

Write answers to the questions in your notebook or on a separate sheet of paper if your instructor wishes to collect them. Your answers will form the basis of class discussion.

1. Describe Harold Krents: state all the facts and inferences you can draw from the selection.
2. What are some of the problems Krents has encountered because of his blindness?
3. What does Krents say was the most "disillusioning experience" of his life? Why does he feel this way?
4. What is Krents's main purpose in writing this essay?

Application

Directions: Discuss the question of whether a blind person can be an effective lawyer. What are some problems he or she would face? In which areas would blindness make no difference at all?

Writing

Directions: Choose one of the people Krents describes—either the airport ticket agent, the waiter in the restaurant, or the woman at the hospital in England. Write that person a letter, reacting to his or her treatment of Krents.

SHORT TAKE

How to Get the Job You Want:
Tips for the Job Hunter

1. *Do your homework.* Check the company's website, stock performance, annual report. Be familiar with its products and/or services. One employer reports that he is turned off by candidates who do not know the most

basic facts about the company. If you can't be bothered to prepare for an interview, it raises serious questions about how well you will perform on the job.

2. *Have your questions ready.* At some point the interviewer will ask if you have any questions. Take advantage of that opening to find out everything you can about the job. You can also use this time to introduce any of your qualifications that haven't come up yet in the interview.

3. *Dress right.* Even if the company is a "casual operation," you can never go wrong if you wear a suit to the interview. Take it easy on the jewelry and makeup.

4. *Use your head.* There are lots of ways to blow an interview. One candidate answered a cell phone call during his interview. Guess whether he got the job.

5. *Be ready for the interviewer's questions.* Here are some frequently asked questions:

> What are your long-range career goals?
>
> Why did you choose the career you are preparing for?
>
> What is your greatest strength?
>
> What is your greatest weakness?
>
> Tell me about yourself.
>
> How has your education prepared you for your career?
>
> In what ways do you think you could make a contribution to our company?
>
> What two or three accomplishments in your life are you the most proud of?
>
> What extracurricular activities have you participated in? What did you learn from them?
>
> Why are you seeking a job with this company?
>
> Describe a mistake you have made and what you learned from it.
>
> Why should we hire you?

OK, let's talk about the future—your future. You've gotten your college degree and—at last!—the job you've always wanted. Now what? Are you happy? Are you satisfied with your career?

Most people expect to find fulfillment in their jobs, but there are no guarantees. This article, which appeared in the Los Angeles Times, *presents the thoughts of business executives, psychologists, and actual workers on finding happiness in work.*

Before you read the article, think about the issue of job satisfaction by answering the following questions.

1. *What are some factors that influence how satisfied a person is with his or her job?*
2. *T or F If you are dissatisfied with your job, there's nothing you can do about it—except quit.*
3. *What is the purpose of a job?*
   a. *personal satisfaction*
   b. *to make money*
   c. *to serve others*
   d. *to avoid boredom*
   e. *social status*
   f. *something else?*
4. *T or F The more overtime you work, the less productive you are.*
5. *Do you think that having interests outside of work contribute to making you a better worker?*

SATISFACTION NOT GUARANTEED, BUT YOU CAN FIND MEANING IN YOUR WORK

Sondra Farrell Bazrod

1   Most Americans grow up with the idea that they will have a satisfying career, yet for many the reality is that work is anything but fulfilling.

2   Experts say, however, that anyone, whether they work on a loading dock or in a corner office, can find satisfaction in their job—or at least find another job that is satisfying. The key is not expecting the job to make you happy.

3   A person needs to find meaning in a job to find satisfaction, said Samuel Culbert, a professor at UCLA's Anderson Graduate School of Management, and they often have to create that meaning for themselves.

4   "I think happiness comes after some things that are far more fundamental," Culbert said. "For example, a job has to be personally meaningful, and some jobs are not. People make them personally meaningful. A job needs to give a person a sense of purpose that he or she is not just a cog in the machinery. Jobs aren't created with the individual in mind."

5   Knowing that he's creating a future for his family provides that meaning for Guillermo Perez, 32, a loading dock foreman.

6   "This company has given me the opportunity of my life to do more and keep succeeding," said Perez, who lives in Covina and works at U.S. Growers Cold

Storage in Vernon. At his previous job at an auto parts ware-house, he said he was working only for a paycheck.

"I had mid-level jobs before," he said. "Now it's been a challenge to keep succeeding. I have a good life and my wonderful wife and three children understand that I work many hours, but our living comes from this job. We have our first house and now we live in a decent neighborhood. [My family] feels more confident about me and their future lives."   7

"Three things can influence your job satisfaction," said Anita Blanchard, an assistant professor of psychology at the University of North Carolina at Charlotte: How significant your job is to other people, how much freedom you have to make decisions, and how many different things you get to do at work.   8

"People who are negative tend to be more dissatisfied, but one way they can improve their outlook and job satisfaction is to think about the positives of the job and think how it is helping people," Blanchard said.   9

And job fit is important.   10

"Everybody has their own unique interest and it's most important to find the job that fills your needs," Blanchard said.   11

Finding that job doesn't necessarily mean making huge changes in a career.   12

For Katrina Elias, 34, now a saleswoman at Beverly Hills Ford, switching from one sales job to another made all the difference in her satisfaction with work.   13

"I sold radio time to small businesses, but I really believed it didn't benefit them," said Elias of North Hollywood. "If you're a salesperson and don't believe in the product, it's a very depressing job. I certainly didn't think I was helping the small businesses. I thought I was ripping them off."   14

As a car saleswoman, Elias said, she "really takes pleasure when a family is excited by the purchase when they drive off. It's a challenge getting people financed who have special needs, but my job was created to help people buy a car. The magic is believing in your product."   15

Seeing your job as a way to help someone is a key way of finding satisfaction, said Sidney Walter, a former UCLA psychology professor who now works as a forensic psychologist for the Department of Health and Human Services.   16

"Unfortunately, many people don't realize this," said Walter, who lives in Chico. "I've asked thousands of people, 'What's the purpose of your job?' and most will answer, 'To make money.' This is true of all types of workers, from executives to janitors."   17

Walter recommends that people discover and accept the purpose of their jobs.   18

"It is not for you to earn money," he said. "It is to serve others. All occupations have the same end purpose—helping others. The teacher to educate, the baseball player to entertain, the shoe clerk to assist, the jailer, vendor, seamstress and spouse to help, assist, to aid others. The basic purpose of all is to help. Until this is recognized and accepted you cannot be happy at your job."   19

And if you're having trouble finding that purpose?   20

"Know all you possibly can about your occupation," Walter said. "What it does, what happens after you are through with your part. During World War II, when the airplane riveters found out what their little contribution did toward   21 the end result, and saw the airplane flying in newsreels, their output increased significantly."

22   Learning on the job—not just about the job—is another way to create a more meaningful work life, said UCLA's Culbert.

23   "A lot of people don't learn because they fear that if they put themselves in a learning mode, they will do something that's a mistake and they'll be criticized or punished for it," Culbert said. "It's self protection. We get defensive even if we want to learn because we're scared, but if you want to have meaning on the job you have to feel it's OK to learn."

24   Meaning, happiness and productivity go beyond pay, Culbert said.

25   Yet the relationship between work and home cannot be isolated, said Blanchard of the University of North Carolina.

26   Los Angeles resident Milton Moreno, 27, said he realizes the need for balance in his life.

27   "When I come home I can't bring my problems from the job so I have to be two people on the same day with two personalities," said Moreno, 24, who has been a cashier and delivery person at Owens Market in West Los Angeles for nine years. "I also can't mix my problems at home with my job or I'll end up with nothing in the long run. I try to take one day at a time."

28   And at a time when workers are being asked to do more, doing less may be one of the quickest ways to job satisfaction.

29   "When I was working at one of my first jobs in a large corporation, I noticed that the people who did the most work and stayed overtime were asked to do even more and became increasingly unhappy," Walter said. "Those who did just enough and did it well were accepted as good workers."

30   Being a workaholic is the only addiction that's applauded, said Jonathon Lazear, author of "The Man Who Mistook His Job for a Life" which chronicles his life as a workaholic.

31   "Statistics indicate that productivity actually decreases the more overtime one is actively working," Lazear said. "But we tell ourselves otherwise."

32   "There's more to life than your job," he said. "Finding balance outside of work will make you a better worker, someone who can bring a fresher perspective to the job."

Vocabulary

Directions: Find each of the key words in the essay. Try to figure out each word's meaning by using the context. Confirm your guess by checking the dictionary. Write the meanings of the words in the margin of the text, near the word. Then record the meanings in the following chart.

Key Word	Paragraph	Meaning
1. cog	4	
2. vendor	19	

Key Word	Paragraph	Meaning
3. isolated	25	
4. chronicles	30	
5. workaholic	30	
Others?		

Guide Questions

Directions: These questions will guide your understanding of what you've read. Write your answers in your notebook or on a separate sheet of paper if your instructor will collect it. Your answers will be the basis of class discussion.

1. Write what you think is the main idea of this essay.
2. In paragraph 4, Samuel Culbert says that some jobs simply are not meaningful, but that people can make them meaningful. How can this be done?
3. How does Guillermo Perez make his job meaningful?
4. What are the three things that can influence your satisfaction with your job according to Anita Blanchard?
5. How can you improve your job satisfaction according to Ms. Blanchard?
6. What do most people say is the purpose of their jobs? Do you agree?
7. Sidney Walter says making money is *not* the main purpose of working. What does he say the main purpose is?
8. According to Walter, how can we become happy in our jobs?
9. What did you learn from this essay about the relationship between home and work?
10. What did you learn about the relationship between working overtime and success and happiness on the job?

Application

Choose some low-paying jobs that you can imagine doing. (Check the reading selection "The High Cost of Being Poor" on page 245 if you need some ideas.) Using what you learned from reading "Satisfaction Not Guaranteed," think of some ways you could make the jobs more satisfying. Write a paragraph summarizing your thoughts.

Marking Text/Summary Writing

Mark the text of this article (if you need to review how to mark text, turn to page 413). Then write a summary of "Satisfaction Not Guaranteed."

Making Connections

Read "Dreams in the Dark" (page 249). Then, thinking about what you learned from reading "Satisfaction Not Guaranteed," give some advice to Gloria Castillo. What would you suggest she do?

Making Connections/Writing

Read "The High Cost of Being Poor" (page 245). Then, imagine a conversation between Barbara Ehrenreich and Sidney Walter (paragraphs 16–19 in "Satisfaction Not Guaranteed"). What do you think Ehrenreich might say to him? How might he respond? Write a paragraph.

SHORT TAKE

Directory of Business Names

Does a person's name affect the career he or she chooses? Consider this list, collected from business directories around the world, of the names of real people in real jobs.

> A dentist in Paris: Docteur Ache
>
> Lawyers in Ireland: Argue and Phibbs
>
> A librarian in Brooklyn: Novella Booker
>
> A disease counselor in California: Mr. Clapp
>
> A pathologist in Florida: Dr. Croaker
>
> An eye doctor in Michigan: Dr. I. Doctor
>
> A judge in Massachusetts: Lawrence J. Felony
>
> A dental technician in Germany: Walburga Floss
>
> A urologist in New Jersey: Dr. Bum Suck Lee
>
> A priest in New York City: Father O'Pray
>
> A gynecologist in New York City: Dr. Zotan Ovary
>
> Plumbers in England: Plummer and Leek
>
> A pathologist in Connecticut: Dr. David P. Stiff

All these names are from John Train's delightful book, *Crazy Quilt* (HarperCollins, 1996).

"To do two things at once—is to do neither," Roman philosopher Publilius Syrus wrote in 100 A.D., and modern science may just be proving him right. Between the cell phone and the PDA, Wi-Fi and lattes—in short, between getting wired and going wireless—we are supposedly doing more in less time than ever. In fact, some believe the more we have to juggle—the more we multitask—the better. But is that really true? A growing body of research suggests that our pursuit of increased productivity through multitasking actually results in diminishing capacity.

THE MULTITASKING GENERATION

Claudia Wallis

It's 9:30 p.m., and Stephen and Georgina Cox know exactly where their children are. Well, their bodies, at least. Piers, 14, is holed up in his bedroom—eyes fixed on his computer screen—where he has been logged onto a MySpace chat room and AOL Instant Messenger (IM) for the past three hours. His twin sister Bronte is planted in the living room, having commandeered her dad's iMac—as usual. She, too, is busily IMing, while chatting on her cell phone and chipping away at homework. 1

By all standard space-time calculations, the four members of the family occupy the same three-bedroom home in Van Nuys, Calif., but psychologically each exists in his or her own little universe. Georgina, 51, who works for a display-cabinet maker, is tidying up the living room as Bronte works, not that her daughter notices. Stephen, 49, who juggles jobs as a squash coach, fitness trainer, event planner and head of a cancer charity he founded, has wolfed down his dinner alone in the kitchen, having missed supper with the kids. He, too, typically spends the evening on his cell phone and returning e-mails—when he can nudge Bronte off the computer. "One gets obsessed with one's gadgets," he concedes. 2

Zooming in on Piers' screen gives a pretty good indication of what's on his hyperkinetic mind. O.K., there's a Google Images window open, where he's chasing down pictures of Keira Knightley. Good ones get added to a snazzy Windows Media Player slide show that serves as his personal e-shrine to the actress. Several IM windows are also open, revealing such penetrating conversations as this one with a MySpace pal: 3

> MySpacer: suuuuuup!!! (Translation: What's up?) 4
> Piers: wat up dude 5
> MySpacer: nmu (Not much. You?) 6
> Piers: same 7

Naturally, iTunes is open, and Piers is blasting a mix of Queen, AC/DC, classic rock and hip-hop. Somewhere on the screen there's a Word file, in which Piers is writing an essay for English class. "I usually finish my homework at school," he explains to a visitor, "but if not, I pop a book open on my lap in my room, and while the computer is loading, I'll do a problem or write a sentence. Then, while mail is loading, I do more. I get it done a little bit at a time." 8

Bronte has the same strategy. "You just multitask," she explains. "My parents always tell me I can't do homework while listening to music, but they don't 9 understand that it helps me concentrate." The twins also multitask when hanging with friends, which has its own etiquette. "When I talk to my best friend Eloy," says Piers, "he'll have one earpiece [of his iPod] in and one out." Says Bronte: "If a friend thinks she's not getting my full attention, I just make it very clear that she is, even though I'm also listening to music."

10   The Coxes are one of 32 families in the Los Angeles area participating in an intensive, four-year study of modern family life, led by anthropologist Elinor Ochs, director of UCLA's Center on Everyday Lives of Families. While the impact of multitasking gadgets was not her original focus, Ochs found it to be one of the most dramatic areas of change since she conducted a similar study 20 years ago. "I'm not certain how the children can monitor all those things at the same time, but I think it is pretty consequential for the structure of the family relationship," says Ochs, whose work on language, interaction and culture earned her a MacArthur "genius" grant.

11   One of the things Ochs' team of observers looks at is what happens at the end of the workday when parents and kids reunite—and what doesn't happen, as in the case of the Coxes. "We saw that when the working parent comes through the door, the other spouse and the kids are so absorbed by what they're doing that they don't give the arriving parent the time of day," says Ochs. The returning parent, generally the father, was greeted only about a third of the time, usually with a perfunctory "Hi." "About half the time the kids ignored him or didn't stop what they were doing, multitasking and monitoring their various electronic gadgets," she says. "We also saw how difficult it was for parents to penetrate the child's universe. We have so many videotapes of parents actually backing away, retreating from kids who are absorbed by whatever they're doing."

12   Human beings have always had a capacity to attend to several things at once. Mothers have done it since the hunter-gatherer era—picking berries while suckling an infant, stirring the pot with one eye on the toddler. Nor is electronic multitasking entirely new: we've been driving while listening to car radios since they became popular in the 1930s. But there is no doubt that the phenomenon has reached a kind of warp speed in the era of Web-enabled computers, when it has become routine to conduct six IM conversations, watch American Idol on TV and Google the names of last season's finalists all at once.

13   That level of multiprocessing and interpersonal connectivity is now so commonplace that it's easy to forget how quickly it came about. Fifteen years ago, most home computers weren't even linked to the Internet. In 1990 the majority of adolescents responding to a survey done by Donald Roberts, a professor of communication at Stanford, said the one medium they couldn't live without was a radio/CD player. How quaint. In a 2004 follow-up, the computer won hands down.

14   Today 82% of kids are online by the seventh grade, according to the Pew Internet and American Life Project. And what they love about the computer, of course, is that it offers the radio/CD thing and so much more—games, movies, e-mail, IM, Google, MySpace. The big finding of a 2005 survey of Americans ages 8 to 18 by the Kaiser Family Foundation, co-authored by Roberts, is not that kids were spending a larger chunk of time using electronic media—that was

holding steady at 6.5 hours a day (could it possibly get any bigger?)—but that they were packing more media exposure into that time: 8.5 hours' worth, thanks to "media multitasking"—listening to iTunes, watching a DVD and IMing friends all at the same time. Increasingly, the media-hungry members of Generation M, as Kaiser dubbed them, don't just sit down to watch a TV show with their friends or family. From a quarter to a third of them, according to the survey, say they simultaneously absorb some other medium "most of the time" while watching TV, listening to music, using the computer or even while reading.

15   Parents have watched this phenomenon unfold with a mixture of awe and concern. The Coxes, for instance, are bowled over by their children's technical prowess. Piers repairs the family computers and DVD player. Bronte uses digital technology to compose elaborate photo collages and create a documentary of her father's ongoing treatment for cancer. And, says Georgina, "they both make these fancy PowerPoint presentations about what they want for Christmas." But both parents worry about the ways that kids' compulsive screen time is affecting their schoolwork and squeezing out family life. "We rarely have dinner together anymore," frets Stephen. "Everyone is in their own little world, and we don't get out together to have a social life."

16   Every generation of adults sees new technology—and the social changes it stirs—as a threat to the rightful order of things: Plato warned (correctly) that reading would be the downfall of oral tradition and memory. And every generation of teenagers embraces the freedoms and possibilities wrought by technology in ways that shock the elders: just think about what the automobile did for dating.

17   As for multitasking devices, social scientists and educators are just beginning to assess their impact, but the researchers already have some strong opinions. The mental habit of dividing one's attention into many small slices has significant implications for the way young people learn, reason, socialize, do creative work and understand the world. Although such habits may prepare kids for today's frenzied workplace, many cognitive scientists are positively alarmed by the trend. "Kids that are instant messaging while doing homework, playing games online and watching TV, I predict, aren't going to do well in the long run," says Jordan Grafman, chief of the cognitive neuroscience section at the National Institute of Neurological Disorders and Stroke (NINDS). Decades of research (not to mention common sense) indicate that the quality of one's output and depth of thought deteriorate as one attends to ever more tasks. Some are concerned about the disappearance of mental downtime to relax and reflect. Roberts notes Stanford students "can't go the few minutes between their 10 o'clock and 11 o'clock classes without talking on their cell phones. It seems to me that there's almost a discomfort with not being stimulated—a kind of 'I can't stand the silence.'"

18   Gen M's multitasking habits have social and psychological implications as well. If you're IMing four friends while watching *That '70s Show,* it's not the same as sitting on the couch with your buddies or your sisters and watching the show together. Or sharing a family meal across a table. Thousands of years of evolution created human physical communication—facial expressions, body language—that puts broadband to shame in its ability to convey meaning and create bonds.

What happens, wonders UCLA's Ochs, as we replace side-by-side and eye-to-eye human connections with quick, disembodied e-exchanges? Those are critical issues not just for social scientists but for parents and teachers trying to understand—and do right by—Generation M.

Vocabulary

Directions: Find each of the key words in the essay. Try to figure out each word's meaning by using the context. Confirm your guess by checking the dictionary. Write the meanings of the words in the margin of the text, near the word. Then record the meanings in the following chart.

Key Word	Paragraph	Meaning
1. hyperkinetic	3	
2. monitor	10	
3. perfunctory	11	
4. quaint	13	
5. simultaneously	14	
6. compulsive	15	
7. wrought	16	
Others?		

Guide Questions

Directions: These questions will guide your understanding of what you've read. Write your answers in your notebook or on a separate sheet of paper if your instructor will collect it. Your answers will be the basis of class discussion.

1. The article begins with a description of a typical evening of the Cox family. Briefly describe the scene.
2. What is your opinion of the IM conversation between Piers and his MySpace pal? How does it compare to your IM conversations?
3. Bronte says that multitasking helps her to concentrate. Do you think it does?
4. Describe the study being conducted by UCLA's Center on Everyday Lives of Families.

5. What have the researchers noticed about what happens at the end of the workday?
6. Explain what is meant by "the phenomenon has reached . . . warp speed" (paragraph 12).
7. Contrast multiprocessing and the use of technology 15 years ago and today.
8. What was the "big finding" of the 2005 survey?
9. The Coxes (and other parents) see both positive and negative aspects to their children's use of technology and multitasking. What good things do they see? What is the downside?
10. Reread paragraph 16. Think about it and discuss it with a classmate. Then write a one- or two-sentence paraphrase of the paragraph.
11. Explain why Jordan Grafman says that "Kids that are instant messaging while doing homework, playing games online and watching TV, I predict, aren't going to do well in the long run."
12. Explain what the author means in paragraph 18 when she says, "Gen M's multitasking habits have social and psychological implications as well."

Application
Talk to your parents or a member of an older generation. Ask them to describe the role that technology played in their lives when they were your age. Write one or two paragraphs comparing and contrasting their experiences with yours.

Writing
Are you a multitasker? If you are, do you think it can be a problem? Write a paragraph discussing your multitasking habits; then add a paragraph in which you discuss the possible dangers that could result.

Feeling a bit hungry? How about a nice snack of seafood-flavored Cheetos? No? Then consider a reindeer sausage pizza with a can of sweet corn for dessert. Or pasta with ketchup on top? All of these culinary treats are popular items in other countries. This essay, first published in The Wall Street Journal *in 1996, describes the challenges of marketing to the wildly different tastes of people in different countries. While for us it might be a fun surprise to find a mayo and potato-topped pizza in Tokyo, international marketers hate surprises. That's why they spend time and money studying the preferences of potential customers all over the world.*

CUSTOM-MADE

Tara Parker-Pope

1   Pity the poor Domino's Pizza Inc. delivery man.

2   In Britain, customers don't like the idea of him knocking on their doors—they think it's rude. In Japan, houses aren't numbered sequentially—finding an address means searching among rows of houses numbered willy-nilly. And in Kuwait, pizza is more likely to be delivered to a waiting limousine than to someone's front door.

3   "We honestly believe we have the best pizza delivery system in the world," says Gary McCausland, managing director of Domino's international division. "But delivering pizza isn't the same all over the world."

4   And neither is making cars, selling soap, or packaging toilet paper. International marketers have found that just because a product plays in Peoria,* that doesn't mean it will be a hit in Helsinki.

5   To satisfy local tastes, products ranging from Heinz ketchup to Cheetos chips are tweaked, reformulated, and reflavored. Fast-food companies such as McDonalds's Corp., popular for the "sameness" they offer all over the world, have discovered that to succeed, they also need to offer some local appeal—like selling beer in Germany and adding British Cadbury chocolate sticks to their ice-cream cones in England.

6   The result is a delicate balancing act for international marketers: How does a company exploit the economies of scale that can be gained by global marketing while at the same time making its products appeal to local tastes?

7   The answer: Be flexible, even when it means changing a tried-and-true recipe, even when consumer preferences, like Haagen-Dazs green tea ice cream, sound awful to the Western palate.

8   "It's a dilemma we all live with every day," says Nick Harding, H.J. Heinz Co.'s managing director for Northern Europe. Heinz varies the recipe of its famous ketchup in different markets, selling a less-sweet version in Belgium and Holland, for instance, because consumers there use ketchup as a pasta sauce (and mayonnaise on french fries). "We're looking for the economies from globalizing our ideas, but we want to maintain the differences necessary for local markets," says Mr. Harding.

---

* "Plays in Peoria" is a common expression which means something is acceptable to most middle-class Americans.

For those who don't heed such advice, the costs are high. U.S. auto makers, for instance, have done poorly in Japan, at least in part because they failed to adapt. Until recently, most didn't bother even to put steering wheels on the right, as is the standard in Japan. While some American makers are beginning to conform, European companies such as Volkswagen AG, Daimler-Benz AG, and Bayerische Motoren Werke AG did it much sooner, and have done far better in the Japanese market as a result.

For Domino's, the balancing act has meant maintaining the same basic pizza delivery system world-wide—and then teaming up with local franchisers to tailor the system to each country's needs. In Japan, detailed wall maps, three times larger than those used in its stores elsewhere, help delivery people find the proper address despite the odd street numbering system.

In Iceland, where much of the population doesn't have phone service, Domino's has teamed with a Reykjavik drive-in movie theater to gain access to consumers. Customers craving a reindeer-sausage pizza (a popular flavor there) flash their turn signal, and a theater employee brings them a cellular phone to order a pizza, which is then delivered to the car.

Local Domino's managers have developed new pizza flavors, including *mayo jaga* (mayonnaise and potato) in Tokyo and pickled ginger in India. The company, which now has 1,160 stores in 46 countries, is currently trying to develop a nonbeef pepperoni topping for its stores in India.

When Pillsbury Co., a unit of Britain's Grand Metropolitan PLC, wanted to begin marketing its Green Giant brand vegetables outside the United States, it decided to start with canned sweet corn, a basic product unlikely to require any flavor changes across international markets. But to Pillsbury's surprise, the product still was subject to local influences. Instead of being eaten as a hot side dish, the French add it to salad and eat it cold. In Britain, corn is used as a sandwich and pizza topping. In Japan, school children gobble down canned corn as an after-school treat. And in Korea, the sweet corn is sprinkled over ice cream.

So Green Giant tailored its advertising to different markets. Spots show corn kernels falling off a cob into salads and pastas, or topping an ice-cream sundae. "Initially we thought it would be used the same as in the United States," says Stephen Moss, vice president, strategy and development, for Green Giant. "But we've found there are very different uses for corn all over the world."

And Green Giant has faced some cultural hurdles in its race to foreign markets. Although vegetables are a significant part of the Asian diet, Green Giant discovered that Japanese mothers, in particular, take pride in the time they take to prepare a family meal and saw frozen vegetables as an unwelcome shortcut. "Along with the convenience comes a little bit of guilt," says Mr. Moss.

The solution? Convince moms that using frozen vegetables gives them the opportunity to prepare their families' favorite foods more often. To that end, Green Giant focused on a frozen mixture of julienned carrots and burdock root, a traditional favorite root vegetable that requires several hours of tedious preparation.

The company also has introduced individual seasoned vegetable servings for school lunch boxes, with such flavors as sesame-seasoned lotus root. Although fresh vegetables still dominate the market, Green Giant says its strategy is starting to show results, and frozen varieties now account for half the vegetable company's sales in Japan.

18   The drive for localization has been taken to extremes in some cases: Cheetos, the bright orange and cheesy-tasting chip brand of PepsiCo Inc.'s Frito-Lay unit, are cheeseless in China. The reason? Chinese consumers generally don't like cheese, because many of them are lactose-intolerant. So Cheetos tested such flavors as Peking duck, fried egg, and even dog to tempt the palates of Chinese. Ultimately, says Tom Kuthy, vice president of marketing for PepsiCo Foods International's Asia-Pacific operations, the company picked a butter flavor, called American cream, and an Asianized barbecue flavor called Japanese steak. Last year, Frito rolled out its third flavor, seafood.

19   In addition to changing the taste, the company also packaged Cheetos in a 15-gram size priced at one yuan, about 12 cents, so that even kids with little spending money can afford them. The bottom line: These efforts to adapt to the local market have paid off. Mr. Kuthy estimates that close to 300 million packages of Cheetos have been sold since they were introduced two years ago in Guangzhou. Cheetos are now available in Shanghai and Beijing as well.

20   Frito isn't through trying to adapt. Now the company is introducing a 33-gram pack for two yuan. Mr. Kuthy also is considering more flavors, but dog won't be one of them. "Yes, we tested the concept, but it was never made into a product," he says. "Its performance was mediocre."

21   Other PepsiCo units have followed with their own flavor variations. In Thailand, Pizza Hut has a *tom yam*-flavored pizza based on the spices of the traditional Thai soup. In Singapore, you can get a KFC Zinger chicken burger that is hot and spicy with Asia's ubiquitous chili. The Singaporean pizza at Pizza Hut comes with ground beef, green peppers and chili. Elsewhere in Asia, pizzas come in flavors such as Mongolian, with pork, chili, and garlic; salmon, with a creamy lobster sauce; and Satay, with grilled chicken and beef.

22   Coming up with the right flavor combinations for international consumers isn't easy. Part of the challenge is building relationships with customers in far-flung markets. For years, the founders of Ben & Jerry's Homemade Inc. had relied on friends, co-workers, and their own taste buds to concoct such unusual ice-cream flavors as Chunky Monkey and Cherry Garcia.

23   But introducing their ice cream abroad, by definition, meant losing that close connection with their customers that made them successful. "For Ben and me, since we've grown up in the United States, our customers were people like us, and the flavors we made appealed to us," says co-founder Jerry Greenfield, scooping ice cream at a media event in the Royal Albert Hall in London. "I don't think we have the same seat-of-the-pants feel for places like England. It's a different culture."

24   As a result, one of the company's most popular flavors in the United States, Chocolate Chip Cookie Dough, flopped in Britain. The nostalgia quotient of the ice cream, vanilla-flavored with chunks of raw cookie dough, was simply lost on the Brits, who historically haven't eaten chocolate-chip cookies. "People

didn't grow up in this country sneaking raw cookie-dough batter from Mom," says Mr. Greenfield.

The solution? Hold a contest to concoct a quintessential British ice 25 cream. After reviewing hundreds of entries, including Choc Ness Monster and Cream Victoria, the company in July introduced Cool Britannia, a combination of vanilla ice cream, strawberries, and chocolate-covered Scottish shortbread. (The company plans to sell Cool Britannia in the United States eventually.)

And in a stab at building a quirky relationship with Brits, the duo opted 26 for a publicity stunt when Britain's beef crisis meant farmers were left with herds of cattle that couldn't be sold at market. Ben & Jerry's creative solution: Use the cows to advertise. The company's logo was draped across the backs of grazing cattle, and the stunt made the front page of major London newspapers.

The company has just begun selling ice cream in France but isn't sure 27 whether the company will try contests for a French flavor in that market. One reason: It's unclear whether Ben & Jerry's wry humor, amusing to the Brits, will be understood by the laconic French. "We're going to try to get more in touch, more comfortable with the feel of the French market first," says Mr. Greenfield.

But for every success story, there have been a slew of global marketing mis- 28 takes. In Japan consumer-products marketer Procter & Gamble Co. made several stumbles when it first entered the market in the early 1970s.

The company thought its thicker, more-absorbent Pampers diapers in big 29 packs like those favored in America would be big sellers in Japan. But Japanese women change their babies twice as often as Americans and prefer thin diapers. Moreover, they often have tiny apartments and no room to store huge diaper packs. The company adapted by making thinner diapers packaged in smaller bags. Because the company shifted gears quickly, Procter & Gamble is now one of the largest and most successful consumer-goods companies in Japan, with more than $1 billion in annual sales and market leadership in several categories.

Vocabulary

Directions: Locate each of the key words in the reading selection. Try to figure out each word's meaning by using the context. Confirm your guess by checking the dictionary or thesaurus. Write the meanings of the words in the margin of the text. Then record the meanings in the following chart.

Key Word	Paragraph	Meaning
1. tweaked	5	
2. mediocre	20	

Key Word	Paragraph	Meaning
3. quintessential	25	
4. slew	28	
Others?		

Guide Questions

Directions: These questions will guide your understanding of what you have read. Write your answers in your notebook, or on a separate sheet of paper if your instructor wishes to collect it. Your answers to these questions will be the basis of class discussion.

1. In a sentence, explain why the author says we should pity the poor Domino's pizza man.
2. Explain the balancing act that international marketers must cope with (paragraph 6). Please use your own words.
3. a. Describe the cultural problem the Green Giant company encountered when it tried to sell frozen vegetables in Japan and how they solved it.
   b. Give one example of how Ben & Jerry's ice cream company solved a similar problem.
4. Describe Proctor & Gamble's marketing mistake in Japan (beginning in paragraph 28). Be sure to use your own words.
5. Write a main idea sentence in your own words that sums up this article.

Marking Text

Mark the text of this essay, "Custom-Made." To review how to mark text, turn to page 413, "Learning Strategy III—Marking Text.

Writing

Directions: Choose one of the following questions and write a paragraph in response.

1. Have you had a personal experience related to the information in the article? If so, tell the story in a paragraph.
2. Assume that you are the president of a company that makes automobiles. What kind of research should you do before trying to sell your cars in a foreign country?
3. Assume you are the president of a company that makes beer. What information about the foreign country should you have before trying to sell your product in that country?

SHORT TAKE

It Got Lost in the Translation

Even experts in business can fall flat on their faces when they forget the importance of language in human affairs. Here are some examples of language goofs by companies involved in international marketing:

> —Several years ago Estée Lauder introduced a new foundation make-up in Germany called Country Mist. In the nick of time, a local manager called U.S. headquarters with a linguistic SOS: *Mist* means "manure" in German. The name was changed to Country Moist.
> —An ad for Nitto Koygo Company, a golf course designer in Tokyo, goes like this: "Preparing for you club-life of luxurious relaxation always there. Feel and Taste it at any one of our golf clubs both in Japan and overseas as well, please."
> —The slogan "Come Alive with Pepsi" almost appeared in the Chinese version of *Reader's Digest* as "Pepsi Brings Your Ancestors Back from the Grave."
> —"Body by Fisher" was translated into "Corpse by Fisher" in Flemish.
> —The French government published an English-language catalog promoting local CAD/CAM products. Referring to one software program, it read: "Different versions are available for educational institutes for symbolic prices."
> —Tokyo Gas Company's slogan in English reads "My Life, My Gas."
> —When Totes Inc. bought the German company Jagra-Haus, it announced the company would be renamed Totes Deutschland. Executives retreated when they learned the new corporate name meant "dead Germany."

SHORT TAKE

International Etiquette for the Business Traveler

Everyone knows that customs differ from country to country, sometimes even from city to city. Etiquette for tourists is essential for a successful vacation, but knowledge of the local customs can make or break a business trip.

Here are a few suggestions for business travelers.

Gifts In China it is considered rude to open a gift in front of the person who gave it. In most parts of Africa, gifts should be opened immediately. In Greece, Spain, or Portugal, never give a gift with the company logo on it—it is considered bad taste.

Business cards The exchange of business cards is very important in Japan. When you give your business card, always use both hands. Be sure to examine and admire the card—the longer you look at it, the more respect you show for the person.

Alcohol Alcohol is discouraged at business lunches in Australia, while in Germany, drinking moderately is acceptable. In Russia drinking is essential—it serves to establish close relationships.

Gender Attention to gender etiquette is crucial in both vacation and business travel. In some countries, where gender roles are rooted in the tenets of religion, a misstep can be disastrous. In the Arab world, shaking hands is mandatory for men in a business meeting, but Arab men may not touch a woman in western dress. In India, men and women do not make physical contact in public, though a handshake may be permissible.

A Few Other Tips

If you travel in Spain, be prepared to eat late. Traditionally dinner is eaten at 10 or 11 p.m. A business dinner can last well into the early morning hours.

In Japan it is not considered rude to ask you how much you earn or how big your house is.

Be prepared for differences in time. If you are invited to a person's home for dinner at 8 p.m., in most of Latin America, don't show up until 9 p.m. or later—you may surprise your host in the shower!

Watch Those Hands!

Gestures can have very different meanings in different cultures. For example:

In Argentina, rotating your finger around the front of the ear means, "You have a phone call." But in the United States it means, "You're crazy!"

Making a circle with your thumb and forefinger means "OK" in the United States, but in Tunisia it means, "I'll kill you!"

In Texas, raising the forefinger and the pinky finger is a gesture used by fans of the University of Texas football team to mean "Hook 'em Horns!" (the longhorn bull is the symbol of the team) but in Italy and other places it means, "Your wife is being unfaithful."

COLLABORATIVE LEARNING

Working in Groups to Guide Your Own Reading

All of the reading selections so far in this unit have been accompanied by questions and exercises that are meant to help you understand and use what you've read. However, in much of your college reading (not to mention in your real life), you will be expected to master the material on your own.

Research has shown that one of the most effective ways to learn is in *groups*. In college, working with classmates can help you to master the material of a college course. The give-and-take that comes naturally when working with other people helps us to avoid falling into bad habits like *passive reading*. (We have all had the awful experience of reading a whole chapter, then realizing that we don't remember one single thing we've read.) Working with other students will help you to avoid such problems. For this assignment, form groups of approximately four students. In your group, read and think about the two following reading selections: "Hispanic USA: The Conveyor-Belt Ladies," by Rose Del Castillo Guilbault, and "Less Is More: A Call for Shorter Work Hours," by Barbara Brandt. Then, create your own vocabulary chart, guide questions, and application and writing assignments.

Follow these steps to complete the assignment:

1. Preview the selection before you read—look at and think about the title, any headings or subheadings, the first paragraph, the last paragraph, and the first sentence of each paragraph.
2. Read through the selection one time quickly.
3. Read the selection a second time, more carefully. This time mark the text. Review how to do this by turning to page 413, "Learning Strategy III—Marking Text."
4. Brainstorm with your group. Ask yourselves: What important issues is the author discussing? What new information did you learn? Can the issues discussed in the selection be connected to those you have already studied? Can any of the information here be applied to situations in your own life?
5. Now, create a set of exercises similar to those you have completed in previous chapters of this book:
   a. **Vocabulary.** Make a list of key words from the text. Set them up in chart format as on page 226.
   b. **Guide Questions.** Write questions that will guide understanding of the major ideas in the reading.
   c. **Application.** Prepare an application exercise that takes one or more of the important ideas in the reading and relates it to real life.
   d. **Writing.** Create a writing assignment to conclude the chapter.

Before you begin, it would be a good idea to review the questions and exercises in the previous reading selections in this book.

When you are finished, submit your work to your instructor. Your instructor may review and combine the work of all the groups and return the exercise to the class. You will then have the opportunity to *answer* the questions you and your classmates have developed.

Now, use your skills as an active, independent reader to tackle the following reading selections. Good luck!

Most of us have had to suffer through summer jobs—usually low-paying, high-boredom work suitable for a temporary, untrained worker. While we may have dreaded the work, the money was welcome and usually essential. In this article, Rose Del Castillo Guilbault describes her last summer job before college. She sorted tomatoes on a conveyor belt, side by side with migrant workers—women who at first embarrassed her, but whom she soon came to like and respect.

HISPANIC USA: THE CONVEYOR-BELT LADIES
Rose Del Castillo Guilbault

The conveyor-belt ladies were the migrant women, mostly from Texas, I worked with during the summers of my teenage years. I call them conveyor-belt ladies because our entire relationship took place while sorting tomatoes on a conveyor belt.   1

We were like a cast in a play where all the action occurs on one set. We'd return day after day to perform the same roles, only this stage was a vegetable-packing shed, and at the end of the season there was no applause. The players could look forward only to the same uninspiring parts on a string of grim real-life stages.   2

The women and their families arrived in May for the carrot season, spent the summer in the tomato sheds, and stayed through October for the bean harvest. After that, they emptied the town, some returning to their homes in Texas (cities like McAllen, Douglas, Brownsville), while others continued on the migrant trail, picking cotton in the San Joaquin Valley or grapefruits and oranges in the Imperial Valley.   3

Most of these women had started in the fields. The vegetable-packing sheds were a step up, easier than the back-breaking, grueling work the field demanded. The work was more tedious than strenuous, paid better, provided fairly steady hours and clean bathrooms. Best of all, you weren't subjected to the elements.   4

The summer I was sixteen, my mother got jobs for both of us as tomato sorters. That's how I came to be included in the seasonal sorority of the conveyor belt.   5

The work consisted of standing and picking flawed tomatoes off the conveyor belt before they rolled off into the shipping boxes at the end of the line. These boxes were immediately loaded onto waiting delivery trucks, so it was crucial not to let imperfect tomatoes through.   6

The work could be slow or intense, depending on the quality of the tomatoes and how many there were. Work increased when the company's deliveries got backlogged or after rainy weather had delayed picking.   7

During those times, it was not unusual to work from 7 A.M. to midnight, playing catch-up. I never heard anyone complain about the overtime. Overtime meant desperately needed extra money.   8

I was not happy to be part of the agricultural work force. I would have preferred working in a dress shop or baby-sitting, like my friends. But I had a dream that would cost a lot of money—college. And the fact was, this was the highest-paying work I could do.   9

10   But it wasn't so much the work that bothered me. I was embarrassed because only Mexicans worked at packing sheds. I had heard my schoolmates joke about the "ugly, fat Mexican women" at the sheds. They ridiculed the way they dressed and laughed at the "funny way" they talked. I feared working with them would irrevocably stigmatize me, setting me further apart from my Anglo classmates.

11   At sixteen I was more American than Mexican and, with adolescent arrogance, felt superior to these "uneducated" women. I might be one of them, I reasoned, but I was not like them.

12   But it was difficult not to like the women. They were a gregarious, entertaining group, easing the long, monotonous hours with bawdy humor, spicy gossip, and inventive laments. They poked fun at all the male workers and did hysterical impersonations of a dyspeptic Anglo supervisor. Although he didn't speak Spanish (other than "*Mujeres, trabajo, trabajo!*" Women, work, work!), he seemed to sense he was being laughed at. That would account for the sudden rages when he would stamp his foot and forbid us to talk until break time.

13   "I bet he understands Spanish and just pretends so he can hear what we say," I whispered to Rosa.

14   "*Ay, no, hija,* it's all the buzzing in his ears that alerts him that these *viejas* (old women) are bad-mouthing him!" Rosa giggled.

15   But it would have been easier to tie the women's tongues in a knot than to keep them quiet. Eventually the ladies had their way and their fun, and the men learned to ignore them.

16   We were often shifted around, another strategy to keep us quiet. This gave me ample opportunity to get to know everyone, listen to their life stories, and absorb the gossip.

17   Pretty Rosa described her romances and her impending wedding to a handsome field worker. Bertha, a heavy-set, dark-skinned woman, told me that Rosa's marriage would cause nothing but headaches because the man was younger and too handsome. Maria, large, moon-faced, and placid, described the births of each of her nine children, warning me about the horrors of childbirth. Pragmatic Minnie, a tiny woman who always wore printed cotton dresses, scoffed at Maria's stupidity, telling me she wouldn't have so many kids if she had ignored that good-for-nothing priest and gotten her tubes tied!

18   In unexpected moments, they could turn melancholic: recounting the babies who died because their mothers couldn't afford medical care; the alcoholic, abusive husbands who were their "cross to bear"; the racism they experienced in Texas, where they were branded "dirty Mexicans" or "Mexican dogs" and not allowed in certain restaurants.

19   They spoke with the detached fatalism of people with limited choices and alternatives. Their lives were as raw and brutal as ghetto streets—something they accepted with an odd grace and resignation.

20   I was appalled and deeply affected by these confidences. The injustices they endured enraged me; their personal struggles overwhelmed me. I knew I could do little but sympathize.

My mother, no stranger to suffering, suggested I was too impressionable 21
when I emotionally told her the women's stories. "That's nothing," she'd say
lightly. "If they were in Mexico, life would be even harder. At least there's opportunities here, you can work."

My icy arrogance quickly thawed, that first summer, as my respect for the 22
conveyor-belt ladies grew.

I worked in the packing sheds for several summers. The last season also 23
turned out to be the last time I lived at home. It was the end of a chapter in my
life, but I didn't know it then. I had just finished junior college and was transferring to the university. I was already over-educated for seasonal work, but if you
counted the overtime, no other jobs came close to paying so well, so I went back
one last time.

The ladies treated me with warmth and respect. I was a college student, 24
deserving of special treatment.

Aguedita, the crew chief, moved me to softer and better-paying jobs within 25
the plant. I went from the conveyor belt to shoving boxes down a chute and
finally to weighing boxes of tomatoes on a scale—the highest-paying position
for a woman.

When the union's dues collector showed up, the women hid me in the bath- 26
room. They had decided it was unfair for me to have to join the union and pay
dues, since I worked only during the summer.

"Where's the student?" the union rep would ask, opening the door to a barrage 27
of complaints about the union's unfairness.

Maria (of the nine children) tried to feed me all summer, bringing extra tor- 28
tillas, which were delicious. I accepted them guiltily, always wondering if I was
taking food away from her children. Others would bring rental contracts or other
documents for me to explain and translate.

The last day of work was splendidly beautiful, warm and sunny. If this had 29
been a movie, these last scenes would have been shot in soft focus, with a crescendo
of music in the background.

But real life is anti-climactic. As it was, nothing unusual happened. The con- 30
veyor belt's loud humming was turned off, silenced for the season. The women
sighed as they removed their aprons. Some of them just walked off, calling *"Hasta
la próxima!"* Until next time!

But most of the conveyor-belt ladies shook my hand, gave me a blessing or 31
a big hug.

"Make us proud!" they said. 32

I hope I have. 33

Vocabulary

Directions: Mark any important words in the reading selection that you don't know. Then
list them in the following chart along with their paragraph numbers. Try to figure out each
word's meaning by reading over the context carefully for clues to help you guess the
meaning of the unfamiliar word. Check your dictionary or thesaurus to confirm your guess.

After you discuss the words with your group members, write the meanings in the margin of the text, near the word. Then enter them in the following chart.

Key Word	Paragraph	Meaning

Guide Questions

Directions: Develop a list of questions that elicit the important ideas in the reading selection. Start at the beginning and work your way sequentially through the text until you have addressed all of the author's major ideas.

Application

Directions: When you have a list of guide questions, read through the selection again. This time, write one or more questions that require the information in the text to be applied to a situation in the real world.

Writing

Directions: Your last task is to prepare a writing assignment. For example, you might ask for a paragraph in which the writer comments on the ideas in the reading selection. You might also ask for a summary of the selection.

Most Americans consider the 40-hour work week to be normal and natural. But many observers think that Americans are working too long and too hard. Here, the author argues that overwork has become a major social problem that has reached crisis proportions. See if you agree with her.

LESS IS MORE: A CALL FOR SHORTER WORK HOURS
Barbara Brandt

America is suffering from overwork. Too many of us are too busy, trying to squeeze more into each day while having less to show for it. Although our growing time crunch is often portrayed as a personal dilemma, it is in fact a major social problem that has reached crisis proportions over the past twenty years. 1

The simple fact is that Americans today—both women and men—are spending too much time at work, to the detriment of their homes, their families, their personal lives, and their communities. The American Dream promised that our individual hard work, paired with the advances of modern technology, would bring about the good life for all. Glorious visions of the leisure society were touted throughout the fifties and sixties. But now most people are working more than ever before, while still struggling to meet their economic commitments. Ironically, the many advances in technology, such as computers and fax machines, rather than reducing our work load, seem to have speeded up our lives at work. At the same time, technology has equipped us with "conveniences" like microwave ovens and frozen dinners that merely enable us to adopt a similar frantic pace in our home lives so we can cope with more hours at paid work. 2

A recent spate of articles in the mainstream media has focused on the new problems of overwork and lack of time. Unfortunately, overwork is often portrayed as a special problem of yuppies and professionals on the fast track. In reality, the unequal distribution of work and time in America today reflects the decline in both standard of living and quality of life for most Americans. Families whose members never see each other, women who work a double shift (first on the job, then at home), workers who need more flexible work schedules, and unemployed and underemployed people who need more work are all casualties of the crisis of overwork. 3

Americans often assume that overwork is an inevitable fact of life—like death and taxes. Yet a closer look at other times and other nations offers some startling surprises. 4

Anthropologists have observed that, in pre-industrial (particularly hunting and gathering) societies, people generally spend 3 to 4 hours a day, 15 to 20 hours a week, doing the work necessary to maintain life. The rest of the time is spent in socializing, partying, playing, storytelling, and artistic or religious activities. The ancient Romans celebrated 175 public festivals a year in which everyone participated, and people in the Middle Ages had at least 115. 5

In our era, almost every other industrialized nation (except Japan) has fewer annual working hours and longer vacations than the United States. This includes 6 all of Western Europe, where many nations enjoy thriving economies and standards of living equal to or higher than ours. Jeremy Brecher and Tim Costello, writing in *Z Magazine* (October 1990), note that "European unions during the 1980s made a powerful and largely successful push to cut working hours. In 1987 German metal-workers struck and won a 37.5-hour week; many are now winning a 35-hour week. In 1990, hundreds of thousands of British workers won a 37-hour week."

7   In an article about work time in the *Boston Globe,* Suzanne Gordon notes that workers in other industrialized countries "enjoy—as a statutory right—longer vacations [than in the United States] from the moment they enter the work force. In Canada, workers are legally entitled to two weeks off their first year on the job. . . . After two or three years of employment, most get three weeks of vacation. After ten years, it's up to four, and by twenty years, Canadian workers are off for five weeks. In Germany, statutes guarantee eighteen days minimum for everyone, but most workers get five or six weeks. The same is true in Scandinavian countries, and in France."

8   In contrast to the extreme American emphasis on productivity and commitment, which results in many workers, especially in professional-level jobs, not taking the vacations coming to them, Gordon notes that "In countries that are America's most successful competitors in the global marketplace, all working people, whether lawyers or teachers, CEOs or janitors, take the vacations to which they are entitled by law. 'No one in West Germany,' a West German embassy's officer explains, 'no matter how high up they are, would ever say they couldn't afford to take a vacation. Everyone takes their vacation.'"

9   And in Japan, where dedication to the job is legendary, Gordon notes that the Japanese themselves are beginning to consider their national workaholism a serious social problem, leading to stress-related illnesses and even death. As a result, the Japanese government recently established a commission whose goal is to promote shorter working hours and more leisure time.

10   Most other industrialized nations also have better family-leave policies than the United States, and in a number of other countries workers benefit from innovative time-scheduling opportunities, such as sabbaticals.

11   While the idea of a shorter workweek and longer vacations sounds appealing to most people, any movement to enact shorter work time as a public policy will encounter surprising pockets of resistance, not just from business leaders but even from some workers. Perhaps the most formidable barrier to more free time for Americans is the widespread mind-set that the forty-hour workweek, eight hours a day, five days a week, fifty weeks a year, is a natural rhythm of the universe. This view is reinforced by the media's complete silence regarding the shorter work-time and more favorable vacation and family-leave policies of other countries. This lack of information, and our leaders' reluctance to suggest that the United States can learn from any other nation (except workaholic Japan), is one reason why more Americans don't identify overwork as a major problem or clamor for fewer hours and more vacation. Monika Bauerlein, a journalist originally from Germany, now living in Minneapolis, exclaims, "I can't believe that people here aren't rioting in the streets over having only two weeks of vacation a year."

A second obstacle to launching a powerful shorter work time movement is   12
America's deeply ingrained work ethic, or its modern incarnation, the workaholic
syndrome. The work ethic fosters the widely held belief that people's work is
their most important activity and that people who do not work long and hard are
lazy, unproductive, and worthless.

For many Americans today, paid work is not just a way to make money but is a   13
crucial source of their self-worth. Many of us identify ourselves almost entirely by the
kind of work we do. Work still has a powerful psychological and spiritual hold over
our lives—and talk of shorter work time may seem somehow morally suspicious.

Because we are so deeply a work-oriented society, leisure-time activities—   14
such as play, relaxation, engaging in cultural and artistic pursuits, or just quiet
contemplation and "doing nothing"—are not looked on as essential and worthwhile components of life. Of course, for the majority of working women who
must work a second shift at home, much of the time spent outside of paid work
is not leisure anyway. Also, much of our nonwork time is spent not just in personal renewal, but in building and maintaining essential social ties—with
family, friends, and the larger community.

Today, as mothers and fathers spend more and more time on the job, we are   15
beginning to recognize the deleterious effects—especially on our young people—
of the breakdown of social ties and community in American life. But unfortunately,
our nation reacts to these problems by calling for more paid professionals—more
police, more psychiatrists, more experts—without recognizing the possibility that
shorter work hours and more free time could enable us to do much of the necessary
rebuilding and healing, with much more gratifying and longer-lasting results.

Of course, the stiffest opposition to cutting work hours comes not from   16
citizens but from business. Employers are reluctant to alter the eight-hour day,
forty-hour workweek, fifty weeks a year because it seems easier and more
profitable for employers to hire fewer employees for longer hours rather than
more employees—each of whom would also require health insurance and other
benefits—with flexible schedules and work arrangements.

Harvard University economist Juliet B. Schor, who has been studying   17
issues of work and leisure in America, reminds us that we cannot ignore the
larger relationship between unemployment and overwork: While many of us
work too much, others are unable to find paid work at all. Schor points out that
"workers who work longer hours lose more income when they lose their jobs.
The threat of job loss is an important determinant of management's power on
the shop floor." A system that offers only two options—long work hours or
unemployment—serves as both a carrot and a stick. Those lucky enough to get
full-time jobs are bribed into docile compliance with the boss, while the spec-
tre of unemployment always looms as the ultimate punishment for the unruly.

Some observers suggest that keeping people divided into "the employed"   18
and "the unemployed" creates feelings of resentment and inferiority/superiority
between the two groups, thus focusing their discontent and blame on each other
rather than on the corporations and political figures who actually dictate our
nation's economic policies.

19   Our role as consumers contributes to keeping the average workweek from falling. In an economic system in which addictive buying is the basis of corporate profits, working a full forty hours or more each week for fifty weeks a year gives us just enough time to stumble home and dazedly—almost automatically—shop; but not enough time to think about deeper issues or to work effectively for social change. From the point of view of corporations and policy-makers, shorter work time may be bad for the economy, because people with enhanced free time may begin to find other things to do with it besides mindlessly buying products. It takes more free time to grow vegetables, cook meals from scratch, sew clothes, or repair broken items than it does to just buy these things at the mall.

20   Any serious proposal to give employed Americans a break by cutting into the eight-hour work day is certain to be met with anguished cries about inter-national competitiveness. The United States seems gripped by the fear that our nation has lost its economic dominance, and pundits, policymakers, and business leaders tell us that no sacrifice is too great if it puts America on top again.

21   As arguments like this are put forward (and we can expect them to increase in the years to come), we need to remember two things. First, even if America main-tained its dominance (whatever that means) and the economy were booming again, this would be no guarantee that the gains—be they in wages, in employment opportunities, or in leisure—would be distributed equitably between upper man-agement and everyone else. Second, the entire issue of competitiveness is suspect when it pits poorly treated workers in one country against poorly treated workers in another, and when the vast majority of economic power, anyway, is in the control of enormous multinational corporations that have no loyalty to the people of any land.

Vocabulary

Directions: Mark any important words in the reading selection that you don't know. Then list them in the following chart along with their paragraph numbers. Try to figure out each word's meaning by reading its context carefully for clues to help you guess the meaning of the unfamiliar word. Check your dictionary or thesaurus to confirm your guess. After you discuss the words with your group members, write the meanings in the margin of the text, near the word.

Key Word	Paragraph	Meaning

Guide Questions

Directions: Develop a list of questions that elicit the important ideas in the reading selection. Start at the beginning and work your way sequentially through the text until you have addressed all of the author's major ideas.

Application

Directions: When you have a list of guide questions, read through the selection again. This time, write one or more questions that require the information in the text to be applied to a situation in the real world.

Writing

Directions: Your last task is to prepare a writing assignment. For example, you might ask for a paragraph in which the writer comments on the ideas in the reading selection. You might also ask for a summary of the selection.

SPECIAL PROJECT

WORK

Career Exploration

For this project you will do research on the career you hope to have when you finish school. The report should answer these questions:

1. What is the nature of the work? What does the worker do all day? Describe a typical day.
2. Where does the work take place? Is it in an office, a clinic, a lab, outdoors? Describe the working conditions.
3. What is the typical annual starting salary? What is the typical salary for someone with 10 years' experience?
4. What is the current employment outlook for this particular career? Are there jobs available?
5. List some of the major employers in this field in your area.
6. What about this job will make you happy and satisfied? Do you think there will be any negative aspects to the job? If so, how will you cope with them?

Many resources are available to help you complete this project. Your school library and your local public library have many magazines and publications related to every job imaginable. Find a magazine or journal read by workers in that field, and become familiar with it.

The Internet offers a wealth of resources for job seekers. A few suggestions follow:

<www.careerbuilder.com>
<www.collegegrad.com>
<www.interbiznet.com>

Government agencies provide websites with general information about jobs and employment:

U.S. Department of Labor	<www.dol.gov>
U.S. Equal Employment Opportunity Commission	<www.eeoc.gov>
U.S. Small Business Administration	<www.sba.gov>

Nonprofit organizations and labor unions also provide information on websites:

AFL-CIO	<www.aflcio.org>
Better Business Bureau	<www.bbb.com>
Communication Workers of America	<www.cwa-union.org>

Most companies have a website where you can find information about products, services, working conditions, and even available jobs. Think of a company or institution that interests you, and try an address or a keyword search. Following are a few examples and their addresses:

American Express Small Business Services	\<www.americanexpress.com/smallbusiness/resources\>
Barnes and Noble	\<www.barnesandnobleinc.com/jobs.html\>
ElderCare	\<www.eldercare.com\>
Four Seasons Hotels	\<www.fourseasons.com/employment\>
Gap Stores	\<www.gapinc.com/careers\>
HSBC	\<www.hsbcusa.com/careers\>
Kinko's	\<www.fedexkinkos.com\>
Liz Claiborne	\<www.lizclaiborne.com\>
Los Angeles Times	\<www.tribjobs.com\>
Microsoft	\<www.microsoft.com/careers\> and \<www.microsoft.com/college\>
Nantucket Nectars	\<www.juiceguys.com\>
National Public Radio	\<http://www.npr.org/about/jobs\>
Procter & Gamble	\<www.pg.com\>
Public Broadcasting Corporation	\<www.pbs.org/aboutpbs/aboutpbs_jobs\>
Samuel Adams Brewery	\<www.samadams.com\>
Starbucks	\<www.starbucks.com/aboutus/jobcenter.asp\>
Target	\<www.target.com\>
The New York Times	\<www.nytco.com/careers\>
Toyota	\<www.toyota.com/jobs\>

UNIT FIVE

CRITICAL READING AND THINKING ABOUT CONTROVERSIAL ISSUES

It is better to debate a question without settling it than to settle it without debate.

—Joseph Joubert

Thinking about Critical Reading and Thinking

Have you ever expressed a strong opinion about a controversial subject, say the death penalty, a political candidate, or gun control? Have you ever been challenged to support your view but been unable to explain your position? How did you feel? Embarrassed? Foolish? Many of us go through life with "unexamined" ideas. We accept views of our parents, teachers, and friends without analyzing them, and only discover our ignorance when we are questioned. Socrates,* perhaps the greatest philosopher who ever lived, tells us "the unexamined life is not worth living." An important part of our college experience should be the examination of ourselves—taking a look at our values, our opinions and beliefs about our world, and why we hold them. In the following story, we see one way of "examining" something. Read the story and decide if you think the blind men's way of looking at the issue of the elephant is a good way to learn about something.

The Blind Men and the Elephant

Once upon a time in a land far away, there was a kingdom of the blind. All of the people were blind, including the king. The king of the land was a very inquisitive man who always wanted to know more about the world. Having heard wondrous tales of an amazing animal called the elephant, he called the three wisest men of the kingdom and ordered them to go and find the elephant so they could come back and tell him what

---

*Socrates (469–399 B.C.) was a Greek philosopher and mentor to Plato. He spent most of his life in profound philosophical discussions. He believed that the highest meaning of life could be attained through self-knowledge.

the elephant was like. The three wise men went off and did, indeed, find the elephant. The first blind man went up to the elephant, felt its tail, and said, "The elephant is very like a rope!" The second man touched the elephant's trunk and said, "The elephant is very like a snake!" The third man touched the elephant's ear and said, "The elephant is very like a fan!"

Now, answer these questions about the story.

1. Which, if any, of the blind men now knows what an elephant is like?
2. When the wise men return and report to the king, will he know what the elephant is like? Why or why not?
3. How could the king find out what the elephant is really like?

Remember that this story is a *fable.* A fable is a story that teaches us a moral or lesson. The characters in such stories are not real, but are symbols of someone or something in real life. Keep the fable in mind as you read the next selection, "Critical Reading—Critical Thinking." You will see that the elephant is a symbol of any important or controversial issue, while the blind men represent the different single perspectives on the issue. We cannot find out what an elephant is really like—or what an issue is really about—unless we actively seek out and then combine all the different perspectives on it.

CRITICAL READING—CRITICAL THINKING

Mary Fjeldstad

One of our greatest challenges as adults is developing a clear understanding   1
about the way things are in the complex, ever-changing world around us. In our
lives, many issues arise that demand our attention, our analysis, and our decision.
Unfortunately, most of us have not been well trained in thinking critically. We
tend to accept the guidance of people whom we respect or who are better informed
than we are. Thus, we often reach adulthood still clinging to the attitudes taught
us by our parents and other authority figures from our youth. Educated persons,
however, are not satisfied with "borrowing" the opinions and ideas of others—
they insist on forming their own. To do so, they must carefully analyze their beliefs.
This is the first step in developing a responsible opinion. Before we can develop
a complete understanding of an issue, we must consider other viewpoints that
may be equally valid. For example, imagine you are looking at a sculpture from
one spot, trying to understand the artist's message. While your view of the sculpture
may be *accurate,* it is not *complete*. It is not until you walk around the sculpture
and see it from different *perspectives* that you can get a full sense of what it really
looks like.

It is the same with most of the important issues and problems in life—one   2
perspective is not enough to give us the whole picture. It is essential to seek
other perspectives on the issues we are trying to understand. What are some
ways we can get information on other perspectives? One way is to use our imaginations. Take, for example, the emotional issue of abortion. To develop an
understanding of the issue, we must examine it from all possible points of view.
What are the possible perspectives on this issue? One perspective is that of the
pregnant woman, another is that of the prospective father, others are those of
the family of each prospective parent, doctors, religious groups, the fetus itself,
and, of course, society as a whole. We can use our imaginations to inform ourselves by mentally putting ourselves in the shoes of each of these persons or
groups. How would I feel if I were the husband of a pregnant woman who
wished to have an abortion? How would I feel as the doctor? Or the minister?
What if the pregnant woman was the victim of a rape? Or a drug addict who
had already given birth to several addicted children or children who were
subsequently abused? What is the impact on society of the decision that will
be made?

Other ways of learning about additional perspectives include reading about   3
them in books, magazines, and newspapers, listening to television and radio
broadcasts, and, of course, discussing them with other people.

Learning about each of the perspectives on an issue helps us to see the arguments.   4
An *argument* in this context means a *reason*—something that supports the way a
person feels about an issue. For example, when you were considering the issue of

whether to go to college, you probably thought of several different arguments supporting a decision to go to school; for example:

1. It will help prepare me for a better job.
2. I will earn more money in the long run.
3. I am bored with my life as it is now.
4. It will help me grow as a person.
5. It will help me develop my mind.
6. I will meet new people with similar interests.
7. I will make new friends.

Although some of these arguments may be more important to you than others, all of them are *reasons* to support the decision to go to college. On the other hand, despite all these good arguments, going to school may still not be the right thing for you. You must examine other sides of the issue: what are some arguments *against* attending college?

5   When you learn about developing and analyzing arguments, you will be learning a skill that is important beyond the world of the classroom. You will need to argue many questions in your life. You will, no doubt, argue about political and moral issues. Someone you love may be considering an abortion, or the school in your neighborhood may decide to hand out condoms to students. You may discover a large industry is dumping toxic wastes in the water near your home. You may apply for financial aid or for a scholarship and be turned down unfairly. You may receive a grade in a course that you feel is lower than you deserve. In each of these situations you will need to consider all of the available information and all of the different perspectives before coming to a decision of your own. Once you have developed an opinion, you will then be able to present your view to others in a reasonable and effective way. Thus, stating arguments is not limited to the sort of issues reported in newspapers and magazines. When you apply for a job, decide to get married, or give advice to a friend, you need to know how to argue effectively.

6   In order to consider all the perspectives of an issue, we must be open to the viewpoints of other people and be willing to listen and exchange ideas with them. This process is called a discussion, or *dialogue.* If you felt strongly about the abortion issue, for example, it might make you feel uncomfortable to listen to someone who disagrees with you. But that is the only way you can be sure your own position is supported and strong. Listening to others' points of view should always make us re-examine our own; we may not change our minds, but we will have a more valuable opinion because it has been examined.

7   The selections in this unit will help you clarify your ideas on some of the important issues of the day. By reading, thinking, and writing about them, you will learn to formulate good arguments of your own—and to hold opinions that are mature and valuable. As you read, keep in mind the words of the great French philosopher René Descartes:

> It is now some years since I detected how many were the false beliefs that
> I had believed to be true since my earliest youth. And since that time,

I have been convinced that I must once and for all seriously try to rid myself of all the opinions which I had formerly accepted, and begin to build anew, if I wanted to establish any firm and permanent structure for my beliefs.

Vocabulary

Directions: Locate each of the key words in the reading selection. Try to figure out each word's meaning by using the context. Confirm your guess by checking the dictionary or thesaurus. Write the meanings of the words in the margin of the text. Then record the meanings in the following chart.

Key Word	Paragraph	Meaning
1. perspective	1	
2. prospective	2	
3. argument	4	
4. dialogue	6	
Others?		

Marking Text

Turn to page 413, "Learning Strategy III—Marking Text." Read and study the information on how to mark your text. Then mark the selection you just read, "Critical Reading—Critical Thinking."

Application

Directions: We experience argumentation all the time in our daily lives—listening to a political candidate trying to persuade us to vote for him or her, a friend trying to convince us to lend him money, classmates trying to convince a teacher to postpone a test, a daughter begging to get a tattoo, a son to buy the latest fashion.

An important skill in school and in life is to be able to understand the arguments people are making in order to persuade us of something. In the following essay, the writer makes several arguments in favor of polygamy. Read the essay carefully; then, in small groups, analyze the arguments made by the author. Pull out the arguments the author makes in favor of polygamy—in this case, of allowing men to take two or more wives. Compare your group's list of arguments with the lists of your classmates.

IN DEFENSE OF POLYGAMY

B. Aisha Lemu

1   Perhaps the aspect of Islam (with respect to women) that is most prominent in the Western mind is that of polygamy. Firstly let me clarify that Islam does not impose polygamy as a universal practice. The Prophet himself was a monogamist for the greater part of his married life, from the age of twenty-five when he married Khadija until he was fifty when she died.

2   One should therefore regard monogamy as the norm and polygamy as the exception.

3   One may observe that, although it has been abused in some times and some places, polygamy has, under certain circumstances, a valuable function. In some situations it may be considered as the lesser of two evils and in other situations it may even be a positively beneficial arrangement.

4   The most obvious example of this occurs in times of war when there are inevitably large numbers of widows and girls whose fiancés and husbands have been killed in the fighting. One has only to recall the figures of the dead in the first and second world wars to be aware that literally millions of women and girls lost their husbands and fiancés and were left alone without any income or care or protection for themselves or their children. If it is still maintained that, under these circumstances, a man may marry only one wife, what options are left to the millions of other women who have no hope of getting a husband? Their choice, bluntly stated, is between a chaste and childless old maidenhood, or becoming somebody's mistress—that is, an unofficial second wife with no legal rights for herself or her children. Most women would not welcome either of these since most women have always wanted and still do want the security of a legal husband and family.

5   The compromise, therefore, is for women under these circumstances to face the fact that, if given the alternative, many of them would rather share a husband than have none at all. And there is no doubt that it is easier to share a husband when it is an established and publicly recognized practice than when it is carried on secretly along with attempts to deceive the first wife.

6   And it is no secret that polygamy of a sort is widely carried on in Europe and America. The difference is that, while the Western man has no legal obligations to his second, third, or fourth mistresses and their children, the Muslim husband has complete legal obligations toward his second, third, or fourth wife and their children.

7   There may be other circumstances unrelated to war—individual circumstances where marriage to more than one wife may be preferable to other available alternatives—for example, where the first wife is chronically sick or disabled. There are, of course, some husbands who can manage this situation, but no one would deny its potential hazards. A second marriage, in some cases, could be a solution acceptable to all three parties.

Again, there are cases in which a wife is unable to have children while the   8
husband very much wants them. Under Western laws, a man must either accept
his wife's childlessness if he can, or, if he cannot, he must find a means of divorce
in order to marry again. This could be avoided in some cases if the parties agreed
on a second marriage.

There are other cases where a marriage has not been very successful and the   9
husband loves another woman. This situation is so familiar that it is known as
the Eternal Triangle. Under Western laws the husband cannot marry the second
woman without divorcing the first one, but the first wife may not wish to be
divorced. She may no longer love her husband, but she may still respect him and
wish to stay with him for the security of marriage, for herself and their children.
Similarly, the second woman may not wish to break up the man's first family.
There are certain cases such as this where both women could accept a polygamous
marriage rather than face divorce on the one hand or an extramarital affair on the
other.

I have mentioned some of these examples because, to the majority of West-   10
erners, polygamy is only thought of in the context of a harem of glamorous young
girls, not as a possible solution to some of the problems of Western society itself.

SHORT TAKE

Argumentation

The word *argumentation* can be confusing. Our first reaction may be to think of
the everyday word *argument*—a disagreement, a quarrel. But writing an argumentation paper has nothing to do with anger or unpleasantness. While we may
throw dishes and slam doors in an argument with our family, *argumentation*
requires that we think and express ourselves clearly, without letting our feelings
interfere. An argumentation paper is an articulate, well-organized statement of
our ideas. It attempts to convince others to consider our point of view, and, perhaps, to persuade them to agree with us.

The most important aspect of argumentation, though, is not winning. It is
gaining the respect of others, convincing them we are worthy of their attention
and consideration. If we can win this, we have won something more valuable than
the vote on the issue at hand. It is essential, then, to treat our opponents with
respect. No one will listen to us if we treat them as if they were fools. Do not be
contemptuous of those who disagree with you. Try not to be narrow-minded. Do
not assume you have a monopoly on the truth. And remember, you cannot expect
others to listen to you if you do not listen to them.

In this consumer age, people demand a perfect product and don't hesitate to sue when they feel they've been saddled with "damaged goods." Does an implied warranty cover children as well? If an adopted child turns out to be different from what the parents expected, should they be allowed to return the goods? The following article from Time *magazine discusses this growing problem in an age of demand for designer cars, houses, clothes, and even children.*

WHEN THE LULLABY ENDS

Andrea Sachs

1   Most eleven-year-olds don't have a lawyer, but Tony is a special case. His adoptive parents decided, five years after his adoption, that Tony had not properly "bonded" with them, and returned him to the state in March. They kept Sam, Tony's natural younger brother. Patrick Murphy, the Chicago public guardian who was appointed to serve as Tony's attorney, says the youngster is an "absolute joy to be around." But there have been scars. Says Murphy: "One of the tragic things is that Tony blames himself."

2   Tony is one of at least one thousand children adopted in the United States each year who will be returned to agencies by their new parents. Some are sent back because of unmet expectations, others because they have severe emotional problems the parents cannot handle. In a risk-averse age when consumer standards have become more exacting and family commitments seem less binding, there is a danger that adopted children could be viewed as commodities that come with an implied warranty. The problem presents a major challenge for the legal system. "This is not a question of damaged goods; it's a matter of what's in the best interest of the child," says Neil Cogan of Southern Methodist Law School.

3   Social workers used to believe that all an adopted child needed was a loving home. But now many admit that even the most committed parents may be overwhelmed by unexpected problems. In 1986 Dan and Rhonda Stanton adopted a blond baby girl they named Stacey René. "We thought we had a perfect baby because she didn't cry," says Dan, an insurance agent in suburban Dallas. Their contentment faded as the months passed and Stacey did not develop properly. She didn't babble and laugh like their friends' babies and couldn't pinch with her individual fingers. The tentative diagnosis: Rett's syndrome, a rare genetic disorder in which the brain stops growing. Devastated, the Stantons took Stacey back to the agency and have not seen her since. "We made a commitment to her, but we were not able to live up to that commitment," says Rhonda. "She turned out to be totally different from what we thought we had adopted."

4   If adoptive parents are saddled with an unforeseen defect, who should shoulder the load? Most experts put the onus on the adoptive parents. "Families, having decided to do an adoption, assume a certain risk," says Professor William Winslade of the University of Texas Medical School in Galveston.

"If it is an incredibly difficult burden, it seems unfair not to give parents, who have provided the benefit to society by making the adoption, some special help. But I don't think the burden should be totally given back to the state either. Parents adopt because they want the joys—and the sorrows—of having children."

About 2 percent of all adoptions in the United States fail. But for older children and children with special needs, the numbers are far higher. For children older than two, 10 percent of the adoptions are dissolved. For ages twelve to seventeen, the rate shoots up to around 24 percent. This poses a special problem, since healthy adoptable babies are increasingly scarce due to the fact that more single women now opt to have abortions or to keep their infants. More families are therefore adopting older or handicapped children. This seems to be a main cause of the growing return-to-sender phenomenon.

As the problem of disrupted adoptions spreads, specialists are looking more closely at agency methods. One cause for failure is a practice that Berkeley professor Richard Barth describes as "stretching." In essence, it is a bait-and-switch game: would-be parents are encouraged to adopt a child different from the one they wanted by the withholding of some negative information. For example, a couple who want a baby are persuaded to take an older child and are never told that several earlier placements have not worked out because of emotional problems. Though the motive is benevolent—finding a home for a hard-to-place child—Barth regards the tactic as unethical.

Some disappointed parents have begun to fight back in the courts. The notion of "wrongful adoption"—which claims that agencies are liable for damages if they place children without fully disclosing their health backgrounds—is gaining legal recognition. Frank and Jayne Gibbs of Philadelphia are suing two agencies for $6 million, following their adoption of a seven-year-old boy who turned out to be violently disturbed. After the adoption, says the couple, they discovered that he had been horribly abused, including an attempt by his natural mother to cut off his genitals.

Many states have passed medical disclosure laws, which make it easier to obtain accurate information about a child. Agencies themselves are attempting to gather more data. The Golden Cradle adoption agency, in Cherry Hill, New Jersey, requires natural mothers to fill out ten-page medical histories that ask about everything from hay fever and heavy drinking to Down's syndrome and blood transfusions. Genetic counselors are often called in as consultants. "We believe an ounce of prevention is worth a pound of cure," says agency supervisor Mary Anne Giello.

Still, there are no warranties on adoptions. Those who set out looking for perfect "designer" children are likely to be disappointed. Nor is it possible—or even necessary—to know everything about a child. "People shouldn't get the idea that they can't be parents unless they have a DNA portrait of a kid," says Professor Joan Hollinger of the University of Detroit Law School. Instead, adoptive parents, armed with as much information as possible, should face the inevitable mysteries—just as all parents do.

Vocabulary

Directions: Locate each of the key words in the reading selection. Try to figure out each word's meaning by using the context. Confirm your guess by checking the dictionary or thesaurus. Write the meanings of the words in the margin of the text. Then record the meanings in the following chart.

Key Word	Paragraph	Meaning
1. risk-averse	2	
2. implied	2	
3. babble	3	
4. onus	4	
5. opt	5	
6. benevolent	6	
7. inevitable	9	
Others?		

Guide Questions

Directions: These questions will guide your understanding of what you have read. Write your answers in your notebook or on a separate sheet of paper if your instructor wishes to collect it. Your answers to these questions will be the basis of class discussion.

1. Eleven-year-old Tony is used as an example in this selection to illustrate a new problem in our society. Explain the problem.
2. Note the use of the word *commodities* in paragraph 2.
   a. Define the word *commodity*.
   b. Look through the selection: what other terms can you find that seem to categorize children as products rather than as persons?
   c. Why is this view of children as products creating a problem with adopted children?
3. How have social workers' views of the needs of adopted children changed?
4. React to the comment by Ms. Stanton in paragraph 3, "We made a commitment to [the baby], but we were not able to live up to that commitment." If Ms. Stanton had said this to you, how would you have answered her?

5. What is the main cause of the new "return to sender" phenomenon, according to the selection?
6. How have some adoption agencies contributed to the problem of failed adoptions?
7. Explain how other adoption agencies have worked to prevent problems.
8. Put yourself in the place of an adoptive parent who discovers that his or her new child has a serious physical or mental disability, and that the adoption agency knew about the problem but never informed you. How would you react? What would you do?
9. What is Professor Hollinger's opinion on adoptive parents returning a child because the child is not exactly what they expected?

Marking Text

Mark the text of "When the Lullaby Ends." (Remember, marking text is explained in the section titled "Learning Strategy III—Marking Text" on page 413.)

Application/Writing

Directions: Discuss *all* of the following questions with your classmates. Then write a response to any *one* of the four questions.

1. Remember that evaluating an issue requires you to view it from all possible perspectives. First, take a look at the "return to sender" situation from the viewpoint of adoptive parents. Read this story:

   After several years of unsuccessfully trying to have a baby, Carol and Jim Field adopt a little girl. At first they are thrilled and happy—she is a beautiful child. Soon, however, it becomes clear that there is something terribly wrong. The baby smiles happily, but never coos or babbles as babies do. She does not respond to colorful toys or to her parents' voices. Fearfully, Carol and Jim consult a doctor who determines that the baby is deaf and blind. Horrified, the Fields seek every kind of treatment that might make their baby hear and see. Finally, they accept that she cannot be helped. Unable to cope with a disabled child, the Fields decide to return the baby to the adoption agency.

   Imagine that you are Jim or Carol. Write a letter to the agency. In the letter explain, first, that you have decided to return the child. Second, explain your reasons for doing so.
2. Now look at Jim and Carol's situation from the perspective of the agency. Write an answering letter in which you explain to the Fields all the reasons they should not return the baby.
3. Write your own letter to Carol and Jim, explaining to them what you think they should do and why.
4. Imagine that it is 20 years in the future. Look at this situation from the perspective of the baby. Pretend you are the child, who is now grown up. Write a letter from her to Carol and Jim reacting to their decision.

As science rushes forward, ethics must hurry to catch up. This article describes recent advances in genetics and the confusing choices they force on us. It appeared in Time *magazine in September 1999.*

IF WE HAVE IT, DO WE USE IT?

Nancy Gibbs

1   We've seen these visions glinting in the distance for some time—the prospect that one day parents will be able to browse through gene catalogs to special-order a hazel-eyed, redheaded extrovert with perfect pitch. Leave aside for the moment whether there really is an "IQ gene" . . . or the argument over what really constitutes intelligence. Every new discovery gives shape and bracing focus to a debate we have barely begun. Even skeptics admit it's only a matter of time before these issues become real. If you could make your kids smarter, would you? If everyone else did, would it be fair not to?

2   It's an ethical quandary and an economic one, about fairness and fate, about vanity and values. Which side effects would we tolerate? What if making kids smarter also made them meaner? What if only the rich could afford the advantage? Does God give us both the power to re-create ourselves and the moral muscles to resist? "The time to talk about it in schools and churches and magazines and debate societies is now," says bioethicist Arthur Caplan of the University of Pennsylvania. "If you wait, five years from now the gene doctor will be hanging out the MAKE A SMARTER BABY sign down the street."

3   What makes the conversation tricky is that we're already on the slippery slope. Doctors can screen fetuses for genetic diseases like cystic fibrosis and Duchenne muscular dystrophy; one day they may be able to treat them in utero. But correcting is one thing, perfecting is another. If doctors can someday tinker with a gene to help children with autism, what's to prevent them from tinkering with other genes to make "normal" children smarter? Technology always adapts to demand; prenatal sex-selection tests designed to weed out inherited diseases that strike one gender or the other—hemophilia, for instance—are being used to help families have the son or daughter they always wanted. Human-growth hormone was intended for children with a proven severe deficiency, but it came to be used on self-conscious short kids—if their parents could afford as much as $30,000 for a year's injections.

4   Self-improvement has forever been an American religion, but the norms about what is normal keep changing. Many parents don't think twice about straightening their kids' crooked teeth but stop short of fixing a crooked nose, and yet, in just the past seven years, plastic surgery performed on teens has doubled. As for intellectual advantages, parents soak their babies in Mozart with dubious effect, put a toy computer in the crib, elbow their way into the best preschools to speed them on their path to Harvard. Infertile couples advertise for an egg donor in the *Yale Daily News,* while entrepreneurs sold the sperm of Nobel laureates.

"What, if anything, is the difference between getting one's child a better   5
school and getting one's child a better gene?" asks Erik Parens of the Hastings
Center, a bioethics think tank. "I think the answer has to do with the difference
between cultivating and purchasing capacities." Buying a Harvard education
may enhance a child's natural gifts, he argues, but it's not the same as buying
the gifts.

Every novel, every movie that updates Frankenstein provides a cautionary   6
tale: these experiments may not turn out as we expect. Genetic engineering is
more permanent than a pill or a summer-school class. Parents would be making
decisions over which their children had no control and whose long-term impact
would be uncertain. "Human organisms are not things you hang ornaments on
like a Christmas tree," says Thomas Murray, Hastings' director. "If you make
a change in one area, it may cause very subtle changes in some other area. Will
there be an imbalance that the scientists are not looking for, not testing for, and
might not even show up in mice?"

What if it turned out that by enhancing intellectual ability, some other   7
personality trait changed as well? "Everything comes at a price," argues UCLA
neurobiologist Alcino Silva. "Very often when there's a genetic change where we
improve something, something else gets hit by it, so it's never a clean thing." The
alarmists, like longtime biotech critic Jeremy Rifkin, go further. "How do you
know you're not going to create a mental monster?" he asks. "We may be on the
road to programming our own extinction."

The broader concern is one of fairness. Will such enhancement be available to   8
everyone or only to those who can afford it? "Every parent in the world is going to
want this," says Rifkin. "But who will have access to it? It will create a new form
of discrimination. How will we look at those who are not enhanced, the child
with the low IQ?" Who would have the right to know whether your smarts were
natural or turbo-charged? How would it affect whom we choose to marry—those
with altered genes or those without? If, as a parent, you haven't mortgaged the
house to enhance your children, what sort of parent does that make you? Will a
child one day be able to sue her parents for failing to do everything they could
for her?

But just for the sake of argument, suppose raising IQ didn't require any   9
permanent, expensive genetic engineering at all. Scientists are studying brain-
boosting compounds. Suppose they found something as cheap and easy as aspirin;
one pill and you wake up the next morning a little bit brighter. Who could argue
with that?

Some people are worried about the trend toward making people more   10
alike—taller, thinner, smarter. Maybe it's best for society as a whole to include
those with a range of needs and talents and predispositions, warts and all. "As
someone who morally values diversity," says ethicist Elizabeth Bounds of Emory
University's Candler School of Theology, "I find this frightening. We run the risk
of shaping a much more homogeneous community around certain dominant
values, a far more engineered community." What sort of lottery would decide who
is to leap ahead, who is to be held back for an overall balance? At the moment,

nature orchestrates our diversity. But human nature resists leaving so much to chance, if there is actually a choice.

11   The debate raises an even more basic question: Why would we want to enhance memory in the first place? We may imagine that it would make us happier, except that we all know smart, sad people; or richer, except that there are wildly successful people who can't remember their phone number. Perhaps it would help us get better grades, land a better job, but it might also take us down a road we'd prefer not to travel. "You might say yes, it would be wonderful if we could all have better memories," muses Stanford University neuropsychiatrist Dr. Robert Malenka. "But there's a great adaptive value to being able to forget things. If your memory improves too much, you might not be a happier person. I'm thinking of rape victims and soldiers coming back from war. There's a reason the brain has evolved to forget certain things."

12   In the end it is the scientists who both offer the vision and raise the alarms. People with exceptional, photographic memories, they note, sometimes complain of mental overload. "Such people," says University of Iowa neurologist Dr. Antonio Damasio, "have enormous difficulty making decisions, because every time they can think of 20 different options to choose from." There is luxury and peace in forgetting, sometimes; it literally clears the mind, allows us to focus on the general rather than the specific and immediate evidence in front of us. Maybe it even makes room for reflection on questions like when better is not necessarily good.

Vocabulary

Directions: Locate each of the key words in the article. Try to figure out each word's meaning by using the context. Confirm your guess by checking the dictionary or thesaurus. Write the meanings of the words in the margin of the text. Then record the meanings in the following chart.

Key Word	Paragraph	Meaning
1. prospect	1	
2. extrovert	1	
3. skeptics	1	
4. quandary	2	
5. tinker	3	
6. dubious	4	
7. alarmists	7	

Key Word	Paragraph	Meaning
Others?		

Guide Questions

Directions: These questions will guide your understanding of what you have read. Write your answers in your notebook or on a separate sheet of paper if your instructor wishes to collect it. Your answers to these questions will be the basis of class discussion.

1. The author begins her examination of this issue with two probing questions: If you could make your kids smarter, would you? If everyone else did, would it be fair not to? At first glance, the answers to these questions seem obvious, but as we read and learn more about the consequences of such decisions, the answer becomes more difficult. Arthur Caplan says, "The time to talk about it in schools and churches and magazines and debate societies is now." Why is it so important to discuss these issues *now?*
2. What does the author mean when she says "we're already on the slippery slope"?
3. Give an example of how "technology always adapts to demand."
4. In paragraph 4, the author says the "norms about what is normal keep changing." Give an example of this from the article. Can you think of an example of your own?
5. Explain the "cautionary tale" of stories like *Frankenstein*.
6. Explain why the issue of fairness is an important part of this discussion.
7. Some people see a threat to diversity in the great advances in technology. Explain what they are worried about.
8. How could anyone argue with the notion of enhancing memory? Is there a downside to the idea of improving memory?

Marking Text

Mark the text of "If We Have It, Do We Use It?" (If you need to review how to mark the text, turn to page 413, "Learning Strategy III—Marking Text.")

Application

The article concludes with the statement, "Maybe it even makes room for reflection on questions like when better is not necessarily good." In a small group, discuss the following issues:

Until just a few years ago, making a baby girl or baby boy was pretty much a hit-or-miss affair. Not anymore. Parents who have access to the latest genetic testing techniques can now predetermine their baby's sex with great accuracy. Before too long, it may be possible to screen kids right after conception for such things as height, body type, hair and eye color, what kind of diseases they may be subject to (and resistant to), and perhaps even their IQ.

Sounds great? But, for the sake of argument, what if lots more couples decided they wanted a boy baby than a girl. Would we face a future population of young men with no women to marry? What would a society overrepresented by males be like?

What if you could choose your baby's hair color and body type? Would you? Should you? Would most people choose to have babies with blonde hair? Blue eyes? Six-feet-tall males? Who could play both basketball and the piano? Do we want a society of people who all look the same and have similar talents?

Should insurance cover the genetic tests? Should the government pay for them? If not, then would only wealthy people have access to these choices? What impact would this have on society?

What would happen if these types of genetic tinkering led to unforeseen problems? What if, say, adjusting the gene that determines height also turned out to produce a deadly heart condition? Who would be responsible? Who would bear the cost of caring for the child?

Writing

Directions: Choose one of the following assignments.

1. Write an essay titled "If We Have It, Do We Use It?" Write at least four paragraphs answering the question by summarizing the concerns raised in the article.
2. Write an essay reacting to one of the issues raised in the article and in your group discussion. For example, you may want to discuss the issue of fairness or of diversity. Or you may want to discuss the dangers of tinkering with genes when we don't yet know what unforeseen consequences there may be. Or you may want to speculate on what you would do if you had the opportunity to alter the genetic makeup of your own child-to-be. Write at least four paragraphs.

Not so long ago, very premature babies were certain to die. The lungs of the tiniest pree-mies lack a surface lubricant that allows the tissue to stretch as the air goes in and out. Without it, the lung tissue rips, and the baby dies. Now, science has developed techniques to save these babies, even those weighing less than two pounds. But what happens after the medical miracles are performed? The children, their parents, and society as a whole are left to face the sometimes grim consequences. This story appeared in The New York Times *in May 2000.*

AS THE TINIEST BABIES GROW, SO CAN THEIR PROBLEMS

Sheryl Gay Stolberg

1   It has been 11 years since Alex Martin was born, a 1-pound 2-ounce bundle of miniature bones and bright red skin, with fingers no bigger than matchsticks and legs so thin they might have fit inside his father's wedding band. His parents, Rick and Allison, waited four months to send birth announcements. "The doctors kept telling us we had to plan for his funeral," Mrs. Martin explained.

2   Today, Alex is a blond-haired, fair-skinned fifth grader, with clear brown eyes, gold-rimmed glasses and a collection of what his mother calls labels: mild cerebral palsy, asthma, hyperactivity and Asperger's syndrome, a form of autism. At an age when most children have conquered fractions, Alex wrestles with addition. He learned to read about a year ago and is racing through the Hardy Boys series. But speaking is a challenge; words roll around like marbles in his mouth.

3   Alex cannot ride a bike. He still wears sneakers that fasten with Velcro, because his fingers cannot master the intricacies of laces. Often, he retreats into a private fantasy world. A recent weekday afternoon found Alex sitting cross-legged in the backyard of his family's home in Raleigh, N.C., spinning stories to an audience of no one as he smashed rocks against the dirt. "Life," Mrs. Martin says, "is overwhelming for him."

4   It is also overwhelming, at times, for his parents, who are discovering first-hand what scientists are beginning to document about babies born as tiny as Alex: their lives often grow more complicated over time. Long after their worries about simply keeping Alex alive have faded, the Martins are faced with new and no less daunting concerns, from whether their son will ever be able to make change at the grocery store, or drive a car or maintain a job, to who will care for him after they die.

5   It has been more than 20 years since doctors began saving extremely premature infants, and about a decade since advances in neonatology vastly improved the survival of babies of very low birth weight—those weighing less than 1,500 grams, or 3 pounds 4 ounces. The tiniest of these babies—micropreemies, they are called—are born as much as 14 weeks early and weigh less than 750 grams, or 1 pound 10 ounces.

6   For the first time, thousands of such children are now well into their school years. The conventional medical wisdom, based on previous studies, had been

that those like Alex, who are not seriously physically disabled, would catch up to other youngsters by age 5. And many do just fine. But as the first large group of tiny babies grows up, new research is showing that academic and behavioral problems often surface in the school years.

7   Researchers had previously had no way of knowing for sure what the long-range effects of complications like bleeding in the brain might be. And they are only now beginning to get a clear picture.

8   "We used to say if they got to 2 or 3 and they were doing fine, they'd be O.K.," said Dr. Deborah E. Campbell, director of the division of neonatology at Montefiore Medical Center in the Bronx. "Now we know that is not necessarily true."

9   In one recent study of 150 teenagers who weighed 2 pounds or less at birth, nearly one-third had significant physical disorders, including cerebral palsy, blindness and deafness. Nearly half were receiving special education assistance, compared with 10 percent in a control group. But the study, which appeared in February in the journal *Pediatrics,* also found that even those children with minor physical problems scored significantly lower on achievement tests than those in the control group.

10   "We can save tiny babies now, which we weren't able to save before, but with the technology there is a price," said the study's author, Dr. Saroj Saigal, a neonatologist at McMaster University in Hamilton, Ontario. Dr. Saigal said she had been flooded with letters, many with the same message: "Behind the success, as this child is called by the medical profession, there are lots of problems."

11   The vast leaps in survival of extremely premature infants came with the widespread use of a synthetic form of surfactant, a chemical that helps babies' lungs absorb oxygen. Before surfactant, about one-quarter of the smallest babies survived; today, about one-half will live.

12   Babies of very low birth weight make up only a tiny fraction of all newborns. According to the National Center for Health Statistics, of the 3.9 million infants born in the United States in 1998, 1.4 percent, or about 56,000, were considered in this category. Of these, 16,647 were micro-preemies.

13   It is difficult for doctors to know if low-birth-weight babies born today will fare any better than those born a decade ago. But Dr. Maureen Hack, a neonatologist at Rainbow Babies and Children's Hospital in Cleveland, who has followed premature infants as they grow, says she suspects the outcomes will be much the same.

14   Dr. Hack said a recent study of infants born weighing less than 1,000 grams found slightly higher rates of cerebral palsy and slightly lower intelligence quotients than in those of the same weight born in earlier decades. "Even though survival has improved, how the children are doing later has at best stayed the same," she said. "You are replacing death with impairment."

15   There is no thornier decision in medicine than the decision to rescue a tiny baby. It is expensive, costing as much as $2,000 a day, and wrenching for doctors and parents. Studies like Dr. Hack's and Dr. Saigal's are intensifying the long-running debate about the ethics of using sophisticated technology to save children with uncertain futures.

For parents, the questions are hardly academic. They feel lucky that their children are alive, although in quiet moments some will confess that they wonder if they made the right choice.   16

"Every day I count my blessings," said Raquel Bolden of Cleveland, whose 8-year-old daughter, Mischa, was one of Dr. Hack's patients. Mischa, who weighed a little more than 2 pounds at birth, has mild cerebral palsy and severe hearing loss.   17

Like most hospitals with neonatal intensive care units, Rainbow Babies and Children's has a follow-up clinic for premature babies, and Mischa was seen there. But as is typical, the tracking at Rainbow stops at age 3. After that, medical and educational professionals lump disabled premature children with the estimated six million disabled youngsters in the United States.   18

When Mischa was younger, Mrs. Bolden said, she worried about her daughter's physical condition. Hoping to improve Mischa's strength, she signed her up for gymnastics and ice skating. "Now," she said, "I'm more worried mentally."   19

In the first grade, Mischa is having trouble with math. Mrs. Bolden, who until recently was a single mother, working and going to school full time, is considering a tutor, though she is not certain how to pay for one. Mischa has trouble filtering out background noise, and Mrs. Bolden said she had fought with school officials to pay for hearing-aid amplifiers.   20

"I read a few preemie books when she was little," Mrs. Bolden said, "but there is no manual when they get older."   21

Decisions about rescuing children like Mischa at birth play out every day in neonatal intensive care units. The one at Montefiore Medical Center, like all such wards, is a place of dreams and heartache.   22

Everything is in miniature. Tiny creatures, their eyes protected by dark patches, their fragile bodies connected to a maze of tubes, sleep in plastic cases, many under the glow of violet lights to cure jaundice. Diapers and pacifiers look as though they were made for dolls. Feedings are measured in half teaspoons.   23

As director of this unit, Dr. Campbell faces the delicate task of answering the questions of new parents who inevitably want to know what the future will bring.   24

"You want to give hope, you want to encourage them," Dr. Campbell said, "but you've got to keep everybody reasoned."   25

Some advocates for parents of premature children say that if doctors were more forthright, parents might make different choices about whether to rescue their babies.   26

"Parents are very rarely told about the long-term, so-called minor disabilities," said Helen Harrison, author of "The Premature Baby Book," a guidebook for parents. "These minor disabilities, of course, can keep children from living independently, or ever having a social life or being able to function in society."   27

Doctors say they do routinely hold discussions with parents on whether to withhold care. But they also say that making predictions is difficult. How well premature infants fare depends on their birth weight—every extra ounce improves their chances—and on whether they suffer any serious complications. It also depends on socioeconomics.   28

29   The Reyes family is a case in point. Jacqueline Reyes is a single mother of two boys who lives in the Soundview section of the Bronx. Her 8-year-old son, Duron, is healthy. But her 5-year-old, Dominic, born weighing a little more than a pound, has severe cerebral palsy. He still wears diapers and cannot sit by himself.

30   On a recent morning, Ms. Reyes took Dominic to the Children's Evaluation and Rehabilitation Center at the Albert Einstein College of Medicine in the Bronx, where doctors are evaluating the boy to get him into kindergarten. As a child with disabilities, Dominic was entitled by federal law to attend preschool at taxpayer expense. But his mother was unaware of the law, and so he never went.

31   Dominic is also entitled to occupational and physical therapy, and Ms. Reyes said therapists did visit him at home for a time, but stopped coming a couple of years ago. Now the doctors at Einstein are considering referring Dominic for surgery to correct a hip problem that the center's director, Dr. Herbert J. Cohen, said might not have developed had the boy's therapy continued.

32   For Ms. Reyes, however, therapy and school are pushed to the back burner by the tasks of daily living like grocery shopping and doing the laundry. Until December, when she showed up at the Einstein center, she did not have a wheelchair for Dominic and simply carried him wherever she went. She lives on the second floor of an apartment building with no elevator and no ramp. When she goes out, she said, she takes her children to the bottom of the stairwell and sits Dominic in his older brother's lap while she runs back up for the chair.

33   Dr. Cohen says the Reyes family is not unusual. Parents of disabled children, particularly the poor, often miss out on services for their children. Once, he said, his center had a program for following infants at high risk of disabilities. But it was disbanded two years ago after cuts in federal and state reimbursements. For children like Dominic, Dr. Cohen said, the future often depends "on how good an advocate the parent is."

34   And even knowledgeable advocates face challenges, as the Martins can attest. Mr. Martin runs the National Computer Center for the federal Environmental Protection Agency and his wife is a former E.P.A. biologist. They have begun an Internet site to provide support for families like theirs.

35   When the Martins moved to North Carolina from the Washington area nearly two years ago, Alex scored below normal on an I.Q. test. Convinced the low score was the result of overmedication for his hyperactivity, the Martins hired a psychologist to repeat the exam; this time, the test scores were normal. Alex's special education teacher, Jan Valletta, said that without the Martins' backing, Alex would have been labeled mentally retarded.

36   "People misjudge Alex," Mrs. Valletta said. "They think from seeing him in the hall that he's retarded, or there's not much there. But Alex is really very intelligent; what makes him different is that he is intelligent, but he cannot communicate."

37   In the time that she has been teaching Alex, Mrs. Valletta says, she has seen vast improvement. She is trying to draw him out of his fantasy world and kindle

his interest in science instead. Alex likes to write, but holding a pen is difficult, so he is getting instruction in typing on the computer. Learning to read has given him confidence, and his social skills are improving.

In the school gym one recent morning, two girls from the regular fifth-grade class took pains to pick Alex when the physical education teacher told them to split up into teams. "The girls," Mrs. Valletta said, "are crazy about Alex."   38

To the Martins, these are encouraging signs. But if the past is any predictor of the future, they know there is uncertainty ahead.   39

"What prematurity is about," Mrs. Martin said, "is risk. And that risk never goes away."   40

Vocabulary

Directions: Locate each of the key words in the reading selection. Try to figure out each word's meaning by using the context. Confirm your guess by checking the dictionary or thesaurus. Write the meanings of the words in the margin of the text. Then record the meanings in the following chart.

Key Word	Paragraph	Meaning
1. intricacies	3	
2. daunting	4	
3. neonatology	5	
4. fare	13	
5. academic	16	
Others?		

Guide Questions

Directions: These questions will guide your understanding of what you have read. Write your answers in your notebook or on a separate sheet of paper if your instructor wishes to collect it. Your answers to these questions will be the basis of class discussion.

1. The story begins with the description of one child, Alex, who was born weighing one pound, two ounces. His mother comments that "life is overwhelming for him." Explain why life is overwhelming, for both Alex and his parents.

2. How has the ability to save the lives of very tiny babies progressed over the past 20 years?
3. What was the "conventional wisdom" about the future of preemies who were not seriously physically disabled?
4. Now that many of these very premature babies are reaching their teens, what are scientists discovering about their physical and mental conditions?
5. Cite Dr. Maureen Hack's conclusion in paragraph 14 on the outcomes of saving very low-birth-weight babies.
6. Explain why "there is no thornier decision in medicine" than that of saving a tiny baby.
7. Explain the point made by some advocates for parents of premature children that "if doctors were more forthright, parents might make different choices about whether to rescue their babies."
8. Why do doctors say it is difficult to make predictions about the children's future?

Application/Writing

Can you imagine yourself in the unimaginable position of the parent of a micropreemie? Of course you would want to be as informed as possible about the risks and benefits of the possible medical procedures. Go back and reread the article carefully. Identify all the arguments you can find that are in favor of rescuing a baby weighing, say, under two pounds. Then identify all the arguments against saving the baby. If you have information from your own knowledge or experience, include it in your discussion.

In a small group, discuss the arguments you have identified with your classmates. Prepare a master list of arguments for your group.

Which set of arguments seems the more persuasive to you? Why? Once you have chosen a position, write an essay arguing the *opposite* of what you chose, either pro or con, regarding the rescue of this imaginary micropreemie.

SHORT TAKE

Controversial Cases

Modern medicine has spawned record numbers of twins, triplets, and even septuplets in recent years, and fertility advances have opened the door to childbirth for much older mothers than ever before.

But along with the miracles have come troubling questions.

Should doctors take into account a woman's age before allowing her to undergo costly fertility treatments?

Does selective abortion of some fetuses save the lives of others or set up an ungodly game of Russian roulette in the womb?

Here's a look at some recent cases that raised troubling questions:

- The nation celebrated with Bobbi and Kenny McCaughey of Iowa when they gave birth to a record seven babies. Doctors cautioned, however, that multiple-birth children often have developmental problems and are more susceptible to problems such as cerebral palsy, blindness, mental retardation, and seizure disorders.
- A Saudi couple—who already had six kids—nearly went broke trying to care for their septuplets. Although the Saudi royal family wound up footing the hospital bill, the stressed-out couple's marriage broke up amid the publicity.
- Arceli Kew, 63, of California became the world's oldest mom after she lied about her age to be admitted to a fertility program. People question whether it was proper to impregnate a woman who may not live long enough to bring up the child.

Huntington's disease, a rare and always fatal hereditary brain disorder, affects about 25,000 Americans. Generally the disease strikes at about middle age. The first signs are twitching, clumsiness, irritability, depression. As the disease progresses, the body moves uncontrollably, twitching and jerking. Facial expressions may become distorted. Speech is slowed and eventually stops as the victim stiffens like a board and becomes unable to swallow. Mental functions also deteriorate, and eventually the ability to reason disappears. Usually the victim must be institutionalized.

The child of a victim of Huntington's has a 50–50 chance of also having the disease. In the 1980s scientists developed a test that will predict if a person will contract Huntington's. News of the test was greeted with relief by family members. Its benefits seemed obvious. If people knew they would develop the disease, they could plan. Should they marry? Should they have children? They could arrange for their future care. They could seek emotional and psychological support.

But the downside soon became apparent. First and most important, there is no cure, no treatment for the disease. And if the test reveals you will get it, you no longer have hope. As one psychologist put it, "Denial is a crucial coping strategy for human beings. How else can those living under a threat like Huntington's be expected to get through the day?"

The families of people who have tested positive for the disease face tremendous sorrow and pressure, too. In some cases, healthy spouses have divorced their doomed partners rather than face a future of pain and expense. So far no one who has tested positive has committed suicide, but it is a fear the doctors live with as they counsel patients about the test.

Would you want to know?

This essay was written by the 16-year-old daughter of a person with Huntington's. It appeared in Newsweek *in 2007.*

A DIFFICULT DECISION

Alexa Shaffer

1   June 28, 2007—To test or not to test. It's a question I debate frequently. I wrestle with it because I have a parent with Huntington's disease, a rare, degenerative neurological disorder that robs people of the ability to walk, talk and function on their own. Like me, all children of a parent with Huntington's have a 50–50 chance of inheriting the mutated gene. I'm 16 and I have not taken the test yet, so I am still uncertain of my fate.

2   My grandfather lived with HD for 15 years; my mom is now in the early stages. I've known about the possibility that I could have the disease for several years and have learned to live with it. Although I have become somewhat comfortable with the idea of what Huntington's will do to my family, I still realize there are many uncertainties in the future: can I live a good life with a positive test result for the mutant gene? Can my family and I cope with a positive result? How will this affect my future relationships and goals? All these questions leave me confused.

As I get older, I have to start making decisions for my future. I have always had my mind set on getting tested as soon as possible, but now I'm having doubts. (Testing isn't recommended for anyone under 18.) I know I still have time to make whichever decision I feel is best, but I also know that deciding is not going to get any easier. I want to continue school, marry and have my own children. Do I pursue these dreams in spite of the possibility of HD, or do I test to determine if I carry the gene? I am, of course, afraid of causing my future children pain. I want to be responsible for my decisions and have as much information as possible.

On the other hand, I'm scared that I may not cope well with the test results, or lose my motivation for life. The last thing I want to happen is to lose hope. I know that whatever the result of the test, I need to stay focused on school and my goals in life. As long as I channel my energy towards causes for HD I hope to stay on the right track.

I also think about my younger sister. She is 11 years old and although she has been well exposed to the world of HD, I can never be sure what she thinks about the situation. Since she is not especially open about the topic, I have trouble understanding her or gauging how much she knows. Another concern I have for her is how she will deal with mom when her symptoms worsen. My sister is so young.

My parents have taught my sister and me that all of the doubts, the "symptom searching" and the stresses can be successfully managed. They've demonstrated this by empowering themselves with involvement in the HD community. As they take us to Huntington's events, I've seen people go through the growth and adjustment caused by the rollercoaster of HD.

When I think about getting tested, I worry that it will put additional emotional stress on my family and friends. What if my parents don't want to know? All of us at risk for HD will eventually reach this fork in the road. Testing is a personal and emotional choice. Each individual has his or her own reasons for wanting or not wanting this information. Although the initial result may feel overwhelming, as I've seen, time is a major factor in the coping process—so is an optimistic outlook. There are no guarantees in life, so even with a positive test result, the world, as I know it, will not come to a halt. Embracing life and living it to its fullest potential is a choice, especially with the difficult reality of HD.

I keep in mind that every day researchers get a step closer to finding a cure. Through fund-raisers we can assist the dedicated medical people who are so passionate about finding a cure. One of my goals is to make my generation the last HD generation.

We need to spread awareness about the disease. I believe that more can and should be done to help those who are suffering from HD and for those at risk. Meantime, I continue to have that inner dialogue: to test or nor to test. I'm still not sure.

Vocabulary

Directions: Find each of the key words in the essay. Try to figure out each word's meaning by using the context. Confirm your guess by checking the dictionary. Write the meanings of the words in the margin of the text, near the word. Then record the meanings in the following chart.

Key Word	Paragraph	Meaning
1. mutant	2	
2. gauging	5	
Others?		

Guide Questions

Directions: These questions will guide your understanding of what you've read. Write your answers in your notebook or on a separate sheet of paper if your instructor will collect it. Your answers will be the basis of class discussion.

1. Describe Alexa and her family.
2. Alexa is struggling with the decision of whether (and when) to have the test. What are the pros and cons to having the test for her?
3. What advice would you give to Alexa?

Application

Use the Internet to find out more about Huntington's and the test to determine its presence. Then, in small groups, develop a list of arguments in favor of taking the test or against taking the test. Present your arguments to the rest of the class.

Writing

Write a short essay arguing either for or against taking the test for Huntington's. State your opinion pro or con in the first sentence, and then list and explain the reasons supporting your opinion.

A child shoots a child, stirring debate on gun control, social safety nets, and good and evil. This article appeared in Time *in March 2000.*

THE KILLING OF KAYLA

Julie Grace, Jay Branegan, and Victoria Rainert

At the end of the movie *The Manchurian Candidate,* Frank Sinatra, unable to fathom the depth and extent of the evil that had been done to the mind of a man programmed to become a killer, cries, "Hell, hell!" People may say the same thing after last week's school shooting of a six-year-old girl by a six-year-old boy. On Tuesday the boy brought a pistol to an elementary school in Mount Morris Township, near Flint, Mich., and shot a classmate, Kayla Rolland, to death. He is too young to be charged with anything, but the county prosecutor has charged the man who left the loaded gun lying around with involuntary manslaughter, contributing to the delinquency of a minor and gross neglect—each of which has a wider application. The story may be too unusual for the drawing of larger lessons, but one reason it is so troubling is that it touches the worst of America's social ills, including the shaping of a boy who became a loaded gun himself.

Who killed Kayla Rolland? A six-year-old classmate did it. On Tuesday morning he went to the Theo J. Buell Elementary School carrying both a concealed Davis .32 semiautomatic handgun, advertised as "the original pocket pistol," and a knife. Another kid reported the knife to a teacher, and it was taken away. The boy held on to the gun. Shortly before 10 A.M., Chris Boaz, a seven-year-old, witnessed the following scene:

The children were changing classrooms, from a small reading group to a computer-training class. This is contrary to the police report that the crime occurred inside a classroom. The kids were on the first level heading to the second when the boy pulled out his pistol. Kayla was walking ahead of him, up the school stairs. He called out, "I don't like you." She had her back to him, then turned and asked, as a challenge, "So?" The boy, who had first pointed the gun at another classmate, swung around and fired a single bullet that entered Kayla's right arm and traveled through her vital organs. Boaz says he saw blood on both sides of Kayla's stomach. She grabbed her stomach, then her neck, gasping for air.

The shooter ran to the bathroom to hide and tossed the gun into the trash. Kayla was treated by paramedics at the school and was taken to Hurley Medical Center, where she was pronounced dead at 10:29 A.M.

Immediately after the shooting, the principal made an announcement over the public-address system ordering teachers to lock all classroom doors. The school was closed at 11 A.M., and police were called for crowd control when distraught parents rushed to pick up their children. The boy, who did not attempt to run away, was taken to the principal's office, where he was questioned, and later to a police station.

The boy's father, Dedric Owens, is in jail for violating parole after serving time for possession of cocaine "with intent to deliver." The boy and his eight-year-old brother had been living with their mother Tamarla until recently, when she was evicted. The two boys then moved into a crack house, where guns were traded for drugs, with their uncle and the 19-year-old man who left the murder weapon, evidently loaded, under some blankets. A search of the house produced a loaded pump-action shotgun and a rock of crack cocaine. The boy and his brother had been sharing a single sofa as a bed.

7   Outside the white clapboard house, dented hubcaps and other discarded auto parts lay strewn among candy wrappers, soda bottles and wires. Broken windows were covered with a blue tarp. A light so dim it might have been a continuation of the dark showed from inside. Of the boy, Genesee County Sheriff Robert Pickerell said, "He was basically living in hell."

8   Who killed Kayla Rolland? The hell in which the boy lived has to be partly responsible, because it helped produce a child full of rage and confusion. The boy was said to have played normal street games. He was also known to have started fights. Boaz said the boy once punched him because he wouldn't give him a pickle. He said the boy was made to stay after school nearly every day for saying "the F word," flipping people off, pinching and hitting. Some weeks before, he had stabbed a girl with a pencil. He had attacked Kayla before and, on the day prior to the killing, tried to kiss her and was rebuffed.

9   Early on the morning of the shooting, he and his brother got into a fight with Boaz's 10-year-old uncle. Boaz's uncle punched the boy, who said, according to Boaz's grandmother, "Do you want me to take my gap [*sic*] out and shoot you?" The boy's father once asked his son, "Why do you fight?" The boy replied, "I hate them."

10   With a record of behavior like this, one might ask why no one was paying more helpful attention to him. The teacher to whom the knife was reported did not take him to the principal's office, where he could have been searched. There is no sign that any social-service organization was watching, or even that one was in the vicinity. His parents were worse than useless to him. Tamarla, a drug addict, admitted that she exposed her children to marijuana regularly. Boaz's mother tried to comfort her son, who is growing increasingly agitated about the killing he saw and does not want to return to school. She explained that the boy who did the shooting "cried out for help, and nobody helped him."

11   Not family. Not school officials. Not any social-service agency. Not the police. The people who lived next door to the crack house reported conditions there many times, but the police did not respond. One neighbor said, "It took a killing to get these people out of here."

12   The last thing that the opponents of gun control wish to hear is that guns too are partly responsible for killing Kayla, but of course they are. In response to the child's death, President Clinton challenged Congress to break the logjam on gun legislation. Senator Orrin Hatch and Representative Henry Hyde, chairmen of the Senate and House Judiciary committees, which have failed since last summer to get through a compromise bill with modest strictures on the sale and possession of weapons and a requirement that guns be sold with trigger locks, agreed last week to meet with the President at the White House. On the "Today" show,

Clinton said that while the bill has stalled, "every single day there are 13 children who die from guns."

Among the compromise bill's more contentious items are the regulation of   13
gun shows and background checks for gun sales. Polls indicate that more people favor stronger gun control and that more are willing to make it a voting issue in the coming elections. But the atmosphere in the Republican Congress remains inhospitable to any effective bill. A proposal to have background checks for a mere three business days barely passed the Senate last year after the killings at Columbine. The day after the President appeared on Today, a representative of the National Rifle Association repeated the equally true and irrelevant argument that what happened in Michigan was the fault of parents, not guns.

The boy did the shooting, but how responsible is he for the act? The law in   14
most states contends that under the age of seven, a child cannot understand the consequences of a criminal act, and indeed, the police said the boy—in spite of his history of violent behavior—did not seem to comprehend the gravity of what he had done. The Genesee County prosecutor said the boy could not have formed criminal intent.

The legal matter here is easier to deal with than the question of his aware-   15
ness of good and evil. The influences on the boy at home could have armed him with the urge for revenge. But how aware was he of a wrong act? And did he understand that death is irreversible? If he did, how can he be absolved of knowing the consequences?

Ron Avi Astor, of the School of Social Work and Education at the University   16
of Michigan, says that "just because a child understands that a gun could cause serious harm and death doesn't mean that society needs to treat the six-year-old in the same way it would a 20-year-old. We understand that children are more vulnerable." He also notes that with more aggressive kids, provocation becomes paramount. The boy who killed Kayla may have felt humiliated—by her, by everything—which became a justification for any act. Astor cautions, though, that culpability is just one piece of the problem. If we do not create a place and a structure for children as a whole, he says, "we'll see groups of children who should have been treated earlier committing horrible acts."

Whatever one concludes about responsibility, this incident will end as too   17
many child killings have ended in recent years—with mournful speeches and eulogies and civic burial mounds made up of heart-shaped balloons, poems, and stuffed animals staring blankly into space. At least that is how it will end for Kayla. For the boy, who can tell? The state will probably take custody of him, his brother and five-year-old sister. It is possible that an enlightened environment somewhere will produce a wholly different child, and just as possible that the wounds go too deep and that he will emerge into adulthood knowing perfectly the meaning and consequences of criminal acts as he blithely commits them.

Last week the nation went through the sort of moment that is growing too   18
familiar not only in content but also in the emotions it engenders. On the same day, one could feel heartbroken and fearful that one's children were in danger in their schools, and yet, also, that this is the way life goes these days, and who,

after all, can do anything about it? If that attitude of inevitability prevails, some would say it answers the question "Who killed Kayla Rolland?"

Vocabulary

Directions: Locate each of the key words in the article. Try to figure out each word's meaning by using the context. Confirm your guess by checking the dictionary or thesaurus. Write the meanings of the words in the margin of the text. Then record the meanings in the following chart.

Key Word	Paragraph	Meaning
1. fathom	1	
2. distraught	5	
3. rebuffed	8	
4. logjam	12	
5. strictures	12	
6. contentious	13	
7. gravity	14	
8. culpability	16	
Others?		

Guide Questions

Directions: These questions will guide your understanding of what you have read. Write your answers in your notebook or on a separate sheet of paper if your instructor wishes to collect it. Your answers to these questions will be the basis of class discussion.

1. Throughout the article the authors repeat the question, "Who killed Kayla?" List and explain each of the possible answers they give.
2. Explain the comment by Chris Boaz's mother in paragraph 10, "[the boy] cried out for help, and nobody helped him."
3. Explain the first sentence in paragraph 12, "The last thing that the opponents of gun control wish to hear is that guns too are partly responsible for killing Kayla. . . ."

4. a. According to the article, what are some of the laws that have been pro-
     posed to control guns?

   b. Have any of these attempts at gun control legislation succeeded?

5. According to the laws in most states, are children under the age of seven
   responsible for their actions? Do you think they should be?

6. What do you think the authors' answer to the question "Who killed Kayla?"
   might be? Can you infer their opinion from evidence in the article? Pay
   special attention to paragraph 18.

Application

Has there been any change in gun control legislation since this article was written in
March 2000? Do some research in the library or on the Internet. Two sites worth looking
at are the following:

www.handguncontrol.org
The website of the largest pro gun control organization in the country. Contains much useful information on legislation and links to articles advocating
gun control.

www.nra.org
The site of the powerful (anti-gun control) National Rifle Association.

Writing

In one or two paragraphs, summarize the answers to the question, "Who killed Kayla?"
that are in the article. Then, in a concluding paragraph, state your own opinion and why
you feel the way you do. Remember to support your opinion with arguments, not with
emotions or unsupported opinion.

If your teacher threatened to give you an F, would it motivate you to work harder? Or would you give up in despair? Would it lower your self-esteem or make you want to prove the teacher wrong? In this essay from Newsweek, *Mary Sherry, a teacher of adult literacy, argues that passing students who have not mastered the work cheats them—of their education—and that it sets them up to fail in the future. Do you think students who don't work hard should be passed anyway? Do you think that the threat of failure is a positive educational tool?*

IN PRAISE OF THE F WORD

Mary Sherry

1   Tens of thousands of eighteen-year-olds will graduate this year and be handed meaningless diplomas. These diplomas won't look any different from those awarded their luckier classmates. Their validity will be questioned only when their employers discover that these graduates are semiliterate.

2   Eventually a fortunate few will find their way into educational-repair shops—adult-literacy programs, such as the one where I teach basic grammar and writing. There, high-school graduates and high-school dropouts pursuing graduate-equivalency certificates will learn the skills they should have learned in school. They will also discover they have been cheated by our educational system.

3   As I teach, I learn a lot about our schools. Early in each session I ask my students to write about an unpleasant experience they had in school. No writers' block here! "I wish someone would have had made me stop doing drugs and made me study." "I liked to party and no one seemed to care." "I was a good kid and didn't cause any trouble, so they just passed me along even though I didn't read well and couldn't write." And so on.

4   I am your basic do-gooder, and prior to teaching this class I blamed the poor academic skills our kids have today on drugs, divorce and other impediments to concentration necessary for doing well in school. But, as I rediscover each time I walk into the classroom, before a teacher can expect students to concentrate, he has to get their attention, no matter what distractions may be at hand. There are many ways to do this, and they have much to do with teaching style. However, if style alone won't do it, there is another way to show who holds the winning hand in the classroom. That is to reveal the trump card of failure.

5   I will never forget a teacher who played that card to get the attention of one of my children. Our youngest, a world-class charmer, did little to develop his intellectual talents but always got by. Until Mrs. Stifter.

6   Our son was a high-school senior when he had her for English. "He sits in the back of the room talking to his friends," she told me. "Why don't you move him to the front row?" I urged, believing the embarrassment would get him to settle down. Mrs. Stifter looked at me steely-eyed over her glasses. "I don't move seniors," she said. "I flunk them." I was flustered. Our son's academic life flashed before my eyes. No teacher had ever threatened him with that before. I regained

my composure and managed to say that I thought she was right. By the time I got home I was feeling pretty good about this. It was a radical approach for these times, but, well, why not? "She's going to flunk you," I told my son. I did not discuss it any further. Suddenly English became a priority in his life. He finished out the semester with an A.

I know one example doesn't make a case, but at night I see a parade of students who are angry and resentful for having been passed along until they could no longer even pretend to keep up. Of average intelligence or better, they eventually quit school, concluding they were too dumb to finish. "I should have been held back," is a comment I hear frequently. Even sadder are those students who are high-school graduates who say to me after a few weeks of class, "I don't know how I ever got a high-school diploma." 7

Passing students who have not mastered the work cheats them and the employers who expect graduates to have basic skills. We excuse this dishonest behavior by saying kids can't learn if they come from terrible environments. No one seems to stop to think that—no matter what environments they come from—most kids don't put school first on their list unless they perceive something is at stake. They'd rather be sailing. 8

Many students I see at night could give expert testimony on unemployment, chemical dependency, abusive relationships. In spite of these difficulties, they have decided to make education a priority. They are motivated by the desire for a better job or the need to hang on to the one they've got. They have a healthy fear of failure. 9

People of all ages can rise above their problems, but they need to have a reason to do so. Young people generally don't have the maturity to value education in the same way my adult students value it. But fear of failure, whether economic or academic, can motivate both. 10

Flunking as a regular policy has just as much merit today as it did two generations ago. We must review the threat of flunking and see it as it really is—a positive teaching tool. It is an expression of confidence by both teachers and parents that the students have the ability to learn the material presented to them. However, making it work again would take a dedicated, caring conspiracy between teachers and parents. It would mean facing the tough reality that passing kids who haven't learned the material—while it might save them grief for the short term—dooms them to long-term illiteracy. It would mean that teachers would have to follow through on their threats, and parents would have to stand behind them, knowing their children's best interests are indeed at stake. This means no more doing Scott's assignments for him because he might fail. No more passing Jodi because she's such a nice kid. 11

This is a policy that worked in the past and can work today. A wise teacher . . . gave our son the opportunity to succeed—or fail. It's time we return this choice to all students. 12

Vocabulary

Directions: Locate each of the key words in the reading selection. Try to figure out each word's meaning by using the context. Confirm your guess by checking the dictionary or thesaurus. Write the meanings of the words in the margin of the text. Then record the meanings in the following chart.

Key Word	Paragraph	Meaning
1. validity	1	
2. impediments	4	
3. trump card	4	
4. flustered	6	
Others?		

Guide Questions

Directions: These questions will guide your understanding of what you have read. Write your answers in your notebook or on a separate sheet of paper if your instructor wishes to collect it. Your answers to these questions will be the basis of class discussion.

1. Explain why Sherry says students in classes like hers will eventually discover that "they have been cheated by our educational system."
2. Sherry uses her own son as an example. How does his experience support her argument in favor of failing students?
3. Explain Sherry's description of the threat of flunking as a "positive teaching tool."
4. In your opinion, what are the pros of passing students who have not mastered the work? What are the cons?

Writing

1. Sherry concludes that failure (or the threat of failure) can be a useful motivational tool. Do you agree? Write one paragraph agreeing or disagreeing with Sherry's conclusion.
2. Sherry says that individual students need to take responsibility for their own learning. How can a student take responsibility for his education? What motivates you to do your best in school? How can you help yourself when you don't feel motivated? Write two or three paragraphs.

SHORT TAKE

Gimme an A—Or Else!

Grade inflation is reaching record levels at American high schools, according to a new survey of incoming freshmen at more than 400 colleges and universities across the country. Almost half of the entering college students had an A average in high school. This number is 18 percent higher than it was in 1968. Linda Sax of the Higher Education Research Institute of the University of California at Los Angeles says, "Something is amiss." Dr. Sax believes that parents and students are pressuring teachers for higher grades because of the intense competition to get into desirable colleges. Teachers feel pressure to avoid damaging students' self-esteem. They are pressured not to ruin students' chances to attend the schools of their choice. A study by the College Board supports the survey's findings. According to the Board's statistics, high school seniors' grades have climbed, but SAT scores have remained the same. The Board's spokesman said the trend began to intensify in the early 1990s when more and more families began taking an interest in their children's choice of schools, and at the same time there was an economic boom allowing parents to choose more expensive schools. He predicted a "correction" soon, saying not all students deserve As.

Before you read this article, think about the impact of television on our lives by answering the following questions.

*Fill in the blanks with your best guess.**

1. *The average American watches _____ hours of TV each day.*
2. *The number of violent acts seen on TV by age 18: _____.*
3. *The number of 30-second commercials seen in a year by the average child: _____.*
4. *By age 65, the average American will have spent _____ years watching TV.*

Answer these questions about your own experience and opinions.

1. *How much television do you watch in a week? _____*
2. *If you have children, how much TV do they watch? _____*
3. *Do you think TV has a positive or negative effect on your life and the lives of your children? _____*
4. *T or F: There is too much violence on TV.*
5. *T or F: TV presents a distorted view of life.*
6. *T or F: Children's viewing of TV should be limited.*
7. *T or F: Children who watch a lot of TV tend to be more violent than those who don't.*

TV

Mary Pipher

1   In a college class I asked, "What would it be like to grow up in a world without media?" A student from the Tonga Islands answered, "I never saw television or heard rock and roll until I came to the United States in high school." She paused and looked around the room. "I had a happy childhood. I felt safe all the time. I didn't know I was poor. Or that parents hurt their children or that children hated their parents. I thought I was pretty."

2   Television has probably been the most powerful medium in shaping the new community. The electronic community gives us our mutual friends, our significant events and our daily chats. The "produced" relationships of television families become our models for intimacy. We know media stars better than we know our neighbors. Most of us can discuss their lives better than we can discuss those of our relatives. We confuse personas and persons. That is, we think a man who plays a doctor on TV actually knows something about medicine. We think a chatty talk show host is truly good-natured. This confusion is especially common with young children, who are developmentally incapable of distinguishing between reality and fantasy. But even adults get mixed up about this.

3   Most real life is rather quiet and routine. Most pleasures are small pleasures—a hot shower, a sunset, a bowl of good soup or a good book. Television suggests that life is high drama, love and sex. TV families are radically different from real families. Things happen much faster to them. On television things that are not visually

---

*See page 335 for answers.

interesting, such as thinking, reading and talking, are ignored. Activities such as housework, fund raising and teaching children to read are vastly underreported. Instead of ennobling our ordinary experiences, television suggests that they are not of sufficient interest to document.

These generalizations even fit the way TV portrays the animal kingdom. Specials on animals feature sex, births and killing. Dangerous and cuddly-looking animals are favored. But in reality, most animals are neither dangerous nor cute. Sharks and panda bears are not the main species on the planet. Most animals, like most people, spend most of their time in rather simple ways. They forage and sleep.   4

TV isolates people in their leisure time. People spend more time watching music videos but less time making music with each other. People in small towns now watch international cable networks instead of driving to their neighbor's house for cards. Women watch soaps instead of attending church circles or book clubs. When company comes, the kids are sent to the TV room with videos. Television is on during meals and kids study to television or radio.   5

Parents are not the main influences in the lives of their children. Some of the first voices children hear are from the television; the first street they know is Sesame Street. A child playing Nintendo is learning different lessons than a child playing along a creek or playing dominoes with a grandfather. Many children have been conditioned via the media into having highly dysfunctional attention spans.   6

Adults too have diminished concentration. Neil Postman in *Amusing Ourselves to Death* writes of the 1858 Lincoln/Douglas debates. The average citizen sat for up to seven hours in the heat and listened to these two men discuss issues. People grasped the legal and constitutional issues, moral nuances and political implications. In addition, they could listen to and appreciate intricate and complex sentences. In the 1990s President Clinton's speeches were decried by the press and the public when they lasted more than an hour. To an audience socialized to information via sound bite, an hour seems like a long time.   7

The time devoted to violence on TV in no way reflects its importance in real life. In real life, most of us exercise, work, visit our friends, read, cook and eat and shop. Few of us spend any significant amount of our time solving murders or fleeing psychotic killers. On television there are many more detectives and murderers than exist in the real world. A rule of thumb about violence is "If it bleeds, it leads." Violence captures viewer attention. Our movies have become increasingly violent, and as James Wolcott wrote in *The New Yorker,* "Violence is the real sex now."   8

Some might argue that there is nothing new under the sun. Of course, in a narrow sense, they are correct. There have always been murderers and rapists, and stories about violence have been themes of literature and song. But things are different now. Children, including toddlers, are exposed to hundreds of examples of violence every day. The frequency and intensity of these images is unprecedented in the history of humanity. We have ample documentation that this exposure desensitizes children, makes it more likely they will be violent and increases their fear levels about potential violence.   9

Another difference is in the attitudes about violence. *Romeo and Juliet,* for example, was a tragedy. The deaths in the play were presented as a cause of enormous   10 suffering to friends and families and as a terrible waste. When Juliet and Romeo died, something momentous happened in the universe. The very gods were upset. Often today, death is a minor event, of no more consequence than, say the kicking of a flat tire. It's even presented as a joke.

11   It is one thing to read Shakespeare, which at least requires that the person can read. It's another to, day after day, see blood splattered across a screen by "action heroes." It is one thing to show, as Shakespeare did, that violence can be the tragic consequence of misunderstandings, and another to show violence as a thrill, as a solution to human problems or merely as something that happens when people are slightly frustrated or men need to prove they are men.

12   Of course, one could argue that parents can keep televisions out of their homes. This is extremely hard for the average parent to do. Even if they succeed, their children go from these "protected environments" to play with children who have watched lots of TV and who behave accordingly.

13   I don't often go to violent movies, but I do have a stake in them. I don't like living in a world where thousands of teenage boys, some of whom own guns, have been reared on them. Walking city streets, I may be accosted by a youth who has spent most of his life watching violent media. Unfortunately, needy children are the ones most affected. Children with the least available parents watch the most TV. Violent television is like secondhand smoke; it affects all of us.

14   Heavy viewers develop the "mean world syndrome." This leads to a vicious-cycle phenomenon. Because children are afraid and the streets are not safe, they come home right after school and stay indoors. They watch more TV, which makes them more afraid and thus more likely to stay indoors. With everyone indoors the streets are less safe. Families watch more TV and are more fearful and so on.

15   Television and electronic media have created a new community with entirely different rules and structures than the kinds of communities that have existed for millions of years. Families gather around the glow of the TV as the Lakota once gathered around the glow of a fire on the Great Plains or as the Vikings once huddled around fires in the caves of Scandinavia. They gather as New England families gathered in the 1800s around a fireplace that kept them warm and safe. But out TVs do not keep us warm, safe and together. Rapidly our technology is creating a new kind of human being, one who is plugged into machines instead of relationships, one who lives in a virtual reality rather than a family.

Vocabulary

Directions: Find each of the key words in the essay. Try to figure out each word's meaning by using the context. Confirm your guess by checking the dictionary. Write the meanings of the words in the margin of the text, near the word. Then record the meanings in the following chart.

Key Word	Paragraph	Meaning
1. forage	4	
2. dysfunctional	6	
3. diminished	7	
4. nuances	7	
5. decried	7	
6. unprecedented	9	
7. accosted	13	
Others?		

Guide Questions

Directions: Answer these questions to make sure that you understand what you've read. Write your answers in your notebook or on a separate sheet of paper if your instructor will collect it. Your answers will be the basis of class discussion.

1. a. In paragraphs 2, 3, and 4, the author contrasts the world of TV with real life. List some of the differences she cites.
   b. Can you think of some specific examples from your own experience as a television watcher that illustrate the author's points in paragraphs 2, 3, and 4?
2. Explain how TV "isolates" people in their leisure time.
3. Why does Pipher say that parents are not the main influence in their children's lives? Do you agree?
4. People complain that politicians and our government representatives communicate to the public in "sound bites." Would Pipher agree?
5. Explain the quote, "If it bleeds, it leads" (paragraph 8).
6. There is an old saying, "There is nothing new under the sun." Pipher argues against this. What evidence does she present?
7. One solution offered is that parents keep TV out of the home (or perhaps strictly limit viewing time). What is the problem with this possible solution?
8. Explain why the author says, "I don't often go to violent movies, but I do have a stake in them" (paragraph 13).

9. Explain the "vicious-cycle phenomenon" described in paragraph 14.
10. Compare and contrast the "community" of past societies with the new TV "community" of today.
11. How does the answer of the student from the Tonga Islands in the first paragraph illustrate the points about TV the author makes in the rest of the essay?

Application

1. Here are some statistics about television compiled by the Nielsen Company. (Nielsen monitors TV viewing by the public.) In a small group, choose a few of the statistics and discuss their implications and your reactions to them.

I. FAMILY LIFE

Percentage of households that possess at least one television: 99
Number of TV sets in the average U.S. household: 2.24
Percentage of U.S. homes with three or more TV sets: 66
Number of hours per day that TV is on in an average U.S. home: 6 hours, 47 minutes
Percentage of Americans that regularly watch television while eating dinner: 66
Number of hours of TV watched annually by Americans: 250 billion
Value of that time assuming an average wage of $5/hour: $1.25 trillion
Percentage of Americans who pay for cable TV: 56
Number of videos rented daily in the U.S.: 6 million
Number of public library items checked out daily: 3 million
Percentage of Americans who say they watch too much TV: 49

II. CHILDREN

Approximate number of studies examining TV's effects on children: 4,000
Number of minutes per week that parents spend in meaningful conversation with their children: 3.5
Number of minutes per week that the average child watches television: 1,680
Percentage of day care centers that use TV during a typical day: 70
Percentage of parents who would like to limit their children's TV watching: 73
Percentage of 4–6-year-olds who, when asked to choose between watching TV and spending time with their fathers, preferred television: 54
Hours per year the average American youth spends in school: 900 hours
Hours per year the average American youth watches television: 1500

III. VIOLENCE

Number of murders seen on TV by the time an average child finishes elementary school: 8,000

Number of violent acts seen on TV by age 18: 200,000
Percentage of Americans who believe TV violence helps precipitate real-life
    mayhem: 79

IV. COMMERCIALISM

Number of 30-second TV commercials seen in a year by an average child:
    20,000
Number of TV commercials seen by the average person by age 65: 2 million
Percentage of survey participants (1993) who said that TV commercials
    aimed at children make them too materialistic: 92
Rank of food products/fast-food restaurants among TV advertisements to
    kids: 1
Total spending by 100 leading TV advertisers in 1993: $15 billion

V. GENERAL

Percentage of local TV news broadcast time devoted to advertising: 30
Percentage devoted to stories about crime, disaster, and war: 53.8
Percentage devoted to public service announcements: 0.7
Percentage of Americans who can name The Three Stooges: 59
Percentage who can name at least three justices of the U.S. Supreme
    Court: 17

2. Watch the local news tonight. Count the number of stories presented.
   At the same time, count the number of stories that deal with violence
   (e.g., murders, rape, fire, accident, crashes, etc.). What percentage of the
   stories dealt with violence?

Writing
Directions: Pipher presents many arguments against TV in today's world. Go through the
essay, find each argument, and create a list. Next, in a group, create a list of arguments
that *support* TV.

*Answers to the questions in the introduction on page 330.

1. *The average American watches* _4_ *hours of TV each day.*
2. *The number of violent acts seen on TV by age 18:* _200,000_.
3. *The number of 30-second commercials seen in a year by the average child:* _20,000_.
4. *By age 65, the average American will have spent* _9_ *years watching* TV.

This information is from the A.C. Nielsen Co.

If someone offered you money or gifts to get an A on your next test, would you work harder? A new practice of offering cash and other rewards to students in return for better performance in school is becoming more and more popular around the country. This article, which appeared in U.S. News & World Report *in 2008, describes some of the efforts and their consequences. What do you think?*

THE VALUE OF GOOD GRADES

Schools offer Happy Meals and cash to improve scores

Eddy Ramirez

1 Susan Pagan of Orlando didn't smile when her 9-year-old daughter Cathy recently brought home a report card that could be traded in for a free McDonald's Happy Meal. The burger-and-fries combo was the girl's reward for making the honor roll. Pagan, who works in advertising, complained to the school district, saying fast food for high marks was a tasteless way to motivate kids. "It's good to reward students but not when schools get companies to advertise directly to our children," she says of the Ronald McDonald cartoon on the report card jacket.

2 Facing mounting pressure to raise students' scores on standardized tests, schools are prodding kids to work harder by offering them clear-cut incentives. Happy Meals are at the low end of the scale. With the help of businesses, schools are also giving away cars, iPods, coveted seats to basketball games, and—in a growing number of cases—cold, hard cash. The appeal of such programs is obvious, but the consequences of tying grades to goods are still uncertain. It's been a common tradition in middle-class families to reward top grades with cash as a way to teach that success in school leads to success in life. But for many disadvantaged minority children, the long-term benefits of getting an education are not so clear, according to experts.

Cash

3 Roland Fryer, a Harvard professor of economics, says it's "absurd" to expect children who grew up in poverty, with parents who, for example, dropped out of school, to appreciate the value of education without giving them immediate rewards for taking school seriously. As the chief equality officer for New York City public schools, Fryer oversees a pilot program that pays students from low-performing schools $25 and $50 for doing well on standardized tests. "We're not undermining this idea of learning for the love of learning," Fryer says. "We're trying to cultivate it by making education tangible for these kids." Before the holidays, Fryer handed out $170,000 in cash (every pupil who completes the test gets $5). The students— fourth and seventh graders—told him they would use the money for a variety of things: new sneakers, a Christmas gift for Mom, and their family's rent.

4 In Dallas, high school students can pocket about $100 for every passing score on college-level examinations. The Advanced Placement Incentive Program "has created a culture where it's cooler to be in an AP class than to be in a regular class,"

says Michael Watkins, associate principal at W. T. White High School. The influx of less prepared minority students has brought down the school's passing rate on AP tests. But, Watkins says, at least those students are getting exposed to challenging classes taught by the best teachers, and that's in turn motivating many to pursue college. It helps that teachers can also cash in on their students' success.

No one knows for sure how well cash and other big-ticket rewards work in education over the long haul. But there are plenty of critics who say that "bribing" kids could have negative effects. In an era of high-stakes testing, rewards conceivably could fuel even more student anxiety, says Virginia Shiller, a Yale University clinical psychologist and author of *Rewards for Kids!* Shiller says that it's worth experimenting with cash incentives but that tying them to perfect attendance or success on a test is not a worthwhile goal. "I'd rather see rewards based on effort and responsibility—things that will lead to success in life," she says.   5

Even if rewards don't lead to individual achievement on a test, they could have a meaningful effect in the school. Rather than give money to his college alma mater, Charles McVean, a businessman and philanthropist, started a peer tutoring program at East High School in Memphis, where he was once a student. The program pays higher-achieving students $10 an hour to tutor struggling classmates and divides them into teams. During the course of the year, students bond and compete. The team that posts the highest math scores wins the top cash prize of $100. McVean calls the combination of peer tutoring, competition, and cash incentives a recipe for "nothing less than magic."   6

For its part, the Seminole County Public Schools system in Florida plans to continue its report card incentive program through the rest of the school year. The local McDonald's restaurants help the cash-strapped district by paying the $1,600 cost of printing the report card jackets. Regina Klaers, the district spokeswoman, says most parents don't seem bothered by the Happy Meals rewards. "There are many ways we try to spur students to do well, and sometimes it's through the stomach, and sometimes it's the probability of students winning a car," she says. "One size doesn't fit all."   7

Vocabulary

Directions: Find each of the key words in the essay. Try to figure out each word's meaning by using the context. Confirm your guess by checking the dictionary. Write the meanings of the words in the margin of the text, near the word. Then record the meanings in the following chart.

Key Word	Paragraph	Meaning
1. incentives	2	
2. coveted	2	
3. pilot program	3	

Key Word	Paragraph	Meaning
4. tangible	3	
5. influx	4	
6. the long haul	5	
7. philanthropist	6	
8. cash-strapped	7	
Others?		

Guide Questions

Directions: These questions will guide your understanding of what you've read. Write your answers in your notebook or on a separate sheet of paper if your instructor will collect it. Your answers will be the basis of class discussion.

1. In a few sentences, summarize the practice that is described in this article.
2. What is the main factor (mentioned in paragraph 2) causing schools to offer kids incentives?
3. Give a few examples of the incentives being offered in some schools.
4. Experts cited in the article draw distinct differences between the attitudes of middle-class and poor families regarding the value of education. Do you agree that a big difference exists?
5. Describe the program in the Dallas high school that offers money for passing AP courses. What has been the benefit? What has been the downside?
6. Do you agree that offering these incentives is "bribing" kids? Please explain.
7. Do you have any experience with a program of rewards for taking school more seriously? Share your insights with your classmates.

Application/Writing

1. Break into small groups. In your group, choose one side of this issue—pro or con—the practice of offering incentives for improved performance in school. Using the information in the article and your own knowledge and experience, create a list of reasons to support your position. Then present your arguments to the rest of the class. Listen to their arguments in return.
2. Based on what you learned in the group exercise, write a paragraph or two stating your opinion on this issue and giving reasons to support your opinion.

This story first appeared in the Boston Globe *in July 1989.*

DREAMING OF DISCONNECTING
A RESPIRATOR

Elissa Ely

Late one night in the Intensive Care Unit, one eye on the cardiac monitor and one on the Sunday paper, I read this story: 1

An infant lies in a hospital, hooked to life by a respirator. He exists in a "persistent vegetative state" after swallowing a balloon that blocked the oxygen to his brain. This "vegetative state," I've always thought, is a metaphor inaccurately borrowed from nature, since it implies that with only the proper watering and fertilizer, a comatose patient will bloom again. 2

One day his father comes to visit. He disconnects the respirator and, with a gun in hand, cradles his son until the infant dies. The father is arrested and charged with murder. 3

In the ICU where I read this, many patients are bound to respirators. I look to my left and see them lined up, like potted plants. Some will eventually be "weaned" back to their own lung power. Others will never draw an independent breath again. 4

In Bed No. 2, there is a woman who has been on the respirator for almost two months. When she was admitted with a simple pneumonia, there were no clues she would come apart so terribly. On her third day, she had a sudden and enigmatic seizure. She rolled rapidly downhill. Her pneumonia is now gone, but her lungs refuse independence: she can't come off the machine. 5

I know little about this patient except that she is elderly and European. (It is the peculiar loss of hospital life that patients often exist here with a medical history, but not a personal one.) I sometimes try to picture her as she might have been: busy in a chintz kitchen smelling of pastries. She might have hummed, rolling dough. Now there is a portable radio by the bed, playing Top Ten, while the respirator hisses and clicks 12 times a minute. 6

The family no longer visits. They have already signed the autopsy request, which is clipped to the front of her thick chart. Yet in their pain, they cannot take the final step and allow us to discontinue her respirator. Instead, they have retired her here, where they hope she is well cared for, and where she exists in a state of perpetual mechanical life. 7

I have dreamed of disconnecting my patient's respirator. Every day I make her death impossible and her life unbearable. Each decision—the blood draws, the rectal temperatures, the oxygen concentration—is one for or against life. No action in the ICU is neutral. Yet many of these decisions are made with an eye toward legal neutrality—and this has little to do with medical truth. The medical truth is that this patient exists without being alive. The legal neutrality is that existence is all that is required. 8

9   Late at night, reading in the ICU, the story of that father—so dangerous and impassioned—puts me to shame. I would never disconnect my patient from her respirator; it is unthinkable. But this is not because I am a doctor. It is because I feel differently toward her than the father toward his son.

10   I do not love her enough.

Vocabulary

Directions: Locate each of the key words in the story. Try to figure out each word's meaning by using the context. Confirm your guess by checking the dictionary or thesaurus. Write the meanings of the words in the margin of the text. Then record the meanings in the following chart.

Key Word	Paragraph	Meaning
1. enigmatic	5	
2. perpetual	7	
Others?		

Guide Questions

Directions: These questions will guide your understanding of what you have read. Write your answers in your notebook or on a separate sheet of paper if your instructor wishes to collect it. Your answers to these questions will be the basis of class discussion.

1. Who is the author of this essay? Where did the author write it?
2. The author provides two examples of persons in a "vegetative state." Briefly describe each person.
3. Explain what Elissa Ely means when she says, "Every day I make her death impossible and her life unbearable" (paragraph 8).
4. The author contrasts "medical truth" with "legal neutrality." What point is she making?
5. React to the author's last sentence, "I do not love her enough."

Application

1. Use the Internet or your library to investigate the current laws on passive euthanasia in your state. For example, would the father who disconnected the respirator in this story be charged with murder in your state?
2. Here is an opportunity to use your thinking skills in real-life situations. Following are some cases in which life-or-death decisions had to be made

by patients, doctors, and family members. Read about each case and ask yourself what your decision would have been. Before you answer, remember to think about the issue from all perspectives. Then, try to imagine all the pro and con arguments. Finally, develop your personal opinion. Write your opinion; then write the supporting arguments that back it up.

Remember: Your goal is to develop a *valid opinion.*

Case 1

Doctors at a university hospital examined a 17-year-old boy whose bone cancer of the upper arm had recurred despite radiation treatments. The physicians advised amputation of the limb and warned that, without the operation, the boy would probably die. But the boy, a star baseball player who had been scouted by several major league teams, begged his parents and the doctors to let him keep his arm so that he could continue to play baseball.

If you were the parents, what instructions would you give the doctors? Remember to state good, solid reasons for your decision.

Case 2

After the age of 18, when she suffered kidney failure, Marilyn Duke had to go to a hospital three times a week for dialysis treatments. (This is a painful procedure in which the patient is hooked up to a machine for several hours while the machine purifies the patient's blood, eliminating wastes. This purification is the normal function of a healthy kidney.)

When she was thirty-three, Marilyn decided she could no longer endure life under these conditions. She told her doctor that she wanted to discontinue the dialysis but, knowing that without medical help she would die in agony, she asked him to ease her pain in her final days. Her doctor said he could treat her only if she was in a hospital. When she returned to the hospital, doctors tried to put Marilyn on the dialysis machine again. She refused to go on the machine and the hospital discharged her. Marilyn died nine days after her last dialysis treatment.

If you were Marilyn, would you have made the same choice? Give arguments to support your choice.

Case 3

A 44-year-old man, a single parent of three children, was hospitalized with brain cancer. Doctors agreed his case was terminal. One night he suddenly suffered cardiac arrest, but an alert intern got the man's heart beating again and the patient lived one more month.

Did the doctor do the right thing in resuscitating the man? Why or why not?

Writing

Write one paragraph either agreeing or disagreeing with Ely's decision not to disconnect her patient's respirator. State your opinion in the first sentence, and follow with your supporting arguments.

SPECIAL PROJECT

Research and Write an Essay
on a Controversial Topic

Throughout this unit, you have been reading and thinking about many different topics and the viewpoints of various writers, and no doubt you considered all this information as it supports (or fails to support) your opinions. In this project, you will have the chance to investigate and write about a topic of your own choice.

You may do this project collaboratively, in a group of two to four persons, or you may work on your own.

Choose a Topic

Select a topic that interests you. You may choose from the list of possible topics provided at the end of this section, or your instructor will suggest a topic.

Research

Look in the library for books, magazines, and newspapers that contain information on your topic. Because you are investigating a current issue, books will probably be less useful to you than magazines and newspapers, but if you find one that is helpful, by all means use it.

Search the Internet for information on your topic. Some suggestions for sources on the Web follow.

Be sure to look for and take notes on information on *both sides* of the issue you are investigating. Only by examining the subject from all perspectives can we hope to develop a worthwhile opinion.

Decide

When you have gathered sufficient information to understand the topic, decide what your position will be. Choose either pro or con. It is not necessary that you truly support this position. In fact, it is probably more valuable to write about the position you do *not* support. In either case, be sure you have sufficient arguments to support your position.

Write

In the first paragraph, state the topic and your position on the topic.

In the body of the essay, include all the arguments (including facts, explanations, and examples) that you discovered when doing your research.

In your final paragraph, restate your main idea and the arguments that you find most persuasive.

References

The last page of the paper should be a list of the references (Works Cited) that you used to write your paper. Include every book, magazine, newspaper, and Internet source.

World Wide Web Sources

For general information:

CNN	<www.cnn.com>
The New York Times	<www.nytimes.com>
Time	<www.time.com>
Newsweek	<www.newsweek.com>
U.S. News & World Report	<www.usnews.com>
National Public Radio	<www.npr.org>
Los Angeles Times	<www.latimes.com>
Boston Herald	<www.bostonherald.com>

For specific information, look for the websites of organizations directly concerned with the issue. For example, the issue of animal rights will be examined at the sites run by the pro-animal rights organization PETA (People for the Ethical Treatment of Animals) at www.peta-online.org and by a group critical of the animal rights movement at www.animalrights.net.

Any listing of specific Web resources is out of date almost as soon as it is published, so consult your instructor and your friendly school or public librarian for assistance.

Evaluating Sources on the Web

As with books, newspapers, and magazines, it is crucial to evaluate the reliability and accuracy of your source. For example, you would probably be safe in assuming a news article from *The Washington Post* is credible. On the other hand, information found in the *National Enquirer* is not. Information on the Internet can be tricky to evaluate. Remember that the Net is a very democratic institution—anyone can put up a site and spout his or her opinion, whether they know anything or not.

Here is a list of questions you can ask about your source to decide if it is reliable:

Is the site run by a known agency or organization?

Is there an author listed for the site or the document?

Does the author have credentials? Does the author seem credible?

Is the document written in good, clear English? If there are grammar or spelling errors, you can assume the article has not been edited and may not be reliable.

Does the article contain real substance, or is it mostly bells and whistles?

Know your source! If you want objective information, that is, just the facts, do not rely on information in sources that have a known bias: For example, you could not expect to find unbiased information on the Democratic party's candidates by reading the Republican party's website. Similarly, do not expect a balanced view of the gun control debate on the website of the National Rifle Association.

List of Possible Topics for Research

Immigration—Should there be limits? What should they be? Should there be amnesty for illegal immigrants?

Welfare/workfare—Should people who receive welfare be made to work for their benefits?

Gun control

Abortion rights

Capital punishment

Legalization of marijuana

Tuition-free higher education

Vivisection—Should animals be used for experimentation of such things as drugs, cosmetics, and household products?

Affirmative action—Should preferences be given to members of groups that have been discriminated against historically?

Should the customs and traditions of other countries be allowed to be practiced by immigrants when they come to this country if the custom violates American laws and/or ethics (examples: polygamy, female circumcision)?

Cloning—of animals, of humans

Grade inflation

Gay marriage

UNIT SIX

READING AND THINKING
ABOUT TEXTBOOKS

He that loves reading has everything within his reach.

—William Godwin

Textbook reading is probably the most challenging type of reading you will do in your life. It poses difficulties for a number of reasons. First, you are usually reading about things that are new to you; there is often a great deal of new information to be learned. Second, the typical chapter in a college textbook is longer than what you normally read in, say, the newspaper or a magazine. Third, there are often many new words and concepts you must learn and remember. So, it is important to use all your study skills when attacking your textbooks.

In this unit you will find chapters from textbooks used in colleges around the country. Each chapter is accompanied by suggestions on previewing, annotating, and learning important terminology. Following each chapter you will find examples of the actual test questions that students who take the course see on their exams. Working with these sample chapters will give you valuable experience with real college materials.

Steps for Studying Textbook Chapters

Begin by reviewing how to preview: previewing is discussed on page 407, "Learning Strategy I—Previewing." Review the four steps for previewing a chapter on page 408.

Next, read, reread, and mark the chapter. Review the steps for marking text on page 413, "Learning Strategy III—Marking Text." Remember, the important first step is to read through the entire chapter one time quickly to get a feel for the information it contains. If the chapter seems very long, divide it up into manageable chunks and attack one chunk at a time. After the first "get-acquainted" reading, go back and read the chapter again. This time, read carefully, underlining and annotating as you go along.

Finally, reflect for a moment on what you have learned. What do you think are the key ideas that you are expected to learn from this chapter? What concepts will you need to remember for the next exam? For the next course in your major? Are there ideas and terms that you will need to know in order to have a successful career? Are there things you would like to remember for the rest of your life?

Remember, *active reading* will help you with the challenging assignments you face in college. *Be active with your textbooks*. While you are underlining and annotating, be sure to mark words you need to look up. Put a question mark next to things you don't understand or that you want to discuss with a classmate or the instructor. Ask yourself questions as you read along and try to find the answers to your questions.

At the end of each of the chapters in this unit, you will see exam questions actually used by the instructors who teach the course in which the text is used. Answering these questions will help you to test the effectiveness of your reading and studying.

Now, use your skills as an active, independent reader to tackle the following textbook chapters. Good luck!

THEORETICAL PERSPECTIVES ON EDUCATION

A Chapter from the Textbook *Essentials of Sociology*, Seventh Edition

David Brinkerhoff, Lynn K. White,
Suzanne T. Ortega, and Rose Weitz

PREVIEWING

The essential first step in studying a textbook chapter should always be to PREVIEW. (If you need to review how to preview, turn to "Learning Strategy I—Previewing" on page 407.)

Here are some questions and suggestions to help you to preview this chapter well.

1. This chapter has many headings and subheadings. Skimming them will give you a good idea of the chapter contents. You may find some headings that you don't understand, for example, "Education as a Capitalist Tool." Or "Symbolic Interactionism: The Self-Fulfilling Prophecy." If you are curious, by all means, go ahead and read the first paragraph or two. But, remember, you'll have two more chances to understand the terms—when you do the first reading of the chapter and then when you go back to read carefully and underline and annotate.

2. As you read the headings, think about this: can you detect any tone or message the authors may be hinting at? Do you think they may have a critical opinion of the U.S. educational system?

3. The authors highlight certain words and phrases—they are in bold type, and some are repeated in the margins along with their definitions. Be sure to pay attention to these words when you go back to study the chapter.

4. Check out the "Connections" and "focus on" boxes for some interesting reading.

Now, turn to page 349 and preview the chapter. When you have finished previewing, go to page 348 to think about what you've learned.

What Did I Learn from Previewing?

The headings and subheadings gave you a clear idea of the chapter's organization and a strong introduction to the authors' tone and message.

Key terms and phrases and their definitions are conveniently highlighted for you in the margins: be sure to pay attention to them as you study.

Most of the potentially confusing terms are explained in the margins, but if you came across any other unfamiliar words while you were previewing, be sure to look them up.

Read the Chapter

Return now to the beginning of the chapter on page 349 and read it carefully.

EDUCATION

This chapter examines the institution of education—a central component of our cultural heritage. It has profound effects on our society and on us as individuals. Most Americans are directly and personally affected by the institution of education—almost all people in the United States have attended school, and all of us are affected by the omnipresence, norms, and values of our educational institutions.

Theoretical Perspectives on Education

The **educational institution** is the social structure concerned with the formal transmission of knowledge. It is one of our most enduring and familiar institutions. Nearly 3 of every 10 people in the United States are involved in education on a daily basis as students or staff. As former students, parents, or taxpayers, all of us are involved in education in one way or another.

What purposes are served by this institution? Who benefits? Structural-functional and conflict theories offer two different perspectives on these questions.

The **educational institution** is the social structure concerned with the formal transmission of knowledge.

Structural-Functional Theory: Functions of Education

A structural-functional analysis of education is concerned with the consequences of educational institutions for the maintenance of society. Structural functionalists point out that the educational system has been designed to meet multiple needs. The major manifest (intended) functions of education are to provide training and knowledge, to socialize young people, to sort young people appropriately, and to facilitate positive and gradual change.

Training and Knowledge

The obvious purpose of schools is to transmit knowledge and skills. In schools, we learn how to read, write, and do arithmetic. We also learn the causes of the American War of Independence and the parts of a cell. In this way, schools ensure that each succeeding generation will have the skills needed to keep society running smoothly.

Socialization

In addition to teaching skills and facts, schools help society run more smoothly by socializing young people to conform. They emphasize discipline, obedience, cooperation, and punctuality. At the same time, schools teach students the ideas, customs, and standards of their culture. In American schools, we learn to read and write English, we learn the Pledge of Allegiance, and we learn the version of U.S. history that school boards believe we should learn. By exposing students from different ethnic and social class backgrounds across the country to more or less the same curriculum, schools help create and maintain a common cultural base.

Sorting

Schools are like gardeners; they sift, weed, sort, and cultivate their products, determining which students will be allowed to go on and which will not. Grades and test scores channel students into different programs—or out of school altogether—on the basis of their measured abilities. Ideally, the school system ensures the best use of each student's particular abilities.

Promoting Change

Schools also act as change agents. Although we do not stop learning after we leave school, new knowledge and technology are usually aimed at schoolchildren rather than at the adult population. In addition, schools can promote change by encouraging critical and analytic skills. Colleges and universities are also expected to produce new knowledge.

Conflict Theory: Education and the Perpetuation of Inequality

Conflict theorists agree with structural functionalists that education reproduces culture, sorts students, and socializes young people, but they view these functions in a very different light. Conflict theorists emphasize how schools reinforce the status quo and perpetuate inequality.

Education as a Capitalist Tool

The **hidden curriculum** socializes young people into obedience and conformity.

Some conflict theorists argue that one primary purpose of public schools is to benefit the ruling class. These theorists point to schools' **hidden curriculum,** the underlying cultural messages that schools teach. In public schools, this curriculum includes learning to wait your turn, follow the rules, be punctual, and show respect, as well as learning *not* to ask questions. All of these lessons prepare students for life in the working class (Gatto 2002). A different hidden curriculum in elite private schools trains young people to think creatively and critically and to assume that they are naturally superior and deserving of privilege. Conflict theorists note that both private and public schools teach young people to expect unequal rewards on the basis of differential achievement and so teach young people to accept inequality (Kozol 2005).

Education as a Cultural Tool

Conflict theorists argue that, along with teaching skills such as reading and writing, children learn the cultural and historical perspective of the dominant culture (Spring 2004). For example, U.S. history texts describe the "Indian Wars" but rarely explain why Native American tribes resorted to warfare and give little or no coverage to the waves of anti-Chinese violence in the United States in the late nineteenth century or the removal of Japanese Americans to relocation camps during World War II. Art and music classes typically ignore the cultures of Latin America and Asia and gloss over the many contributions African Americans have made in the United States.

■ In all societies, education is an important means of reproducing culture. In addition to skills such as reading and writing, children learn many of the dominant cultural values. In Japan, school uniforms emphasize group solidarity over individual achievement.

Education as a Status Marker

One supposed outcome of free public education is that merit will triumph over origins, that hard work and ability will be allowed to rise to the top. Conflict theorists, however, argue that basing decisions regarding who should get the best jobs and highest status on individuals' educational credentials does little to equalize economic opportunity. Instead, a subtle shift has taken place. Instead of inquiring who your parents are, prospective employers ask what kind of education you have and where you got it. Because people from affluent families tend to end up with the best educational credentials—the median family income for Harvard students *who apply for financial aid* is about $150,000 (Leonhardt 2004)—the emphasis on credentials serves to keep "undesirables" out. Conflict theorists argue that educational credentials are mere window dressing; apparently based on merit and achievement, credentials are often a surrogate for race, gender, and social class (Brown 2001). In the same way that we use the term *racism* to refer to bias based on race, sociologists use the term **credentialism** to refer to bias based on credentials: *Credentialism* is the assumption that some are better than others simply because they have a particular educational credential.

Credentialism is the assumption that some are better than others simply because they have a particular educational credential.

Unequal Education and Inequality

The use of education as a status marker is reinforced by the very unequal opportunities for education available to different social groups and communities (Kozol 2005). In poor communities, students sit in overcrowded classrooms, where undertrained, substitute, or newly-graduated teachers are encouraged to focus on rote memorization

■ It is difficult for any children to learn in crowded classrooms that lack proper heating or cooling. It is even more difficult when students are taught by beginning or substitute teachers and must share out-dated textbooks with other students. Such conditions are considerably more common in poor and minority communities.

© Bob Daemmrich/The Image Works

Connections

Personal Application

What social-class advantages or disadvantages did you bring with you to college? Did you grow up with parents who read the *New York Times*, or with parents who couldn't read, or couldn't read English? Did your parents pay for you to receive extra tutoring, music lessons, theater tickets, a computer of your own, or a junior year abroad? Or did your parents need you to work to help them pay the household bills? Did your high school have all the latest facilities, or a leaky roof and out-of-date textbooks? These advantages and disadvantages will continue to affect you as you go through college.

rather than creative thinking skills. Students can choose to take auto mechanics or cosmetology, but their school is not likely to offer calculus, creative writing, or advanced placement (AP) classes. And regardless of which classes are offered, students find it difficult to learn when their classrooms lack proper heating or cooling and they must share out-dated textbooks with other students. In contrast, in affluent communities, students sit in state-of-the-art classrooms and science laboratories and can choose from a variety of languages, challenging topics, and AP classes. A staff of advisors will help them gain admission to the most prestigious college that fits their needs and abilities; at the most selective U.S. colleges, 55 percent of freshmen come from families earning in the top 25 percent of income (Leonhardt 2004). Similarly, in mixed-income communities the wealthier students typically receive a far better education, with a very different range of classes, than do the poorer students (Bettie 2003).

Ethnic differences in access to educational opportunities mirror social class differences. Public school segregation was outlawed by the U.S. Supreme Court in 1954, and segregation did decline significantly over the next 30 years. Since the mid-1980s, however, judicial support for desegregation programs has declined, and school segregation has steadily increased for both Hispanic and African American students (Frankenberg & Lee 2002). Fewer than 15 percent of students are white in some public schools, from Boston to Birmingham. The higher the percentage of minority students at a school, the lower the chances that the school will offer students the opportunities they need to learn, to graduate high school, or to go on successfully to college. Within a given school as well, minority students are typically offered far fewer opportunities than are white students (Bettie 2003).

Symbolic Interactionism: The Self-Fulfilling Prophecy

In the modern world, the elite cannot directly ensure that their children remain members of the elite. To pass their status on to their children, they must provide their children with appropriate educational credentials. To an impressive extent, they are able to do so: Students' educational achievements are very closely related to their parents' social status.

How does this happen? Whereas conflict theorists emphasize how the *structure* of schools leads to these unequal results, symbolic interactionists focus on the *processes* that produce these results. Perhaps the most important such process is the self-fulfilling prophecy.

Self-Fulfilling Prophecy

One of the major processes that takes place in schools is, of course, that students learn. When they graduate from high school, many can type, write essays with three-part theses, and even do calculus. In addition to learning specific skills, they also undergo a process of cognitive development in which their mental skills grow and expand. In the ideal case, they learn to think critically, to weigh evidence, and to develop independent judgment.

An impressive set of studies demonstrates that cognitive development during the school years is greatest when teachers set high expectations for their students and, as a result, give their students complex and demanding work. Teachers are most likely to do this when students fit teachers' expectations for how "smart" students should look and behave. This is most likely when students are white and middle- or upper-class.

One explanation for this is that teachers share the racist and classist stereotypes common in our society. Another explanation is that white, well-off students are likely to have more cultural capital—attitudes and knowledge common in elite culture (Bourdieu 1984; Bettie 2003). They are more likely to have been introduced at home to the sort of art, music, and books that middle-class teachers value. They also are more likely to dress and behave in a way that teachers appreciate. This cultural capital helps them in their interactions with teachers and convinces teachers that they are worth investing time in (DiMaggio & Mohr 1985; Farkas et al. 1990; Kalmijn & Kraaykamp 1996; Teachman 1987).

In contrast, teachers (most of whom are white) are especially likely to assume that African American and Mexican American students are unintelligent and prone to trouble (Ferguson 2000; Bettie 2003). As a result, teachers often focus more on disciplining and controlling minority students than on educating them.

This process is a perfect example of a self-fulfilling prophecy. Those who are now teachers themselves grew up in a society still characterized by racist, sexist, and classist biases. When teachers biases' lead them to assume that certain students cannot succeed, the teachers give those students less opportunity to do so. So girls don't get taught calculus, boys (whether African American or white) don't learn how to cook, and working-class students (whether male or female, white or nonwhite) are encouraged to take cooking or auto mechanics rather than physics. This process helps to keep disadvantaged students from succeeding.

Current Controversies in American Education

In recent years, various proposals have emerged to improve the quality of education in the United States and to give young Americans the tools needed to be more competitive in an increasingly global job market. Three proposals that have been widely adopted are tracking, high-stakes testing, and school choice.

Tracking

Tracking occurs when evaluations made relatively early in a child's career determine the educational programs the child will be encouraged to follow.

Tracking is the use of early evaluations to determine the educational programs a child will be encouraged or allowed to follow. When students enter first grade, they are sorted into reading groups on the basis of ability. By the time they are out of elementary school, some students will be directed into college preparatory tracks, others into general education (sometimes called vocational education), and still others into remedial classes or "special education" programs. At all levels, and regardless of their actual abilities, minority and less affluent students are more likely to be put into lower tracks (Bettie 2003; Kao & Thompson 2003; Harry & Klingner 2005).

Ideally, tracking is supposed to benefit both gifted and slow learners. By gearing classes to their levels, both groups should learn faster and should benefit from increased teacher attention. In addition, classes should run more smoothly and effectively when students are at a similar level. In some ways, this is indeed true. Nevertheless, one of the most consistent findings from educational research is that students are helped modestly by assignment to high-ability groups but hurt significantly if put in low-ability groups (Kao & Thompson 2003).

An important reason students assigned to low-ability groups learn less is because they are taught less. They are exposed to less material, asked to do less homework, and, in general, are not given the same opportunities to learn. Because teachers expect low-track students to do poorly, the students find themselves in a situation where they cannot succeed—a self-fulfilling prophecy.

Less formal processes also operate. Students who are assigned to high-ability groups, for instance, receive strong affirmation of their academic identity; they find school rewarding, have better attendance records, cooperate more with teachers, and develop higher aspirations. The opposite occurs with students placed in low-ability tracks. They receive fewer rewards for their efforts, their parents and teachers have low expectations for them, and there is little incentive to work hard. Many will cut their losses and look for self-esteem through other avenues, such as athletics or delinquency (Bettie 2003). However, these negative effects of tracking diminish in schools where mobility between tracks is encouraged, teachers are optimistic about the potential for student improvement, and schools place academic demands on students who are not in college tracks (Gamoran 1992; Hallinan 1994).

High-Stakes Testing

Both federal and many local laws now require schools to measure student performance using standardized achievement tests. In many school districts, students must now pass these "high stakes" tests before they can move on to a higher grade. In addition, teachers and schools increasingly are evaluated, punished, or rewarded based on results from standardized examinations.

American Diversity:

focus on

What Do IQ Tests Measure?

- How many legs does a Kaffir have?
- Who wrote *Great Expectations*?
- Which word is out of place? sanctuary—nave—altar—attic—apse
- If you throw the dice and 7 is showing on top, what is facing down? 7—snake eyes—boxcars—little joe's—11

If you answered two, Dickens, attic, and 7, then you get the highest possible score on this test. What does that mean? Does it mean that you have genetically superior mental ability, that you read a lot, or that you shoot craps? What could you safely conclude about a person who got only two questions right?

The standardized test is one of the most familiar aspects of life in American schools. Whether it is the California or the Iowa Achievement Test, the SAT or the ACT, students are constantly being evaluated. Most of these tests are truly achievement tests; they measure what has been learned and make no pretense of measuring the capacity to learn. IQ tests, however, are supposed to measure the innate capacity to learn—mental ability. On these tests, African

American, Hispanic, and Native American students consistently score below white students, and working-class students score substantially below middle-class students. The obvious question is whether these tests are fair measures. Do African American, Hispanic, Native American, and working-class youths have lower mental ability than middle-class or white youths?

Before we can answer this question, we must first ask another: What is mental ability? It is an aspect of personality, "the capacity of the individual to act purposefully, to think rationally and to deal effectively with his environment" (Wechsler 1958, 7).

Do questions such as those that opened this section measure any of these things? No, they do not. We can all imagine people who act purposefully, think rationally, and deal effectively with the environment but do not know who wrote *Great Expectations* and are ignorant about dice or church architecture. These people may be foreigners, they may have lacked the opportunity to go to school, or they may have come from a subculture where dice, churches, and nineteenth-century English literature are not important.

For this reason, good IQ tests try to measure the ability to think and reason independently of formal education. Do these tests achieve

their intention? Do they measure the ability to reason independently of years in school, subcultural background, or language difficulties? Again, the answer seems to be no.

There are two ways in which these tests are not culture-free. The first is that they reflect not only reasoning and knowledge but also competitiveness, familiarity with and acceptance of timed tests, rapport with the examiner, and achievement aspiration. Students who lack these characteristics may do poorly even though their ability to reason is well developed.

The more serious fault with such nonverbal tests is their underlying assumption. Reasoning ability is not independent of learning opportunities. How we reason, as well as what we know, depends on our prior experiences. The deprivation studies of monkeys and hospitalized orphans (see Chapter 3) demonstrate that mental and social retardation occur as a result of sensory deprivation. Just as the body does not develop fully without exercise, neither does the mind. Thus, reasoning capacity is not culture-free; it is determined by the opportunities to develop it. For this reason, there will probably never be an IQ test that measures test takers' true *abilities*, rather than measuring their previous learning opportunities.

The emphasis on documenting school achievement through standardized test performance has pressed schools to pay more attention to the quality of the education their students receive and has encouraged them to make sure that all students receive good training in basic skills such as reading, writing, and arithmetic.

But high-stakes testing also has had unanticipated negative consequences (Berliner & Biddle 1995). Few schools have received additional resources to meet these new goals. As a result, schools have dropped classes in art, music, physical education, foreign languages, and even history and science so they can use these teachers for classes in reading, writing, and arithmetic—even when the teachers lack the training to teach these subjects (Berliner & Biddle 1995). Furthermore, teachers can afford to spend time only on teaching those aspects of the subjects that appear on the tests. In addition, teachers now must devote time simply to teaching test-taking skills. Meanwhile, the testing process itself costs school districts considerable time, energy, and money.

High-stakes testing also means that some students will be held back a grade and thereby stigmatized as failures. At the end of the 2002/2003 school year, for example, 23 percent of Florida third graders were held back because they failed to score high enough on the state reading test (Winerip 2003). Yet research suggests that holding students back can *reduce* their long-term academic performance and *increase* their chances of dropping out. Moreover, those who fail are disproportionately lower class and minority, for a variety of reasons. Similarly, when standardized achievement exams are used to determine who should graduate, be admitted to college, or receive financial aid, they typically increase inequality between races and social classes (McDill, Natriello, & Pallas 1986). Finally, there is some evidence that, to artificially improve their schools' rankings on high-stakes tests, schools are encouraging or even forcing low-performing students to leave school before taking the tests—turning potential dropouts into "push-outs" (Lewin & Medina 2003).

School Choice

School choice refers to a range of options (vouchers, tax credits, magnet and charter schools, home schooling) that enable families to choose where their children go to school.

Concern about the quality of American public education has led to a variety of proposals and programs for increasing school choice. **School choice** refers to a range of options (including tuition vouchers, tax credits, magnet schools, charter schools, and home schooling) that enable families to choose where their children go to school. Tuition vouchers and income tax credits are designed to help families pay for private (and, in some cases, religious) schools. Magnet schools are public schools that try to attract students through offering high-quality special programs or approaches; most commonly these schools emphasize either basic skills, language immersion, arts, or math and science. Charter schools are similar to magnet schools but are privately controlled. Charter schools receive some public funding and are subject to some public oversight, such as requirements that they offer certain courses and that their students meet specified measures of academic performance.

Proponents of school choice argue that when schools compete with each other for students, they provide better quality services, in the same way that Ford and Chevrolet compete to provide better cars (Chubb & Moe 1990; Schneider, Teske, & Marschall 2000). The school choice movement reflects the animosity toward "big government" that has been building in the United States for the last quarter century and is part of a broader movement toward **privatization:** the process of taking goods and services out of governmental control and instead treating them like any other marketable commodity. School choice has found supporters on the left as well as the right: black separatists, liberal believers in free-form "alternative schools," and Evangelical Christians all may prefer that their children attend schools where their own values are reinforced.

Although there is some merit to the arguments for school choice, it is difficult to scientifically document its benefits. The problem is that students who participate in school choice programs differ from other students from the beginning. Their parents are often more educated than other parents. More importantly, by definition their parents are committed to seeking out the best education for their children, knowledgeable about the options available, and willing to invest time and effort in obtaining the best options for their children. As a result, no matter what schools their children attend, they will likely do well.

Opponents of school choice identify several unintended negative consequences of these programs. First, these programs reinforce social inequality. Because tuition vouchers and tax credits do not cover the full cost of tuition and transportation, only middle- and upper-income children can afford to use them. Second, because white and affluent parents typically prefer not to send their children to schools with many poor or nonwhite students, school choice programs unintentionally increase segregation (Saporito 2003). Third, school choice programs reduce Americans' commitment to public education and to maintaining high-quality schools in all neighborhoods.

Privatization is the process of taking goods and services out of governmental control and instead treating them like any other marketable commodity—something to be bought and sold in a competitive market.

College and Society

Before World War II, college and even high school graduation was only common among the elite. Since then, however, there has been a tremendous growth in high school and college education, and today almost half of recent high school graduates ages 18 to 21 are enrolled in college. As Figure 1 shows, all segments of the population have been affected by this expansion in education, but significant differences still remain (Kao & Thompson 2003).

Who Goes?

Until recently, non-Hispanic white males were the group most likely to be enrolled in college, but this has changed (Figure 2). Because young men can earn good incomes right out of high school, many decide against going to college—even though in the long run they would earn far more money if they did so (Lewin 2006). Young women, on the other hand, have little chance of earning a good income unless they go to college. As a result, rates of college attendance for women in all ethnic groups have increased steadily, while rates among men have stayed stable. However, white men are still the most likely to receive professional and doctoral degrees and to graduate in the fields that promise the highest incomes.

FIGURE 1

Educational Achievement of Persons 25 and Older by Race and Ethnicity, 1960–2004

Among whites, the proportion of adults graduating from high school has almost doubled since 1960; among African Americans, the proportion has quadrupled. Nevertheless, African Americans and Hispanics continue to have less education than do whites.

SOURCE: U.S. Bureau of the Census 2006.

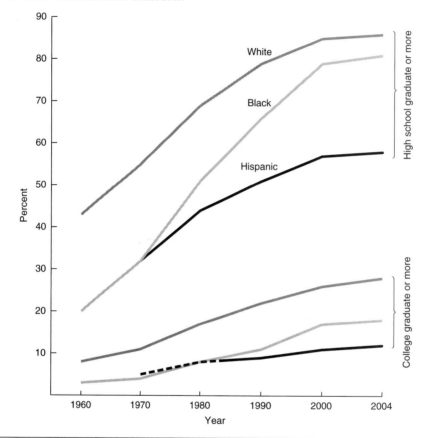

Overall, though, sex differences in college attendance are fairly small compared to ethnic and social class differences (Lewin 2006; Mead 2006). Native Americans are the least likely to graduate high school. African Americans are still slightly less likely than whites or Asians to do so, and Hispanics are considerably less likely to do so, partly because many emigrated here as adults (U.S. Bureau of the Census 2006).

Why Go?

There is no question that a college education pays off economically. As Table 1 shows, college graduates are more likely to get satisfying professional jobs with good benefits and are less likely to be unemployed. They also earn nearly double the income of high school graduates.

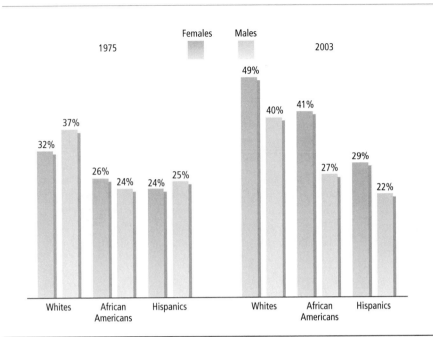

1975   Females   Males   2003

49%
40%   41%
37%
32%
29%
26%   24%   24%   25%   27%   22%

Whites   African   Hispanics   Whites   African   Hispanics
Americans   Americans

FIGURE 2

Percentage of Recent High School Graduates Enrolled in College, by Race, Ethnicity, and Sex, 1975 and 2003 Comparisons by sex, race, and ethnicity show increasing similarity in the likelihood that high school graduates from each category will attend college. SOURCE: U.S. Bureau of the Census 2006.

TABLE 1

Socioeconomic Consequences of Higher Education, 2003–2004
Going to college pays off—literally. Those who graduate college earn nearly twice as much as high school graduates, are more likely to be employed, and are more likely to have a professional job.

Education	Median Annual Income*	% with Managerial/Professional Job**	% Unemployed**
9–12 years, no degree	$18,990	6%	8.5%
High school graduate	28,763	16	5.0
Less than 4 years college	39,015	33	4.2
College graduate	55,751	72	2.7

*2003 data
**2004 data

SOURCE: U.S. Bureau of the Census 2006.

A college education also offers many less tangible benefits. At its best, college teaches students not only specific skills in math, science, and other fields, but also how to think logically and critically about all aspects of the world. Research shows that students also emerge from college more knowledgeable about the world around them, more active in public and community affairs, and more open to new ideas than those who don't have a college degree (Funk & Willits 1987; Weil 1985); they also lead healthier lives and live longer (Ross & Mirowsky 1999).

College conveys psychological and social benefits as well (Kaufman & Feldman 2004). During college, students learn to talk and behave in ways that older adults will interpret as smart and middle class (such as substituting "How are you?" for "Yo, whas up?"). College also teaches students to believe they are intelligent and are entitled to middle-class jobs. As a result, college graduates are more confident and more likely to apply for such jobs. At the same time, because American culture stresses that college graduates are more likely than others to have the skills needed for prestigious, high-paying jobs, college graduates are more likely to receive such jobs even if their actual skills are questionable (Brown 2001).

Mark the Text

Now that you've previewed and read the chapter one time, go back and mark the text—underline important ideas, write notes in the margin, circle key words, write question marks next to anything you don't understand. (To review how to mark text, turn to page 413, "Learning Strategy III—Marking Text.") Remember, when it's time for an exam, you won't need to read the chapter all over again—you'll only need to review your underlining and notes.

Vocabulary

You've seen that the authors call your attention to key terms and concepts by writing them in bold type and, in most cases, repeating them in the margin. Make sure you master these terms; if you have any questions about a term, mark it so you'll remember to ask a classmate or your instructor about it.

Exam Questions

This textbook is used in many colleges across the country. Here are some questions that the instructors who teach the course ask on exams. Answer the questions to check that you've understood the main ideas of the chapter.

Multiple Choice/True False/Short Answer Questions

1. The chapter offers two theoretical perspectives on education. The two perspectives are the _____ theory and the _____ theory.

2. According to conflict theorists, _____ socializes young people into obedience and conformity.

   a. tracking
   b. the hidden curriculum
   c. formal curriculum
   d. multicultural education

3. Tracking

   a. is the practice of evaluating children relatively early in their school experience and encouraging them to follow a particular educational program.
   b. is the practice of studying adults' achievements in a longitudinal study to determine the effects of intelligence on economic attainment.

   c. is the formal term used for holding children back a grade
      in school.

   d. is none of these choices.

4. The use of educational credentials to measure social origins and
    social status is known as:

   a. tracking
   b. credentialism.
   c. the hidden curriculum.
   d. cultural capital.

5. Which of the following statements is true?

   a. Non-Hispanic white males are likely to go to college.
   b. Just slightly less than half of all high school graduates
      between the ages of 16 and 24 are enrolled in colleges or
      universities.
   c. African Americans and Hispanics are now more likely than
      whites to go to college.
   d. Nearly 75% of all those who graduated from high school in the
      1990s enrolled in a college or university.

6. True of False: White men are the most likely group to receive
    professional and doctoral degrees.

7. The term *School Choice* refers to

   a. tuition vouchers
   b. tax credits
   c. magnet schools
   d. charter schools
   e. home schooling
   f. all of the above

8. List some of the less tangible benefits of a college education.

9. History books in the United States:

   a. tend to ignore the history of minorities in the U.S.
   b. tend to present an objective perspective from all
      viewpoints.
   c. are consistent with the values that all children learn
      at home.
   d. presented a more well-rounded history 25 years ago than they
      do today.

10. True or False: Studies show that cognitive development in
    school is greatest when teachers have high expectations of their
    students.

11. College graduates earn approximately _____ high school graduates.

    a. double the income of

    b. the same income as

    c. 50% more income than

    d. 25% more income than

12. True or False: Today almost half of recent high school graduates ages 18 to 21 are enrolled in college.

13. True of False: Rates of college attendance for women in all ethnic groups have increased steadily, while rates among men have stayed basically the same.

Thinking Critically Questions

1. List some of the negative consequences of high stakes testing.

2. Compare and contrast magnet schools and charter schools.

3. Have you experienced tracking? Were you helped or harmed by tracking? If you have not experienced it, answer this question based on someone you know.

4. How would you reorganize elementary and secondary classrooms to best meet the needs of all students?

5. Summarize the benefits of attending college.

LANGUAGE AND CULTURE

A Chapter from the Textbook
Looking Out/Looking In, Eighth Edition

Ronald B. Adler and Neil Towne

PREVIEWING

Your first step in studying a chapter in your textbook should always be to *preview*. (If you need to review how to preview, turn to "Learning Strategy I—Previewing" on page 407.)

The questions and suggestions here will help you to preview this chapter well.

1. Read the title. What do you think the chapter will be about?
2. Read the first four paragraphs quickly. They will introduce you to the tone and content of the chapter. (If you enjoy the examples of "bungled translations" in the first paragraph, you'll also like reading "It Got Lost in the Translation" in *The Thoughtful Reader* on page 279).
3. Read the subtitles of the chapter. Are there any words or phrases that you don't understand? If so, be sure to mark them so you can ask about them in class.
4. Are any tables or charts included in the chapter? What do they contain?
5. How do the authors indicate the words or terms they feel are important?
6. List the other helpful features (such as a glossary, a summary, margin notes, etc.) that the chapter contains.

Now, turn to page 365 and preview the chapter. When you have finished previewing, go to page 364 to think about what you've learned.

What Did I Learn from Previewing?

Reflect for a moment on what you learned from previewing this chapter. First, the title "Language and Culture" should have triggered many associations in your mind. For example, if you have read any of the selections in Unit Two or Unit Three of *The Thoughtful Reader,* try to make connections between them and the information in this textbook excerpt.

The subtitles "Verbal Communication Styles" and "Language and World View" serve as an outline to the content of the chapter.

The key terms the authors think you should know are written in boldface type. Two of the key terms, *low-context* and *high-context* communication styles, are presented in a table.

Finally, a summary repeats the highlights of the chapter.

Read the Chapter

Return now to the beginning of the chapter and read it carefully.

LANGUAGE AND CULTURE

INTRODUCTION

Anyone who has tried to translate ideas from one language to another knows that conveying the same meaning isn't always easy. Sometimes the results of a bungled translation can be amusing. For example, the American manufacturers of Pet milk unknowingly introduced their product in French-speaking markets without realizing that the word *pet* in French means "to break wind." Likewise, the English-speaking representative of a U.S. soft-drink manufacturer naively drew laughs from Mexican customers when she offered free samples of Fresca soda pop. In Mexican slang the word *fresca* means "lesbian."

Even choosing the right words during translation won't guarantee that non-native speakers will use an unfamiliar language correctly. For example, Japanese insurance companies warn their policyholders who are visiting the United States to avoid their cultural tendency to say "excuse me" or "I'm sorry" if they are involved in a traffic accident. In Japan, apologizing is a traditional way to express goodwill and maintain social harmony, even if the person offering the apology is not at fault. But in the United States an apology can be taken as an admission of guilt and result in Japanese tourists being held accountable for accidents in which they may not be responsible.

Difficult as it may be, translation is only a small part of the differences in communication between members of different cultures. Differences in the way language is used and the very world view that a language creates make communicating across cultures a challenging task.

VERBAL COMMUNICATION STYLES

Using language is more than just choosing a particular group of words to convey an idea. Each language has its own unique style that distinguishes it from others. Matters like the amount of formality or informality, precision or vagueness, and brevity or detail are major ingredients in speaking competently. And when a communicator tries to use the verbal style from one culture in a different one, problems are likely to arise.

One way in which verbal styles vary is in their *directness*. Anthropologist Edward Hall identified two distinct cultural ways of using language. **Low-context cultures** use language primarily to express thoughts, feelings, and ideas as clearly and logically as possible. Low-context communicators look for the meaning of a statement in the words spoken. By contrast, **high-context cultures** value language as a way to maintain social harmony. Rather than upset others by speaking clearly, communicators in these societies learn to discover meaning from the context in which a message is delivered: the nonverbal behaviors of the speaker, the history of the relationship, and the general social rules that govern interaction

TABLE 1   Low- and High-Context Communication Styles

Low Context	High Context
Majority of information carried in explicit verbal messages, with less focus on the situational context	Important information carried in contextual cues (time, place, relationship, situation); less reliance on explicit verbal messages
Self-expression valued; communicators state opinions and desires directly and strive to persuade others to accept their own viewpoint	Relational harmony valued and maintained by indirect expression of opinions; communicators abstain from saying "no" directly
Clear, eloquent speech considered praiseworthy; verbal fluency admired	Communicators talk "around" the point, allowing the other to fill in the missing pieces; ambiguity and use of silence admired

between people. Table 1 summarizes some key differences between the ways low- and high-context cultures use language.

North American culture falls toward the low-context end of the scale. Residents of the United States and Canada value straight talk and grow impatient with "beating around the bush." By contrast, most Asian and Middle-Eastern cultures fit the high-context pattern. In many Asian cultures, for example, maintaining harmony is important, and so communicators will avoid speaking clearly if that would threaten another person's face. For this reason, Japanese or Koreans are less likely than Americans to offer a clear "no" to an undesirable request. Instead they would probably use roundabout expressions like "I agree with you in principle, but . . ." or "I sympathize with you. . . ."

The same sort of clash between directness and indirectness can aggravate problems between straight-talking, low-context Israelis who value speaking clearly and Arabs, whose high-context culture stresses smooth interaction. It's easy to imagine how the clash of cultural styles could lead to misunderstandings and conflicts between Israelis and their Palestinian neighbors. Israelis could view their Arab counterparts as evasive, while the Palestinians could perceive the Israelis as insensitive and blunt.

Even within a single country, subcultures can have different notions about the value of direct speech. For example, Puerto Rican language style resembles high-context Japanese or Korean more than low-context English. As a group, Puerto Ricans value social harmony and avoid confrontation, which leads them to systematically speak in an indirect way to avoid giving offense.

Another way in which language styles can vary across cultures is whether they are *elaborate* or *succinct*. Speakers of Arabic, for instance, commonly use language that is much more rich and expressive than most communicators who use English. Strong assertions and exaggerations that would sound ridiculous in English are a common feature of Arabic. This contrast in linguistic style can lead to misunderstandings between people from different backgrounds. As one observer put it,

> First, an Arab feels compelled to overassert in almost all types of communication because others expect him to. If an Arab says exactly what he means without the expected assertion, other Arabs may still think that he means the opposite. For example, a simple "no," by a guest to the host's requests to eat more or drink more will not suffice. To convey the meaning that he is actually full, the guest must keep repeating "no" several times, coupling it with an oath such as "By God" or "I swear to God." Second, an Arab often fails to realize that others, particularly foreigners, may mean exactly what they say even though their language is simple. To the Arabs, a simple "no" may mean the indirectly expressed consent and encouragement of a coquettish woman. On the other hand, a simple consent may mean the rejection of a hypocritical politician.

Succinctness is most extreme in cultures where silence is valued. In many Native American cultures, for example, the favored way to handle ambiguous social situations is to remain quiet. When you contrast this silent style to the talkativeness that is common in mainstream American cultures when people first meet, it's easy to imagine how the first encounter between an Apache or Navajo and an Anglo might feel uncomfortable to both people.

Along with differences such as directness and indirectness and elaborate and succinct styles, a third way languages differ from one culture to another involves *formality* and *informality*. The informal approach that characterizes relationships in countries like the United States, Canada, and Australia, and the Scandinavian countries is quite different from the great concern for using proper speech in many parts of Asia and Africa. Formality isn't so much a matter of using correct grammar as of defining social position. In Korea, for example, the language reflects the Confucian system of relational hierarchies. It has special vocabularies for different sexes, for different levels of social status, for different degrees of intimacy, and for different types of social occasions. For example, there are different degrees of formality for speaking with old friends, nonacquaintances whose background one knows, and complete strangers. One sign of being a learned person in Korea is the ability to use language that recognizes these relational distinctions. When you contrast these sorts of distinctions with the casual friendliness many North Americans use even when talking with complete strangers, it's easy to see how a Korean might view communicators in the United States as boorish, and how an American might see Koreans as stiff and unfriendly.

LANGUAGE AND WORLD VIEW

Different linguistic styles are important, but there may be even more fundamental differences that separate speakers of various languages. For almost 150 years, some theorists have put forth the notion of **linguistic determinism:** that the world view of a culture is unavoidably shaped and reflected by the language its members speak. The best-known example of linguistic determinism is the notion that Eskimos have a large number of words (estimated at everything from seventeen to one hundred) for what we simply call "snow." Different terms are used to describe conditions like a driving blizzard, crusty ice, and light powder. This example suggests how linguistic determinism operates. The need to survive in an Arctic environment led Eskimos to make distinctions that would be unimportant to residents of warmer environments, and once the language makes these distinctions, speakers are more likely to see the world in ways that match the broader vocabulary.

Even though there is some doubt that Eskimos really have so many words for snow, other examples do seem to support the principle of linguistic determinism. For instance, bilingual speakers seem to think differently when they change languages. In one study, French-Americans were asked to interpret a series of pictures. When they spoke in French, their descriptions were far more romantic and emotional than when they used English to describe the same kinds of images. Likewise, when students in Hong Kong were asked to complete a values test, they expressed more traditional Chinese values when they answered in Cantonese than when they spoke English. In Israel, both Arab and Jewish students saw bigger distinctions between their group and "outsiders" when using their native language than when they spoke in English, a neutral tongue. Examples like these show the power of language to shape cultural identity . . . sometimes for better, and sometimes for worse.

Linguistic influences start early in life. English-speaking parents often label the mischievous pranks of their children as "bad," implying that there is something immoral about acting wild. "Be good!" they are inclined to say. On the other hand, French adults are more likely to say *"Sois sage!"*—"Be wise." The linguistic implication is that misbehaving is an act of foolishness. Swedes would correct the same action with the words *"Var snäll!"*—"Be friendly," "Be kind." By contrast, German adults use the command *"Sei artig!"*—literally "Be of your own kind"—in other words, get back in step, conform to your role as a child.

The best-known declaration of linguistic determinism is the **Sapir–Whorf hypothesis,** formulated by Edward Sapir and Benjamin Whorf. Following Sapir's theory, Whorf observed that the language spoken by Hopi Native Americans represents a view of reality that is dramatically different from more familiar tongues. For example, the Hopi language makes no distinction between nouns and verbs. Therefore the people who speak it describe the entire world as being constantly in process. Whereas we use nouns to characterize people or objects as being fixed or constant, Hopi view them more as verbs, constantly changing.

In this sense our language represents much of the world rather like a snapshot camera, whereas Hopi reflects a world view more like a motion picture.

Although there is little support for the extreme linguistically deterministic viewpoint that it is *impossible* for speakers of different languages to view the world identically, the more moderate notion of **linguistic relativism**— that language exerts a strong influence on perceptions — does seem valid. As one scholar put it, "The differences between languages are not so much in what *can* be said, but in what it is *relatively easy* to say." Some languages contain terms that have no English equivalents. For example, consider a few words in other languages that have no English equivalents:

> *Nemawashi* (Japanese): The process of informally feeling out all the people involved with an issue before making a decision
>
> *Lagniappe* (French/Creole): An extra gift given in a transaction that wasn't expected by the terms of a contract
>
> *Lao* (Mandarin): A respectful term used for older people, showing their importance in the family and in society
>
> *Dharma* (Sanskrit): Each person's unique, ideal path in life, and knowledge of how to find it
>
> *Koyaanisquatsi* (Hopi): Nature out of balance; a way of life so crazy it calls for a new way of living

Once words like these exist and become a part of everyday life, the ideas that they represent are easier to recognize. But even without such terms, each of the concepts above is still possible to imagine. Thus, speakers of a language that includes the notion of *lao* would probably treat its older members respectfully and those who are familiar with *lagniappe* might be more generous. Despite these differences, the words aren't essential to follow these principles. Although language may shape thoughts and behavior, it doesn't dominate them absolutely.

The importance of language as a reflection of world view isn't just a matter of interest for anthropologists and linguists. The labels we use in everyday conversation both reflect and shape the way we view ourselves and others. This explains why businesses often give employees impressive titles, and why a woman's choice of the label "Ms." or "Mrs." can be a statement about her identity.

Relational titles aren't the only linguistic elements that may shape attitudes about men and women. Language reforms like avoiding "he" as a gender-neutral pronoun can lead to less discriminatory thinking. A recent study examined precisely this question. Students were corrected every time they used "he" as a generic pronoun in their writing. At the end of a semester, results showed that the corrections did reduce the use of gender-biased language. However, students did not change their mental images or their attitudes toward language reforms.

Along with **gender labeling, ethnic group labeling** can both affect and reflect the way members of an ethnic group define themselves. Over the years, labels of racial identification have gone through cycles of popularity. In North America,

LOOKING AT DIVERSITY

The Bilingual World of the Deaf

Larry Littleton lost his hearing at age seven after contracting spinal meningitis. He spent the next eight years relying exclusively on lip reading to understand others' speech and using his own voice to express ideas. At age fifteen he learned American Sign Language and finger spelling. Larry has worked for Southern California Edison conducting energy audits, and he volunteers his time speaking to students and community groups.

Most people don't realize that American Sign Language (ASL) is a complete language with its own vocabulary. Some of the symbols we use even have different meanings in ASL than they do in other sign languages. For example, I just came back from Australia, where the sign that we use to mean "sex" means "fun," and the one that means "socks" to us means "learn" to them. You can imagine how confused I was when an Australian used his sign language to ask me, "Are you having fun learning while you're here?" and I thought he was asking, "Are you having sex in socks while you're here?"

Being a bilingual speaker who understands both ASL and English helps me appreciate how different the two languages are. For one thing, I think ASL is a more expressive language. English speakers depend on words to get ideas across. In ASL, a lot more of the meaning comes from how you act out a sign. For example, in ASL the difference between "I'm a little sorry," "I'm sorry" and "I'm terribly sorry" come from your facial expression, your posture, and the way you gesture as you make the sign. I guess you could say that being expressive may be *useful* in spoken language, but it's *essential* in ASL.

Besides being more expressive than English, ASL is more concise. I just read about a study of one elementary-school classroom with a hearing teacher and an ASL interpreter. In one week the speaking teacher used almost eighty-six thousand words; but the interpreter only used forty-three thousand words to get across the same message to the deaf students. Maybe the interpreter missed some ideas, but I also think the difference came because sign language is so concise and expressive. Let me show you an example. In speaking I could tell you "Sorry, I've lost my train of thought." In ASL, the whole idea gets communicated almost instantly, in one sign [he demonstrates]. Here's another example: I can make one sign [he gestures] that means the same as the seven words: "Don't worry: It's not a big deal."

ASL is good at communicating concepts, but it doesn't work as well when the message contains specific details. When people who are deaf need to get across a precise message—a phone number or somebody's name, for example, they usually fingerspell. Fingerspelling has its own set of symbols for each letter of the alphabet, and you communicate by spelling the word out one letter at a time. Fingerspelling isn't really a different language from English: it's just a different way of "writing."

I think ASL and spoken languages both have strengths. Because they're precise, spoken languages are useful when you need to get across specific details. But when you want to be expressive, I think ASL works much better. I know one ASL interpreter whose translations are beautiful: Almost everything she says comes across like poetry or music. I also think sign languages are more universal. A while ago I was traveling in Europe with a bunch of hearing people. When we got to countries where nobody could speak the local language, my signing got us through a lot of tough situations. I think that's because using sign language develops a communicator's creativity and expressiveness. The same thing happened when I was in Thailand last year. Almost nobody spoke English in the village where I lived, but I got along pretty well because I have had so much practice expressing my ideas with my face and gestures, and also because I spend so much time and energy observing how others act.

I think everybody can benefit from being bilingual, and ASL is a wonderful second language to learn. Besides developing your expressiveness, it can help you appreciate that people who are deaf have the same ideas and feelings that hearing people do.

the first freed slaves preferred to be called *Africans.* In the late nineteenth and early twentieth centuries *colored* was the term of choice, but later *Negro* became the respectable word. Then, in the sixties, the term *Black* grew increasingly popular — first as a label for militants, and later as a term preferred by more moderate citizens of all colors. More recently *African American* has gained popularity. Recent surveys have found that between 60 and 72 percent of Blacks surveyed prefer the term *Black,* while between 15 and 25 percent prefer *African American.* (The rest either had no opinion or chose other labels.)

Decisions about which name to use reflect a person's attitude. For example, one recent survey revealed that individuals who prefer the label *Black* choose it because it is "acceptable" and "based on consensus" of the larger culture. They describe themselves as patriotic, accepting of the status quo, and attempting to assimilate into the larger culture. By contrast, people who choose the term *Afro-American* derive their identity from their ethnicity and do not want to assimilate into the larger culture, only succeed in it.

SUMMARY

Different languages often shape and reflect the view of a culture. Low-context cultures, like the United States, use language primarily to express feelings and ideas as clearly and unambiguously as possible. High-context cultures, such as Japan and Saudi Arabia, however, avoid specificity in order to promote social harmony. Some cultures value brevity and the succinct use of language, while others have high regard for elaborate forms of speech. In some societies, formality is important, while others value informality. Beyond these differences, there is evidence to support linguistic relativism — the notion that language exerts a strong influence on the world view of the people who speak it.

KEY TERMS

ethnic group labeling

high-context cultures

gender labeling

linguistic determinism

linguistic relativism

low-context cultures

Sapir–Whorf hypothesis

Mark the Text

Now that you have previewed and read the chapter, you are ready to master the ideas that it contains. As you read through a second time, mark the text—underline important ideas, write notes in the margin, circle key words, write question marks next to anything you don't understand. (To review how to mark the text, turn to page 413, "Learning Strategy III—Marking Text") When you have finished marking the text, discuss any questions you have with your classmates. And remember—when exam time comes along, you only need to review the marks and comments you have written.

Vocabulary

Note that, in this textbook chapter, the authors give you a list of the *key terms*—important words they think you should know and remember. Be sure to find and mark each term in the text. Mark any term you don't understand so you'll remember to ask a classmate or the instructor for an explanation. It would be a good idea to keep a special section of your notebook where you write the terms and their meanings.

Exam Questions

Each instructor will have his or her own style of testing. Following are several examples of exam questions used by instructors who actually teach the course in which this text is used. Test your understanding of the chapter by answering these questions.

Short Essay Questions

1. Contrast low-context cultures with high-context cultures. Write two to four sentences.
2. Define and explain the concept of linguistic relativism.
3. In *The Thoughtful Reader,* read "Speaking Different Languages," on page 207. Using the information in this textbook chapter, "Language and Culture," explain the problem the American woman had in Turkey. Write one paragraph.

Matching

Match the terms in column 1 with their definitions in column 2.

1	2
＿＿ 1. high-context cultures	a. theory of linguistic determinism in which language is determined by a culture's perceived reality
＿＿ 2. low-context cultures	b. cultures that avoid direct use of language, relying on the context of a message to convey meaning
＿＿ 3. linguistic determinism	c. the theory that a culture's world view is unavoidably shaped and reflected by the language its members speak

_____ 4. linguistic relativism

d. cultures that use language primarily to express thoughts, feelings, and ideas as clearly and logically as possible

_____ 5. Sapir–Whorf hypothesis

e. a moderate theory that argues that language exerts a strong influence on the perceptions of the people who speak it

True/False

Mark the following statements as true or false.

_____ 1. According to research, the name you use to describe your ethnic group can reflect your attitude about many aspects of life.

_____ 2. The United States would fall into the category of low-context cultures.

_____ 3. Ambiguity and vagueness are forms of language that are to be avoided at all costs.

_____ 4. A person from the United States is more likely to value direct language than is someone from Japan.

TECHNOLOGY, CULTURAL CHANGE, AND DIVERSITY

A Chapter from the Textbook
Sociology in Our Times, Sixth Edition

Diana Kendall

Now, turn to page 376 and preview the chapter. When you have finished previewing, go to page 375 to review what you've learned.

What Did I Learn from Previewing?
The headings and subheadings gave you an excellent idea of the chapter's organization and content.

Key terms and phrases and their definitions are clearly pointed out for you in three ways: they are shown in boldface; they are summarized in boxes in the margin of the text and then listed along with their page numbers at the end of the chapter.

Read the Chapter
Return now to the beginning of the chapter and read it carefully.

TECHNOLOGY, CULTURAL CHANGE, AND DIVERSITY

Cultures do not generally remain static. There are many forces working toward change and diversity. Some societies and individuals adapt to this change, whereas others suffer culture shock and succumb to ethnocentrism.

Cultural Change

Societies continually experience cultural change at both material and nonmaterial levels. Changes in technology continue to shape the material culture of society. *Technology* **refers to the knowledge, techniques, and tools that allow people to transform resources into usable forms and the knowledge and skills required to use what is developed.** Although most technological changes are primarily modifications of existing technology, *new technologies* refers to changes that make a significant difference in many people's lives. Examples of new technologies include the introduction of the printing press more than 500 years ago and the advent of computers and electronic communications in the twentieth century. The pace of technological change has increased rapidly in the past 150 years, as contrasted with the 4,000 years prior to that, during which humans advanced from digging sticks and hoes to the plow.

All parts of culture do not change at the same pace. When a change occurs in the material culture of a society, nonmaterial culture must adapt to that change. Frequently, this rate of change is uneven, resulting in a gap between the two. Sociologist William F. Ogburn (1966/1922) referred to this disparity as *cultural lag*—**a gap between the technical development of a society and its moral and legal institutions.** In other words, cultural lag occurs when material culture changes faster than nonmaterial culture, thus creating a lag between the two cultural components. For example, at the material cultural level, the personal computer and electronic coding have made it possible to create a unique health identifier for each person in the United States. Based on available technology (material culture), it would be possible to create a national data bank that included everyone's individual medical records from birth to death. Using this identifier, health providers and insurance companies could rapidly transfer medical records around the globe, and researchers could access unlimited data on people's diseases, test results, and treatments. However, the availability of this technology does not mean that it will be accepted by people who believe (nonmaterial culture) that such a national data bank constitutes an invasion of privacy and could easily be abused by others. The failure of nonmaterial culture to keep pace with material culture is linked to social conflict and societal problems. As in the above example, such changes are often set in motion by discovery, invention, and diffusion.

norms established rules of behavior or standards of conduct.

sanctions rewards for appropriate behavior or penalties for inappropriate behavior.

folkways informal norms or everyday customs that may be violated without serious consequences within a particular culture.

mores strongly held norms with moral and ethical connotations that may not be violated without serious consequences in a particular culture.

taboos mores so strong that their violation is considered to be extremely offensive and even unmentionable.

laws formal, standardized norms that have been enacted by legislatures and are enforced by formal sanctions.

technology the knowledge, techniques, and tools that allow people to transform resources into a usable form and the knowledge and skills required to use what is developed.

cultural lag William Ogburn's term for a gap between the technical development of a society (material culture) and its moral and legal institutions (nonmaterial culture).

Discovery is the process of learning about something previously unknown or unrecognized. Historically, discovery involved unearthing natural elements or existing realities, such as "discovering" fire or the true shape of the earth. Today, discovery most often results from scientific research. For example, discovery of a polio vaccine virtually eliminated one of the major childhood diseases. A future discovery of a cure for cancer or the common cold could result in longer and more productive lives for many people.

As more discoveries have occurred, people have been able to reconfigure existing material and nonmaterial cultural items through invention. *Invention* is the process of reshaping existing cultural items into a new form. Guns, video games, airplanes, and First Amendment rights are examples of inventions that positively or negatively affect our lives today.

When diverse groups of people come into contact, they begin to adapt one another's discoveries, inventions, and ideas for their own use. *Diffusion* is the transmission of cultural items or social practices from one group or society to another through such means as exploration, war, the media, tourism, and immigration. Today, cultural diffusion moves at a very rapid pace in the global economy. The popularity of shopping malls in many nations around the world is a good example of this diffusion, as discussed in Box 1.

Cultural Diversity

Cultural diversity refers to the wide range of cultural differences found between and within nations. Cultural diversity between countries may be the result of natural circumstances (such as climate and geography) or social circumstances (such as level of technology and composition of the population). Some nations—such as Sweden—are referred to as *homogeneous societies,* meaning that they include people who share a common culture and who are typically from similar social, religious, political, and economic backgrounds. By contrast, other nations—including the United States—are referred to as *heterogeneous societies,* meaning that they include people who are dissimilar in regard to social characteristics such as religion, income, or race/ethnicity (see Figure 1).

Immigration contributes to cultural diversity in a society. Throughout its history, the United States has been a nation of immigrants. Over the past 175 years, more than 55 million "documented" (legal) immigrants have arrived here; innumerable people have also entered the country as undocumented immigrants. Immigration can cause feelings of frustration and hostility, especially in people who feel threatened by the changes that large numbers of immigrants may produce (Mydans, 1993). Often, people are intolerant of those who are different from themselves. When societal tensions rise, people may look for others on whom they

© Spencer Grant/PhotoEdit

In heterogenous societies such as the United States, people from diverse cultures encourage their children to learn about their heritage. This East Indian mother and daugher in California dance with flower petals.

BOX 1   Sociology in Global Perspective

The Malling of China: What Part Does Culture Play?

What is five stories tall, the length of six football fields, and more than one and a half times bigger than the Pentagon? What has 230 escalators, more than 1,000 stores, 20,000 workers, and shops with names such as Ralph Lauren and Chanel?

Although many of us would think that the answer to this question is a shopping mall in the United States, the mall described here is the Golden Resources Shopping Mall, located in Beijing, China. Golden Resources is currently the world's largest shopping mall, at six million square feet (Marquand, 2004). Other giant shopping theme parks, or "temples of consumerism," are opening throughout China in an effort to lure consumers to settings that often resemble Las Vegas or Disneyland (Barboza, 2005).

Under communism, China had no shopping malls. Today, China is a hotbed for capitalist expansion, and shopping malls are viewed as "cash cows" by developers and entrepreneurs (Whiting, 2005). Many malls in China are being built by U.S. developers such as the Simon Property Group and Taubman Centers, Inc. In addition, many mall stores in China, such as Old Navy, Louis Vuitton, and Chanel, originated in the United States, Italy, France, or other nations of Western Europe. Although the first shopping malls were developed in the United States (Kowinski, 2002), the "shop till you drop" spirit evoked by these shopping complexes has spread throughout the world as malls have sprung up in Western Europe, Mexico, South America, the former Soviet Union, and Japan.

Is the malling of China and other nations an example of *cultural imperialism*—the extensive infusion of one nation's culture into other nations? Or is "malling" nothing more than *cultural diffusion*—the transmission of cultural items or social practices from one group or society to another? Some analysts believe that "malling" and "branding" (the selling of a name-brand product for a higher price when a generic one would serve the same purpose) are not forms of cultural imperialism because people in nations such as China welcome the vast malls and see them as a source of cultural pride and as a sign of their own economic progress. However, other analysts disagree with this assessment because they believe that part of China's culture is disappearing forever. Open-air food markets and old department stores that traditionally sold Chinese clothing and other merchandise indigenous to the Chinese culture have been replaced by chain stores and big-box retailers such as Wal-Mart, many of which are operated by giant U.S. corporations. From this perspective, culture is "for sale" in the giant shopping malls because malls are more than just a collection of stores that share a common geographic location. Theme-park shopping malls, for example, are carefully designed psychological selling machines that sell not only products and services but also cultural symbols of the good life and of social acceptance by one's peers. This is a powerful form of selling culture to people who desperately want to become players in the twenty-first-century global economy.

Is consumerism a *cultural universal* shared by people worldwide as they gain new opportunities to shop and have a vast array of merchandise set before them to choose from? Although "shop till you drop" consumerism may be possible for some middle- and upper-income families in China and other nations, many of the world's people cannot purchase the basic necessities of life, much less buy mall-hyped items such as the following, which are available at Beijing's Golden Resources Shopping Mall: "goat-leather motorcycle jackets, Italian bathroom sinks, hand-made violins, grandfather clocks, colonial-style desks, and Jaguars" (Marquand, 2004: 1). An ad for Golden Resources proudly proclaims that it is "the mall that will change your life" (Marquand, 2004: 1). If we think about this statement from a sociological perspective, it raises interesting questions for all of us: Will the malling of China change the way of life and culture of people in that nation? Has the malling of America changed our culture and influenced how we spend our time? What do you think?

and wives should remain at home. Children (about seven per family) are cherished and seen as an economic asset: They help with the farming and other work. Many of the Old Order Amish speak Pennsylvania Dutch (a dialect of German) as well as English. They dress in traditional clothing, live on farms, and rely on the horse and buggy for transportation.

The Amish are aware that they share distinctive values and look different from other people; these differences provide them with a collective identity and make them feel close to one another (Kephart and Zellner, 1994). The belief system and group cohesiveness of the Amish remain strong despite the intrusion of corporations and tourists, the vanishing farmlands, and increasing levels of government regulation in their daily lives (Kephart and Zellner, 1994).

ETHNIC SUBCULTURES   Some people who have unique shared behaviors linked to a common racial, language, or nationality background identify themselves as members of a specific subculture, whereas others do not. Examples of ethnic subcultures include African Americans, Latinos/Latinas (Hispanic Americans), Asian Americans, and Native Americans. Some analysts include "white ethnics" such as Irish Americans, Italian Americans, and Polish Americans. Others also include Anglo Americans (Caucasians).

Although people in ethnic subcultures are dispersed throughout the United States, a concentration of members of some ethnic subcultures is visible in many larger communities and cities. For example, Chinatowns, located in cities such as San Francisco, Los Angeles, and New York, are one of the more visible ethnic subcultures in the United States. By living close to one another and clinging to their original customs and language, first-generation immigrants can survive the abrupt changes they experience in material and nonmaterial cultural patterns. In New York City, for example, Korean Americans and Puerto Rican Americans constitute distinctive subcultures, each with its own food, music, and personal style. In San Antonio, Mexican Americans enjoy different food and music than do Puerto Rican Americans or other groups. Subcultures

provide opportunities for expression of distinctive lifestyles, as well as sometimes helping people adapt to abrupt cultural change. Subcultures can also serve as a buffer against the discrimination experienced by many ethnic or religious groups in the United States. However, some people may be forced by economic or social disadvantage to remain in such ethnic enclaves.

Countercultures

Some subcultures actively oppose the larger society. A *counterculture* **is a group that strongly rejects dominant societal values and norms and seeks alternative lifestyles** (Yinger, 1960, 1982). Young people are most likely to join countercultural groups, perhaps because younger persons generally have less invested in the existing culture. Examples of countercultures include the beatniks of the 1950s, the flower children of the 1960s, the drug enthusiasts of the 1970s, and contemporary members of nonmainstream religious sects, or cults that establish communes or enclaves where members live apart from other people and engage in practices that may or may not conform to societal norms. Some countercultures (such as the Ku Klux Klan, militias, neo-Nazi skinheads, and the Nation of Islam) engage in revolutionary political activities.

Culture Shock

Culture shock **is the disorientation that people feel when they encounter cultures radically different from their own and believe they cannot depend on their own taken-for-granted assumptions about life.** When people travel to another society, they may not know how to respond to that setting. For example, Napoleon Chagnon (1992) described his initial shock at

> **subculture** a category of people who share distinguishing attributes, beliefs, values, and/or norms that set them apart in some significant manner from the dominant culture.

seeing the Yanomamö (pronounced yah-noh-MAH-mah) tribe of South America on his first trip in 1964.

The Yanomamö (also referred to as the "Yanomami") are a tribe of about 20,000 South American Indians who live in the rain forest. Although Chagnon traveled in a small aluminum motorboat for three days to reach these people, he was not prepared for the sight that met his eyes when he arrived:

> I looked up and gasped to see a dozen burly, naked, sweaty, hideous men staring at us down the shafts of their drawn arrows. Immense wads of green tobacco were stuck between their lower teeth and lips, making them look even more hideous, and strands of dark-green slime dripped from their nostrils—strands so long that they reached down to their pectoral muscles or drizzled down their chins and stuck to their chests and bellies. We arrived as the men were blowing ebene, a hallucinogenic drug, up their noses. . . . I was horrified. What kind of welcome was this for someone who had come to live with these people and learn their way of life—to become friends with them? But when they recognized Barker [a guide], they put their weapons down and returned to their chanting, while keeping a nervous eye on the village entrances. (Chagnon, 1992: 12–14)

The Yanomamö have no written language, system of numbers, or calendar. They lead a nomadic lifestyle, carrying everything they own on their backs. They wear no clothes and paint their bodies; the women insert slender sticks through holes in the lower lip and through the pierced nasal septum. In other words, the Yanomamö—like the members of thousands of other cultures around the world—live in a culture very different from that of the United States.

Even as global travel and the media makes us more aware of people around the world, the distinctiveness of the Yanomamö in South America remains apparent. Are people today more or less likely than those in the past to experience culture shock upon encountering diverse groups of people such as these Yanomamö?

Ethnocentrism and Cultural Relativism

When observing people from other cultures, many of us use our own culture as the yardstick by which we judge their behavior. Sociologists refer to this approach as *ethnocentrism*—**the practice of judging all other cultures by one's own culture** (Sumner, 1959/1906). Ethnocentrism is based on the assumption that one's own way of life is superior to all others. For example, most schoolchildren are taught that their own school and country are the best. The school song, the pledge to the flag, and the national anthem are forms of *positive ethnocentrism*. However, *negative ethnocentrism* can also result from constant emphasis on the superiority of one's own group or nation. Negative ethnocentrism is manifested in derogatory stereotypes that ridicule recent immigrants whose customs, dress, eating habits, or religious beliefs are markedly different from those of dominant-group members. Long-term U.S. residents who are members of racial and ethnic minority groups, such as Native Americans, African Americans, and Latinas/os, have also been the target of ethnocentric practices by other groups.

An alternative to ethnocentrism is ***cultural relativism**—the belief that the behaviors and customs of any culture must be viewed and analyzed by the culture's own standards.* For example, the anthropologist Marvin Harris (1974, 1985) uses cultural relativism to explain why cattle, which are viewed as sacred, are not killed and eaten in India, where widespread hunger and malnutrition exist. From an ethnocentric viewpoint, we might conclude that cow worship is the cause of the hunger and poverty in India. However, according to Harris, the Hindu taboo against killing cattle is very important to their economic system. Live cows are more valuable than dead ones because they have more important uses than as a direct source of food. As part of the ecological system, cows consume grasses of little value to humans. Then they produce two valuable resources—oxen (the neutered offspring of cows) to power the plows and manure (for fuel and fertilizer)—as well as milk, floor covering, and leather. As Harris's study reveals, culture must be viewed from the standpoint of those who live in a particular society.

Cultural relativism also has a downside. It may be used to excuse customs and behavior (such as cannibalism) that may violate basic human rights. Cultural relativism is a part of the sociological imagination; researchers must be aware of the customs and norms of the society they are studying and then spell out their background assumptions so that others can spot possible biases in their studies. However, according to some social scientists, issues surrounding ethnocentrism

and cultural relativism may become less distinct in the future as people around the globe increasingly share a common popular culture. Others, of course, disagree with this perspective.

KEY TERMS

technology p. 376

cultural lag p. 376

discovery p. 377

Invention p. 377

diffusion p. 377

cultural diversity p. 377

homogeneous societies p. 377

heterogeneous societies p. 377

subculture p. 380

ethnic subculture p. 381

counterculture p. 381

culture shock p. 381

ethnocentrism p. 382

cultural relativism p. 383

counterculture a group that strongly rejects dominant societal values and norms and seeks alternative lifestyles.

culture shock the disorientation that people feel when they encounter cultures radically different from their own and believe they cannot depend on their own taken-for-granted assumptions about life.

ethnocentrism the assumption that one's own culture and way of life are superior to all others.

cultural relativism the belief that the behaviors and customs of any culture must be viewed and analyzed by the culture's own standards.

Mark the Text

Now that you've previewed and read the chapter one time, go back and mark the text—underline important ideas, write notes in the margin, circle key words, write question marks next to anything you don't understand. (To review how to mark text, turn to page 413, "Learning Strategy III—Marking Text.") Remember, when it's time for an exam, you won't need to read the chapter all over again—you'll only need to review your underlining and notes.

Vocabulary

It should be very easy to master the new terms in this chapter. You may want to write the words and their definitions in your notebook to further reinforce them in your mind. Remember, if you have any questions about a term, mark it so you'll remember to ask a classmate or your instructor about it.

Exam Questions

This is a popular textbook used in many Introduction to Sociology courses around the country. Here are some questions that the instructors who teach the course ask on exams. Answer the questions to check that you've understood the main ideas of the chapter.

Multiple-Choice Questions

1. A heterogeneous society is one in which:

    a. people share a common culture and are typically from similar social, religious, political, and economic backgrounds.
    b. people in each economic class share a common culture and are typically from similar social, religious, political, and economic background.
    c. people are dissimilar in regard to social characteristics such as religion, income, or race/ethnicity.
    d. people are similar in social characteristics, but visibly look different.

2. Which one of the following is *not* considered to be a counterculture?

    a. The Amish
    b. Neo-Nazi skinheads
    c. The Ku Klux Klan
    d. The Nation of Islam

3. An alternative to ethnocentrism is:

    a. racism.
    b. prejudice
    c. cultural relativism.
    d. xenophobia.

Essay Questions

1. Identify and explain the process of cultural change.
2. Compare and contrast ethnocentrism and cultural relativism.
3. Can you think of an example of a downside of cultural relativism?
4. Give an example of *discovery* as a cause of cultural change.
5. Contrast *homogeneous* and *heterogeneous* societies.
6. Napoleon Chagnon experienced culture shock when he went to visit the Yanomamö. Do you think the Yanomamö were shocked to meet Chagnon?
7. Describe some of the technological changes that you have experienced since you began high school.
8. Do you think there is a cultural lag at your college? For example, do the incoming students have more expertise in learning technology than the faculty? Or is it the reverse?
9. What are some examples of subcultures that exist at your school?

Questions for Critical Thinking

1. Would it be possible today to live in a totally separate culture in the United States? Could you avoid all influences from the mainstream popular culture or from the values and norms of other cultures? How would you be able to avoid any change in your culture?
2. Do fads and fashions reflect and reinforce or challenge and change the values and norms of a society? Consider a wide variety of fads and fashions: musical styles; computer and video games and other technologies; literature; and political, social, and religious ideas.
3. You are doing a survey analysis of recent immigrants to the United States to determine the effects of popular culture on their views and behavior. What are some of the questions you would use in your survey?

MOTIVATING EMPLOYEES

A Chapter from the Textbook
Introduction to Business, Fourth Edition

Jeff Madura

PREVIEWING

Your first step in studying a chapter in your textbook should always be to *preview*. (If you need to review how to preview, turn to "Learning Strategy I—Previewing" on page 407.)

The questions and suggestions here will help you to preview this chapter well.

1. This textbook has many features that will be helpful to you. It begins with a case study of a company and its needs in developing a strategic plan. Be sure to check the flowchart on the first page.
2. Skim the first section, "The Value of Motivation," to get a sense of the information you'll learn in the chapter. What major question will the chapter answer?
3. Read the headings and subheadings. Then, list the "Theories of Motivation" the chapter will cover.
4. Are there any other special features, such as charts, graphs, or exercises?
5. How does the author indicate key terms that are important?

Now, turn to page 388 and preview the chapter. When you have finished previewing, go to page 387 to think about what you've learned.

What Did I Learn from Previewing?

The headings and subheadings gave you a clear idea of the chapter's content and its organization.

The text has many charts and "exhibits." Reading the information in these graphics will help you understand and retain the information in the text, so be sure to read them carefully. The "Self-Scoring Exercise" lets you think about some of the issues in the text and how they apply directly to you.

Note that key terms are printed in bold type and reprinted in the margins of the text—so you know that these words are of major importance.

If you came across any unfamiliar words while you were reading the headings and subheadings, be sure to look them up; for example, did you understand the word *hierarchy* on page 391?

Read the Chapter

Return now to the beginning of the chapter and read it carefully.

Motivating Employees

A firm has a strategic plan that identifies opportunities and indicates the future direction of the firm's business. When the firm develops strategies to achieve the strategic plan, it relies on its managers to utilize employees and other resources to make the strategies work. Consider the situation of Players Company, which produces and sells sporting goods. Its performance is highly dependent on the efforts of its employees. Players Company must decide:

▶ What possible methods could it use to motivate its employees.

▶ What type of motivation will be most effective.

▶ How it can ensure that its employees are satisfied with their jobs.

▶ How motivation can improve its value.

If Players Company can successfully motivate its employees, it benefits in two ways. First, if the employees are motivated to work, they will accomplish more tasks, and Players will need fewer employees. Second, if its salespeople are motivated to sell

sporting goods, Players' sales volume, and therefore its revenue, will be higher. If Players Company can ensure that its employees are satisfied with their jobs, it will be able to retain employees for a longer period of time and will reduce the expenses associated with training new employees.

The types of decisions described above are necessary for all businesses. This chapter explains how firms can motivate and satisfy employees in a manner that maximizes the firm's value.

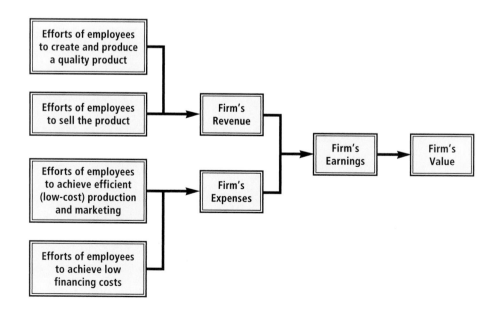

The Value of Motivation

1

Explain how motivating employees can increase the value of a firm.

Many businesses are successful not just because of their business ideas, but also because of their employees. But employees need to be motivated as well as to have the proper skills to do their jobs. Employees at some firms have adequate skills for their jobs, but they lack the motivation to perform well. Consequently, these employees offer only limited help in the production process.

Some firms believe that if they can hire people who are naturally motivated, the employees will perform well in the workplace, but this will not always happen. Although some people naturally make more of an effort to perform well, they will still need a work environment that motivates them.

Consider Anna and Marie, who are equally intelligent and tend to exert the same amount of effort in the workplace. Anna and Marie are hired by two different firms in the same industry for the same type of job. They work the same number of hours and receive the same salary, but their workplaces differ as follows:

	Firm A (which hires Anna)	Firm B (which hires Marie)
Employee work interaction	Frequent	Seldom
Employee social interaction	Frequent	Seldom
Input provided by managers to employees	Frequent	Seldom
Input requested from employees by managers	Frequent	Seldom

Given these conditions, Anna will be much more motivated to perform well than Marie. If Anna and Marie swap jobs, Marie will now be much more motivated than Anna. The point is that the firm has a major influence on the motivation of the employees. To the extent that a firm can motivate its employees, it can increase the productivity of each employee. Consequently, it can achieve a higher production level with a given number of employees, which results in higher profits.

How does a firm motivate its employees? There is no single motivational tool that works perfectly for all employees. The ideal form of motivation may vary among employees. Some of the more popular theories of motivation are described next. These theories can be useful for determining the advantages and limitations of various types of motivation.

Decision Making

Responding to a Lack of Motivation

Players Company (described in the introduction to the chapter) produces and sells sporting goods. Last year it hired eight recent college graduates for various entry-level managerial positions. Each person was a business major with a high grade-point average and very strong letters of recommendation. All of the new hires reported to Joel Kemp. All of them quit their jobs within a year of being hired. Paula Powell, the vice-president of human resources, was shocked that all the new hires quit, so she contacted them to learn their reasons for quitting. They offered different reasons, but all the reasons reflected a lack of motivation. When Paula told Joel Kemp about these responses, he replied, "We paid them well. That should be enough motivation." Paula Powell decides that some changes will be necessary to motivate new employees before Players Company hires any more people.

1. Do you think that the eight entry-level managers would have been more motivated if they had received higher salaries?

2. Joel Kemp suggests that after Players Company hires its next batch of entry-level managers, it should consider hiring a motivational speaker for one day to make a motivational speech. Do you think that this would motivate the entry-level managers?

ANSWERS: 1. No. A higher salary will not substitute for a workplace that motivates employees. 2. No. A motivational speech will not be effective if the workplace does not motivate employees.

2

Describe the theories on motivation.

job satisfaction
the degree to which employees are satisfied with their jobs

Theories on Motivation

The motivation of employees is influenced by **job satisfaction,** or the degree to which employees are satisfied with their jobs. Firms recognize the need to satisfy their employees, as illustrated by the following statements from recent annual reports:

"You will see a greater focus on employee satisfaction . . . which will lead us to higher quality, better growth, and improved profitability."

— Kodak

"Bethlehem's success ultimately depends on the skill, dedication, and support of our employees."

— Bethlehem Steel

Since employees who are satisfied with their jobs are more motivated, managers can motivate employees by ensuring job satisfaction. Some of the more popular theories on motivation are summarized here, followed by some general guidelines that can be used to motivate workers.

Hawthorne Studies

In the late 1920s, researchers studied workers in a Western Electric Plant near Chicago to identify how a variety of conditions affected their level of production. When the lighting was increased, the production level increased. Yet the production level also increased when the lighting was reduced. These workers were then subjected to various break periods; again, the production level increased for both shorter breaks and longer breaks. One interpretation of these results is that workers become more motivated when they feel that they are allowed to participate. Supervisors may be able to motivate workers by giving them more attention and by allowing them to participate. These Hawthorne studies, which ignited further research on motivation, are summarized in Exhibit 1 and suggest that human relations can affect a firm's performance.

Maslow's Hierarchy of Needs

In 1943, Abraham Maslow, a psychologist, developed the **hierarchy of needs** theory. This theory suggests that people rank their needs into five general categories. Once they achieve a given category of needs, they become motivated to reach the next category. The categories are identified in Exhibit 2, with the most crucial needs on the bottom. **Physiological needs** are the basic requirements for survival, such as food and shelter. Most jobs can help achieve these needs.

Once these needs are fulfilled, **safety needs** (such as job security and safe working conditions) become the most immediate goal.

hierarchy of needs
needs are ranked in five general categories. Once a given category of needs is achieved, people become motivated to reach the next category.

physiological needs
the basic requirements for survival

safety needs
job security and safe working conditions

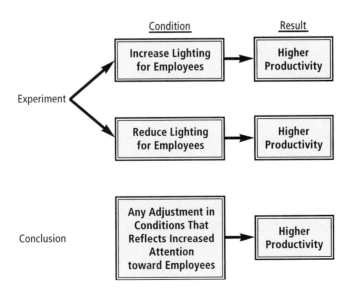

Exhibit 1

Summary of the Hawthorne Studies

Exhibit 2

Maslow's Hierarchy of
Needs

Self-Actualization — Maximization of potential

Esteem Needs — Respect, prestige, recognition, power

Social Needs — Social interaction, acceptance by others

Safety Needs — Job security, safe working conditions

Physiological Needs — Food, shelter, clothing

social needs
the need to be part of a group

esteem needs
respect, prestige, and recognition

self-actualization
the need to fully reach one's potential

Some jobs satisfy these needs. People also strive to achieve **social needs,** or the need to be part of a group. Some firms attempt to help employees achieve their social needs, either by grouping workers in teams or by organizing social events after work hours. People may also become motivated to achieve **esteem needs,** such as respect, prestige, and recognition. Some workers may achieve these needs by being promoted within their firms or by receiving special recognition for their work. The final category of needs is **self-actualization,** which represents the need to fully reach one's potential. For example, people may achieve self-actualization by starting and successfully running a specific business that fits their main interests.

The hierarchy of needs theory can be useful for motivating employees because it suggests that different employees may be at different places in the hierarchy. Therefore, their most immediate needs may differ. If managers can identify employees' needs, they will be better able to offer rewards that motivate employees.

Herzberg's Job Satisfaction Study

In the late 1950s, Frederick Herzberg surveyed 200 accountants and engineers about job satisfaction. Herzberg attempted to identify the factors that made them feel dissatisfied with their jobs at a given point in time. He also attempted to identify the factors that made them feel satisfied with their jobs. His study found the following:

Common Factors Identified by Dissatisfied Workers	Common Factors Identified by Satisfied Workers
Working conditions	Achievement
Supervision	Responsibility
Salary	Recognition
Job security	Advancement
Status	Growth

Employees become dissatisfied when they perceive work-related factors in the left column (called **hygiene factors**) as inadequate. Employees are commonly satisfied when the work-related factors in the right column (called **motivational factors**) are offered.

Herzberg's results suggest that factors such as working conditions and salary must be adequate to prevent workers from being dissatisfied. Yet better-than-adequate working conditions and salary will not necessarily lead to a high degree of satisfaction. Instead, a high degree of worker satisfaction is most easily achieved by offering additional benefits, such as responsibility. Thus, if managers assign workers more responsibility, they may increase worker satisfaction and motivate the workers to be more productive. Exhibit 3 summarizes Herzberg's job satisfaction study.

hygiene factors
work-related factors that can fulfill basic needs and prevent job dissatisfaction

motivational factors
work-related factors that can lead to job satisfaction and motivate employees

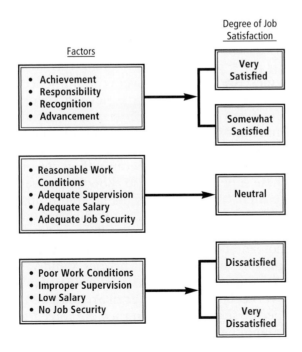

Exhibit 3

Summary of Herzberg's Job Satisfaction Study

Notice how the results of Herzberg's study correspond with the results of Maslow's hierarchy. Herzberg's hygiene factors generally correspond with Maslow's basic needs (such as job security). This suggests that if hygiene factors are adequate, they fulfill some of workers' more basic needs. Fulfillment of these needs can prevent dissatisfaction as employees become motivated to achieve a higher class of needs. Herzberg's motivational factors (such as recognition) generally correspond with Maslow's more ambitious hierarchy needs.

Several U.S. firms, including Ford Motor Company, have implemented workshops to stress teamwork and company loyalty. These workshops build self-esteem by focusing on employees' worth to the company. In this way, the workshops may enable employees to achieve a higher class of needs, thereby increasing job satisfaction.

McGregor's Theory X and Theory Y

Another major contribution to motivation was provided by Douglas McGregor, who developed Theory X and Theory Y. Each of these theories represents supervisors' possible perception of workers. The views of Theories X and Y are summarized as follows:

Theory X	Theory Y
Employees dislike work and job responsibilities and will avoid work if possible.	Employees are willing to work and prefer more responsibility.

The way supervisors view employees can influence the way they treat the employees. Supervisors who believe in Theory X will likely use tight control over workers, with little or no delegation of authority. In addition, employees will be closely monitored to ensure that they perform their tasks. Conversely, supervisors who believe in Theory Y will delegate more authority because they perceive workers as responsible. These supervisors will also allow employees more opportunities to use their creativity. This management approach fulfills employees' needs to be responsible and to achieve respect and recognition. Consequently, these employees are likely to have a higher level of job satisfaction and therefore to be more motivated.

Exhibit 4 provides a summary of Theories X and Y. Most employees would prefer that their supervisors follow Theory Y rather than Theory X. Nevertheless, some supervisors may be unable to use Theory Y in specific situations, when they are forced to retain more authority over employees rather than delegate responsibility.

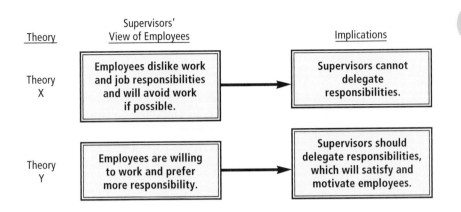

Exhibit 4

Summary of McGregor's Theories X and Y

Theory Z

In the 1980s, a new theory on job satisfaction was developed. This theory, called Theory Z, was partially based on the Japanese style of allowing all employees to participate in decision making. Participation can increase job satisfaction because it gives employees responsibility. Job descriptions tend to be less specialized, so employees develop varied skills and have a more flexible career path. To increase job satisfaction, many U.S. firms have begun to allow employees more responsibility.

Expectancy Theory

Expectancy theory suggests that an employee's efforts are influenced by the expected outcome (reward) for those efforts. Therefore, employees will be more motivated to achieve goals if they are achievable and offer some reward.

As an example, consider a firm that offers the salesperson who achieves the highest volume of annual sales a one-week vacation in Paris. This type of reward will motivate employees only if two requirements are fulfilled. First, the reward must be desirable to employees. Second, employees must believe they have a chance to earn the reward. If the firm employs 1,000 salespeople, and only one reward is offered, employees may not be motivated because they may perceive that they have little chance of being the top salesperson. Motivation may be absent even in smaller groups if all employees expect that a particular salesperson will generate the highest sales volume.

Motivational rewards are more difficult to offer for jobs where output cannot easily be measured. For example, employees who repair the firm's machinery or respond to customer complaints do not contribute to the firm in a manner that can be easily measured or compared

expectancy theory
Holds that an employee's efforts are influenced by the expected outcome (reward) for those efforts

Self-Scoring Exercise

The Frazzle Factor

Read each of the following statements, and rate yourself on a scale of 0 to 3, giving the answer that best describes how you generally feel (3 points for always, 2 points for often, 1 point for sometimes, and 0 points for never). Answer as honestly as you can, and do not spend too much time on any one statement.

Am I Angry?

_____ 1. I feel that people around me make too many irritating mistakes.
_____ 2. I feel annoyed because I do good work or perform well in school, but no one appreciates it.
_____ 3. When people make me angry, I tell them off.
_____ 4. When I am angry, I say things I know will hurt people.
_____ 5. I lose my temper easily.
_____ 6. I feel like striking out at someone who angers me.
_____ 7. When a co-worker or fellow student makes a mistake, I tell him or her about it.
_____ 8. I cannot stand being criticized in public.

Am I Overstressed?

_____ 1. I have to make important snap judgments and decisions.
_____ 2. I am not consulted about what happens on my job or in my classes.
_____ 3. I feel I am underpaid.
_____ 4. I feel that no matter how hard I work, the system will mess it up.
_____ 5. I do not get along with some of my co-workers or fellow students.
_____ 6. I do not trust my superiors at work or my professors at school.
_____ 7. The paperwork burden on my job or at school is getting to me.
_____ 8. I feel people outside the job or the university do not respect what I do.

Scoring

To find your level of anger and potential for aggressive behavior, add your scores from both quiz parts.

40–48: The red flag is waving, and you had better pay attention. You are in the danger zone. You need guidance from a counselor or mental health professional, and you should be getting it now.

30–39: The yellow flag is up. Your stress and anger levels are too high, and you are feeling increasingly hostile. You are still in control, but it would not take much to trigger a violent flare of temper.

10–29: Relax, you are in the broad normal range. Like most people, you get angry occasionally, but usually with some justification. Sometimes you take overt action, but you are not likely to be unreasonably or excessively aggressive.

0–9: Congratulations! You are in great shape. Your stress and anger are well under control, giving you a laid-back personality not prone to violence.

with other employees. Nevertheless, their performance may still be measured by customer satisfaction surveys or by various other performance indicators.

Equity Theory

The **equity theory** of motivation suggests that compensation should be equitable, or in proportion to each employee's contribution. As an example, consider a firm with three employees: Employee 1 contributes 50 percent of the total output, Employee 2 contributes 30 percent, and Employee 3 contributes 20 percent. Assume that the firm plans to allocate $100,000 in bonuses based on the relative contributions of each employee. Using the equity theory, the $100,000 would be allocated as shown in Exhibit 5.

If employees believe that they are undercompensated, they may request greater compensation. If their compensation is not increased, employees may reduce their contribution. Equity theory emphasizes that employees can become dissatisfied with their jobs if they believe that they are not equitably compensated.

Supervisors may prevent job dissatisfaction by attempting to provide equitable compensation. A problem, however, is that the supervisor's perception of an employee's contribution may differ from that of the employee. If a firm can define how employee contributions will be measured and compensate accordingly, its employees will be better satisfied and more motivated.

equity theory
suggests that compensation should be equitable, or in proportion to each employee's contribution

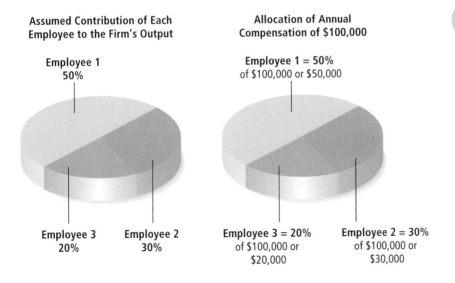

Assumed Contribution of Each Employee to the Firm's Output

Employee 1
50%

Employee 3
20%

Employee 2
30%

Allocation of Annual Compensation of $100,000

Employee 1 = 50%
of $100,000 or $50,000

Employee 3 = 20%
of $100,000 or
$20,000

Employee 2 = 30%
of $100,000 or
$30,000

Exhibit 5

Example of Equity Theory

Exhibit 6

Summary of Reinforcement
Theory

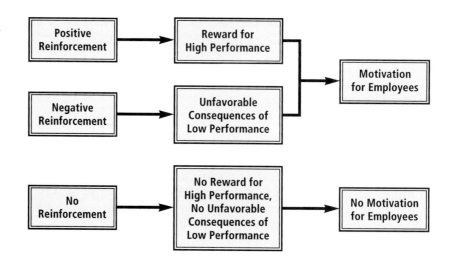

Reinforcement Theory

reinforcement theory
suggests that reinforcement can
influence behavior

positive reinforcement
motivates employees by
providing rewards for high
performance

negative reinforcement
motivates employees by encouraging them to behave in a
manner that avoids unfavorable
consequences

Reinforcement theory, summarized in Exhibit 6, suggests that
reinforcement can influence behavior. **Positive reinforcement** motivates employees by providing rewards for high performance. The
rewards can range from an oral compliment to a promotion or large
bonus. Employees may react differently to various forms of positive
reinforcement. The more they appreciate the form of reinforcement,
the more they will be motivated to continue high performance.

   Negative reinforcement motivates employees by encouraging
them to behave in a manner that avoids unfavorable consequences. For
example, employees may be motivated to complete their assignments
today to avoid having to admit the delay in a group meeting or to avoid
negative evaluations by their supervisors.

   Various forms of negative reinforcement can be used, ranging
from a reprimand to job termination. Some supervisors may prefer
to consistently offer positive reinforcement for high performance
rather than penalize for poor performance. However, offering positive reinforcement for all tasks that are adequately completed may
be difficult. Furthermore, if an employee who has performed poorly
is not given negative reinforcement, others may think that employee
was given preferential treatment, and their general performance
may decline as a result.

Motivational Guidelines Offered by Theories

If supervisors can increase employees' job satisfaction, they may
motivate employees to be more productive. All of the theories on

Theory	Implications
Theory developed from Hawthorne studies	Workers can be motivated by attention.
Maslow's hierarchy of needs	Needs of workers vary, and managers can motivate workers to achieve these needs.
Herzberg's job satisfaction study	Compensation, reasonable working conditions, and other factors do not ensure job satisfaction but only prevent job dissatisfaction. Thus, other factors (such as responsibility) may be necessary to motivate workers.
McGregor's Theory X and Theory Y	Based on Theory X, workers will avoid work if possible and cannot accept responsibility. Based on Theory Y, workers are willing to work and prefer more responsibility. If Theory Y exists, managers can motivate workers by delegating responsibility.
Theory Z	Workers are motivated when they are allowed to participate in decision making.
Expectancy theory	Workers are motivated if potential rewards for high performance are desirable and achievable.
Equity theory	Workers are motivated if they are being compensated in accordance with their perceived contribution to the firm.
Reinforcement theory	Good behavior should be positively reinforced and poor behavior should be negatively reinforced to motivate workers in the future.

Exhibit 7

Comparison of Motivation Theories

motivation are briefly summarized in Exhibit 7. Based on these theories, some general conclusions can be offered on motivating employees and providing job satisfaction:

1. Employees commonly compare their compensation and perceived contribution with others. To prevent job dissatisfaction, supervisors should ensure that employees are compensated for their contributions.

2. Even if employees are offered high compensation, they will not necessarily be very satisfied. They have other needs as well, such as social needs, responsibility, and self-esteem. Jobs that can fulfill these needs may provide satisfaction and therefore provide motivation.

3. Employees may be motivated if they believe that it is possible to achieve a performance level that will result in a desirable reward.

Summary

1 If a firm can motivate its employees, it can increase productivity of each employee. Consequently, it can achieve a higher production level with a given number of employees, which results in higher profits. The ideal form of motivation may vary among employees.

2 The main theories on motivation are as follows:

▶ The Hawthorne studies suggest that employees are more motivated when they receive more attention.

▶ Maslow's hierarchy of needs theory suggests that employees are satisfied by different needs, depending on their position within the hierarchy.

Firms can satisfy employees at the low end of the hierarchy with job security or safe working conditions. Once basic needs are fulfilled, employees have other needs that must be met. Firms can attempt to satisfy these employees by allowing social interaction or more responsibilities.

▶ Herzberg's job satisfaction study suggests that the factors that prevent job dissatisfaction are different from those that enhance job satisfaction. Adequate salary and working conditions prevent job dissatisfaction, while responsibility and recognition enhance job satisfaction.

▶ McGregor's Theories X and Y suggest that when supervisors believe employees dislike

work and responsibilities (Theory X), they do not delegate responsibilities and employees are not motivated; when supervisors believe that employees prefer responsibilities (Theory Y), they delegate more responsibilities, which motivates employees.

▶ Theory Z suggests that employees are more satisfied when they are involved in decision making and therefore may be more motivated.

▶ Expectancy theory suggests that employees are more motivated if compensation is aligned with goals that are achievable and offer some reward.

▶ Equity theory suggests that employees are more motivated if their compensation

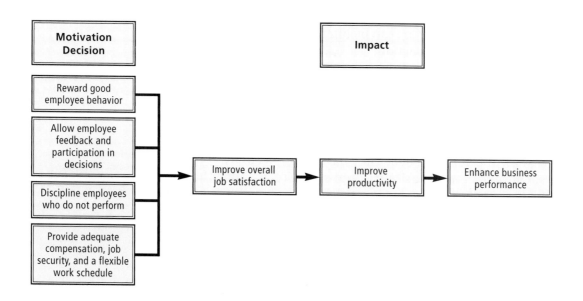

is aligned with their relative contribution to the firm's total output.

▶ Reinforcement theory suggests that employees are more motivated to perform well if they are rewarded for high performance (positive reinforcement) and penalized for poor performance (negative reinforcement).

3 A firm may not be able to motivate some employees, regardless of its efforts or the methods used to motivate them. If no form of motivation is effective, the threat of being fired may serve as a last resort to motivate these employees.

How the Chapter Concepts Affect Business Performance

A firm's decisions regarding the motivation concepts summarized here affect its performance. If a firm can motivate its employees, it can improve employee morale and increase productivity. While there are many motivation theories, the proper form of motivation varies with the firm's characteristics and may even vary among employees.

Key Terms

equity theory

esteem needs

expectancy theory

hierarchy of needs

hygiene factors

job satisfaction

motivational factors

negative reinforcement

physiological needs

positive reinforcement

reinforcement theory

safety needs

self-actualization

social needs

Mark the Text

Now that you've previewed and read the chapter one time, go back and mark the text—underline important ideas, write notes in the margin, circle key words, write question marks next to anything you don't understand. (To review how to mark text, turn to page 413, "Learning Strategy III—Marking Text.") Remember, when it's time for an exam, you won't need to read the chapter all over again—you'll only need to review your underlining and notes.

Vocabulary

You've seen that the author calls your attention to key terms and concepts by writing them in bold type and, in most cases, repeating them in the margin. As extra help, he also summarizes key terms at the end of the chapter. Make sure you master these terms; if you have any questions about a term, mark it so you'll remember to ask a classmate or your instructor about it.

Exam Questions

This chapter is taken from a textbook that is used in many colleges around the country. Following are some exam questions given by instructors who teach the course. Test your mastery of the chapter by answering the questions.

True or False

1. Maslow's hierarchy of needs identifies superior compensation as the key to employee motivation.
2. According to Frederick Herzberg, hygiene factors are work-related factors that will motivate and please employees.
3. The management strategy of empowerment is favored by Theory X managers.
4. A supervisor who believes in McGregor's Theory Y will likely monitor employees closely to ensure that their work is completed.
5. Equity theory suggests that an employee's efforts are influenced by the expected outcome of those efforts.
6. Negative reinforcement motivates employees by encouraging them to behave in a manner that avoids unfavorable consequences.

Multiple Choice

1. By _____ employees to properly perform the tasks they are assigned, management can maximize the firm's value.

   a. motivating
   b. threatening
   c. coercing
   d. manipulating
   e. harassing

2. One implication of the Hawthorne studies is that workers can be motivated by receiving:

   a. attention.
   b. money.
   c. stock.
   d. bonuses.
   e. profit sharing.

3. Maslow's hierarchy of needs theory can be useful for motivating employees because it suggests that:

   a. people are motivated to achieve their work-related hygiene factors.
   b. managers respond to the need for corporate profitability.
   c. employee needs are stable.
   d. employees are motivated by unsatisfied needs.
   e. money is the most important motivating factor.

4. Social interaction and acceptance by others are examples of:

   a. physiological needs.
   b. esteem needs.
   c. safety needs.
   d. social needs.
   e. self-actualization needs.

5. Needs that are satisfied with food, clothing, and shelter are called _____ needs.

   a. safety
   b. social
   c. affiliation
   d. self-esteem
   e. physiological

6. Herzberg's hygiene factors most closely correspond with Maslow's:

   a. physiological needs.
   b. psychological needs.
   c. social needs.
   d. esteem needs.
   e. self-actualization needs.

7. According to Herzberg, employees are commonly most satisfied when offered:

   a. adequate supervision.
   b. adequate salary.
   c. recognition.
   d. job security.
   e. safe working conditions.

8. All of the following are methods used to enhance job satisfaction except:

   a. employee involvement programs.
   b. Theory X management.
   c. job security.
   d. adequate compensation programs.
   e. flexible work schedules.

9. Theory Z suggests that employees are more satisfied when:

   a. they receive above-average pay raises.
   b. their compensation is consistent with their efforts.
   c. managers restrict the delegation of authority.
   d. they are involved in decision making.
   e. appropriate hygiene factors are available.

10. Which of the following theories of management suggests that workers will be motivated if they are compensated in accordance with their perceived contributions to the firm?

    a. expectancy theory
    b. equity theory
    c. need theory
    d. Theory Y
    e. reinforcement theory

11. The reinforcement theory that motivates employees by encouraging them to behave in a manner that avoids unfavorable consequences is _____ reinforcement.

    a. positive
    b. neutral
    c. equity
    d. negative
    e. expectancy

Review and Critical Thinking Questions

1. Identify the categories of Maslow's hierarchy of needs theory.
2. Briefly describe Herzberg's job satisfaction study on worker motivation.
3. Distinguish between McGregor's Theory X and Theory Y perceptions of management.
4. Describe how expectancy theory can motivate behavior.
5. Briefly summarize the equity theory of motivation.
6. Describe the reinforcement theories of motivation and explain how a manager could utilize them.
7. Describe some methods that will enhance job satisfaction and motivate employees.

Discussion Questions

1. You are a manager who recognizes that your employees are primarily motivated by money. How could you motivate them at work?
2. Would motivational techniques be more important for the Atlanta Braves than for an organization such as General Motors? Explain your answer.
3. You are a manager of a video store. Which theory of motivation do you think would best apply to your employees?
4. Would you consider using negative reinforcement to improve the performance of lazy employees? Explain your answer.

Case: Using Motivation to Enhance Performance

Tom Fry is a plant manager for Ligonier Steel Corporation, located in Ligonier, Pennsylvania. The plant is small, with 250 employees. Its productivity growth rate has stagnated for the past year and a half.

Tom is concerned and decides to meet with employees in various departments. During the meeting, employees disclose that they do not have a chance to interact with one another while on the job. Furthermore, because they do not receive any recognition for their suggestions, their input of ideas for improvement has stopped.

After a week elapses, Tom calls a meeting to announce a new program. He plans to offer rewards for high performance so that employees will be motivated to surpass their quotas. Bonuses will be awarded to employees who exceed their quotas. Tom believes this program will work because of his perception that "money motivates employees."

A few months later, Tom notices that productivity has increased and that employees are enjoying the bonuses they have earned. Tom decides to provide an additional means of motivation. He wants employees to continue to interact with one another to solve work problems and share information. Supervisors now recognize individual accomplishments. They praise employees who make suggestions and identify an employee of the month in the company newsletter to recognize outstanding performance. Tom strongly supports this feature of the program.

The goal is for employees to grow and develop to their fullest potential. Individuals may be retrained or go back to college to permit job growth within the plant. Employees' ideas and contributions are now perceived as a way to enhance their individual career paths. The results have been overwhelming. Tom Fry, supervisors, and employees are all enjoying the benefits that have made Ligonier Steel a satisfying place to work.

Questions

1 Describe the motivation theory that applies to this case.

2 What needs can employees at Ligonier Steel satisfy in performing their jobs?

3 Describe how bonuses motivated the employees at Ligonier Steel.

4 Describe other rewards besides bonuses that can motivate work behavior in this case.

5 Ligonier does not use any negative reinforcement. Does this case illustrate any disadvantages of providing only positive reinforcement?

Internet Applications

1. http://www.fortune.com/fortune/bestcompanies

Which companies are the top companies to work for? What kinds of benefits do they provide for their employees? Which companies would you like to work for?

2. http://www.nceo.org

Click on "ESOPs." Briefly describe what an employee stock ownership plan is. How might an ESOP encourage employees to be more motivated? How do ESOPS relate to the theories of motivation discussed in the chapter? What is an ownership culture, and how does it create an environment where employees are more empowered?

3. http://www.motivation-tools.com

Click on "Elements of Motivation." What are the three elements of motivation? What are the seven rules of motivation? Do you think motivation results from an individual's own drive, or is it primarily driven by external factors? How can the seven rules of motivation result in better performance for a company?

LEARNING STRATEGIES

Strategies to help you get the most out of your reading.

LEARNING STRATEGY I—PREVIEWING

So many of us are frequent television viewers; we have become accustomed to letting information and entertainment come to us, without any effort on our part. But if we read the same way we watch TV, we will miss a lot. Reading well requires us to become partners with the author, to be active participants in the creation of meaning. There are many strategies we can use to be better readers. One of them, previewing, helps us get ready to read actively.

Does this sound familiar? It's your first week of a new semester. You've just spent a wheelbarrow-full of money on your new books. You are full of enthusiasm and have promised yourself you are really going to study hard this term. You open a book to do your first reading assignment and begin to study and what happens? Your mind begins to wander. You come to the end of a page, and even though you know your eyes have passed over every single word on the page, you have no idea what you've read.

Of course, this has happened to everyone: don't panic! There are ways to help yourself, but be prepared: reading for school is different from reading for pleasure. It requires more effort, more concentration—and a plan.

One reason we sometimes find it hard to absorb what we read is that we are reading materials totally new to us. This is especially true in college introductory courses where we are beginning a subject we may never have studied before. Have you noticed that it's easier to read a difficult, perhaps very technical, article about a subject you know well (say baseball, or computers, or fashion), than it is to read a very simple article on an unfamiliar topic (like ecology, perhaps, or astronomy)? The reason is simple: the more you know about a topic, the easier it is to read about that topic. In other words, the more background information you possess, the easier it is to read.

How is this going to help you when you're confronted with a college textbook on a subject you're not familiar with? Previewing the material before reading it is a first step toward acquiring background knowledge. Previewing will introduce you to the goals of the book, its structure, and helpful tools for learning that are contained in the book. Previewing will also "turn on the engine" of your brain, get you thinking, help you remember anything you *do* know about the topic, and, in general, get you ready to study.

Previewing the Textbook

These are the steps to follow to get ready to read your textbook:

First, read and think about the book's title. Are there any words in it you don't know? Look them up. Try to remember what you already know about the subject.

Second, quickly skim the preface or introduction. The author may give some helpful information about the goals and structure of the book.

Third, skim through the table of contents. This will show you the organization of the book and the topics that will be covered.

Fourth, check the table of contents for a glossary. It can appear either at the end of the book or after each chapter. A glossary can be very helpful; it contains definitions of important words used in the book. Using the glossary saves you the time of looking up words in the dictionary and the confusion that often results when a dictionary lists more than one definition; the glossary will list only one — the one used in the textbook.

Fifth, check the table of contents for an index. An index lists all the topics mentioned in the book in alphabetical order, plus their page numbers. Using an index can save lots of time when you are looking for information on one specific subject.

Sixth, check to see if there is an appendix. What does it contain? Sometimes the information in an appendix can be very helpful. For example, a history text's appendix may contain maps to help orient you; an accounting text's appendix may include sample financial statements.

Finally, look quickly through the book. Check to see if there are helpful features, such as summaries at the ends of chapters, or headings and subheadings.

Now spend a moment thinking about what you've just done. Are any of the topics in the title or table of contents familiar to you? Try to remember anything you can about them. Ask yourself what you expect to learn from this book.

You've probably spent 4 or 5 minutes previewing the textbook—a small investment of time that will speed up your studying in the long run.

Previewing Each Chapter

When you are ready to study a chapter in a textbook, you'll find previewing a very helpful strategy to "turn on" your brain, help you remember what you already know about the subject, and get ready to absorb new information. These are the steps to follow to prepare yourself to read a chapter:

First, read the title. Think about what it means. If you know anything about the subject, spend a moment to recapture from your memory as much information as you can. If there are any words you don't understand, look them up in the glossary or dictionary.

Second, read the headings and subheadings. This will show you the organization of the chapter and introduce you to the topics to be covered.

Third, see if there is a summary. If there is, read it carefully. It should provide you with a good overview of the chapter and will probably be the most useful part of the chapter later, when it comes time to review.

Fourth, check any questions or exercises before or after the chapter. These questions generally are meant to highlight the most important ideas in the chapter, so it is helpful to keep them in mind as you read.

Previewing the chapter will probably take you 3 or 4 minutes. Sometimes, students are impatient and say they'd rather spend these few minutes "really reading" rather than previewing. Studies have shown, however, that students who preview first will read faster, with better comprehension, and remember more. Not a bad return on a few minutes' investment!

Guide Questions

Directions: Write answers to the following questions.

1. a. Describe the problem many students have when they study a textbook.
   b. Do you ever have this problem?
2. a. Which topic would you find it easier to read about: television or U.S. geography? Why?
   b. Which topic would be easier to read about, baseball or the Bible? Why?
3. Explain why previewing can help you read better.
4. List the steps in previewing a textbook.
5. List the steps in previewing a chapter.

Application

Directions: Now that you have read and understood the ideas in "Previewing," it's important to use them at once. The following exercises, "Previewing a Textbook" and "Previewing a Chapter," will help you apply the methods you have just read about.

Previewing a Textbook

Directions: Choose one of the textbooks you will be using this term and answer the following questions about it.

1. a. State the title of the textbook.
   b. Are there any words in the title you don't understand?
   c. Is the title clear? For example, why do you think *this* textbook is called *The Thoughtful Reader?*
2. Name the author or authors.
3. Name the course in which you will use this book.
4. Who is the instructor of the course?
5. Identify the company that published the book.
6. Cite the publication date.
7. Quickly skim the Preface (which may also be called Introduction, Foreword, or To the Student). What does the author say is his or her goal in writing the book?
8. Turn to the table of contents. List three topics from the table of contents.

9. Are there any words in the table of contents that you don't understand? List them.
10. Does the book have a glossary?
11. Does the book have an index?
12. Does the book have an appendix? What does it contain?
13. Flip through the book. Do the chapters have any helpful features, such as boldface type, headings, summaries, questions, or illustrations? State which features the book has.
14. How much of the book will your instructor ask you to read this term? If you don't know, ask!

Previewing a Chapter

Directions: Preview a chapter of this book or a chapter from one of the other textbooks you are using this semester by answering the following questions. Your instructor will tell you which chapter to preview.

1. Read the title and subheadings (if any).
    a. Are there any words you don't know?
    b. What are they? Look them up and write their meanings.
    c. What topic will be discussed?
    d. What do you already know about the topic?
2. Does the chapter contain a summary?
3. Does the chapter include comprehension questions or other exercises? What are they?
4. List helpful features that the chapter contains, such as boldface type, illustrations, a glossary, margin notes, and so on.

LEARNING STRATEGY II—NARRATIVE AND EXPOSITION

Narrative

Much of the reading we do is the reading of *narratives*. To *narrate* is to tell a story. The fairy tales and bedtime stories parents read to their children are narratives. They have characters; things happen to these characters; usually a tone or feeling emerges in the story. Often there is a lesson for the reader to learn.

When you read a narrative, think about:

Who are the characters?

What happens to them?

What is the setting?

Does any special mood (e.g., happiness, sadness, anger, frustration, etc.) or tone emerge?

Is the author making a point? Is there something he or she wants us to remember from the story?

Is there a crisis? A turning point? What happens?

How relevant is the story to the world today? To you personally?

What are some examples of narrative that you have read?

Exposition

Exposition is a type of writing that presents information and teaches ideas. Most textbooks use exposition: they present facts, theories, processes, etc.

Exposition is different from narrative. Narrative tends to be easier to read; we are all familiar with stories—we have heard them all our lives. The familiar form of narrative is simply a beginning, middle, and end. Generally it is easy to follow along, enjoying the ride, without too much worry about understanding and remembering the facts.

Exposition, on the other hand, can take many different forms. Also, your goal in reading exposition is usually different: you are reading to learn.

Different forms of exposition include the following:

a list of reasons

causes and effects

comparison and contrast

a process or method of doing something

analysis—*why* does something exist or happen?

definition

example

When you are reading exposition, think about these questions:

What are the major ideas the author is presenting?

What kind of support does the author offer for these major ideas?

What form does the author use (e.g., list, cause and effect, etc.)?

What are you expected to learn and remember?

Most of the textbooks you will read in college are examples of exposition. What other exposition have you read recently?

LEARNING STRATEGY III—MARKING TEXT

Marking text is an excellent way to stay active and involved while studying. It's easy to fool ourselves into thinking that we're studying when all we are really doing is passing our eyes over print. This helps explain why sometimes we can read a whole chapter and realize at the end that we can't remember a single thing we've read! By being *physically* involved—by underlining, marking, and making notes—we are forced to be involved with the text and really pay attention to what we're reading. The more involved we are, the better chance we have of *remembering* what we read.

Why Mark the Text?

1. It forces us to be active, not passive, readers.
2. It gives us a chance to note any questions we have as we read along.
3. It is a real plus when it comes time to study for an exam.

How to Mark a Text

1. <u>Underlining</u> is the most common and popular way of marking. Underline ideas that are important. Ask yourself: Is this new information? Do I need to know and remember this? Will it possibly appear on an exam? Will it be needed for a writing assignment?
2. **But Don't Just Underline:** If you find a particularly important idea, indicate that by double underlining or put an asterisk (*) next to it. You want to distinguish really important points from all the other ideas you've underlined.   **
3. **Label your Underlining**. Next to your underlining, in the margin of the page, write a note explaining why you underlined it: this could be just a label or a few words summarizing it.   *Explain <u>why</u> you underlined*
4. (Circle) words you don't understand. Later, you can go back and look them up or ask the teacher or a classmate about them.
5. Write a **question mark (?)** next to ideas you don't understand. As with circled words, the mark will remind you to ask about them later.   *?*

Help! How Do I Decide What to Underline and Mark?

Here are some tips to help you mark your textbooks:

1. Read the whole chapter very quickly first without marking anything. If the chapter is long, divide it into sections, and attack one section at a time. Don't try to mark the text on the first read-through—you will almost certainly make mistakes. It is impossible to know what is important (and thus what should be marked) if you don't first have a good feel for the author's message. If there are any "Objectives" or "Focus Questions" at the beginning of the chapter, be sure to read them.
2. On the second reading, underline and mark the information you think you'll need to understand and remember. Don't forget to circle unfamiliar words and put question marks next to confusing ideas.

3. Keep the title and any subheadings in mind as you read along.
4. Pay special attention to the first sentences of paragraphs as you read. Major points are often stated in the first sentence.
5. Note any words in **boldface,** *italics,* or underlined. If the author gives special attention to these words, you should, too.
6. Look for "signal words" that often introduce major ideas, for example: *first, second, third,* and so on; *next; furthermore; another; finally; in addition; therefore; to summarize.*
7. As you underline new ideas, new terminology, or important concepts, write notes in the margin to explain why you've underlined.

Warning:
Be careful not to mark too much! If you underline too much, it is just as useless as not marking anything at all.

Practice
Try out all you've learned by marking the text on the next page.

GESTURES

Gestures are an important form of nonverbal communication. Gestures are usually defined as movements of the arms and hands, but can include whole body movements and posture, too. People who study language and communication say that humans communicated through gestures for many thousands of years before spoken language developed. In fact, they are so basic to our nature that people who have been blind from birth use them.

There are three main types of gestures. The first is called **illustrators.** Illustrators accompany speech and add meaning to the spoken word, but do not have meaning all by themselves. The next time you ask someone for directions, try to notice all the gestures they use—pointing, waving, stepping forward and backward. Or watch people on the phone, waving their hands and moving their heads and body, raising their eyebrows, smiling or frowning, even though obviously no one can see the movements. Without the spoken words, the gestures by themselves are meaningless.

Certain cultures are known to be more expressive with their hands than others. People from the Mediterranean—such as Italians, French, and Spanish—use their hands more than do Americans or English. Americans, do, however, use illustrators often when they are excited or angry. Most of us use illustrators, and people can often be identified just by their gestures. Thus, impersonators use gestures when they imitate famous people. Students usually identify the gestures of their teachers and can imitate them easily.

A second type of gestures is called **emblems.** These are movements that have a direct meaning and can function as replacements for words. Nodding the head means "yes," shaking the head means "no," a flat palm aimed at the listener means "stop," and of course everybody knows the meaning of a raised middle finger.

A third category is the **adaptors.** These are a quite different type of gesture; they are unconscious body movements made in response to something in the environment. For example, we might fiddle with our hair or tap a foot when something makes us feel nervous. We shiver or fold our arms around our body when it's cold. These movements are not consciously intended to convey meaning to others, though sometimes the same gestures can be used on purpose. We might cross our arms around our body to show we feel "cold" toward another person or that we feel the need to protect ourselves from him or her. We might tap our foot to signal impatience or examine our fingernails to show ennui.

It is interesting to note that *too few* gestures can be as significant as *too many.* Limited gesturing may signal a lack of interest, sadness, boredom, or low enthusiasm.

It is important to remember that gestures, while they may not signal a direct, concrete meaning, are important to understanding in interpersonal communication.

How Well Did You Do?

Compare your text marking with this model.

GESTURES

* Main idea → Gestures are an important form of nonverbal communication. Gestures are usually defined as movements of the arms and hands, but can include whole body movements and posture, too. People who study language and communication say that humans communicated through gestures for many thousands of years before spoken language developed. In fact, they are so basic to our nature that people who have been blind from birth use them.

* definition

blind people use gestures

There are three main types of gestures. The first is called **illustrators.** Illustrators accompany speech and add meaning to the spoken word, but do not have meaning all by themselves. The next time you ask someone for directions, try to notice all the gestures they use—pointing, waving, stepping forward and backward. Or watch people on the phone, waving their hands and moving their heads and body, raising their eyebrows, smiling or frowning, even though obviously no one can see the movements. Without the spoken words, the gestures by themselves are meaningless.

* 3 Types:

(1) illustrators

Some cultures more expressive with hands

Certain cultures are known to be more expressive with their hands than others. People from the Mediterranean, such as Italians, French and Spanish use their hands more than do Americans or English. Americans, do, however, use illustrators often when they are excited or angry. Most of us use illustrators and people can often be identified just by their gestures. Thus, impersonators use gestures when they imitate famous people. Students usually identify the gestures of their teachers and can imitate them easily.

A second type of gestures is called **emblems.** These are movements that have a direct meaning and can function as replacements for words. Nodding the head means "yes," shaking the head means "no," a flat palm aimed at the listener means "stop" and of course everybody knows the meaning of a raised middle finger.

(2) emblems

A third category is the **adaptors.** This is a quite different type of gestures; they are unconscious body movements made in response to something in the environment. For example, we might fiddle with our hair or tap a foot when something makes us feel nervous. We shiver or fold our arms around our body when it's cold. These movements are not consciously intended to convey meaning to others, though sometimes the same gestures can be used on purpose. We might cross our arms around our body to show we feel "cold" toward another person or that we feel the need to protect ourselves from him or her. We might tap our foot to signal impatience or examine our fingernails to show (ennui).

(3) adaptors

?

Too few vs Too many

It is interesting to note that *too few* gestures can be as significant as *too many.* Limited gesturing may signal a lack of interest, sadness, boredom, or low enthusiasm.

conclusion → It is important to remember that gestures, while they may not signal a direct, concrete meaning, are important to understanding in interpersonal communication.

LEARNING STRATEGY IV—WRITING A SUMMARY

What Is a Summary?

A summary is a brief, concise statement, in your own words, of the most important points of a passage (a chapter, an article, an essay, a paragraph, etc.).

Did you know that you are already an expert summarizer? You summarize in your day-to-day life all the time. For example, if a friend asks you about the 2-hour movie you saw last night, you don't spend 2 hours telling her—you summarize. (You'd lose your friend pretty quickly if you didn't.) If you e-mail or write a letter to a relative telling him what you did last week, you summarize. Another example of summarizing is when you write down a telephone message. Can you think of some other examples?

As an expert summarizer, all you need to do now is learn to apply the skill you already have to your college reading and writing.

Why Summarize?

Summary writing offers college students many advantages. The first is that it forces you to truly understand what you have read. If you don't understand, you will not be able to put the text into your own words. Second, writing a summary will help you to remember what you have read. Third, the summaries you write of your textbook chapters or articles are excellent tools for studying when exam time comes along. Wouldn't it be easier to reread your own summaries than to plow through the entire chapter again? Finally, writing summaries will help you to improve your writing skills, because a good summary must be clear and coherent, just as we would like all of our writing to be.

How to Summarize

First, remember to follow the steps for previewing and marking text that you studied in earlier Learning Strategies I and III (pages 407 and 413):

1. Preview the chapter.
2. Read the chapter through one time quickly. If it is long, divide it into manageable chunks.
3. Read the chapter a second time carefully; during this second reading, underline and mark the text.

When you have finished marking the text, follow these steps to **write a summary.**

1. Begin your summary by writing the main idea. (Remember to paraphrase.)

 What is a main idea? A main idea (also called the thesis, the central idea, the main point) is an umbrella sentence. We call it an umbrella sentence because, just like a real umbrella, it "covers" everything beneath it. The main idea is large enough to "cover" all the other ideas in the reading selection.

2. Next, follow your main idea with the important supporting ideas you underlined and marked. (Remember to use your own words as much as possible.) *This is your first draft.*
3. Proofread. Check to make sure you've included all the major ideas, that you have not included unnecessary detail (e.g., small examples, lengthy explanations, repetitions, etc.). Check your grammar and spelling.
4. Write the final draft.

Practice these four steps by writing a summary of the essay "Gestures." Use the marked text of "Gestures" on page 416.

How Well Did You Do?

Compare your summary with this model.

GESTURES

Gestures are an important form of nonverbal communication. Gestures are movements of the arms and hands, but can include whole body movements and posture. Experts say humans used gestures to communicate for thousands of years before they started speaking. Even blind people use them.

There are three categories of gestures. The first, **illustrators,** accompany speech and add meaning to speech, but don't contain meaning themselves. Some cultures, such as the French, Spanish, and Italian, use more hand gestures than others. Most people use illustrators. We can often identify individuals just by their gestures.

A second category of gestures is **emblems,** movements that have a direct meaning and can actually replace words. For example, nodding the head means "yes."

A quite different type of gestures is **adaptors,** unconscious body movements that are a response to something in the environment, for example, tapping your foot when something makes you nervous.

Using *too few* gestures may be as meaningful as *too many;* it may indicate a lack of interest, sadness, or boredom.

Finally, while gestures may not have a direct, concrete meaning, they are important to interpersonal communication.

More Practice

Practice all the steps by writing a summary of following article.

Step 1—Preview, then read the article quickly.

HUMAN RELATIONS IN BUSINESS

Lorence Long

LaGuardia Community College

Think of the human relations challenges in business! Here are just a few:

Telling the boss she is wrong, without getting her angry;

Encouraging a subordinate to tell you what you need to know to solve a problem that involves your own behavior;

Helping a customer to make a purchase, without overdoing it;

Expressing your criticism of a peer who is not carrying his share of the work, without turning the rest of the office against you (or him);

Handling your supervisor's overtures, which the supervisor says will improve your position in the office, but which might cost you some self-respect.

Some students (and some instructors) may focus so intently on the skill and knowledge of preparing for the business world that they neglect the human relations dimensions of the work situation.

Recent research indicates that human relations are very important in business. Last October, the *Wall Street Journal* asked 782 company chief executives to identify the most important personal traits linked to success. The executives specified "integrity" and "ability to get along with others" as by far the most important success-related characteristics.

Further, when these same people were asked to identify the failings of weak managers in their firms, they cited "inability to understand others" and "inability to work with others" as two of three most common failings. (The most common fault was described as "limited point of view.")

Many people think that they are constitutionally unable to learn how to relate to people more effectively. "I'm just a numbers person," they say in explaining their uncomfortable dealings with others. But human relations skills are like any others: they can be learned, and practice helps to improve performance.

One skill that is helpful in working with people is being able to observe accurately. Most of the time, we see events around us from a very personal viewpoint. Our observations are usually laced with assumptions and inferences that distort our ability to see what is happening. Practice in accurate observation helps us to respond more appropriately to the people around us.

A second skill is that of listening. A major corporation—Sperry—has been spreading across the advertising pages its conviction that listening to each other is the most important skill we can learn. We can learn to hear what the other person is saying without defensiveness or judgmental attitudes. We can learn ways to respond, so that the other person knows that we have heard what he or she was trying to say.

A third area for learning in human relations is that of assertiveness: expressing our needs, feelings, and ideas clearly, but without stifling others or putting them down. Many interpersonal problems arise from our inability to say what is on our minds in a way that other people—bosses, subordinates, peers—can accept.

A fourth area is related to our ability to recognize the culturally conditioned values of people we work with, and to be able to take them into account. Especially when these values clash with our own, we need to be sensitive to the implications of this conflict for our work.

Research indicates that human relations skills are as important as any other to business success and are worthy of serious study.

Step 2—Reread the article, and mark the text.

HUMAN RELATIONS IN BUSINESS

Think of the human relations challenges in business! Here are just a few:

> Telling the boss she is wrong, without getting her angry;
>
> Encouraging a subordinate to tell you what you need to know to solve a problem that involves your own behavior;
>
> Helping a customer to make a purchase, without overdoing it;
>
> Expressing your criticism of a peer who is not carrying his share of the work, without turning the rest of the office against you (or him);
>
> Handling your supervisor's overtures, which the supervisor says will improve your position in the office, but which might cost you some self-respect.

Intro

Some students (and some instructors) may focus so intently on the skill and knowledge of preparing for the business world that they neglect the human relations (dimensions) of the work situation.

aspects?

character-istics?

Recent research indicates that human relations are very important in business. Last October, the *Wall Street Journal* asked 782 company chief executives to identify the most important personal (traits) linked to success. The executives specified "integrity" and "ability to get along with others" as by far the most important success-related characteristics.

main idea

Further, when these same people were asked to identify the failings of weak managers in their firms, they cited "inability to understand others" and "inability to work with others" as two of three most common failings. (The most common fault was described as "limited point of view.")

Many people think that they are constitutionally unable to learn how to relate to people more effectively. "I'm just a numbers person," they say in explaining their uncomfortable dealings with others. But human relations skills are like any others: they can be learned, and practice helps to improve performance.

1st skill:
observing

One skill that is helpful in working with people is being able to observe accurately. Most of the time, we see events around us from a very personal viewpoint. Our observations are usually laced with assumptions and inferences that distort our ability to see what is happening. Practice in accurate observation helps us to respond more appropriately to the people around us.

2nd skill:
listening

A second skill is that of listening. A major corporation—Sperry—has been spreading across the advertising pages its conviction that listening to each other is the most important skill we can learn. We can learn to hear what the other person is saying without defensiveness or judgmental attitudes. We can learn ways to respond, so that the other person knows that we have heard what he or she was trying to say.

3rd skill:
assertiveness

A third area for learning in human relations is that of assertiveness: expressing our needs, feelings, and ideas clearly, but without stifling others or putting them down. Many interpersonal problems arise from our inability to say what is on our minds in a way that other people—bosses, subordinates, peers—can accept.

4th skill:
be
sensitive
to others'
values

A fourth area is related to our ability to recognize the culturally conditioned values of people we work with, and to be able to take them into account. Especially when these values clash with our own, we need to be sensitive to the implications of this conflict for our work.

Research indicates that human relations skills are as important as any other to business success and are worthy of serious study.

Step 3—Write the main idea.

In this case the author has kindly written a main idea statement for us. The first sentence of the third paragraph is an "umbrella" sentence that "covers" all the information in the article:

. . . human relations are very important in business

Changing it to our own words, we can write our own main idea:

Human relations skills are important to success in the business world.

 Remember—a main idea is an umbrella sentence. Like a real umbrella, it should be large enough to "cover" all the other ideas in the reading selection.

Step 4—Follow the main idea with the important points you noted when you marked the text. Paraphrase them.

These skills can be learned and improved with practice. The first important human relations skill is the ability to observe accurately. The second important skill is listening well. A third skill is assertiveness—expressing ourselves without hurting or offending others. A fourth skill is the ability to recognize and appreciate the values of other people, especially if they differ from our own.

Steps 5 and 6—*Proofread and then write the final draft. This is how your summary would look:*

Human relations skills are important to success in the business world. These skills can be learned and improved with practice. The first important human relations skill is the ability to observe accurately. The second important skill is listening well. A third skill is assertiveness—expressing ourselves without hurting or offending others. A fourth skill is the ability to recognize and appreciate the values of other people, especially if they differ from our own.

LEARNING STRATEGY V—DIRECTION WORDS

When your instructor asks you to *paraphrase* information or to *define* a term or to *analyze* a problem, do you know exactly what to do? Words like *paraphrase, define,* and *analyze* are called **direction words**. These words are used frequently in college. You will see them on exams and homework assignments and hear them in class lectures. Knowing their meanings and how to use them will help you to answer questions correctly. The following is a list of the most common direction words and their meanings. An example of how each word is used is given. Study the examples to make sure you understand each word.

Analyze—To break down into parts in order to better understand the whole

Q: Analyze the decision to increase property taxes in the town of East Liniment.

A: The population of East Liniment has increased 20 percent over the past 5 years. The majority of residents are young families. This has necessitated building a new elementary school and a new high school. In addition, a $2 million expansion has been proposed for the town library. Increasing the currently modest property tax rate was felt by the local officials to be the best source of revenue to meet these needs.

Cite—To name or to quote (as a fact, authority, or example)

Q: Cite the author of the "Law of Effect."

A: Edward L. Thorndike is the author of the "Law of Effect."

Classify—To arrange according to some stated category

Q: Classify the patient's stage of development according to Erikson's stages of development.

A: According to Erikson's stages of development, this patient is an infant, and thus is dependent on others for care.

Compare—To state the similarities between two things; **contrast**—to state differences between two things

Q: Compare and contrast your role as a parent with your role as a student.

A: Both roles require a sense of responsibility and commitment. Guiding, advising, and supporting your children in every way requires constant vigilance and attentiveness, which at times is difficult when you feel tired and burdened with other responsibilities.

As a parent, you cannot always foresee and plan for unexpected events. Your son's soccer game or an unexpected illness can arise and require that you change previous plans. As a student, once you become familiar with the course requirements at the start of the semester, you can work out a fairly consistent schedule, which includes class times, study times, and other school-associated activities. However, despite the differences, both roles require self-discipline and the ability to be flexible.

Define—To give a concise, clear meaning as briefly as possible (as in a dictionary)

Q: Define *microbiology*.

A: Microbiology is the study of life too small to be seen with the naked eye.

Describe—To paint a picture using words

Q: Describe the plants on the street where you live.

A: The street has an abundance of trees and flowering plants. The trees are deciduous; that is, they shed their leaves in the fall. However, the change in leaf color is not as dramatic as one sees farther north. At the base of each tree is a simple fence enclosing a variety of flowering plants—tulips, pansies. Several of the tenants living on the first floor of the apartment houses have placed window boxes containing mostly geraniums, pansies, and ivy.

Diagram—To draw a, chart, or graph, including labeling and a brief explanation or description for clarity

Q: Diagram the route from East Liniment Community College to your home at 11-22 46th Street.

A:

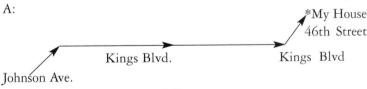

*My House
46th Street

Kings Blvd.   Kings Blvd

Johnson Ave.
*East Liniment Community College

Evaluate—To examine something and then make a judgment about it

Q: Evaluate your decision to work part-time and attend college full-time.

A: My decision was both easy and difficult. My full-time job was well-paying and I never had to think about having enough money for new clothes, a movie, and eating in a restaurant. At the same time, opportunities for further advancement were limited. I realized that further education was the only solution to expanding my opportunities. My decision involved a compromise. It required that I cut back on nonessential purchases and plan a more disciplined budget. However, I am already realizing that the sacrifices I am making are well worth my efforts.

Explain—To make something understandable, to give reasons for something

Q: Explain why you decided to enroll as a student at East Liniment Community College.

A: I decided to enroll as a computer science major at East Liniment Community College for several reasons. I have always enjoyed mathematics and spend a lot of time trying to understand how the computer works. My talents seem to be strong in the areas of mathematics and technology. In addition, the job market in computer programming is wide open. I feel that when I graduate, I will have the opportunity not only to work in a field that I enjoy but also will be well-compensated financially.

Identify/Name—To state something; to give the name of something

Q: Identify four students in your science laboratory.

A: John Jackson, Ludmilla Marcus, Edward Rodriguez, and Jane Simon are all students in my science lab.

Illustrate—To make something clear by giving examples

Q. Illustrate how studying mathematics can help you in your daily life.

A. I was making a recipe that would yield six servings but I only wanted to make it for two people. I needed my math to figure out how to adjust the amounts of all the ingredients.

List—To present information in an itemized series or table

Q: List the nine stages of development from infancy to old age.

A: The nine stages of development are infancy, early childhood, preschool, middle childhood, adolescence, early adulthood, middle adulthood, late middle age, late adulthood.

Paraphrase—To put something into your own words

Q: Paraphrase the following quote taken from your textbook. "Alveoli are air sacs that make up the lung tissue; within them, oxygen and carbon dioxide are exchanged between the lungs and blood."

A: The lungs are the organs where oxygen and carbon dioxide are exchanged with the blood. The specific structures in the lungs where the exchange takes place are called alveoli. These represent tiny air sacs.

React—To state your view of an issue and the reasons you feel the way you do

Q: React to the news that tuition will rise in the coming year.

A: I am distressed and angry at the news of a rise in tuition. We students are already suffering financially, with the high cost of living in general, high tuition costs, the price of textbooks, and more. An increase in tuition may mean some students will have to work more hours, and their studies will suffer. Some may have to drop out of school.

Summarize—State the important ideas in a condensed form, presenting only the main points or highlights

Q: Summarize the issues addressed by the two presidential candidates at the debate.

A: The major issues addressed by the presidential candidates in the debates included the future of social security, the future of Medicare, the possibility of prescription drug coverage, and tax rebates for childcare. Tax cuts and the budget deficit were also discussed.

Practice Using Direction Words

Directions: Read and study each direction word and its definition and example. When you are convinced that you know what each word requires, do the following exercise.

1. *Identify* three authors of reading selections on the topic of *culture* in this textbook.
2. *Illustrate* what is meant by the statement "Life is 10 percent what happens to you and 90 percent how you react to it."
3. *Describe* one of the other students in this class.
4. *Define* education.
5. *Paraphrase* the old saying, "Genius is 90 percent perspiration and 10 percent inspiration."
6. *Explain* the value of good communication skills.
7. *Name* the instructors of the courses you are taking now.
8. *Compare* and *contrast* your experiences in high school and in college.
9. *Analyze* your decision to attend college.
10. *List* three courses outside your major that you would like to take.
11. *React* to the statement "Every student in the United States should study a foreign language."
12. *Cite* three reasons that some college students drop out of school.

LEARNING STRATEGY VI—FIGURATIVE LANGUAGE

Figurative language is used so much in English that it is hard to imagine a conversation in which at least one example does not appear. "The line at the bursar's office was a zoo!" "The air conditioning broke down and the office was an oven." "My little brother is a pain in the neck!" Stevie Wonder sang, "You are the sunshine of my life. . . ." "Excuse me, I have a frog in my throat." "I'd like to help you, but my hands are tied."

One type of figurative language, the simile, is extremely common. Similes generally use the words *like* or *as*. Similes usually involve a simple comparison: "Whew! I worked like a dog last night!" "She eats like a horse, but stays as thin as a rail." "The news of the air crash spread like wildfire." "Searching for my dropped contact lens at the beach was like looking for a needle in a haystack." Forrest Gump observed that "Life is like a box of chocolates; you never know what you're going to get."

Another type of figurative language, the metaphor, is a bit more complex. Like the simile, it involves a comparison of one thing to another; but in a pure metaphor, the comparison is more complicated, more layered. Think about Shakespeare's *Romeo and Juliet*. As Romeo sees Juliet come onto her balcony at dawn, he says, "What light through yonder window breaks? It is the east and Juliet is the sun!" Romeo is comparing Juliet to the sun, but it is not a simple comparison. If Romeo compares his beloved to the sun, it is not the same as simply saying she is bright or warm. What does his metaphor make us think, make us feel? The sun is so many things: it gives light; it is bright; it gives warmth; it is beautiful; it is dependable. The sun is the giver of life! So, when Romeo says these scant four words, "Juliet is the sun," we learn a wealth of things about his feelings for her. Metaphor allows us to say a lot in few words; it makes our speech and writing so much more interesting.

Figurative Language in Poetry

Following are examples of figurative language written by famous poets. Explain what you think each poem means.

> *Hope is the thing with feathers*
> *That perches on the soul,*
> *And sings the tune without the words,*
> *And never stops at all.*

> —Emily Dickinson

> *A wicked whisper came and made my heart as dry as dust.*

> —Samuel Taylor Coleridge

> *Last summer you left*
> *my life quivering*
> *like a battlefield.*
> *I wore headaches like garments.*

> —Colleen McElroy

An aged man is but a paltry thing,
a tattered coat upon a stick, . . .

—William Butler Yeats

Metaphor in Prose

Here are some famous examples of metaphor by prose writers. Explain what each one means.

Hope is a good breakfast, but it is a bad supper.
—Francis Bacon

Speak softly and carry a big stick.
—President Theodore Roosevelt

A house divided against itself cannot stand.
—President Abraham Lincoln

What comparison is each of these writers making? What effect does the comparison have on the reader?

An Exercise in Understanding Figurative Language in Poetry

Here are two famous poems written by the great American writer Langston Hughes. Discuss each of the poems in view of what you have learned about figurative language.

ISLAND

Wave of sorrow,
Do not drown me now:

I see the island
Still ahead somehow.

I see the island
And its sands are fair:

Wave of sorrow,
Take me there.

HARLEM

What happens to a dream deferred?

Does it dry up
like a raisin in the sun?
Or fester like a sore—
And then run?

Does it stink like rotten meat?
Or crust and sugar over—
like a syrupy sweet?

> *Maybe it just sags*
> *like a heavy load.*
>
> *Or does it explode?*

What comparisons does the writer make? What do you think his poems mean? Why do you think he used the comparisons he did?

An Exercise in Recognizing Figurative Language

Over the next few days, keep in mind what you have learned about figurative language. As you read the newspaper, magazines, listen to the radio, watch TV, and talk with friends, be aware of the many metaphors we use in everyday life. Keep a notebook with you to jot down the metaphors and similes you hear and read. When you have a good collection, create a chart like the following one. List the metaphors and similes in the left column and their sources in the right column. There are two examples in the chart to get you started. You should collect at least ten examples of your own.

Examples of Figurative Language	Sources
1. "The city woke up under a blanket of snow this morning."	The weatherman on Channel 4 said this on February 2nd at 6:20 p.m.
2. Cubs Sweep Series with White Sox	This was a headline in the sports section of the August 14th *Chicago Tribune*.
3.	
4.	
5.	
6.	
7.	
8.	
9.	
10.	
11.	
12.	

LEARNING STRATEGY VII—TEST-TAKING

Test! That word every student fears and dreads. Yet, in a way, a test is a great opportunity. It is the place where we can demonstrate, both to ourselves and to the instructor, that we have learned, that we know what we need to know. Most of us, however, are not good test-takers. We haven't learned the strategies of successful test-taking. Knowing these strategies can make a big difference in our performance.

Here are a few tips to improve your test-taking skills.

Before the Test

1. Study smart. Review the information in this textbook in Learning Strategy III. If you have marked your textbook chapters well, you have already gone a long way toward success on a test. You have decided what material is important and what is not. Review your marked text. Then, if you have class notes, reread them. Are some of the ideas you underlined in the text repeated in class notes? If they are, be sure to review them carefully.

   Did the instructor give you guidelines for studying? Remember, you have the right to ask your teacher what the exam will cover and what form it will take. If your instructor did not tell you, ask!

2. Study early. Don't wait until the night before. If you begin to study early you will avoid that panicky feeling that comes with last-minute cramming. Also, if you come across something you don't understand, you will have time to find the answer.

3. Take advantage of the practice tests that many textbooks offer. Or, your instructor may make old exams available to you. Getting comfortable with the format of the test will be a big step toward success. Test-taking is a skill—practice helps.

The Day of the Test

1. Come on time. (But don't come too early.) Arriving late to a test is a sure way to increase your anxiety, not to mention the time you lose. But if you arrive too early, you may become nervous as you wait. Try to arrive a few minutes before the test is scheduled to begin. Organize your belongings and get comfortable. Take deep breaths and visualize yourself doing well. After all, if you have studied well, there is no reason you won't perform well.

2. Come prepared. Bring a watch. Will you need your own paper? A calculator? A dictionary? Do you have a pencil or a pen?

3. Listen carefully to the instructor's (or monitor's) directions. If there is an answer form, make sure you know how to fill it out. Is it OK to guess? Or will wrong answers count against you?

4. Read all the directions on the test before you begin to answer.

5. Preview the entire test. How many questions are there? Compute how much time you should spend on each one. For example, an exam consisting of 40 multiple-choice questions with a 20-minute time limit means you have 30 seconds to spend on each item.

6. Don't spend too much time on one item. If you don't know the answer, don't waste time puzzling over it. Move on to the next question. If you have time at the end, go back to questions you did not know.

7. If you finish early, check over your answers. If you see an obvious mistake, change it. But beware—most studies show that your first answer is usually the correct one.

8. Don't let other test-takers distract you. Try to sit where you will not see other people, usually near the front of the room. Turn your chair toward the wall if you can. The more you insulate yourself from other people, the less distracted you will be. Sometimes another student will finish the test very early. Ignore it. You can't know why that person finished so quickly. Perhaps he or she did not study and simply gave up.

9. Learn from the results. When you get your test back, use it as a learning tool. Look at each item you got wrong and figure out why it was wrong. Did most of the questions you answered wrong come from information presented in class lectures? Perhaps you need to work on your note-taking skills. If most came directly from the text, you will know where to concentrate your studying next time.

GLOSSARY

abstract An abstract word refers to a quality, condition, or idea that cannot be perceived by the senses. *Abstract* is the opposite of *concrete*. Examples of abstract words: love, happiness, justice, truth, fear.

allusion An allusion is a reference to another idea, something the writer assumes the reader is familiar with.

analogy An analogy is a comparison of one thing to another thing. Analogies are generally used to explain the nature of something unfamiliar to us by comparing it to something we already know. For example, in the novel *Being There,* author Jerzy Kosinski describes the economy by using the analogy of a garden; just as there are cycles (or seasons) in a garden, there are cycles (times of growth and times of stagnation) in the economy. Analogies can be helpful in understanding a difficult concept, but they are not always *true.* (The economy and the garden are quite different things.) Other examples of analogies: comparing the human mind to a computer, the heart to a pump, life to a journey.

annotation Annotation means marking the text by underlining, writing comments, noting questions, and so on.

antonym An antonym is a word that is opposite in meaning from another word. Examples of pairs of antonyms: hot /cold; high / low; sharp/dull.

argument In discussions, an argument is a reason given to support a position or opinion.

concrete Something concrete is something you can see, touch, hear, smell, or taste. *Concrete* is the opposite of *abstract*. Examples of concrete words: chair, wine, elephant.

connotation Connotation refers to the emotional effect a particular word or phrase has on a person. Two words can have the same denotation, but different connotations. For example, *thin* and *skinny* have basically the same denotation, but different connotations. Likewise, *fat, chubby, heavyset,* and *full-figured* all have the same basic meaning but arouse different feelings or attitudes in the mind of the listener or reader. Compare to *denotation.*

denotation The denotation of a word is its literal, dictionary meaning.

exposition Exposition is a form of writing whose purpose is to present information. It can take many forms. Exposition contrasts with narrative, which tells a story.

jargon   Jargon is the specialized language of a specific group or profession. The fields of law, medicine, and computers are well known for their jargon. The jargon of a group is usually unfamiliar to people outside the group.

main idea   In an essay or article, the main idea is a brief statement of the author's main point or thesis.

metaphor   A metaphor is a figure of speech that compares one thing to another by saying that thing *is* the other. Shakespeare is the source of many of our most familiar metaphors: "All the world's a stage"; "What's in a name? . . . a rose by any other name would smell as sweet." Calderón de la Barca said, "Life is a dream." Other familiar metaphors: "Life is just a bowl of cherries"; "Time is money."

narrative   Narrative is a form of writing that tells a story.

oxymoron   An oxymoron is a word or phrase that combines two opposites in meaning. Examples: "James Bond was a well-known secret agent"; "The menu offered fresh-frozen jumbo shrimp" (two oxymorons in one phrase). A famous oxymoron is the Greek word *sophomore,* which is a combination of two words: *wise* and *fool.*

paradox   A paradox is a statement that seems to contradict itself, but is nevertheless true. One of the most famous paradoxes in literature is the opening of *A Tale of Two Cities,* by Charles Dickens: "It was the best of times, it was the worst of times, it was the age of wisdom, it was the age of foolishness, it was the epoch of belief, it was the epoch of incredulity, it was the season of Light, it was the season of Darkness, it was the spring of hope, it was the winter of despair, we had everything before us, we had nothing before us, we were all going direct to Heaven, we were all going direct the other way . . ."

simile   A simile is a figure of speech in which a comparison is made using the words *like* or *as.* Examples: "I was as hungry as a bear"; "Her tears flowed like wine."

summary   A summary is a concise restatement in your own words of another writer's ideas.

symbol   A symbol is something (e.g., an object, a person, a word, a number) that stands for, or represents, something else.

synonym   A synonym is a word that means the same as another word. Examples of synonym pairs: old/elderly, doctor/physician, teacher/instructor, student/pupil.

thesis   In an essay, the thesis is a brief statement of the main point of the essay.

CREDITS

AUTHOR/TITLE INDEX